YOUNG CENTER BOOKS IN ANABAPTIST & PIETIST STUDIES

Donald B. Kraybill, *Series Editor*

Growing Up Amish

SECOND EDITION

The Rumspringa Years

Richard A. Stevick

Johns Hopkins University Press
Baltimore

© 2007, 2014 Johns Hopkins University Press
All rights reserved. Published 2014
Printed in the United States of America on acid-free paper
2 4 6 8 9 7 5 3

First edition published as *Growing Up Amish: The Teenage Years*, 2007

Johns Hopkins University Press
2715 North Charles Street
Baltimore, Maryland 21218-4363
www.press.jhu.edu

Library of Congress Cataloging-in-Publication Data

Stevick, Richard A., 1939–
Growing up Amish : the Rumspringa years / Richard A. Stevick. — Second edition.
   pages cm. — (Young Center books in Anabaptist & Pietist studies)
Earlier edition has subtitle: the teenage years.
Includes bibliographical references and index.
ISBN-13: 978-1-4214-1371-6 (pbk. : alk. paper)
ISBN-13: 978-1-4214-1372-3 (electronic)
ISBN-10: 1-4214-1371-X (pbk. : alk. paper)
ISBN-10: 1-4214-1372-8 (electronic)
1. Rumspringa. 2. Amish teenagers—United States—Social life and customs. 3. Amish
teenagers—United States—Social conditions. 4. Amish teenagers—Religious life—United
States. 5. Amish—United States—Social life and customs. 6. Youth—United States—Social
life and customs. I. Title.
E184.M45S75 2014
289.7092—dc23
[B]   2013033889

A catalog record for this book is available from the British Library.

Frontispiece: *These teenagers take advantage of their increased freedom to play in a girls' evening softball league in Holmes County, Ohio.* (Mike Schenk / Wooster (OH) Daily Record)

Special discounts are available for bulk purchases of this book. For more information, please contact Special Sales at 410-516-6936 or specialsales@press.jhu.edu.

Johns Hopkins University Press uses environmentally friendly book materials, including recycled text paper that is composed of at least 30 percent post-consumer waste, whenever possible.

To our grandchildren:

Katherine, Allison, Zahra, Kavitha, Wesley, David,

Wyn, Madelaine, and Brendan

Contents

Preface

If they still take us back after being on television,
they'll take us back no matter what we do.
—Mose Gingerich, from *Amish in the City*

When I began this revision of *Growing Up Amish* in January 2012, a number of friends expressed surprise that I was working on this project less than a decade after the original edition came out in early 2007. "After all," they asked rhetorically, "what significant changes could occur among Amish youth in a few years?" Admittedly, much appears to be the same as it was even a decade ago: children learn to work hard early on, they complete school by the age of fourteen or fifteen, and a year or two later they begin their *Rumspringa*, that brief period of comparative freedom for Amish youth to date, seek a mate, and explore the outside world before they choose or reject the Amish faith and culture. Most eventually do join the church, find a "special friend," and "settle down" to become the latest generation to embrace the Amish way, just as their parents, grandparents, and generations of other forebears did. Yet other things have changed with the *Youngie*, as Amish youth are known, in a relatively short time, and this revision will provide some answers to my friends' questions.

One of the events that led to this revision was that my editor at Johns Hopkins University Press, Greg Nicholl, was intrigued by an article that he discovered in the *Lancaster Sunday News* in June 2011 about Amish youth on Facebook and the Internet.[1] He rightly concluded that this subject was both interesting and an important development in the Amish community. In the 2007 first edition, I had not even mentioned Facebook's predecessor, Myspace, and had given only eight words of coverage to cell phone use. Those subjects were off my radar when I did most of my initial research during the decade surrounding the millennium. Now the scene has changed dramatically, as thousands of youth in the large settlements are dedicated Internet and Facebook users, thanks to their sophisticated smartphones and e-savvy Amish peers.

While working on his Facebook-Amish article, reporter Gil Smart contacted ten Facebook users with Amish-related names to ask if they would be willing to communicate with him. Predictably, not one replied. Amish youth, even those "cruising the fast lanes," routinely protect their culture, family, and friends. Smart was correct, however, in surmising that many Amish youth were seriously involved in Facebook. My experiences in charting Amish youths' electronic journeys for the last eighteen months has led me to believe that each of the three big Amish settlements in Indiana, Ohio, and Pennsylvania currently have more than 1,000 Facebook Youngie.

Discerning that fact, however, turned out to be much more difficult than I had anticipated. First, I needed to get on Facebook. A young professor friend helped me sign up as a bona fide user. As a member of the "Grandparents' Generation" and one who is marginal at best on the Internet, I first had to learn to navigate the intricacies of Facebook and, later, how to understand and utilize this resource's potential to learn more about what Amish elders would call the "fast (or fast-track) Rumspringa." A young colleague taught me how to seek "Friends" and how to respond to requests from others to be their Facebook "Friend." At first I rarely checked my status or did anything on my account. I did not even know the difference between a profile picture and a cover photo. I never uploaded any photos to my Facebook page. This hands-off approach changed quickly when I realized the potential available on Facebook to learn about Internet Amish youth. The invitation from Johns Hopkins University Press to research and write about the Amish-Facebook connection sealed the deal.

My first breakthrough came when a young man who grew up in Lancaster County befriended me. In the process, he bequeathed access to his list of 532 Facebook "Friends" to me, 80 percent of whom were Amish. Later, his seventeen-year-old rumspringa sister identified all of her 800-plus "Friends" as to their heritage (reared in Amish homes or not), state of residence, youth gang, and church membership. Then my friend Jim Cates, a psychologist and founder of the Amish Youth Vision Project in northern Indiana, arranged for me to meet with him and two of his rumspringa "Friends," an act of great generosity and grace. With their connections, I was also able to delve into the Indiana Amish Facebook world.

My initial introduction to the Amish "electronic generation" happened in Pinecraft, Florida, the traditional Amish vacation spot for Amish and Mennonite snowbirds, as well as for an assortment of Amish and Mennonite youth who come to socialize, play volleyball, and take a break from northern winters. The first interview I did was in January 2012, with a Lancaster County teenager who agreed to talk with me and my wife about Amish youth involvement with cell phones, the Internet, and other issues. Within five minutes, I observed our young Amish visitor pausing to check the text messages on her smartphone and then responding to them while we attempted to talk. After a few more minutes of this, I decided to see what she would do when I stopped talking whenever she became absorbed in receiving or sending messages. After the second or third 15- or 20-second pause, she looked up, realizing what was happening. "Oh, don't worry," she reassured me." I am good at multitasking." I told her that I would wait while she was attending to her messages, but she put her phone away, at least for most of the rest of our conversation. That experience was my first encounter with the role that this kind of technology was assuming among most fast-track Amish youth.

Since all Facebook users can block access to any information contained on their profile page from anyone but their "Friends," I was surprised to learn that, for whatever reason, most Amish youth do not exercise that option. Eventually I sifted through the hundreds of names from my two lists and compiled a non-random collection of over 300 confirmed Amish Facebook users, mostly from the big three settlements. I started my study by looking at the Facebook profile pictures selected by the users. Simply being on Facebook set these youth apart from the majority of Amish youth and placed them in a different category. They were not necessarily at the extreme end of Amish rumspringa youth, but they were certainly in a place with potentially high exposure to mainstream and popular culture. Consequently, I have been able to get a closeup look at how those two cultures intersect and, in the process, follow the trajectories of many youth in the rumspringa fast track. Among other things, these users' public profiles allowed me to chart their reported hobbies, reading preferences, and habits, as well as their favorite sports, music, television programs, and films. Additionally, I observed their manner of dress, perused photo albums from their trips and parties, and, by simple name analysis, identified the number of their non-Amish-reared "Friends."

As my computer search time on all things Amish continued, I realized how much media interest in the Amish, and especially in Amish youth, had grown in the last decade. Unlike my search results from ten years ago, I not only found information about the Amish in general, but also a greater focus on rumspringa youth and on those who had left the church or had never joined. For example, an early 2013 search for "Amish youth" on Amazon. com produced 312 hits, ranging from the scholarly to the sensationalized. This includes books by former Amish with memories of bucolic childhoods and youth to scathing descriptions of abuse or violence suffered within dysfunctional Amish families or communities. Both fiction and nonfiction books on the Amish were represented. One need not go to Amazon.com to realize the extent of Amish-based works, however. A stroll through most bookstores reveals that books on Amish youth sell. More than two dozen writers routinely turn out hundreds of titles under the rubric of Amish romance fiction, and the number of new books published has been growing exponentially since 2009.[2] As one might expect, the authors' abilities to write quality fiction that rings with authenticity and portrays a credible rumspringa experience vary widely.

The public seems to be especially captivated by those rumspringa years. A young Amish man described a search he did on Wikipedia for the term "Amish." He reported that "Rumspringa" was the third-most-searched subject, following the generic term "Amish" and details of the Nickel Mines shooting of five Amish schoolgirls in 2006.[3] Many writers seem to be attracted either to the extreme end of Amish youthful excesses or to the outlandish or bizarre. An example of this is in the novel *Rum Springa*, in which the main character, an Amish teenage girl from a large settlement, is courted by her childhood English school chum, who turns out to be a lesbian. Amazon.com featured two more novels entitled *Rumspringa*, one released in 2011 and the second in 2012. Other writers specialize in detailing the real or alleged experiences of the "fast crowd," to use the common Amish term. Many readers are apparently fascinated by the novelty of plain youth engaged in the wild behavior that some of the rowdiest Amish youth exhibit. On the other hand, many writers are equally interested in what draws so many of the youth back into the Amish fold after they dabble in or imbibe deeply of mainstream culture and the pleasures of the world.

One area in popular culture that reveals mainstream interest in Amish youth and young adulthood is the spate of so-called reality shows that feature rumspringa youth, rowdy behavior, and the crucial decision of returning or not returning to their families, church, and plain lifestyle. We will explore this phenomenon in more detail in chapter 1 by looking at the succession of Amish reality shows following Lucy Walker's 2002 documentary, *Devil's Playground*, a film that depicts in vivid detail the lives of several northern Indiana teenagers at the hedonistic extreme of their Rumspringa.

Amish parents and ministers are also deeply interested in the youth, but for a much different reason. The Amish are most content when everything is in order and under control, including their rumspringa-aged children. During the years between their offspring's sixteenth birthday and marriage, the freedom to explore can either strengthen or sever familial and cultural ties. Parents instinctively know that the future of the Amish and their way of life ultimately depends on their sons' and daughters' choices during those critical decision-making years. The most reflective adults realize that they are always only a generation or two from the loss of all that they and their forebears have guarded, nurtured, and lived for over the three centuries of their existence. Though the loss of Amish youth from the fold would be a mere blip in the lives of the sensationalists who distort and exploit the young, Amish elders would regard the demise of their culture as catastrophic and tragic.

A major interest that has fueled my continued studies of Amish youth (and has remained throughout the process of this revision) is what impact

Internet involvement is having on its youthful Amish users, now and in the future. The influence of the Internet is of concern to all conscientious parents, mainstream or Amish. Although relatively few parents from either culture would be likely to encounter the studies and books that report the latest findings on the Internet's effects on individuals and society, newspaper and magazine articles frequently raise issues not only related to its content (e.g., pornography, advertising, age-inappropriate material), but also to its unknown or unintended byproducts (e.g., reduced attention span, decreased ability to concentrate, fewer face-to-face contacts, addiction, and possible negative alterations in brain functioning and effectiveness).[4]

To date, no formal studies have been conducted on the impact of the Internet on Amish youth, but it is likely that the issues just raised will affect youth from both mainstream and Amish cultures. A salient question for Amish parents is how their children's Internet use might influence and change their Amish values, behaviors, and, eventually, their culture. Will those wired rumspringa youth with smartphones and instant Internet access be less likely to settle down, give up this technology, and choose the Amish way than their technology-free peers? And even if the tech-savvy and experienced users do remain Amish, will regular exposure to mainstream culture via the Internet change the users' values and contentment? If such changes can alter Amish culture in directions counter to their commitment to plain and simple living, those Amish parents and leaders who understand this will need to think seriously and act effectively to stop this breakdown. The easy but unsatisfactory answer for now is "Time will tell." For the "time being,"[5] which refers to "time-limited beings" but also means "now," I am hopeful that this revised edition will provide clues for understanding the changes that loom and also grapple with the emerging questions regarding the future of Amish culture as we know it.

Acknowledgments

I could not have written this revised edition without the help of many individuals. I am grateful to my original Johns Hopkins University Press editor, Greg Nicholl, who approached me with the idea not only to revise the book, but especially to focus on the intersection of Amish youth and the electronic world of smartphones, computers, and the Internet. From the book's inception until he left the Press in 2013, Greg encouraged my efforts and provided helpful counsel and direction. Likewise I am indebted to Sara Cleary, his successor at the Press, who immediately and enthusiastically picked up where Greg left off, continuing at the same high level of competence and encouragement throughout the rest of the project. The skilled input and guidance from both of these editors made this a much better book. Both of these professionals' insights, competence, and attitude have defined for me what a truly competent editor should be. Many thanks, Greg and Sara.

I am also grateful for the excellent and untiring help I received from Seleena Lindsey and Diane Hunsinger of Messiah College's faculty services. Even though I am now an emeritus rather than full-time professor, these women were not only supportive of my professional needs but willingly offered immediate help whenever I needed it. Little wonder that they were officially honored for their consistently excellent work by their supervisors, peers, and clientele at Messiah College.

Heartfelt thanks also go to professional colleagues who gave willingly of their time to update me in their areas of expertise, especially as it related to Amish youth. Among them were Charles Bauman, Edsel Burdge, James Cates, Karen Johnson-Weiner, David McConnell, and Steven Nolt. Special thanks are due to my friend and colleague, Charles Jantzi, professor of psychology at Messiah College, who was my go-to person for advice and current information on the Internet and social media. Kudos also apply to his student assistant, Michelle Yoder, who located and organized an enormous amount of data regarding Amish youth activity on the Internet. Special thanks also go to the Young Center of Elizabethtown College and their administrative assistant, Edsel Burdge, who was my other go-to person. Edsel was always available, always helpful, always cheerful, and a worthy successor to the late Stephen Scott. Thank you so much, Edsel.

Needless to say, I could not have accomplished this task without the help of scores of Amish friends and acquaintances, young and old, in the last two years. Some of them spent literally hours talking with me, answering my questions, and responding to my prose. My wife and I were also invited to their singings, volleyball games, church services, a funeral, and a wedding. These folks frequently shared their concerns and hopes surrounding their futures, that of their children, the Amish in general, and themselves. Erik Wesner, editor of the Amish America blog site, graciously gifted me by introducing me to some of his Amish friends who also befriended me and proved to be exceptionally helpful, both in updating my knowledge and in critiquing my manuscript.

I am also thankful for the encouragement of my family to undertake and complete this important and challenging project, even though I am in my retirement years. My wife, Pauline, who has now read the manuscript several times since its inception, provided careful scrutiny, excellent criticism, and explicit feedback throughout the entire process. Thanks to her, this book is much clearer and more accurate than it would have been without her faithful ministrations. I hope to reciprocate in many ways as she writes her next book.

Another surprising aid to my increased clarity and accuracy is that for this edition, most of my Amish sources, other than those living on the plainest end of the spectrum, have permitted me to use a small digital recorder when we talked. This change in Amish attitudes served to reduce my need to constantly take notes or try to remember exact wordings during the interviews. Now my quotations can come from transcripts rather than memories. Almost everyone I asked granted me permission to record our discussions, and I never taped secretly. I am thankful for this unanticipated gift.

My last acknowledgement goes to my copyeditor, Kathleen Capels, who provided the most careful and comprehensive editing of anyone I have ever worked with. Kathleen has an inborn sense for the flow of a manuscript and a musician's ability to intuit and offer up the exact words to express my intended thoughts. With her eye for detail and her considerable semantic skills and sensitivity to words and syntax, only she knows how much she has helped in strengthening the cohesion, clarity, and flow of my endeavors. Any lapses in these areas are mine, not hers. Thank you, Kathleen, for both your help and encouragement. My friend Donald Kraybill's observation that there are no great authors, just great editors, is certainly true in Kathleen's case.

In their own ways, all of the individuals cited above helped me complete this book. My hope is that its content will not only be worthy of note and engagement, but will also be instructive to both non-Amish and Amish readers. If this volume provokes its readers to think about the strengths, challenges, and threats to our respective communities, we just may be more likely to act in ways that will strengthen the integrity and goodness of our lives, whatever our cultural differences.

Growing Up Amish

Although this young man is adhering to the traditional dress and transportation expectations of the Amish, during their late teenage years, significant numbers of Amish youth, especially in the large settlements, dress like mainstream youth, drive cars, and pursue prohibited pastimes.
(Daniel Rodriguez)

Amish Life

Plain but Not So Simple

All good things go to ruin if we don't work on them.
—Amish parent

Amish Youth: In the Spotlight, under the Lens

When I first began studying the Amish in the early 1990s, I was hard pressed to find extensive or even superficial attention focused on their teenage years. Although several writers had documented their experiences at an Amish wedding, the couples are considered to be adults, and their marriages signal to the community that the newlyweds have completed their adolescence and are fully entering Amish adulthood.[1] In the past, accurate historical knowledge about the youth culture of the Amish was limited to a few pages (at best) in the most highly regarded books of the time. Virtually no films, television programs, or popular books touched on any of the important aspects of that critical period when Amish youth decide whether or not to follow the Amish way. Amish youth are the business of their Amish parents or their community, and nobody else's. Amish adults work hard to keep the happenings of their youthful offspring, especially the wayward young, as privileged information within the community.

Despite their best endeavors, however, today almost every aspect of Amish adolescence is scrutinized, analyzed, or exploited by the media or academia—their friendships, their pastimes, their indiscretions, and their future either as committed Amish church members or as casualties along the way. Witness the abundance of television shows that purportedly deal in one way or another with most of the above experiences. United Paramount Network (UPN) paved the way with their youth-centered reality show, *Amish in the City*, in the first decade of this century. What followed was a succession of other self-proclaimed reality series, such as *Amish: The World's Squarest Teenagers* in 2010 from Channel 4, London; the Learning Channel's *Breaking Amish* in 2012; and the most bizarre to date, *Amish Mafia* (also from the Learning Channel in 2012), a preposterous and fabricated offering having almost nothing to do with reality. This latter program claimed to expose the hidden underbelly of lawless Amish youth and adults, and the existence of stern-faced, ex-Amish enforcers. These "Mafia" members purportedly brought swift and sometimes violent resolution for Amish bishops who needed their help to quiet recalcitrant members or enforce unpopular decisions on an innocent and unsuspecting community. All of my knowledgeable Amish friends perceived this "reality" show as fiction. One of my teenaged friends captured the sentiments of the Amish community when she remarked, "*Amish Mafia* would be funny, Rich, except for the fact that a lot of people are going to believe that these things are actually true."

Today, in contrast to a decade or two ago, books on Amish youth also abound. Publishers have discovered that emerging interest in this topic is a bonanza for new and electronic book sales and profits. Look, for example, at the "bonnet fiction" offerings, with dozens of titles sporting covers graced by stunning-looking Amish females ready for romancing by eager Amish or English suitors ("English" is the term used by the Amish to describe the non-Amish). Since 2006, more than two dozen writers have written nearly 300 titles under the rubric of Amish romantic fiction.[2] The three best-selling authors (Beverly Lewis, Wanda Brunstetter, and Cindy Woodsmall) have sold nearly 25 million copies, with Lewis accounting for nearly two-thirds of that total.[3]

What happened to catapult Amish youth and their teenage years squarely in the public eye, both here and abroad? Seeds were undoubtedly planted in 1998, with the shocking news that the FBI had arrested two young men and a minor—all of whom had grown up in Amish homes—for dealing in drugs both with the notorious Pagans motorcycle gang and with members of Amish youth groups in Pennsylvania. Not only did reporters from around the world flock to Lancaster County, but these revelations and attendant publicity also shook the Lancaster Amish adult community to the core, and sent reverberations throughout all the large Amish settlements. The other major fallout was that it sparked curiosity about the period known as *Rumspringa*, a term most Americans had never heard of before the drug bust.

The word *Rumspringa* comes from German and literally and simply translates as "running around." Outsiders whose understanding comes primarily from watching Amish-themed reality shows or from reading popular accounts of this transitional stage cannot be blamed if they have a distorted understanding of the typical rumspringa experience. The UPN website defined Rumspringa as "running wild." One reviewer wrote, "Rumspringa is an Amish version of spring break and Mardi Gras rolled into one."[4] An unidentified writer coined the term "time-out period" to describe Rumspringa as an opportunity the community granted its young people to experience worldly pursuits. Another writer, using the contemporary German spelling, described Rumschpringe as "the Amish equivalent of teenage rebellion." Still another reviewer concluded, "During Rumspringa, the Amish are . . . encouraged to experience the world of the 'English' to expose themselves to temptations before they make an adult commitment."[5] An Amish teenager walking along the sidewalk in Intercourse, Pennsylvania, reported that she was subjected to a drive-by shouting when a passing motorist rolled down his window and yelled "Rumspringa" at her. Although the term simply refers to the transition period that lasts from when the youth turn sixteen or seventeen until they marry another church member or settle down, many Amish do not use the word Rumspringa in regular conversation. Instead, they refer to it as "going with the young folk" or "being with the *Youngie*."

Rumspringa Goes Viral

This widespread interest and misperception of the typical rumspringa experience most likely occurred in 2002, with the release of Lucy Walker's documentary, *Devil's Playground*, a graphic description of the wild end of Amish youthful dissipation. With a bit of luck, three years of perseverance, and an impressive ability to gain the trust of these pushing-the-envelope youth, Walker's videographer acquired unprecedented access to film all sorts of youthful excesses. Virtually every expert on Amish culture agrees that *Devil's Playground* portrays the extreme end of Amish youth behavior, especially in the large settlements. Nonetheless, Walker's film, covering two years in the lives of five northern Indiana youth, established the idea that Rumspringa and wildness were synonymous. From the DVD's jarring cover image of an Amish girl in plain attire lighting up a cigarette in the back seat of a car, to a scene with four girls drinking beer at a party, to a shot of boys huddled around a bong (a water-cooled device for smoking marijuana), the message is clear: these teens have cast aside their plain inhibitions for a hedonistic lifestyle. Walker juxtaposes these and more extreme images of drunkenness, "hooking up" and premarital sex, and serious drug use with scenes of rural tranquility.[6]

Following on the heels of *Devil's Playground*, freelance writer Tom Shachtman published *Rumspringa: To Be or Not to Be Amish*, a book with a similar theme that relied heavily on the 300 hours of filming shot by Walker's videographer. Shachtman likewise emphasized the extreme end of Amish youthful misbehavior. Despite their disclaimers, these two works were instrumental in shaping the public's perception that the majority of Amish youth spent their rumspringa years in deviance or the full pursuit of pleasure. Since then, as we will see in chapter 8, the term "Rumspringa" has become imbedded in popular culture.

In the second decade of this century, the reality-show producers and promoters continue to add to the viewing public's misperception of Amish youth. Sidestepping the fact that 85 percent of Amish youth choose to stay Amish, the so-called reality media mostly focus on those who are seeking to break free of those cultural, religious, and familial constraints. Never mind that these shows are a caricature of reality, stocked with characters long departed from the culture and loaded with scripted scenes and lines that defy Amish reality. For whatever reasons, the intersecting of callow Amish youth with jaded young worldlings plays to our prurient interests, or at least to the novelty inherent in such a clash of world views and behaviors. UPN's success in cashing in with unexpectedly high numbers of viewers undoubtedly spawned the virtual smorgasbord of offerings to amuse the most bored channel-surfing viewers.[7]

These often-fraudulent offerings reveal less about the Amish and far more about the programs' many mainstream viewers (and the companies that pander to them), with their contrived situations, scripted crises, and supposedly Amish characters who have donned a fresh set of newly fitted (and better-fitting) Amish clothing and act as if they are in the throes of existential decision making. Nevertheless, the very popularity of such shows confirms the public's widespread fascination with Amish youth culture and deviant behaviors within it, even as the programs continue to fuel such interest. Why would producers have little desire in showing a true representation of everyday Amish life? The answer is apparent to anyone who really understands Amish culture. Picture the typical viewer watching the normal plain and simple Amish lifestyle taking place in the slow lane, even if the program focused on youth. Sunday-night singings would be hopelessly boring—two hours of singing hymns in a stuffy room, and then a courting couple riding home from the event and playing Monopoly in the living room—as would an Amish wedding reception, consisting largely of eating and then singing German hymns. Besides, obtaining the cooperation of typical Amish youth and adults to assist in such films would be incredibly time intensive and difficult. Information about their Youngie is routinely guarded within the Amish culture, and even when rumspringa youth are breaking parental and church expectations, they overwhelmingly refuse to assist filmmakers. Clearly, film producers and marketers want something sexier than girls wearing bonnets and boys driving buggies in order to capture and maintain the attention and imagination of jaded television viewers.[8]

Amish Youth Discover the City

In terms of a relatively accurate portrayal of Amish youths' behavior, most observers agree that the first such offering, the *Amish in the City* series, provided the most realistic dilemmas and authentic character portrayals.[9] It featured five young adults who had grown up in Amish homes in the Midwest and six non-Amish counterparts; they supposedly approximated a cross-section of middle-class American twenty-somethings. UPN prepared an upscale house in the Hollywood Hills so the two groups could live together. During the next several weeks, the network dispatched their camera crews to document the encounters of the innocents and the sophisticates, both within the home and in interactions with the diversity and allurements of glitzy life in Los Angeles.

Most new reality shows receive minimal attention from the mainstream media, but before *Amish in the City* aired, writers and producers from a variety of news organizations, including the *Washington Post*, the *Washington Times*, the *Philadelphia Daily News*, the *Christian Science Monitor*, MS-NBC News, National Public Radio, and even London's *Sunday Telegraph* not only took note of the new series, but often questioned UPN's motivation and taste in producing it. Even some politicians raised similar issues when word of the network's intentions leaked out. U.S. Representative Joe Pitts of Pennsylvania and fifty of his Republican colleagues petitioned UPN to cancel the show, out of respect for Amish values. Pitts and his group charged that the media would make a mockery of down-home Amish values and would subject his plain constituents to public scorn and the ridicule of late-night comics. It turns out that their fears were unnecessary.

From the very first episode, the five young people from Amish families quickly established themselves as the home-team favorites. Despite their lack of sophistication ("Who is Reggae?" and "What is sushi?"), they demonstrated a refreshing curiosity regarding their surroundings and their companions, while displaying affable cooperation and good-natured courtesy. Most of the time, the Amish five were low-maintenance participants, compared with their often whining, bored, entitled, and self-preoccupied counterparts. The Amish youth had been "pulled up right," meaning "reared well" in the Pennsylvania Deitsch language. Representative Pitts must have been pleased with his television Amish.[10]

Parental Joy, Parental Anguish

The parents of the six non-Amish participants were undoubtedly pleased that their children were on national television, and they probably recorded every episode. Besides the notoriety and the $20,000 that each of the young people purportedly received, such national exposure might prove to be a foot in the door for a future career, or even stardom. Such opportunities are not to be taken lightly. The English parents would surely have watched each episode with great interest.

In contrast, not one of the Amish parents, if they had even contemplated watching television, would have wanted to see even a single episode of *Amish in the City*, because it would have been too painful. Even though they would have known nothing about reality television, these parents would have experienced deep sadness and shame since first learning of their children's involvement with the medium. For these mothers and fathers, this was more bad news that simply confirmed their worst fears—the worldly journey that had begun during their children's teenage years was leading into apostasy and perhaps even to damnation. All of the Amish parents undoubtedly also struggled with self-condemnation, remorse, and guilt, and they were surely plagued by the recurring question, "Where did we go wrong?" All of them knew by heart the Bible verse, "Train up a child in the way he should go, and when he is old, he will not depart from it" (Proverbs 22:6).[11] Even though they may have done their best, in their own eyes, if not in the eyes of the community as well, they had failed in their training.

The parents of one of the Amish youth in the series, Miriam, may have been especially hurt, because her father was a bishop, a position of additional responsibility and accountability in the church. The parents of the other Amish youth would have been equally worried, however, not just about the temptations their wayward children would face, but also by their own awareness that if their sons or daughters married outside the Amish faith, they would surely be lost from the fold. Mose, an affable twenty-four-year-old and the oldest of the five, was regarded by most viewers as the star of the series. He faced the most serious consequences, because he had already joined the church at age seventeen and had to endure shunning by his family and friends, a consequence that goes with breaking one's lifetime vows to God and the church.[12]

For all of the Amish-themed reality shows that followed in the next few years, their one undisputed element of real life would be that the Amish parents of the youth in these shows would experience the same gnawing sense of failure and shame that their predecessors had felt. Almost all the cast member in the various programs had indeed grown up in Amish families, but they numbered among the 15 percent who, for whatever reason, turn away from their families, friends, and heritage. Despite any out-of-wedlock children, drug use, DUI convictions, or immersion in mainstream culture, however, each prodigal (fallen) son or daughter would be welcomed back if they would repent, "give themselves up" to the authority invested in the church, and affirm their desire to be united with God and the church, a highly unlikely scenario for any of them. The only welcome-back exception would be for those who were divorced. Because of the Amish communities' unbending opposition to divorce and remarriage, those who had divorced their spouses would be unable to return unless they remarried their ex-spouse, or rejoined after their ex-spouse died.[13]

With such deliberate misrepresentations abounding in the television versions of Amish youth, the romanticized depictions in typical Amish bonnet fiction, and the news media's preoccupation with deviant youth, it is little wonder that the average viewer, reader, or writer would harbor a distorted view of the true nature of a typical Amish rumspringa experience. An important way to dispel the myths about any culture is to examine the history of that culture and identify those elements that contribute to what it is today. This we now do.

Deep Roots

Although each of the ex-Amish actors above, like all Amish everywhere, received a limited formal education and acquired a very circumscribed knowledge of urban life and culture, most Amish, young and old, have some interest in both oral and written history. These television-show participants undoubtedly would have learned something about their ancestors' early history in Europe and America. In a culture that reveres tradition, knowing one's past is more than a matter of idle curiosity. For the Amish, recalling their stories helps define who they are and gives them a standard for judging whether they are drifting into mainstream worldliness or following the biblical injunction of "keeping the faith once delivered to the saints" (Jude 3). According to sociologist Donald B. Kraybill, the Amish constantly navigate through the pressures of modernity, and now postmodernity, by weighing present realities with their historical core values. Without this intentional reflection and assessment, they are in danger of losing their distinctiveness and, ultimately, their culture. Kraybill believed that this combination of scrutiny, vigilance, and compromise has contributed to their survival.[14]

The Radicals

Although the non-Amish generally regard Amish people with respect in today's world, the Amish have not always been an esteemed part of the greater community or of their country. Historically, both secular and religious authorities regarded the forebears of today's peaceful Amish as dangerous radicals when they emerged in Switzerland during the early sixteenth century. Shortly after the reformer Martin Luther ruptured Christendom by challenging the established church in 1517, certain Swiss reformers decided that Luther's Reformation failed to go far enough or deep enough. Although they adhered to Luther's belief in the ultimate authority of scripture (*sola scriptura*) and in the repudiation of the Roman Catholic Church, they also criticized the Protestant reformers Luther, John Calvin, and Ulrich Zwingli for their refusal to sever ties with political powers. These radical Swiss reformers agreed with the Protestant belief that the state was instituted by God to provide structure and maintain order, even by force, if necessary. The dissenters, however, insisted that true Christians should separate themselves from earthly powers. As followers of Christ, they adhered to the concept that they should not be actively involved in any government that used force or violence to achieve its objectives. In essence, they believed in two separate kingdoms: the kingdom of this world and the kingdom of

God. Those in God's kingdom were to be peaceable, non-violent, and non-resistant.[15]

From their reading of the New Testament, the Swiss radicals also concluded that only adults could make a meaningful confession of Christian faith. They believed that infants and children lacked the understanding to make an intelligent and informed commitment to Christ and the church. This radical idea contradicted the Lutheran, Reformed, and Roman Catholic practice of infant baptism. Not only did these dissidents rebaptize each other in 1525, but they also required all converts to be baptized again, thus earning the derogatory term "Anabaptists" (re-baptizers).[16]

Perilous Times

Because of their beliefs and practices, thousands of Anabaptists were tortured and many were drowned or burned at the stake, persecuted by both Catholics and Protestants. Because baptismal records established future tax rolls, civil authorities were incensed by the potential loss of taxpayers. Since the Anabaptists initially rejected all forms of violence, including involvement in the military, the state also joined in their persecution, fearing that it would lose future soldiers who would be needed to fight the Ottoman Turks. As a result of an uncharacteristically violent uprising by a heretical Anabaptist fringe group, civil and religious authorities in the German city of Münster retaliated by executing many Anabaptist dissidents.[17] These persecutions are recounted in numerous songs in the *Ausbund* (the Amish hymnal) and in the graphic narratives in *Martyrs Mirror*, a book owned by many Amish families today.[18] Adversity scattered the survivors, and new groups took root in France, Germany, and Holland.[19]

Persecution of these Swiss Anabaptists, also known as the Swiss Brethren, waxed and waned for nearly a century, depending on then-current tensions or the whims of the powerful. Bloodless internal conflicts also wracked the Anabaptists. Nearly 170 years after the birth of the Anabaptist movement, some of their descendants, called Mennonites after an early leader, Menno Simons (1496–1561), faced a serious challenge by a zealous Swiss-Alsatian Anabaptist minister, Jakob Ammann. He charged that Mennonite leaders had been drifting away from the teachings of the Bible and

Menno Simons and were becoming lax on important issues, such as separation from the world, communion practices, excommunication, and shunning.

The heart of the conflict stemmed from the issue of shunning excommunicated members. Ammann and his followers believed that disobedient church members should not only be excommunicated (put out of the
fellowship), but also be socially avoided, as taught in the New Testament
and elaborated in the *Dordrecht Confession*, an early Dutch-Mennonite document.[20] Ammann brashly charged Swiss Anabaptist leaders to either discipline lax ministers and members or face excommunication by Ammann
and his followers. The Swiss leaders and Ammann's group eventually split
over their disagreements, and the more conservative offshoot in both Switzerland and Alsace became known as the Amish.

A Separate People

In light of the history of early and widespread persecution of the Anabaptists, the Amish belief in separation—that is, in segregation from the world
and in the separation of church and state—is understandable. Today most
Amish are decidedly wary of government, and relatively few vote in state
and national elections.[21] They follow the biblical injunctions in Matthew
22:21 and Romans 13:6–7 to pay taxes, but they have traditionally rejected
the federal social security system, believing that they should care for their
own. For the same reason, they also rarely accept unemployment or health
care assistance from the government.[22] Since the mid-twentieth century,
their distrust has often extended to public school boards and local officials,
who had sometimes arrested, jailed, and fined Amish fathers for refusing to
send their children to large consolidated schools or to high school. In many
places, the Amish avoid public education, because of their persistent fear of
the worldly ideas and secularizing effects of higher education.

The desire of the Amish to be separate from the world (Romans 12:2) also
helps explain their hallmark bonnets and broad-brimmed hats, suspenders
and aprons, and straight pins or hooks-and-eyes instead of buttons. Their
dress and characteristic grooming help maintain their identity and emphasize their distinctiveness. In the twentieth century, their commitment to

separation also translated into the rejection of "worldly" technologies and practices, such as car ownership, power-line electricity, telephones in their houses, and commercial insurance. Kraybill has pointed out that the Amish do not automatically equate modern technology with sinful practices, but they do seek to limit anything that they believe will weaken or corrupt the community or endanger their society and their youth.[23]

Other aspects of their past also influence Amish society. Many of the men started out as farmers or craftsmen in northern Europe; when they migrated to America they maintained their attraction to rural life, their passion for agriculture, and their penchant for hard work. Even though many Amish have had to give up farming for lack of available farmland, they have traditionally viewed farming as the ideal occupation, and farms as an especially suitable environment for rearing a family. Parents can always find work for their children on a farm, and manual labor is part of the Amish rural heritage. They see the rural environment as a wholesome place, in contrast to the city, which they regard as both physically dangerous and morally corrupt.

Another remnant from their European heritage is their language. All Amish speak a German or Swiss dialect in the home and use a mixture of dialect and High (sixteenth-century) German in their church services. In the most conservative circles, many Amish believe that their young children are protected from worldly influences by not knowing English during their early years. As an Amish man explained, "If children grow up with only [Pennsylvania] German, they will be protected from television or a cursing neighbor. It is protective." Thus their offspring, especially the oldest ones, typically do not learn English until they enter school.

The Amish Core

The faith and practices of the Amish stem from their literal understanding of the Bible, especially the New Testament teachings of Jesus. Because they take the Gospels seriously, particularly the Sermon on the Mount, they oppose war and retaliation, refuse to take oaths, and strive for a simple and peaceable life.[24] Within the church and the home, the Amish unabashedly support a patriarchal system, again based on their understanding of the scriptures.[25] Males are expected to be the head of the household and of the church. Females, married or single, are to wear head coverings, to reflect an attitude of prayer and submission (1 Corinthians 11:2–16).[26]

Socialization into community mores begins early, because all able-bodied people, including infants, are expected to attend the local church service. Unless individuals marry or move elsewhere, they attend church all their lives with the same friends, neighbors, and relatives. Services are held every other week in members' homes, barns, or shops.[27] The local congregation, called a church district, is an ecclesiastical unit based on geography and proximity. Typically it consists of twenty to forty families that live within a geographic boundary small enough to permit members to reach each other's houses by horse and carriage for church on Sundays.

Attending church from childhood, however, does not make a child a member of the church. Each young man and woman decides, usually during their late teens or early twenties, whether they will take membership instruction, make lifetime vows to follow Christ and the church, and be baptized into the faith. To freely choose to be baptized as an adult is one of the defining principles of Anabaptism.

An Array of Communities

If an outsider were to visit church services in several of the thirty states where the Amish live, a typical visitor would probably observe few differences from one place to the next. The tone, the order of the service, the cadences, and the songs and prayers would all be remarkably similar. Also, to the uninitiated, most Amish look alike. All wear plain clothes, use horse-drawn transportation, resist many aspects of modern technology, and speak in "Dutch."[28] Thus it is easy to conclude that if the Amish look and talk alike, they must act alike. Even scholars who study a single Amish community may tend to generalize about all Amish, based on their limited experiences. Such generalizations and tendencies help explain why outsiders are surprised when they first encounter the diversity that exists, both in the Amish communities and in the behavior of their youth.

Today more than 2,000 Amish church districts or churches are scattered throughout nearly 500 settlements in thirty states and in Ontario, Canada

(Young Center).[29] The local church district is the unit that organizes Amish life, and each has its own set of ministers and its own rules, called the *Ordnung*. The Ordnung, although rarely written down, is the agreed-upon set of rules that prescribes behavior in individual districts. With such a large number of churches, some diversity in customs and practices naturally emerges, because each local church district has considerable autonomy in establishing its own Ordnung.[30]

Other factors also lead to varying traditions and behavior. Amish groups in the same settlement sometimes belong to different affiliations (clusters of church districts that are governed by a shared Ordnung). The Big Valley of central Pennsylvania has several Amish affiliations, each with its own set of standards.[31] Members in each affiliation drive the distinctive carriages that identify their particular group: the Renno Amish drive all-black carriages, the Byler people ride in yellow-topped carriages, and the so-called "Nebraska" Amish have white-topped carriages. One can also identify these three affiliations by the color and style of their clothing, by their hairstyles, and by their use or avoidance of certain technologies. In contrast to the Renno and Byler Amish, the Nebraska men dress in brown coats rather than black, and the women wear head scarves instead of the traditional organdy head coverings. The Renno and Byler groups may use gas refrigerators, but most of the Nebraska Amish forbid their use. Many other differences also exist.

Adams County, Indiana, has five affiliations, or distinct groups,[32] and in the Ohio settlement in Holmes/Wayne/Stark Counties, at least a dozen Amish affiliations coexist, often side by side. They range from the ultraconservative Swartzentruber Amish, who reject almost all modern technology, to the progressive New Order Christian Fellowship, or, more commonly, *New* New Order Amish. Most of the latter have either cell phones or landline telephones in their homes, electricity in their houses, computers in their businesses, and tractors on their farms.[33] Differences in recreation, dating, and wedding customs also exist among the youth in these affiliations. The distinctions generally center on what each affiliation regards as moral or immoral behavior and on how each group expresses its Christian faith.

The New Order Amish originated in Ohio in the late 1960s, splitting from the Old Orders over moral and theological issues, especially as they related to acceptable behavior among the youth.[34] New Order founders objected to several traditional Old Order practices, such as tobacco use and certain courtship behaviors. The New Order Amish also adopted non-traditional practices, such as Sunday school and Wednesday-night church gatherings for the youth. Additionally, they spoke out strongly against the weekend party scene. These ideological and moral distinctions, more than external differences, became the defining issues that ultimately divided the two groups.[35]

A Snapshot of Two Communities

Adult-Centered Communities

Wherever the settlement or whatever visual images are associated with Amish communities, outsiders may be tempted to envision a picture-perfect Amish life, unchanged over the centuries. Especially in small traditional communities, Amish life may appear to be untouched by the present. On Saturday nights, families will complete their farm or shop work in preparation for "the Lord's Day." Most of the evening's activity will center around the table, where the family may read, play games, or talk about plans for the next day. If the next day is an "off-Sunday" instead of a "church Sunday," courting couples will see each other at the home of the young woman.

On church Sundays, virtually all teens attend the three-hour worship service. The youth closely resemble their parents and grandparents in modes of dress and grooming. Like their fathers, the young men wear their hair in the traditional blunt cut, a squared-off Dutch-boy style. The young women part their long hair in the middle and pull it back in a bun, also in the traditional fashion. They wear opaque or even dark stockings, and dresses that reach at least midway down their calves. During the singing of the traditional slow songs from the *Ausbund*, a venerable German hymnbook, even the youth who do not sing usually turn to the announced pages, and all sit quietly during the sermons.

Following church, most of the young people remain for the light communal meal. Afterward they might chat with friends, go hiking, or, in the larger settlements, play volleyball until supper or the beginning of the

Sunday-evening youth singing. These peaceful Sunday scenes are reminiscent of the simple rural life of a century ago, with its horse-and-buggy pace and its cross-generational mix of family, relatives, and friends. Many communities do, in fact, approach this ideal, particularly in the more isolated settlements in Kentucky, Michigan, Missouri, New York, and Wisconsin, but also in the conservative sections and among the plainer youth groups in the large settlements.

Peer-Centered Communities

But life on the inside is rarely as simple or as perfect as it appears from the outside. Picture the same scene on any Saturday night in a large Amish settlement in Indiana, Ohio, or Pennsylvania, where thousands of Amish youth live in close proximity, not only to each other but also, for those youth who have cars, within easy driving distance of surrounding urban centers such as Fort Wayne, Cleveland, or Philadelphia. Closer to home, clusters of Amish teenagers may lounge outside the local 7-Eleven store. Some have come to town by horse and buggy, but most drive cars, pickup trucks, or SUVs. For girls who are dressed Amish, their organdy head coverings may be precariously perched far back on their heads, and the hems of their dresses may be shortened or lengthened, depending on the current mainstream fashions. They may also wear ankle socks instead of the traditional stockings. In the largest settlements, some of the teenage girls may change into English clothes in the restroom of a local convenience store or fast-food restaurant, but they most commonly do so at a girlfriend's house if her parents are out. In parts of Indiana, some of the most daring or rebellious young women may leave home already dressed in their English attire. In many informal gatherings, teenage Amish girls are indistinguishable from their English cohorts, showing up in jeans and sweats, designer t-shirts or sleeveless blouses, and even shorts and tank tops, depending on the season or the weather.

Almost all the teenage boys in the "fastest" groups sport barber haircuts or variations on the latest English hairstyles, even—at the extremes—Mohawks or highlighted hair. Some of the most daring boys get piercings and earrings. A few may have hidden their plain clothing in plastic bags in the back of their buggies or other vehicles, in family mailboxes, or even between corn rows before they left home, but many will be dressed in their English clothing before they leave. Baseball caps, often turned backward, have replaced straw hats, and belts take the place of suspenders. Many teenage boys smoke cigarettes—fewer of the girls do—while discussing the latest standing of their local Amish ball team; checking their smartphones for the current status of their favorite professional baseball, football, or basketball teams; texting a girlfriend or cousin; or seeing who has posted a message to them on Facebook or Twitter.

Others talk about the band hop, hoedown, or party starting later that night, an event that will attract scores, if not hundreds, of young people and may feature live music, dancing, alcohol in abundance, and even drugs. Parties may last until 3:00 or 4:00 a.m., so fewer than half of the youth may show up for church in some districts. Those who do attend often doze through the singing, take a smoking break during the scripture reading, and slump or sleep through the main sermon. Afterward, many teens will skip the communal meal to join their friends from other church districts for an afternoon of softball, volleyball, or ice hockey, depending on the season. Some of the youth, especially the males, may still be feeling the effects from Saturday night or may begin drinking again in the afternoon.

Just as the earlier pastoral scene failed to depict all small-settlement youth, this large-settlement scene represents perhaps only the estimated 15–20 percent of youth who ignore community standards. Yet most Amish agree that these two vignettes accurately represent life today in both kinds of settlements. Whether compliant or rebellious, most youth in each type of settlement are deeply invested in the heady experience of Rumspringa.

Why the Differences?

When asked to speculate on why such differences exist among communities in the behavior of their youth, most Amish parents and ministers do not mention specific rules or a lack of them, instead quickly attributing the causes to adult or community failures. They talk about dissension in the church, lax discipline by leaders, careless parents, or inconsistent adults. Many Amish also believe that those settlements where most of the fathers are farmers have fewer problems with their youth than those where fathers are employed in factories, on construction crews, or in similar work venues away from home.

Others cite factors such as the settlement's density and its size. "When it comes to the young folk," declared a bishop from Arthur, Illinois, "the larger the settlement, the larger the problems." Similarly, a minister mused, "It's easier to corral ten calves than a hundred." The size of the settlement actually does appear to be the single best predictor of youth behavior. Settlements that consist of one church district with a few families (such as in Oceola, Missouri), or only two or three church districts (such as Somerset County, Pennsylvania), tend to have few problems with their youth. On the other hand, the largest three settlements—Elkhart/LaGrange Counties in Indiana, Holmes/Wayne/Stark Counties in eastern Ohio, and Lancaster County in Pennsylvania—regularly encounter not only more problems with their youth, but also the conspicuous or illegal behaviors that catch the attention of the public and the media.[36]

Although most mainstream people would regard the three largest Amish enclaves as rural, their residents have been dubbed the "urban Amish," because of their large numbers of residents and relative proximity to sizeable non-Amish population centers. Together, these three settlements consist of several different Amish affiliations, contain hundreds of church districts, and are home to nearly two-thirds of all Amish. All other settlements are significantly smaller than the big three and are typically more isolated from urban areas.[37]

The relationship between settlement size and youth behavior most likely stems from demographic changes that occurred in the 1930s and 1940s. During the early decades of the twentieth century, when church districts were small and grew slowly, an Amish young person's peers consisted primarily of family members and childhood friends from the local church district and immediate vicinity. Before 1950, the Amish population in America barely exceeded the population of a single large settlement today, and, according to an Amish historian who lived during that period, was fairly static.[38] Improved health care and strong retention contributed to the exponential population growth among the Amish, which is especially apparent in the large settlements.[39] Because of this growth, the demand for good farmland began to outstrip the supply. Farm sizes began to shrink as parents divided their property among their children.[40]

As their communities grew, more families moved into non-farming occupations, since many more non-farming-family plots than farms could be squeezed into a given area. Thus the growing numbers of people, coupled with smaller farms and non-farming households, resulted in a greater density of Amish families in the larger settlements. Instead of church districts being fifteen or twenty miles across, some became as small as four or five square miles. And, instead of needing to travel long distances to visit friends, young people were able to easily associate with a variety of peers living only a short buggy ride away. These changes produced social influences with enormous implications for youth and their parents.

As the Amish population expanded in the large settlements during the early 1950s, a few young people began to break away from the single, large Sunday-night singing to socialize with smaller groups of peers.[41] This had rarely, if ever, happened before among the Amish. Another change that led to wider peer contacts began after World War II, when some of the teenage males began driving cars during Rumspringa.[42] Until then, a youth's birth community, more than one's social preferences, shaped the selection of one's friends. The new postwar demographics and increased mobility provided greater opportunities to find like-minded companions who shared and reinforced one's particular interests, values, and proclivities.[43]

It is unlikely that mid-twentieth-century Amish leaders and parents realized the impact these demographic changes would have on their communities. As young people began socializing with other youth farther from home, accountability diminished. At the same time, these teenagers discovered other peers whom they had not even known before but who, like themselves, had left their home-church district to enjoy the excitement and stimulation afforded by clusters of like-minded youth. A bishop's wife flatly declared, "It's the anonymity our youth have that leads to trouble." In the larger settlements, the growing numbers of young people, coupled with their having a choice of potential companions, ushered in significant changes in social interactions that transformed Amish youth culture. The antecedents of the current social networks and behavior in large settlements started to emerge with the peer choices made more than a half century ago by the grandparents of today's Amish teenagers.

Whose Standards, Anyway?

In Amish circles, especially in the large settlements, adults frequently express concerns about the attitudes and behaviors of the youth. Leaders may not connect past demographic changes with what is happening on weekends, but the behavior of the youth, or Youngie as they are affectionately called in dialect, is a frequent topic. A perplexed father from a large settlement wondered: "Why do our young people have to carry on like this? So many of the youth in this community do not care what us parents or church leaders think or believe. They only care about what their friends will think or say and about having a good time." Many adults have added their concerns about adolescents in the large settlements and speculate as to why more problems and fun-seekers emerge there than in the smaller settlements.

Although neither Amish adults nor youth would use the terms "adult-centered" or "peer-centered," most would recognize that these concepts describe the difference in the orientation of the youth in large and small settlements. During Rumspringa, adult-youth interaction tends to be much higher in the small settlements than in the larger ones. In chapter 7, we will see that every week many large-settlement youth associate with each other for almost the entire weekend, while their small-settlement counterparts typically spend only a few hours a month with their peers, at the singing socials. Small-settlement youth have more opportunities to absorb adult standards and thus behave and think more conservatively. On the other hand, youth with extensive peer contact and a wide variety of possible friends may act in ways that are less acceptable to adults.

A major indicator of adult-centered settlements is the continuity of behavior from teen years to adulthood. "Continuity" refers to a fairly smooth or seamless transition from childhood to adulthood in areas of dress, mode of transportation, recreation, and dating and courting practices.[44] Conservative youth behave in ways that are consistent with adult behavior and expectations. When these sixteen-year-olds begin "going with the youth," their actions primarily reflect the traditional standards of their parents and grandparents. Likewise, conservative young people sound more like the adults in their community, especially when they condemn certain changes, which they refer to as "drift," meaning the growing tendency of Amish youth to violate church rules or disobey their parents. A seventeen-year-old boy from a small settlement who had recently visited one of the larger settlements exclaimed: "I think it's awful the way the young folk behave over there. They drink and smoke and carry on at the singings. It's a disgrace." He also added, "When some young people from their settlement visited us, they got bored right away; they didn't know what to do out here." His grandfather would have undoubtedly agreed with the young man's assessment.

Peer-centered settlements demonstrate much more discontinuity between adult expectations and the actions of their youth. When these sixteen-year-olds begin their Rumspringa, many show a dramatic change in behavior, especially the males. Besides ignoring or modifying traditional standards of dress, they frequently engage in activities that would result in excommunication for church members.

Determining whether a community is adult-centered or peer-centered is not simply a matter of settlement size, however, because adult-peer orientation also reflects a community's local history, traditions, and moral beliefs. Peers can either oppose or reinforce adult values and mores in communities of any size. Because of strong negative peer pressures, some small settlements also struggle with the rowdy behavior more common in large settlements. Although one of the young women who participated in *Amish in the City* grew up in a large settlement, two of the small-settlement young men experienced many of the same behaviors that more typically characterize the fringes of the larger settlements. Also, two of the participants in *Breaking Amish* grew up in very small and relatively isolated settlements in Pennsylvania.

Despite these exceptions, most Amish would agree that settlement size is a useful factor in predicting youthful attitudes and behaviors.[45] But many other factors, past and present, help build an Amish mindset that retains the faithful and brings the wayward back into the fold. Among these, we turn first to the religious underpinnings on which Amish society is constructed.

In the three-hour biweekly church services, everyone, except for young children, enters and sits together by age and by sex. Here unmarried young women walk into the barn, a typical site where church may be held in the summer.

(Doyle Yoder)

-ᴥᴥᴥ Chapter Two ᴥᴥᴥ

Religion
Transmitting the Faith

I remember the day when I was baptized. I felt clean as a whistle.
—Amish grandfather

A Faith-Filled Community

Although most standard texts on adolescent development devote little attention to religious practices and faith issues, any study of Amish youth that neglects this subject would be seriously deficient. Much has been written to describe Amish worship rituals and beliefs, but little attention has been directed to moral or spiritual development, the transmission of faith to the young, and the religious practices of the youth.[1] Most young people, no matter how neglectful or wayward, would agree with the words of an elderly bishop: "Our faith is at the heart of Amish life, the foundation on which we seek to build our relationships, vocations, family, and communal life. If anyone fails to understand that, they will never really understand who we are and what we are about."

A non-Amish observer accustomed to the compartmentalizing of secular and religious life might assume that in the highly structured Amish society, every facet of community life rigorously instructs and enforces the tenets of the Amish faith. Outsiders might expect Amish practices to resemble the extremism of David Koresh's Branch Davidian compound or Sun Myung Moon's Unification Church. Actually, for a religious culture that strives to leave nothing to chance or to the outside world, Amish communities provide relatively little *formal* religious instruction in the home or even in Amish schools. As David Weaver-Zercher has observed, faith within the Amish community is more caught than taught. It is part of their "habits of the heart."

Amish parents admonish their children and youth to obey God and their parents, revere the scriptures, recognize God as the creator and sustainer of life, and submit themselves to Christ and the teachings of the Bible. Amish mothers are often the chief readers of Bible stories, and other stories with moral lessons, to their young children.[2] In most communities, however, formal religious instruction occurs only after the youth, usually in their late teens, have expressed their intention to join the church. Prior to that, according to Donald B. Kraybill and Carl F. Bowman, "religion is not formally taught in the school or in other Amish settings."[3] Formal instruction in the faith occurs only during the eighteen-week preparatory class for church membership.

Youth and Worship

Although church leaders do not adapt the traditional forms and practices of the Amish faith to the interest level or preferences of the young, an estimated 85 percent choose to join the church and remain Amish for life.[4] Nor does the church employ age-appropriate curricula, junior church, or interactive instruction. Infants, children, and youth sit through adult-centered services, along with their grandparents, parents, siblings, and neighbors. They sing the same songs and hear the same sermons as the adults. Moreover, everyone expects the young to sit quietly through a long, thoroughly predictable, adult-oriented worship service. A bishop observed, "The reason there are so many good archery hunters among the Amish is because they are used to sitting still for three hours in church."

As a further challenge, all hymns, prayers, and scriptures are written in sixteenth-century High German, the language Martin Luther used to translate the Bible. Since the Amish never use this idiom in daily discourse, the youth face a challenge similar to that of mainstream youth listening to Chaucer's *Canterbury Tales*. "When I was younger," a man recalled, "I had to concentrate so hard to understand High German that I would eventually give up and start to think about the upcoming Phillies' game in the afternoon." A twenty-five-year-old man admitted, "Our family sometimes reads the Bible at home in English, but in church I understand very little of the scripture readings and hymns." When asked how members learn the older form of German, he replied that most absorb it throughout their adult years.[5]

Ministers preach in the Pennsylvania German vernacular, their first language, but the two customary sermons may last nearly an hour and a half, which is beyond the attention span of many adults, let alone children and youth. In the plainest settlements, some ministers still exhort attendees in an old-fashioned singsong or chantlike style, rarely establishing eye contact with the faithful. A few even preach with their eyes closed. Finally, everyone must endure the discomfort of cramped seating, hard benches (except for the oldest members, who are allowed to sit in chairs), and, depending on the season, a hot stuffy house, dusty barn, or drafty shop. Despite these conditions, the Amish transmit their faith effectively, at least if their high retention rate is any indication.

In most settlements, children and almost all of the youth regularly attend church. Although those in this latter age group always sit with their peers, they rarely "carry on" (disturb worship by talking). Parents admit, however, that it is hard to know how many youth are actually engaged in the prayers and sermons. During the reading of the scriptures in some settlements, half or more of the young men leave for an ostensible bathroom break. If posture or eye contact is an indicator, youth generally appear to be less involved in worship than the adults, but that also varies from place to place. One parent indicated: "I think they are listening. When they get home, young people can be quite critical of boring sermons. They will also get upset when ministers harp on things such as dress or the behavior of the Youngie. 'They should be preaching from the Bible,' our youngest son says."

The Faithful "Curriculum"

Most Old Order communities do not supplement their Sunday services with any of the standard Protestant programs, such as Sunday schools, summer-vacation bible schools, or bible-study groups. The Amish have traditionally associated Sunday schools with the more liberal Anabaptists and mainline churches.[6] This negative attitude toward Sunday schools was expressed by an Amish minister, who voiced his disapproval of non-ordained persons instructing in matters of faith. Another elder stated, "We are concerned about what might be taught to our children and the lack of safeguards against error." Finally, a leader argued that if Sunday school was such a good idea, it would have been part of the New Testament church.[7]

This belief that ordained leaders and the family carry the primary responsibility for religious interpretation and instruction may explain why Amish schools provide little specific religious teaching. This differs significantly from many non-Amish conservative religious groups that regard parochial schools as crucial for teaching and propagating their faith. The curriculum in many private religious schools presents doctrinal beliefs in a systematic fashion, while that in most Amish schools is more low-key. Additionally, the teachers are usually women, and many Amish consider it inappropriate for females to instruct their students on religious topics (1 Corinthians 14:34–35). The widespread Amish belief is that explicitly religious instruction should be the role of the ordained ministers.

This does not mean that school classes are devoid of religious content. In most Amish schools, teachers start the day by reading a biblical passage, leading the children in singing hymns and gospel songs, and reciting the Lord's Prayer. Teachers typically assign "memory verses" from the King James Version of the Bible, especially from the Sermon on the Mount, a favorite Anabaptist passage. In some communities, pupils in the upper grades memorize both scripture and songs in High German for the equivalent of one or two class periods per week. Teachers are instructed to simply make the assignments and not explain the scriptural passages. A section addressed to teachers from the booklet *Standards of the Old Order Amish and Old Order Mennonite Parochial and Vocational Schools of Pennsylvania* admonishes: "Instructors are advised not to include Sunday school lessons, not induce the child to be scripture-smart for religious show. Scripture teaches simplicity by examples. Do not beguile [*sic*] that which belongs to the Church and its leaders." In certain areas of Lancaster County, some ministers and school board members have argued that writings about God are too sacred to be printed in textbooks. Consequently, their curriculum and textbooks are generally morality based rather than specifically religious. They emphasize the values of hard work, thrift, honesty, and humility, with some references to the Bible.

Teaching by Word and Deed

Ideally, the community expects all adults to teach the faith through examples of consistent living. They believe that the young come to spiritual maturity more from what they see than from what they hear. The Amish consider one's life to be the most important text, and these lives are to be marked by humility and yielding—"giving oneself up," to use a key phrase that expresses their putting God, the church, and others ahead of their personal agendas and whims. As parents and teachers like to say to their children, "Jesus, Others, You—that's the secret of joy." The German word used to express this approach is *Gelassenheit* (giving oneself up to God's will and to the church).[8] What is always regarded as more important than admonitions and slogans, however, is the example of adults behaving with humility and integrity. Amish adults believe that their living in submission to God's will and each other "prepares the soil," plants the seeds of faith, and nurtures the spiritual development of the young. "Our major task," explained one father, "is to pass our faith on to our children."[9]

In many Old Order settlements, parent traditionally use off-Sunday mornings at home for religious readings and reflection. "We were taught that off-Sunday should be used for the family *Sunndaagschul* [Sunday school]. We would read the Bible, memorize bible verses in English or German, and pray together, but we were not supposed to explain the word of God—just read it," stated a grandfather from a large settlement. Most Old Order Amish believe that religious discussions are more appropriate among adults, and that the final interpretation comes from ordained ministers in communal worship. Parents are expected to teach their children in the "nurture and admonition of the Lord" (Ephesians 6:4), providing a loving Christian family and being faithful examples and mentors for their children. Parents are also guardians, protecting their offspring from unhealthy worldly influences and reinforcing the teachings of the church. In daily discourse, parents admonish their children to live obedient, faithful, and moral lives. One Amish man recalled his parents' strictures and reminders of forty years ago: "God sees what we do. . . . He can see into our hearts. . . . When we do wrong, it is sin. . . . Don't lie. . . . Don't harm others. . . . Play nice with other children. . . . Keep yourself clean. . . . Look constantly to God. . . . Remember that Christ has the forgiveness for sins."

Depending on the family and the particular community, many households systematically start or end the day by reading a passage from the Bible and a prayer from *Die Ernsthafte Christenpflicht*, a German prayer book.[10] In the Old Order homes where daily devotions are practiced, fathers typically read the scriptures and prayers in High German. Except for the more progressive New Order Amish, in most settlements extemporaneous prayers are the exception. This lack of intentional religious discourse cannot be equated with an absence of devotion; rather, it may simply indicate that a majority of the Amish accept the religious teachings and practices of the church with few serious questions or reservations. Amish adults are not wont to encourage their youth to analyze their beliefs and practices and subject them to critical scrutiny. Consequently, most youth apparently embrace their religious faith without serious questioning and simply absorb it from the landscape of daily life.[11]

This does not mean, however, that conscientious parents are disengaged from their children's moral and spiritual development. In most families parents are involved in the careful selection and monitoring of reading materials available to their children. Many families have a copy of *Martyrs Mirror*, with its 1,100-plus pages describing the persecution and suffering of the early Anabaptist martyrs through graphically described accounts and vivid engravings. Since the 1960s, Amish periodicals such as *Young Companion* and *Family Life* have been popular in many homes.[12] In the first decade of this century, Amish individuals have started other publications, such as *Ladies Journal, Connections*, and *Tagaliches Manna* (Daily Bread), a daily devotional. The stories and articles in these publications emphasize

adherence to Christian ideals and high moral standards. Unlike mainline
and evangelical church publications, typical Amish magazines rarely feature scriptural analyses or even biblical stories. Rather, they are filled with
short stories (morality tales) and brief essays by Amish and Old Order Mennonites, often written anonymously to minimize pride or pretentiousness.
Articles emphasize religious values and themes, such as the responsibility
of parents, obedience to those in authority, submission to God's will, non-
resistance, and separation from worldly temptations and activities.

The Ultimate Decision

About the time Amish children finish their formal schooling in early adolescence, they are considered to be approaching the "age of accountability,"
the stage at which they are assumed to fully know right from wrong and understand the implications of their choices. After youth begin attending the
singings, adults consider them to be accountable and answerable for their
choices and behaviors. It is at this time that many bishops and ministers,
especially in the smaller settlements, increasingly admonish the youth to
set aside any sinful behaviors, start counting the cost, and give themselves
up to become a baptized member of the church. Although most Old Order
ministers preach about the necessity of the new birth, their emphasis is
much more on being baptized into the community of faith than the evan-
gelicals' emphasis on a personal-salvation experience with God.

The age at which young people decide to join the church varies. In most
Old Order groups, parents hope that their children will take instruction and
then receive baptism between the ages of sixteen and nineteen. In some
large settlements, however, youth typically join the church between the ages
of eighteen and twenty-one. Females almost always join the church at a
younger age than males. Youth in small, isolated settlements or in New
Order churches normally join earlier than young people from the larger
settlements. Leaders in the larger communities observe that in the last generation or two, the faster youth (especially males) are waiting longer to join
than their parents and grandparents did. A significant minority of young
males have even been delaying membership instruction beyond their midtwenties, a trend that seems to be growing in the large settlements. The

Amish generally attribute this delay to the young men's desire to "keep their vehicles and have a good time for a while longer." Some adults regard sports as detrimental to joining "on time." One young man confessed that he was not going to join as planned because the Cleveland Cavaliers and LeBron James had a good chance of winning the NBA title, and he wanted to be able to watch them to the end. On the other hand, many Amish adults believe that the general trend has begun to move toward earlier membership, especially in settlements or youth groups that require church membership as a prerequisite for dating and courtship.

The Amish Catechism and Preparing for Baptism

No young person joins the church without first receiving teaching in religious beliefs and practices from the local bishop and ministers. During the first hymn on a spring Sunday morning, the self-declared candidates for church membership join their clergy in the "council room," usually an upstairs bedroom of the home. The first day of the instructional class marks an important day in the life of the church, one of both anticipation and apprehension. The ministers, and even the parents, do not always know who will decide to take instruction and who will delay for yet another year or more.[13] One minister reported: "My wife and I were holding our breath Sunday morning, watching to see if our son would enter the room with the youth or remain outside with the candidates, waiting to meet the ministers. He was only sixteen, and we weren't sure he was ready. When we went out to lead the waiting candidates up to the council room, I was greatly relieved to find him there along with the others who were starting in the instruction class." In all settlements, parents hope and pray that their children's closest friends and relatives take instruction at the "right age," since youth tend to join at the same time as their closest friends.

Some parents, especially in the large settlements, experience the disappointment of facing another year or two of waiting, hoping, and praying if their children fail to take the membership step. One father hoped that his son might give up playing in the local softball league in order to enter the current class, but admitted that it was very unlikely: "He is really good, and softball has taken over in his life. It looks like he is out [of church] for another year." Meanwhile, a bishop asked, "If a young man is not willing to give up softball, what kind of church member is he going to make, anyway?" Imagine what that bishop's reaction would have been to the LeBron James fan. The parents' greatest worry that is that if their child is refused membership, particularly more than once, he or she might decide to leave the Amish in the interim period.

Those who decide to take instruction meet every other Sunday with the bishop, ministers, and deacon during the first twenty-five or thirty minutes of the service, while the rest of the church members continue with their accustomed morning songs. At the beginning of every instructional meeting, each candidate affirms, "I am a seeker desiring to be part of this church of God." In most districts, the classes are devoted to explaining the articles of the *Dordrecht Confession*, two articles per class, for a total of nine sessions over an eighteen-week period. This 1632 confessional document summarizes the historic beliefs and practice of the early Dutch Anabaptists.[14] The eighteen articles begin with the foundational belief in God the Creator and proceed through the second coming of Christ as the final judge. They also explain the basis for the Amish adherence to the typical Anabaptist practices of adult baptism, separation from the world, non-swearing of oaths, non-participation in civil government, non-resistance, foot washing, excommunication, and shunning (social avoidance).[15] Although these youthful candidates may not know scriptural references or be able to recall specific points, they are already familiar with the themes. They have repeatedly heard all of the beliefs and practices from the *Confession* in past sermons at church and in conversations at home. Thus both the content of the classes and one's willingness to submit oneself to instruction by those who have been ordained by God to lead the church set the pattern for the right beliefs and acceptable behavior.

Working with Recalcitrant Youngie

When they reach this stage, candidates for membership are expected to be in compliance with the local church Ordnung, especially those who have been lax or have strayed in their behavior.[16] Ministers and church members seek evidence of sincerity, especially from those who have owned cars, dressed English, or partied hard. By the end of the eighth session, if the young men have failed to let their hair grow to the proper length, or the young women's hemlines are too long or too short, they will be instructed to comply so that they will not be "held back" from baptism. The decision to accept the candidates is made by church members in the Sunday council meeting two weeks prior to the baptism. All members vote on the candidates' worthiness for membership. If some are still regarded as failing to meet church standards, their vows may be postponed for six weeks, or until they demonstrate their serious intentions and adjust their behaviors. If an issue can be satisfactorily resolved immediately, these young people will normally be "taken up" with their peers at the baptismal service two weeks later. Writing about such a situation, a young man explained: "If there is an improvement in whatever the problem is, they are baptized [with the others on] the same day. I would say 99 percent of the time it would be this way."[17] Some young people react like two sixteen-year-olds in a large settlement. They simply dropped out of instruction after the deacon confronted them about their worldly behavior at Saturday-night parties. To their parents' great relief, they returned, albeit two years later, for instruction, baptism, and a secure place in the church and the community.

In Lancaster County, a test of the seriousness of the youthful candidates is that they are expected to stay home with their families on the first, third, and ninth instructional weekends, as well as stay home on the Friday and Saturday nights immediately before their Sunday baptism. If all goes well, on the Saturday prior to baptism, the youth and their parents meet with the ministers one final time to review the *Dordrecht Confession* and the vows they will take. The ministers again ask the candidates if they still wish to be baptized and join the church. This is also the time when the bishop asks each young man if he is willing to be ordained and serve in the ministry if the lot, or choice, should ever fall on him.[18] In Lancaster County, at least, a young man must also affirm his willingness to grow a beard at the appropriate time. Such scrutiny and attention to details show how seriously the community regards church membership vows. The entire candidate group is voted on and must receive a unanimous vote for membership, in order for all of them to be taken up that day. Those who are still regarded as not being in full compliance will be "worked with," and if they change, they may be baptized as soon as the next church service. If they still fail to receive unanimous support, they will normally have to wait at least until the next spring, when a neighboring district offers its instruction class. Otherwise, they must wait two years for instruction in their own district.[19] Again, such delays are relatively rare.

The Sacred Day

On the day of baptism, the service runs considerably longer than normal. After more than three hours of singing, prayer, scripture reading, and two long sermons, the candidates—who have all been sitting together, bent forward with heads down, in the traditional posture of submission and humility, for part of the time—kneel to answer the following questions asked by the presiding bishop:

Q. Can you also confess with the Ethiopian eunuch: Yes, I believe that Jesus Christ is the Son of God?
A. *Yes, I believe that Jesus Christ is the Son of God.*
Q. Do you also recognize this to be a Christian order, church, and fellowship under which you now submit yourselves?
A. *Yes.*
Q. Do you renounce the world, the devil with all his subtle ways, as well as your own flesh and blood, and desire to serve Jesus Christ alone, who died on the cross for you?
A. *Yes.*
Q. Do you also promise before God and His church that you will support these teachings and regulations with the Lord's help,[20] faithfully attend the services of the church, and help counsel and work in it, and not forsake it, whether it leads to life or death?
A. *Yes.*

The members then stand and, with the baptismal candidates still kneeling before the bishop, he declares, "Upon your faith, which you have confessed before God and many witnesses, you are baptized in the name of the Father, the Son, and the Holy Spirit. Amen."[21] As the bishop mentions each member of the Trinity, the deacon (who has been standing nearby) steps forward and pours a small amount of water from a cup or pitcher through the bishop's cupped hands, which have been resting on the candidate's head. After all candidates are baptized, the bishop grasps the right hand of each kneeling young man and raises him to his feet, saying, "In the name of the Lord and the church, my hand is extended to you; stand up. I extend to you the hand of fellowship. Rise up." He then gives each new male member a handshake and presses a holy kiss on his lips, saying, "You are no longer strangers and foreigners, but fellow citizens with the saints and of the household of God." The bishop's wife extends the same greeting to each new female member.[22]

Strangers No More

Baptism affects each candidate differently. One father, recounting his baptism forty-five years earlier, recalled, "I remember the day when I was baptized. I felt clean as a whistle—I could have died right then and I knew that I would have gone straight to heaven." "You don't always stay at that level," he added. "For some people, they are converted right then. For others, I believe it's the start of something gradual." A young woman who was featured in the film *The Amish* described her experience as follows:

> When I was kneeling down on the floor, I remember thinking my feet hurt because I was sitting on them. And then I was like, "Man, all these people are praying for me." And just wow! It just felt good. And I'm still down on my knees, and then one of the ministers brings the bucket of water and cups their hands above my head, and he says, "I baptize you in the name of the Father," and then they pour water, "Son," pours more, and then, "the Holy Ghost." I remember thinking, "Whoa, there's a lot of water in my lap!" And then I'm baptized, and then he helps me stand up and says, you know, now I'm a member of the church, and "You are no more a stranger, you're a sister in the church now." I just wanted to go . . . flutter around and be happy, I guess. On the way home, I just wanted to sing.[23]

An Old Order Lancaster County mother spoke of her coming to faith in her late teens, before she was baptized: "I can remember the night that I feel I accepted Christ. I was outside. I was walking. Yeah. It's almost too personal to talk about. But there were some things that I had done that I knew weren't right, and I just remember crying out to God, and it just seemed like I was flying. I could just . . . I was so free; you know, I just knew God had forgiven me. Just knew he had. I felt that saving grace. And yeah, I just felt that I could—I think I could live this life."[24] Others have described their coming-to-faith experiences happening before they ever attended instruction class or became baptized. Another Lancaster County mother explained how her life changed because of a dream. "I was sixteen or seventeen, and I would come home from a weekend with my friends feeling terrible about the things I was doing. But I would be back at the same things the next weekend. One night I had a dream that I was waiting in line at the final judgment, but when Jesus got to me, he looked doubtful and said that he would have to think about it. He said my record was not too good. I woke up and determined to change. Within a month I was going in a different direction, and I was eventually baptized." However one responds, the intensity, the instruction, the scrutiny, and the solemnity surrounding baptism underscore the seriousness the Amish place on an informed, volitional, and lifetime covenant in becoming part of the church.

Passing On the Faith

Because the candidates receive less than eight hours of formal religious instruction, other factors must account for the success that Amish communities and families have in transmitting their faith. The Amish believe that all of life has religious significance and should be lived carefully and intentionally for the Lord. They implicitly acknowledge God's sovereignty in both the mundane and extraordinary events of life. They recognize God's hand in providing the daily blessings of good weather and good health, as well as his sustaining grace in times of drought or disaster. They see evidence of God in the cycles of life, the circles of the seasons, their daily work, and their designated lot in life. The entire community authenticates these shared beliefs and reaffirms them individually and corporately. The Amish are imbued with the sense that they have been privileged and are responsible for being God's children "in the midst of a crooked and perverse nation" (Philippians 2:15).

The Amish ideal is submission to God's will, to divinely appointed leaders, and to the community of faith. This means that after one joins the church, he or she promises to remain Amish until death. These lessons are not lost on the children and youth. God's will, whether revealed through the Bible and the church or through selection to the ministry by the casting of lots, transcends temperament, personal preference, or convenience. As parents submit themselves to the teaching and discipline of the church, they, in turn, are teaching their children about ultimate priorities, faith, and commitment. No wonder that the majority of their children follow their way of faith. Through "precept and example," the soil has been prepared to nurture the seeds of faith and commitment. When youth fail to follow the expected trajectory, many in the community assume that the parents have been at fault by "pushing the fences" (cutting corners), hence the resultant hesitation or confusion on the part of the young person.

As Kraybill has pointed out, spirituality for the Old Order churches is more communal and traditional than individual, and the children learn through modeling and assimilation more than from direct instruction.[25] The responsibility of transmitting the faith to the next generation belongs not only to individual couples, but also to their extended family and the entire community. Everyone understands the parameters and expectations. As one aged grandmother remarked, "We have some who don't do [practice], but we have none who don't know."[26] To assure that no one forgets, before each spring and fall communion, ministers review the Ordnung with the entire church and then ask each individual member, young and old, if he or she is in agreement with it.[27] Thus the church's expectations and the vows of faithfulness are renewed twice each year at the semiannual church council.

The New Order Amish Alternative

Although the more progressive New Order churches share many of the fundamental practices and assumptions of their Old Order counterparts, the religious environment for youth growing up in New Order churches differs in several ways from the most tradition-minded Old Orders groups. One is the age at which young people typically join the church. In most settlements, New Order youth join around the age of sixteen, two or three years earlier than their typical Ohio Old Order counterparts. Some have even joined as young as fourteen years of age.[28] Another difference between Old and New Orders is in the content and sheer number of New Order publications that are explicitly religious and theological. New Order leaders are much more intentional in discussing and disseminating their religious convictions, both to members and to outsiders. Several New Order ministers and lay leaders have written and published booklets on plain dress, godly homes, theological errors, and the dangers of bed courtship (for a discussion of the latter, see chapter 9).[29]

New Order expectations for living separate and faithful lives include a strong emphasis on an explicit new-birth experience and the belief that one can know that he or she is in "right standing" with God. These theological issues also characterize the relatively progressive Beachy Amish, a small, plain-dressing offshoot that permits car ownership.[30] Similar to the Beachy Amish, most New Order members support the idea of prison ministries, missionary activities, and witnessing to their faith, that is, explaining to outsiders their need for salvation through repentance of their sins, acceptance of God's salvation, and obedience to Christ. Some New Order members may even offer outsiders religious tracts or pamphlets that discuss the necessity of being born again to go to heaven. In contrast, Old Order members generally talk about their "hope of salvation" or the quiet witness of a faithful life but do so only when they are directly questioned about their beliefs and lifestyle. When asked about his Christian life, an Old Order man answered: "Ask my friends, family, and people I work with. They know how I live, and they should be able to answer that question."[31] Once again, praxis trumps theology.

Although the format of worship remains virtually the same in both groups, visitors often note a different tone, tempo, and emphasis between them. New Order services are characterized by faster singing, a more conversational tone in the sermons, and the use of more English words.[32] A New Order minister who visited a Swartzentruber Amish service reported: "During the sermon, I happened to catch the bishop's eye while he was speaking. He totally lost his train of thought when we established eye contact. Their ministers are not used to that."[33] Even the level of involvement of the young people in church services appears to be different. In general, New Order youth participate in singing more consistently than their Old Order cousins. Also, comparatively few New Order youth leave during the scripture reading for the traditional bathroom break. "If our young people begin leaving too often or staying too long," said one New Order man, "the ministers will bring it up in the members' meeting following the church service."[34]

New Order churches still maintain the cultural distinctiveness of plain dress, house church, German singing and preaching, and horse-and-buggy transportation. Their theological distinctions, however, have led to practices more typical of their conservative Mennonite cousins, or even to religious practices typical of some conservative evangelical or fundamentalist groups. New Order parents are expected to conduct family worship or devotions each day. Unless outside employment interferes, everyone living at home attends. In at least one district, parental failure in this area brought censure by the ministers. This kind of scrutiny of family worship practices would be rare among the Old Order Amish, although many Old Order families also have daily devotions. Unlike most of their traditional Old Order neighbors, many New Order parents prefer to read the Bible and pray in English. Additionally, they are more likely to discuss with their children the meaning and implications of the scriptural passages that have been read. They may even ask family members to offer a spontaneous prayer, another practice absent in most Old Order settings. Another basic difference is that both New Order adults and youth have traditionally voiced their disapproval of tobacco and alcohol; involvement in worldly activities, such as card playing or reading romance or western novels; or dancing of any kind. They also advocate strict courtship requirements that discourage any physical involvement, such as holding hands or kissing.[35]

New Order Youth Concerns

New Order Amish adults have also typically been more intentional in focusing on the needs and concerns of their youth. Adult leaders often invite the young people at their annual youth gatherings to submit questions to a panel of ministers. These questions provide a window into the moral issues and religious concerns that engage their youth. Some examples were: "What are some subtle sins that we should be careful not to let creep into our youth group? In what areas could we as youth improve in the church? How can we best keep from drifting along with the tide? What is the best way to keep our flesh [human temptations] crucified? Can you give some advice as how to keep our thought life pure and holy?" Conspicuously absent in this sample were questions challenging the status quo or demanding explanations from the ministers concerning why certain practices were forbidden. Rather than revealing dissatisfaction with group expectations or prohibitions, these questions focused more on personal and religious concerns. The questions, at least from this group, reflected a sense of accountability to God for high moral and spiritual standards, as opposed to simply abiding by traditional expectations. These young people were not trying to wrest concessions from reluctant leaders or seeking to "crowd the fence." Rather, they expressed a desire to align their inner lives and outward behavior with their understanding of the Bible and the teachings of the church.[36]

Such spiritual concerns are not limited to one group or affiliation of Amish. But given the differences that exist between New and Old Order groups, New Order youth, in general, appear to be more deliberately invested in religious matters than their Old Order counterparts. Although most New Order communities have accepted telephones, tractors, and power-line electricity, their young people must still conform to most other traditional Amish practices—plain dress, the Pennsylvania German dialect, horse transportation, non-resistance, and excommunication—which set them apart from the world, mainstream Christianity, and most other Anabaptist groups. In addition, most New Order churches emphasize rigorous moral standards in dating and in their recreational activities more than their Old Order neighbors do. Most importantly, like the adults, the youth need to profess having a personal experience of God's salvation and are encouraged to practice "private daily devotions" consisting of bible study and prayer. They are also expected to demonstrate a willingness to share their faith with those who have not been "saved" or converted.

These internal and external demands combine to make their faith and its practice, which must always be in the foreground, more salient on both cognitive and emotional levels. For New Order youth, experiencing their faith, with its inherent joys and responsibilities, may be similar to that of conscientious young people in evangelical churches. On the other hand, most Old Order youth feel fewer demands to verbalize their faith or engage in evangelizing. The deep meanings of their faith are not found in individual experience, cognitive claims, or verbal statements. At first blush, such differences between the two groups might suggest that New Orders would retain a higher percentage of their youth, but, ironically, this is not the case, as we shall see later in this chapter.

New Order–Old Order Tensions

Differences between the two groups loomed large enough to strain their relationship for several years in the 1970s and 1980s. When the New Order split first occurred in Ohio in the 1960s, members reported that some rowdy or overzealous Old Order youth occasionally disrupted their singings. These young people called the singers "goodie-goodies" and criticized them for having a holier-than-thou attitude, the same charges and names used when the New Order group split from the older orders in Pennsylvania.[37] Recalling those days, a New Order minister said: "I believe those things actually made us stronger. Nowadays, our young people have it so easy that they can just drift along without being challenged."

In their zeal, New Order members would often question the sincerity of some Old Order youths' decision to join the church. The New Order critique would be similar to that of a writer in *Family Life*: "When I was taking instructions for baptism, there were several in my [Old Order] group who were not permitted to date until they were baptized. On the evening of the day of their baptism, all of them dated. How sad that they should cast a dark shadow of suspicion upon their motives for being baptized."[38] Elmo Stoll, an Old Order bishop from Canada who eventually left the Amish, also questioned some of the practices of his day in a column in *Family Life*: "Young people sow their wild oats, living undisciplined and lustful lives until they want to get married. Then all of a sudden, they decide to join the church. Many people suspect deep down inside that they are joining the church to get married, and not because they have repented of their sins. Yet parents and ministers go along with this mockery, remarking to one another how thankful they are that the young people still have a desire to join the church. Sure enough, they are barely baptized until they get published [have their engagement officially announced] and married."[39] Stoll would not have been surprised to hear the Old Order father of a twenty-one-year-old admit, "Roy is sorry now that he didn't 'follow church' last time around, because I think he has marriage on his mind."

Most Amish can recite, or at least have heard of, instances where some youth purportedly had one last Saturday-night fling before showing up for baptism and church membership the next day. Since such parties frequently involve alcohol, they occasionally end in accidents or death on the Saturday night before the Sunday that the young person was to be taken up into membership. Ministers undoubtedly recount these incidents to emphasize the seriousness that one should have in taking the vows of membership, but they also cause New Order members to wonder aloud how much Old Order "faithfulness" is primarily external and cultural: "Too many of them think they will get to heaven by simply living the Amish lifestyle." One elderly convert to the New Order charged that "for too many of them, it's simply following the culture instead of the Holy Spirit."[40] Another insisted, "The reason they have trouble with their young folk is that they have not been born again."

While admitting that some of these stories are true, Old Order members often regard the New Order adherents as simply "Mennonites in Amish clothing" or "Beachy Amish without the cars," in danger of sliding down the slippery slope of liberalism and a loss of Amish identity. They charge the New Orders with "abandoning the ancient landmarks" and simply us-ing talk of spirituality and grace as a cover for their underlying desire for technology and the material trappings permitted in the more liberal groups. Not all Old Order members regard their New Order neighbors and relatives negatively, however. In candid moments, some ministers confess that they wish their teens were as well under control as the youth in the New Order. They admit that far fewer New Order teenagers have driver's licenses than do their own teenagers, and they recognize that this aspect, and various other differences, is attractive to many Amish parents.[41] One Old Order mother in a large settlement confessed, "I would rather see my children become New Order than join one of the Old Order youth groups that carries on like some of them do around here."[42]

On the other hand, Old Order members report private conversations with some of their New Order neighbors who express regret for ever having switched, because their children tend to leave the Amish in far greater numbers than those belonging to the Old Order. Some New Order districts or settlements in the past have lost more than half of their youth, compared with an estimated 20 percent in the most progressive Old Order groups (those with the highest defection rates among the Old Order communities).[43] Needless to say, these losses both perplex and disturb New Order parents and leaders. They also provide Old Order parents with convincing evidence that if they want their youth to be Amish, their best hope is to remain faithful to their Old Order heritage.

Nevertheless, most Amish—Old Order or New Order—affirm that affiliation, family, community life, and the security of tradition are all inadequate foundations or rationales for their group's survival. "When seekers from the outside come to us wanting to be Amish," explained a bishop, "they are often attracted for the wrong reasons. They could have fallen in love with one of our Youngie. Or they may have fallen in love with what they think is a simpler way of life. What they fail to recognize is that our Christian faith is at the center. Horses, buggies, and kerosene lanterns will quickly grow stale without the faith foundation." Most Amish would agree with his assessment, not only for seekers, but also for their own sons and daughters. They are convinced that ultimately their faith in Christ provides the core that nurtures them as believers and serves as the magnet that draws their wandering youth back to the fold. They find it unthinkable that any Amish community could continue without the centrality of that faith. But as realists, they also know that a host of variables, including personality, temperament, human nature, and cultural influences and practices, can either diminish or nurture a strong Amish identity. It is to the latter that we now turn our attention.

Developing an Amish identity begins early in childhood, and—despite teenage experimentation with non-Amish practices, such as driving cars or partying— by late adolescence, most youth affirm this identity by receiving membership instruction and being baptized into the Amish faith.

(Sean J. Hagins)

Adolescence

Building an Amish Identity

*It's a mistake for parents to think they can teach
their children right and wrong when they turn sixteen.
You have to start when they are in diapers.*
—Amish father

Identity and Autonomy

When I began my study of Amish youth and the Internet, especially
their involvement with Facebook, I had the challenge of discerning, from among those who were current rumspringa Amish, those who
grew up in Amish homes but were on their way out or had already left, and
those who had a distant Amish heritage but had nothing left but names in
past community directories or in the "Fisher Book" (the unofficial Lancaster
County genealogical guide) to trace their connections.[1] With few exceptions,
especially in the largest Indiana and Ohio settlements, youthful Facebook
profile pictures were of little help to me. They were virtually interchange-
able with profile shots of students from the college where I teach. Haircuts,
attire, and reported activities also provided no hints. This left me with the
challenge of determining who were and who were not Amish. Occasionally

a young person would leave a helpful clue, such as entering "Amish" as a religious category or listing "Amish parties" under "Likes." Although such evidence was circumstantial, it proved to be accurate enough to be a good starting point in seeking the specific backgrounds of these Facebook youth.

The task of Amish youth—at either end of the rumspringa spectrum—in attaining their psychological identity is more difficult than was my task of determining who was or was not Amish. Although few in the culture might articulate the importance of identity formation for their children and youth, virtually all correctly discern that the establishment of an Amish identity is crucial for the retention of their young and the continuation of their society. In the same way, most developmental psychologists contend that attaining a clear identity is a crucial adolescent developmental task. The Amish tendency is to regard identity as one's literal place in both an extended family and the community, while psychologists focus on those attributes and choices that make an individual unique and provide the sense of self that distinguishes him or her from everybody else.[2]

Erik Erikson, the most influential psychologist in identity theory, contends that the resolution of identity is a universal psychosocial crisis for adolescents. If they resolve the crisis successfully, they will attain what psychologists call an achieved identity and have a focused life.[3] If they do not resolve it, they will most likely flounder in a state of identity confusion or diffusion. Fear, withdrawal, and hedonism impede the formation of a positive identity. James Marcia argues that the key to successful identity resolution hinges first on exploring one's options and subsequently choosing—or failing to choose—among them.[4] In both theories, the importance of struggling with alternatives and making one's selections is central in achieving an authentic identity.

Identity theorists almost universally discuss this concept in the context of an individualistic, pluralistic society. They focus on "self" issues, such as self-esteem, self-concept, and self-efficacy—important subjects in mainstream American culture. In contrast, the Amish always think in terms of a web of relationships, rather than a complex stage of development or words beginning with the hyphenated "self-" prefix.

Also when the Amish think about a person's identity, they are more likely to be picturing a plural rather than a singular context. They connect someone to his or her place within an extended family that reaches back for generations. It is not uncommon to hear an Amish man inquire, "How is Bill Joe Josie's Junior getting along?" Newlyweds Samuel Stoltzfus and Rebecca Lapp are "Caleb's Elam's Samuel" (grandfather-father-son), and "Daniel's Reuben's Rebecca" (her paternal lineage). In a society that seeks to know both families' members and stories, weddings unite two families and their histories forever, every bit as much as they join two individuals. An example of what Pauline Stevick calls "the web of relationships" comes from a scribe's letter in the 9 August 2000 issue of the weekly newspaper *Die Botschaft* (Message): "We extend our sympathy to the Jake Smucker family. Jake died suddenly July 28. Jake served as preacher for 42 years. Jake's wife was in Doddy Sams relation. Her mother, Sadie King, married to Chris L. King, was grandmother's Salome's niece. A daughter of Joel Fisher's Lovina, the second wife of Chris K. Stoltzfus. This is the Lovina that was the second wife of Daniel S. Esh."[5] Obviously the Amish care deeply about relational connections.

In the same manner, an important part of Samuel's and Rebecca's identities is their church affiliation, and even their church district. In the Big Valley of Pennsylvania, being a "Nebraskan white-topper" and not a "Byler yellow-topper" provides instant recognition and information about a person's cultural identity to all Amish in the valley, both within and outside their particular group. Everyone knows that the "low" Nebraska Amish dress and live more plainly than their more progressive "high" Byler neighbors. Each affiliation's Ordnung delineates the expectations and distinctive attributes of that particular group, key components of each member's identity.

Identity in a Communal Society

Whether conservative or progressive, however, the strictures against choosing self-gratification or searching for self-actualization reflect the communal nature of Amish society. As cross-cultural psychologist Harry Triandis points out, in communal or collectivist societies (such as in Japan, India, or West Africa), the group's well-being and priorities take precedence over an individual's desires and preferences.[6] Choice is appropriate solely within group-approved options, and then only if it maintains and strengthens the group. Understanding this difference is central in comprehending the heart of Amish identity.

In a collectivist society like that of the Amish, the young people's task is not to distinguish themselves from others by their uniqueness and achievement, but rather by their willingness to support and strengthen the group. This happens by "giving yourself up," as they call it. Despite their unique personal preferences, tastes, and personalities, they are expected to accept their church's collective Ordnung, with its explicit rules for dress and behavior. An Amish person's identity is achieved through tempering much of his or her personal autonomy. Because the Amish know that humans are weak and that sacrifices are difficult, they believe that forming an Amish identity is too important to be left solely to the individual and his or her family. Ideally, all members—individually and collectively—share the responsibility of helping each child and youth form a firm identity as a member of their Amish community.

In mainstream society, young people may flounder for years as they seek to know who they are and where their niche is in a complex, individualistic world. Many modern youth find the struggle long, lonely, and too often unsuccessful. At puberty, they may begin both their movement toward independence from parents and their growing involvement with peers, but they might not gain financial independence and intimate relationships until their midtwenties or later. In contrast, Amish young people almost never begin to seriously socialize with their peers until they are sixteen or seventeen. By this age most are working full time as adults, and by the time they are twenty-one or twenty-two, most have joined the church, are married, and are starting families. Instead of an exploratory period of a decade or more on their way to full-fledged adulthood, most Amish youth typically spend no more than five years in this pursuit: from the time they enter their Rumspringa until they reach full Amish adult status.[7] Everyone, young and old, knows exactly what their society expects of them.

Unlike mainstream youth, who are confronted with a multitude of vocational, value, and lifestyle choices, the ultimate task of an Amish young person is deciding whether or not to accept an Amish identity. This culminates either in being baptized and joining the church, or in assuming a non-Amish identity that results in leaving one's community. This is the most critical decision an Amish youth will ever make. Becoming a church member means embracing the expectations of one's community. Not joining the church, or joining but then leaving, almost never occurs without great pain and existential struggle. An Amish identity takes root deeply into one's psyche, or soul.

Components of an Amish Identity

A teenager's family is an important source in forming his or her identity. Children and youth from loving Amish families begin to effortlessly assume an Amish identity. Those children from highly regarded families are also likely to form positive self-identities, since they benefit directly from the accomplishments and status of their parents and grandparents. "Everyone knows that Klines are bright and that Smuckers are exceptionally hard workers." Young people whose parents fail to meet community ideals may struggle more with attaining a positive identity, both personally and socially, because of their familial liabilities.

In Amish society, a family's success is usually measured, among other things, by hard work, thrift, good management, and the outcome of their children. Consequently, a major component of one's identity is influenced by how industrious and intelligent a worker he or she is. Since most Amish children learn to work early in their lives, and thus develop a sense of their own efficacy and competence, by their midteens almost all are able transition smoothly into adult work responsibilities. For example, a fifteen-year-old girl in Franklin County, Pennsylvania, taught twenty-five children in grades one through eight. When she started, she was scarcely a year older than her oldest students. During the girl's second year of teaching, her twelve-year-old sister transferred into her one-room school to help the older girl by teaching the school's eight first-graders how to read. Parents of the schoolchildren reported that the sisters did well. If Amish youth are not supposed to be proud of their work, they are certainly permitted to feel satisfaction in applying themselves diligently and accomplishing tasks like these. Since these young hard workers are esteemed by both their peers and adults, they have a good foundation on which to develop a positive and robust sense of self-worth.

Another major identity component for Amish youth, whether positive or negative, is shaped by their choice of peers, especially in the large settlements. In Lancaster County, peer groups (youth groups) are called "gangs," and in northern Indiana, similar groups are called "crowds." In both places, these gatherings of cohorts provide an important arena for shaping one's identity, especially through one's age-mates and best friends. In a Lancaster County daughter settlement, a father observed, "Youth from farm families tend to hang out with each other, and those whose dads work away find their friends in that group." As in mainstream society, Amish young people tend to gravitate toward those who are like themselves, a situation that further reinforces their identities. "I hang out with the rowdy boys," explained an eighteen-year-old from Montour County, Pennsylvania, who lived in a small, conservative daughter (offshoot) settlement from the Lancaster County settlement. "Almost all the other Youngie do what they are supposed to do, but my friends and me like to have fun together. Sometimes it gets us in trouble." Despite the increased impact of peers, especially during the rumspringa years, the power of their community and their families exerts a constant counterbalance to the excesses of the young, tacitly and intentionally reminding them of adult values and expected behavior.

Identity and Dressing Amish

The symbolic aspects of their attire promote and reinforce the desired Amish identity. The majority of Americans, from children to grandparents, distinguish themselves through their dress. What a person wears often reveals his or her personal or family income, social class, extravagances, love of adventure, travel history, political or sexual preferences, or non-conformity. Amish clothing, on the other hand, is designed to minimize individual tastes and differences. It demonstrates one's willingness to squelch personal preferences and uniqueness by accepting the group's attire and the community's expected standards of decency. By reducing individual or economic differences, an Amish person's garments symbolize his or her membership in the group, rather than being apart from or above it. Whether one is a teenager or a grandparent, conformity in dress reinforces a person's identity as an obedient and yielding member of the community.

Far More than Fabric

Another aspect of Amish identity that is strengthened through dress is their intentional separation from the dominant culture. Amish garb functions as a distinctive marker to others and to themselves of the gap between the two societies. For the Amish, seeing themselves and their peers in capes and bonnets, or in old-fashioned broadfall pants and broad-brimmed hats, serves as a constant visual reminder of their uniqueness. Their attire reaffirms both their separate status and their shared values as a countercultural group, even as it distinguishes one Amish affiliation from another. Wherever Amish travel, most instantly recognize one another as a likely source of support, rapport, camaraderie, and help. An Amish father related his experience of spotting an Amish couple at the far end of a bus terminal in Chicago: "We never seen these people before, but we knew them." One bishop urged his members to think of their garb as a uniform symbolizing their separation from the world and their accord with their community.

Amish clothing supports the culture's core values. Their apparel is so simple and plain, and their styles change so slowly, that most wives, mothers, and daughters are confident that they can provide whatever clothing they and their entire family need. The Amish know precisely what materials and colors are acceptable. No one needs to waste money on expensive, store-bought clothes. Observant Amish do not have to keep up with the latest fashions or worry about disposing of outmoded clothing. Instead, they pass usable clothes along to younger siblings or relatives. Once the garments are worn out, the women can transform the material into quilts or rugs. Amish clothing affirms their collective identity as frugal, practical people.[8]

Clothing styles also demonstrate the community's high regard for tradition and the past. One outsider, invited to attend an Amish church service, remarked that when she first saw the group, she felt that she had entered a painting by a Dutch Old Master, with the congregation's subdued colors and peasant styles. Such plainness reflects their simple rural beginnings and provides another visual link with the past. It is an affirmation to everyone that the old days and the old ways are almost always best.

Although parents and elders may deliberately teach some of these distinctive aspects, such as the importance of modesty and simplicity of dress, the young more often absorb these standards through daily living. Parents need not tell their growing children that their apparel will immediately mark them as different. As they mature, the young people implicitly recognize the contrasts between themselves and the tourists or the community's English neighbors, with their jewelry, shorts, slacks, and ostentatious colors and patterns. Fancy clothing, with buttons and bows or neckties and belts, has always belonged to the worldly minded, not to the plain people of God.[9] The Amish also believe that any apparel that is form fitting or revealing, whether it is shorts, short skirts, or sleeveless or low-cut blouses, indicates a worldly and wayward heart. Because children and youth are immersed from infancy in these communal clothing expectations and examples, the formation of their Amish identity is constantly strengthened and reinforced.

Despite community standards and parental reminders, a significant minority of youth, especially in the large settlements, express their independence by departing from the plain and simple dress standards during their transitional rumspringa period. These independent-minded youth are generally invisible to mainstream society, since they often mimic the currently popular styles in the rest of the country. These fashion statements may be directed toward parents and other adults, to demonstrate the young people's independence, however temporary. It is more likely, though, that such deviance in dress may be designed to make a similar show of independence to their peers, or perhaps to seek acceptance by conforming to the standards of their more daring peers. In this case, the medium most likely is the message: "Look how cool I am. I'm not afraid to defy my parents or the ministers. And I can certainly pass for English if I want to." A desire to be well accepted, admired, and cool is certainly not confined to English adolescents.

A Healthy Sense of Self

Non-Amish observers, accustomed to the autonomy and choice inherent in an individualistic culture, might wonder if communal restrictions result in stunted or cookie-cutter personalities and impaired self-esteem. If such is the case, most outsiders who have face-to-face or extended contact with Amish children and youth fail to detect such outcomes. Instead, observers often comment that Amish young people appear to have high levels of maturity and confidence.[10] They also note the poise with which the youngsters and teens relate to peers and adults, both friends and strangers. Little formal research has focused on the social skills and psychological well-being of Amish youth, but relatively few of them appear to be depressed, sad, lonely, or hostile.[11] If anything, their sense of who they are seems to be both clear and positive.[12]

Not surprisingly, Amish parents, teachers, or ministers rarely talk about building their children's self-esteem. That idea, with its self-focus, is contrary to their way of thinking. They believe that children will learn to feel good about themselves by finding and fulfilling their God-given roles within the Amish community. If the majority of Amish youth are, in fact, psychologically robust, this should not come as a surprise. Compared with the complex and often vague demands placed on youth in competitive mainstream society, those faced by Amish youth are clear and within reach of most. As Donald B. Kraybill has observed, "Achieving the Amish dream is much more attainable for the typical Amish individual than achieving the American dream is for the average mainstream individual."[13] Work competence is both within reach and acquired by virtually all Amish youth, and this sense of confidence and agency undoubtedly contributes positively to their self-esteem and the formation of their Amish identity.[14]

Another achievable expectation is in their garb. In mainstream society, a person's attitude toward his or her physical appearance is the single best indicator of self-esteem, according to Susan Harter's research.[15] Advertisers foster insecurity among youthful consumers by creating needs that can only be met by purchasing the right look or product. Unless Amish teenagers have overly restrictive parents who demand conformity to more conservative adult standards, typical youths can more easily meet peer expectations, despite their economic status or fashion limitations. Because Amish children and the majority of Amish youth escape the bombardment of the unrealistic and often unattainable standards of material affluence portrayed in the media, they are less likely to feel deprived because they cannot afford expensive jewelry, makeup, designer jeans, certain brands of footwear, or NFL team jackets. Likewise, their lack of exposure to fashionably thin models and media stars may help explain the relative scarcity of anorexia and bulimia in these communities. This seems to be especially true in the more traditional Amish groups, where physical attractiveness appears to be less important to self-worth and identity than desirable character traits, a humble demeanor, moral development, and maturity.[16]

An exception to my belief that young women from the plainest settlements would be less likely to struggle with body-image issues and eating disorders was documented by a research team from Vanderbilt University. A physician from the university's hospital first encountered a teenage Amish female patient from a Swartzentruber community in Tennessee. He quickly learned that four other teenage girls in that same settlement exhibited anorexic behavior. Although community members attributed the problem to parasites, the medical specialists at Vanderbilt concluded that it was a form of mass hysteria.[17] Until that incident, virtually no one within the medical profession had reported treating Amish patients for eating disorders, other than obesity or diabetes.

Like many aspects of Amish life, this sensitive area had been kept private within families facing such difficulties. And, predictably, Amish communities have kept this information away from outsiders, whether they be neighbors, physicians, or academics. A 1999 article, "A Thin Shadow," featured the first Amish reference to the dangers of an excessive concern about thinness. The first extensive treatment of eating disorders appeared in *Family Life* in 2006, where the entire "Problem Corner" section was devoted to anorexia and bulimia among Amish and Old Order Mennonite young women. In response to the article, ten females wrote in, all of whom had either personally experienced this disorder or had a family member who did. The editor received more letters on the subject than he could print. Meanwhile, many Amish and outside observers believe that the plain people have proportionately fewer incidences of these disorders than do mainstream adolescents. An Amish writer speculated: "Girls in your society have to be more concerned about their appearance than our girls do. Your girls have to attract a boy from such a wide field. Our girls have a much smaller field to worry about and they can be pretty sure that somewhere in their group is a boy for them." In my two decades of working among the Amish, including my work at an Amish mental-health treatment center, I have encountered fewer than a dozen occurrences of eating disorders. My sense is that

Amish young women have generally been protected from the toxic effects of a popular culture that values and promotes thinness in females. The possibility of underreporting always exists, but in time it should become apparent whether there is an increase in these disorders or simply a more open attitude for plain people to disclose eating disorders.

A critical factor that helps minimize destructive mainstream cultural influences is if children and youth sense that they are highly valued and loved by their families and others in their communities. Amish society's love for children manifests itself in a number of ways. The Amish traditionally fail to understand why English couples would routinely want to postpone having a family. An Amish parent stated, "Newlyweds expect and want to begin having children as soon as they get married."[18] Even Amish couples who learn that their baby will be born with severe birth defects do not consider abortion. Rather, their "special ones" (children with physical and mental disabilities) appear to be treated with particular care by the community. Instead of stigmatizing individuals with disabilities, the Amish often express the belief that families with these challenging children and youth are chosen by God to care for these needy ones. Many Amish settlements have special schools for their impaired children and youth. If a family has a deaf child, community members will sometimes even learn sign language, along with the family. Whenever children are wanted, loved, and nurtured by a caring mother, father, extended family, and the community, they are likely to develop both a confidence in their self-worth and a positive sense of themselves as Amish.

Gender Matters Really Matter

As in all societies, a major component of Amish identity is found in one's gender role. For the Amish, these roles are clearly delineated and based on their traditional understanding of the Bible. They interpret the scriptures as teaching the husband's headship in the family and the submission of wives to their husbands. Women are expected to be helpmeets and supporters of their husbands, and husbands, in turn, are to love their wives as Christ loved the church and gave himself for it (Ephesians 5:25). Likewise, Amish women are to respect and support male leadership and authority in the church.[19] Women may nominate men for the ministry, even though females can never serve in that position themselves. Amish society clearly defines and models expected sex-role attitudes and behavior for youth and adults. People who deviate from these roles and act like "bossy wives" or "henpecked husbands" are often stigmatized.

Sex-role distinctions exist in virtually all areas of Amish culture. Dress and grooming standards for males and females are highly specialized and maintained. The Amish cite Deuteronomy 22:5 from the Old Testament as their basis for prohibiting females from wearing jeans or slacks: "The woman shall not wear that which pertaineth unto a man, neither shall a man put on a woman's garment: for all that do so are an abomination unto the Lord thy God." Following the instructions of Saint Paul in the New Testament, married and unmarried women and girls must wear a head covering, or *Kapp*, as a sign of piety, submission, and prayer.[20] Although some teenage girls will discreetly trim their locks so their head covering fits better or shape the front of their hairstyle into bangs, they are not supposed to cut their hair, because "if a woman have long hair, it is a glory to her: for her hair is given her for a covering" (1 Corinthians 11:15). By the same token, males are not to have long hair: "Doth not even nature itself teach you that, if a man has long hair, it is a shame unto him?" (1 Corinthians 11:14). Men and boys wear traditional bangs in front, and square- or blunt-cut hair on the sides and back. After joining the church or marrying, young men further differentiate themselves from women by growing beards.[21]

In most settings, males and females customarily interact and relate in same-sex groups. This separation is apparent even in church, where the married males enter and sit separately from the married females; the unmarried males and unmarried females enter and sit separately; and the boys and girls, except for the youngest, do the same. After church, everyone eats at same-sex tables and later socializes primarily with their own gender. In some settlements, sex segregation continues during Sunday-afternoon youth activities and through the evening singing. Courting couples rarely pair off until they are ready to go home. Even at the most social types of gatherings, such as auctions and family reunions, males and females usually cluster in same-sex groups. Boys and girls may mix at work bees and

Sunday-afternoon volleyball games, but actual pairing off is almost always reserved for courting couples or assigned pairs at wedding meals.

Sex-role differentiation also impacts the world of work. From early childhood on, children learn that males and females have different work domains. On the farm, the men and boys work in the barn and the fields, and the women and girls care for the house, yard, and garden. Crossovers occur, however, if a farmer has no or few sons. Then his wife and daughters will help with the milking and care of the animals. In especially busy times, women will even assist with the field work, such as planting, haying, or harvesting. Likewise, men will sometimes help in the kitchen with food preparation or washing dishes, especially when the children are young. In families where all of the children are males, the boys are expected to help their mothers in certain "female" tasks. "All of us were boys, and we had to take turns cooking, helping with the washing, and doing other things for our mother," a grandfather reported. A father explained, "Some boys help to wash dishes and do laundry if there are few girls in a family. But the boys want no one to see them doing those chores." As in mainstream society, females more frequently cross over to help in traditional male activities than the reverse.

In work outside of the home, gender-role differences are again apparent. Husbands more typically work away from home than wives, especially when the children are young. Men generally work in shops, on construction sites, or in factories. Women, on the other hand, usually work as teachers, housekeepers, clerks, or waitresses. In certain communities, some men will teach school, and single women might work in factories, but these exceptions are usually limited. Mothers with young children rarely work away from home, although in recent years women in some communities have begun developing home-based business enterprises of their own.[22] Both sexes in certain settlements may travel to distant farmers' markets to run their stands, but they rarely work away from home for more than two or three days per week and try not to stay away overnight. In all domains, however, males have more freedom and latitude in their work choices than females.

A gender difference in Amish children and youth emerges in their interaction with same-sex friends. At school, boys and girls play softball together, and, after they turn sixteen, teenagers of both sexes play volleyball together in the more progressive settlements. Otherwise, adolescent Amish males generally relate to each other through physical activities such as hunting, ice hockey, and softball or other sports. Where Amish youth participate in organized sports, boys almost always play and girls watch, although in northern Indiana and Ohio, teenage girls have a softball league of their own; in 2009, the majority of the teams were Amish.[23] Typically, however, girls will intermittently cheer the boys on, but observers note that the girls are often more focused on their conversations with each other than they are on the game.

This gender difference in female intimacy and male activity even manifests itself in the decor of teenagers' bedrooms, especially in the large settlements. The walls or bulletin boards of a typical girl's room feature birthday cards and notes; wedding announcements and mementos; and handwritten letters from her "secret pal," her best friend, and pen pals or relatives from other communities.[24] She typically chooses a theme color, and her quilt or bedspread, wall coverings, throw rugs, artificial flowers, vases, and china accent this shade. In the large settlements, she might display framed photos of her gang or best friends on a shelf or on her desk.

In contrast, Amish boys, especially in the faster crowds of large settlements, will typically adorn their rooms with mementos such as hunting trophies, guns, archery equipment, or athletic gear and souvenirs, depending on their interests. The bedroom of one nineteen-year-old in a large settlement reflected his preoccupation with sports. It was flooded with sports paraphernalia and clothing. An expensive Weider weight-training station dominated the room. Photos of professional athletes from the Pittsburgh Pirates and Steelers, an "I play to win" poster, and a football clock decorated the walls. A phalanx of eight trophies from his softball league lined his desk and bookshelves—one trophy was nearly two feet tall. With the exception of a work jacket and a couple of pairs of Wrangler jeans, almost all of his clothes were sports-related—four Pittsburgh Steelers hats and a Steelers warmup jacket, a Nike cap and Nike sneakers, his local team's warmup jacket and hat, and a sports-equipment bag. A large Magnavox boom box sat on the bed, connected by a heavy yellow extension cord to some distant

outside outlet. No straw hat or suspenders were in sight. With the exception of a bottled-gas lamp, a battery-operated horse-collar clock on the wall,
and a picture of his ten-year-old sister in plain garb stuck in the corner of
his dresser mirror, almost nothing in his room resembled the plainness of
a boy's room in a conservative group. By adding a TV and DVD player or
computer, it could have easily passed for the bedroom of an active mainstream nineteen-year-old male.[25] Although such worldly trappings would
never be tolerated among preadolescent children, more progressive parents
may simply choose to stay out of their teenagers' bedrooms, or at least refrain from checking in drawers or under the bed, convenient spots to stash
forbidden electronic devices, cell phones, or reading matter.

Autonomy: Independence within a Communal Society

Perhaps because of their Anabaptist emphasis on an adult decision to join
the church and follow Christ, most Amish allow their youth more latitude
and independence for exploration and experimentation than one might expect, especially in the larger communities. Many parents make an abrupt
shift in their treatment of their teenagers when the young people reach
sixteen or seventeen and begin their rumspringa period. Throughout their
children's formative years, the most common Amish parenting approach
would be labeled authoritarian or traditional, according to family specialist
Diana Baumrind.[26] Parents are the undisputed authorities, and they expect
immediate obedience. Until their children are ten or eleven, most parents
will not hesitate to spank them for disobedience or defiance.[27] After their
children begin going with the young folks, however, most parents tend to
be more permissive as they recognize the new status of their sixteen- or
seventeen-year-olds.

The most tangible way in which parents acknowledge their children's
newfound status is to allow them the freedom to socialize with their friends
without being dependent on their parents or older siblings for transportation. Normally this freedom is demonstrated by parents giving a horse and
carriage to each son when he begins going to the singings. Unless their parents cannot afford it, almost all males over sixteen may lay claim to this traditional form of transportation. Those youth running in the fastest circles

may reject their parents' offer and opt to buy a motor vehicle of some sort as soon as they have the money and can legally do so. Whether traveling by 1 or by 200 horsepower, these teenagers have increased privacy and freedom with their new mobility.

Girls rarely have their own carriages, at least in the early stages of Rumspringa, so they are dependent on their brothers or male relatives for rides to singings and other events until the girls begin courting.[28] Nonetheless, females, along with their male cohorts, are granted the freedom to fully enter social life and attend singings With their newly gained freedom, males are much more likely than females to deviate from adult and community expectations in the areas of dress, car ownership, alcohol consumption, friendship with outsiders, and church membership. The tendency for disproportionately more single males to leave the Amish than females probably reflects the males' greater need for independence and autonomy.[29]

Exerting One's Independence

Besides having new opportunities to travel with their peers, youth have other realms in which to express their autonomy. Because attire and appearance are such central components of Amish life and expectations, some youth find this a convenient target for expressing their independence, especially in the larger communities. In many settlements, many teenage boys trade their plain clothes for what they believe to be the English look: in some cases, knit shirts, black jeans, and sneakers; in other cases, stylish polo shirts, khaki cargo pants, and sandals or expensive athletic footwear, depending on their peer group. To the embarrassment of their parents, a few young men have even sprouted forbidden moustaches.

Teenage girls, who tend to dress more conventionally, may still hitch up or lengthen their skirts, shave their legs, sport gold pins on their sweaters or jackets, and wear flip-flops or sandals, even in some of the conservative circles. Also, if females dress in English attire, it happens most often when they are out with their peers. One girl related how she told her date to wait for her at the end of the lane. Before she met him, she quickly changed into English clothes and stored her Amish garments in a bag in the carriage or a car.

Although virtually no Amish youth wear English clothing to church, many of them will still exert independence in other ways on Sundays. In some areas of Lancaster County, the young men file into the service last, and church does not begin until they are seated. At times, the host father must go out and prod them to enter in a timely fashion. In parts of northern Indiana, many youth arrive at the Sunday service an hour and a half after the opening hymn, although it's unclear how this became accepted youth behavior. Once inside and seated, many or most of the youth may simply sit passively instead of singing the hymns. During the scripture reading, some will leave for a supposed bathroom break, returning twenty minutes later smelling of tobacco smoke. Once the sermons begin, youth often slump on the benches, head in their hands, elbows on their knees. As soon as the last song is sung and the service ends, they will exit immediately. If the host fails to serve the meal promptly, or if the first seating of elders lingers too long at the tables, many youth will simply leave to join their friends from other church districts. All of this serves as an unspoken but clear reminder to the parents and elders that these youth are ultimately in charge of their own destinies. The tacit message is, "Don't push too hard, because we are no longer under your control or under the control of the church."

Parents and church leaders are well aware that the youth are in a sometimes unpredictable borderland where the scrutiny of parents is diminished and control by the church has not yet taken over. The young person who wishes to become a member of the Amish church, however, will ultimately yield to that control. What helps in that final transformation is that during their formative childhood years, most youth have learned unquestioned obedience to their parents. This childhood training undoubtedly prepares the young people to later submit to the demands of the community. Sometimes rules will be bent, such as while traveling or visiting other Amish affiliations with different standards, but within an individual Amish community, the Ordnung can be changed only by the consensus of the group. Until that happens, the expectation is that the rules are to be binding on all members, old and young alike.

Accepting the Boundaries

Consequently, young people aspiring to church membership rarely struggle about whether they should go to high school or college, become physicians or lawyers, marry outsiders, move away from the Amish community, or postpone having children until after they have been married for a while. One reason is that their primary reference group almost always consists of other Amish youth and adults. Therefore most do not feel deprived because they must work so hard, end their formal education at age fourteen or fifteen, or drastically restrict their vocational choices.

Having a group of serious-minded peers also helps diminish the impact of mainstream values and influences. For most youth, "joining church" is a natural choice that indicates a willingness to curtail one's autonomy and accept the community's strictures. All other choices naturally flow out of this ultimate decision—whether or not to become a baptized Amish member. When an individual joins the church, there is to be no turning back from that covenant, and no exceptions are allowed. As one elder stated, "Joining church is a spiritual marriage, and just as in an earthly marriage, we cannot divorce the church and still be Amish."

The Balancing Act

Given the limited range of choices in this collectivist society, is identity development as important for Amish youth as it is for mainstream teenagers? Certainly everyone, English or Amish, needs to know how he or she is different from everybody else, so in that sense, forming one's identity is a universal task. But are identity issues equally important for all cultures? Undoubtedly, in traditions that stresses uniformity and conformity, the task of developing one's identity differs from what happens in mainstream society, with its emphasis on individualism and independence. For the majority of youth who choose to remain Amish, it would appear that acquiring a clear identity would be a relatively easy task, because of limited choices and well-defined expectations.

Once again, though, things are rarely as simple as they seem. Sociologist Denise Reiling studied Amish life and culture for nearly ten years in a settlement that bordered northern Indiana and southern Michigan. During that time, she devoted more than 300 hours interviewing a randomly selected group of sixty Amish-reared youth and adults about their Rumspringa. She reported that in her sample, "identity during this decision-making period [of whether to be baptized or leave the community] was reported to be highly ambiguous. Almost every participant's description depicted this decision-making period as one of limbo, wherein the child does not identify as Amish, even though continuing to live in an Amish home and to engage in Amish cultural practices. . . . Virtually every participant reported that they experienced social isolation during this time, which generated a high level of depression and anxiety."[30] Reiling concluded that these participants experienced strong levels of "negative affective response" and "angst." She attributed these effects, at least in part, to the length and seriousness of the deviant activities of the youth of that particular group, and to the conflict between the Amish cultural expectation of obedience to God and the church and what Reiling regarded as the unspoken parental expectations that their teens should experience a sow-their-oats Rumspringa to weed out the unworthy and strengthen those who choose to eventually join.

Even in settlements where most youth do not participate in deviant activities or feel conflicted about adult expectations, those Amish young people with a strong need for personal independence or those who are dissatisfied with their way of life have a much more complex task, fraught with the potential for psychological and emotional distress or damage. A poignant illustration of this complexity occurs in *No Strange Fire*, by Ted Wojtasik, a novel about the Nebraska Amish. When Jacob, the youthful protagonist, abandons his predictable and prescribed Amish world, he struggles with a deep sense of loss on entering the new world of ambiguity, confusion, and alienation. Two autobiographies written in the second decade of this century by former Amish also illustrate the difficulty of leaving the Amish culture. Ira Wagler initially found it easy to make the break but exceedingly hard to stick with his decisions. He left four times before finally cutting his ties with the church.[31] The other autobiography chronicled the Amish years of Salome Miller Furlong, who desperately wanted to break free from an abusive family setting but who also returned to her family for nearly two years before making a final break.[32] Despite the fact that one can find many ex-Amish who express satisfaction with their having left, almost none leave the culture without serious struggles and difficult adjustments to mainstream society.[33]

One indication of how deeply the Amish identity runs may be found in the way that even those youth who are flaunting their community's rules react to outsiders seeking to learn about the inner workings of Amish life. When a doctoral-student acquaintance of mine sought information from a former musician in an Amish band regarding Amish musical preferences and practices at hoedowns and parties, he reported that he was "stonewalled." He finally completed his dissertation, but only by collecting most of his data from adults who had left the Amish through the years.[34] Another researcher attempted to interview a former Amish band member who purportedly had a vision of hell during a bad drug trip. Although the young man was asked to talk only about the kinds of music his band played, he declined to give any details, "because that is our business." Shortly thereafter, he received instruction, was baptized, and joined the church. Even if some youth were impressed by the media attention after the 1998 drug bust in Lancaster County, most Amish youth distanced the swarm of reporters that crisscrossed the county. Amish young men, dressed in English clothes and driving cars, still refused to disclose to reporters what happened at their hoedowns and parties.[35]

This non-cooperation on the part of these rowdy youth reflects an instinctive loyalty acquired in their separatist community. Despite youthful dalliance or deviance, in a relatively short time most of them abandon their worldly ways and return to their Amish roots.[36] This fundamental sense of who they are, now and in the future, is both pervasive and powerful enough to maintain their primary identity as Amish. This identity provides the core that allows them to give up their autonomy, the right to do anything they please, and to accept the restrictions and proscriptions of the community. This relinquishment is necessary if they are going to be contented, committed members of this communal subculture. In addition to the home and the church, one of the places where the young are intentionally taught to give up their prideful, self-centered ways and fit in with their society's expectations for children is in the eight years of schooling that the community provides. We turn now to Amish education.

Almost all Amish teachers are young women in their late teens who were chosen by the local school board because of their brightness, maturity, and commendable lives.
(Lucian Niemeyer, LNS Art)

Chapter Four

Schooling

Read'n, Rite'n, 'Rithmatic— but Shunning Darwin

That school is modeling what we profess to value.
We have a lot to learn from them!
—A professor of education, visiting a one-room Amish school

A Carefully Tended Education

In mainstream society, many young people are only halfway through their formal education when they enter puberty. Not so in Amish society, where all youth complete their formal education by age fifteen at the latest. The Amish think that eight grades are more than adequate to prepare youth to earn a livelihood, fill adult roles, and function as responsible, God-fearing church members, both in their community and in the larger society. Moreover, they believe that high school and higher education produce *Hochmut* (high-mindedness and pride), the antithesis of simplicity and humility. John A. Hostetler has noted: "The word *education* as used in American society is regarded with suspicion by most Amish people. To them it signifies ego advancement, independence, and cutting the ties that bind one to the community of faith and work."[1] In the crucial task of transmitting their culture and faith to the next generation, Amish education is both traditional and intentional: traditional in that it has changed relatively little over many generations, and highly intentional in that virtually nothing is left to chance in their eight years of schooling.[2]

A nineteenth-century child would probably feel at home in an Amish classroom today. One teacher typically instructs eight grades of a no-frills curriculum in a one- or two-room schoolhouse. A cursory look at contemporary Amish life, however, reveals many changes outside the classroom. The decline of farming, the rise of Amish industries and an entrepreneurial class, increased mobility and travel between settlements, and more discretionary wealth describe but a few of the discernible changes in most communities.[3] Similarly, incremental but continuing acceptance of technology and scientific farming methods—such as automatic milkers, bulk milk tanks, hay balers, diesels, weed whackers, artificial insemination of dairy cattle, electrical-power inverters, LED lights, solar panels, cell phones, smartphones, battery-operated word processors, and now computers—slip into many communities.[4]

The Amish school, nevertheless, has remained relatively impervious to the realities of these changes. In some communities the leaders have attempted, with varying degrees of success, to revive the *Alice and Jerry* series from the 1930s, with its small-town and rural-life settings. Some conservative Amish, such as the Swartzentrubers, still use reprints of the 1853 revision of *McGuffey's Readers* in the early grades, and the Amish-produced textbooks used by the majority of their schools today still reflect little about the changes affecting daily Amish life.

Compared with mainstream classes, Amish classes are characterized by considerably more recitation and rote memorization. Nor would an Amish teacher (usually a female) ever offer a unit on scientific discovery or critical thinking. She avoids a curriculum that might produce a questioning attitude that rejects traditional Amish values and behaviors. She would be distressed if even one of her brightest and best eighth graders began challenging Amish traditions or sought more education in high school or college. The teacher's task is to reinforce the status quo. As Hostetler has noted, "the Amish educate for social cohesion and not for technical competence."[5]

Until the school consolidation movement began in the 1940s, Amish children attended public schools along with the children of their rural English neighbors. These predominantly one-room neighborhood schools were funded and staffed by small, local school districts. When public-school boards decided to consolidate and bus children to distant buildings with hundreds of other children, Amish parents and ministers objected, because this went counter to the Amish values of smallness, proximity, and local control. In addition, states began enacting mandatory attendance laws that would require Amish youth to enroll in high school. From the East through the Midwest, these changes put the Amish and local and state educational establishments on a collision course. School officials warned the Amish that they were required to cooperate. When the parents refused, authorities arrested, fined, and sometimes jailed the recalcitrant fathers. Officials and parents eventually reached a compromise, permitting the Amish to establish their own schools, with the pupils taught by uncertified Amish teachers.[6] In 1972, the U.S. Supreme Court (in *Wisconsin v. Yoder*) ruled that in the interests of freedom of religion, the Amish had a right to restrict their formal education to eight grades.[7]

These constraints in Amish education still produce tensions at times.[8] Limiting education to eight grades strikes many moderns as archaic, if not abusive. Middle-class Americans, with their deep commitment to secondary and higher education, typically find this restriction one of the hardest to understand or accept. "What an unfair stifling of talent and a tragic loss for that individual and society! What if a bright Amish student wants to go to high school or college or would like to be a doctor, nurse, or engineer?" outsiders ask. Some critics charge that the Amish have deliberately structured their educational system to limit their children's capacity for critical thinking. Others regard it as a sinister form of social control, designed to trap young people in the Amish fold by inadequately preparing them to compete in a complex, high-tech world.[9]

Because the Amish believe that their children need to be protected from the corruption and sinfulness of worldly ideas taught in secondary schools, few appear defensive or disturbed over these allegations. Most are convinced that eight years of practical education are more than adequate for their children to lead fulfilled, productive, faithful lives, and the majority of Amish express satisfaction with the quality of their education. If demographic and quantitative data accurately reflect school success, the Amish appear to be correct about their degree of education being sufficient for their lives. Unemployment is virtually unknown, and although their cash flow may be limited, few, if any, Amish are destitute, even in areas where farming and small-business opportunities are marginally productive.

In terms of their scores on standardized achievement tests, Amish students, who are referred to as "scholars" by their parents and grandparents, have equaled, if not surpassed, the national norms in most subject areas, even though English is the Amish students' second language. In achievement tests administered in 1969, Hostetler and Huntington found that of the six subtests measured in the Iowa Test of Basic Skills (ITBS), Amish children scored as well as or better than their public-school counterparts in every area except English vocabulary.[10] The Amish scored higher in spelling, word usage, and arithmetic, and no differences were found in reading comprehension or the use of reference materials. Results from other standardized tests were similar. The authors concluded: "These standardized test results indicate that the Amish parochial schools, now taught by teachers educated in Amish schools, are continuing to give their students an adequate academic education, even when judged by measures designed to test students in our modern, technological society. Amish parochial schools are preparing their students for successful, responsible adulthood within their own culture and within the larger society."[11] If anything, ITBS tests from 2009 and 2011 reveal even stronger performances, with average achievement scores for Amish students from Indiana and Iowa being up to two years higher than the scores for public school students taking the same test.[12]

Although reading achievement test scores—and reading itself—continue to decline overall for American public school students, the majority of Amish children read at or above grade level. From my observations over the years, many Amish become "bookworms" (to use their term); most function effectively in English; and their mathematical skills are more than adequate for carpentry, business, and household finances. In many communities, adults who need bookkeeping and accounting skills or more advanced math usually teach themselves, learn from a relative or coworkers, or take correspondence or extension courses at home. In cases when church members need a high school diploma or specific certification for their employment, a few communities, such as the more progressive districts in northern Indiana and central Ohio, permit them to meet this requirement by passing the GED (high school equivalency exam) or by unobtrusively taking approved postsecondary correspondence or certification courses.[13] This, however, would be unheard-of in traditional settlements.

Today, as in the past, most Amish are still decidedly wary of secondary education's emphasis on individual expression and independent thought. They see it as the antithesis of a community-based society that values humility and cooperation. They also worry about the influence of non-Amish teachers and peers and a totally secular curriculum. In addition, they regard secondary schooling's focus on critical thinking and its intensified peer pressures as especially dangerous to the young and the traditional Amish way of life. In general, most of the Amish believe that any schooling beyond the eighth grade leads to pride and self-sufficiency instead of humility and God-centeredness. "After all," they would argue, "1 Corinthians 8:1 asserts that 'knowledge puffeth up.'"

The Classroom and Curriculum

In all states, the law requires that classes in Amish schools be taught in English.[14] In conservative circles, firstborn Amish children often understand only Pennsylvania German when they enter school, although many first-graders with older siblings have already learned English at home. Some four- or five-year-olds have even learned to read in English from their parents or older siblings before entering first grade. Besides the three Rs, children in most Amish private schools study penmanship, geography, German, and more. Most Swartzentruber and some Big Valley, Pennsylvania, school boards reject music and geography. In one of Pennsylvania's Nebraska affiliations, an Amish teacher bought a globe and brought it to his school to teach geography. A few days later, three parents arrived one morning and asked him to get rid of the globe. A significant number of the plainest Amish reputedly believe that the Bible teaches that the earth is flat. Most Amish school boards do not prohibit studying nature, but many regard anything smacking of dinosaurs as suspect, worldly, and dangerous, since it flies in the face of the Amish belief in a 6,000-year-old earth.

When a parent was asked what science subjects were taught in their school systems, he wrote tersely, "No science classes taught!" Few, if any, Amish schools use science textbooks, and most distrust science as it is taught in the public schools. They regard it as being not only impractical but, most importantly, promoting the theory of evolution. Nevertheless, many Amish, old and young, are interested in aspects of science when they are outside of school. A retired teacher wrote: "We do not use science textbooks, but I believe we have teachers and students who would love to discuss 'moon landings' and other topics of this nature. There are those who are well-read and quite broad-minded."[15] A Lancaster County bishop indicated that "thirty years ago" the antiscience bias was stronger, because their people did not understand the nature of science and equated it with Darwin.

Despite Amish suspicions of science, evolution, and higher education, many first-time visitors to an Amish school express surprise at the level of student engagement they observe in many classrooms. While touring through Lancaster County, a professor from Texas Tech University who specialized in educational research visited a one-room school. In relating his experiences to me, he was visibly moved in recounting the interactions of the students with each other and of the pupils with their teacher. Although the teacher was obviously in charge, all her pupils called her by her first name or simply "Teacher." In addition, she knew the families of each student. The visitor watched as the eighth graders listened to the second graders read or helped them with their times tables and spelling words.

If the professor had interviewed other teachers in the area, he would have learned that parents are welcomed at school and that teachers routinely encourage the parents to be involved in their children's education. A mother from Indiana said: "I'm expected to stop by on occasion to touch base with the teacher and keep up with what's going on. You don't just send your kids off to school and expect the teacher to raise them. It's a parent's responsibility."[16] The teacher reported that "100 percent of my parents are behind me and involved with the school." The parents visited the school from time to time to encourage their children and help where needed. At least one exception to this norm is a Swartzentruber settlement in New York State, where the half-dozen recorded visitors in two years were mostly from outside the community.[17] Not infrequently, many teachers invite their pupils to their homes for dinner or a birthday celebration. At least once a year, many invite every student, in groups of five or six, to stay overnight, and some teachers invite their pupils home during the summer. Another visiting educator remarked: "That school is modeling what we profess to value. The classes are manageable, and the teacher cares about each pupil, both as an individual and a learner. She clearly knows what she is about. It is obvious that students feel valued, competent, and safe with her and with each other. We have a lot to learn from them!"

Two other areas where Amish and mainstream schools differ are in their attitudes toward homework and corporal punishment. Regarding homework, Amish parents generally want their children to be able to complete their schoolwork during school hours so that they will be free to help with chores and interact with their families at home. As for corporal punishment, a paddle or a switch is used at times, but most teachers regard it as a discipline of last resort. They prefer to keep students in the classroom during recess or after school, the latter practice being easily possible when children walk or bicycle to school.

In parts of Indiana and Ohio, a significant number of Amish children still attend public schools. This usually happens in areas where the Amish are highly concentrated among neighbors who have historically accepted and understood the distinctiveness of their culture, such as in Holmes County, Ohio, where almost one-third of the Amish students go to public schools. Charles Hurst and David McConnell have pointed out that sometimes disagreements surface between Amish public school and private school parents.[18] The 70 percent who send their children to Amish private schools express their belief that their children are better prepared for the Amish way of life than those who attend public schools. Most of these parents worry about the public-school students' exposure to technology in general, and to computers and the Internet in particular. In many, if not most, public schools with Amish pupils, these children have frequent contact with computers, if not actual instruction in their use. Parents choosing to send their children to public school, however, often cite their own positive experiences there and believe that their children will be better prepared to function capably in an increasingly demanding economic and technological environment. In most places today, however, the majority of Amish still prefer locally controlled private schools that are under the oversight of an Amish-elected school board. Three to six fathers serve as board members, whose task is to monitor the selection of teachers, curriculum, and texts.

In many settlements, curricular materials are chosen by a "Book Society" composed of several designated men who have oversight and control. They generally select books and materials from two or three main sources. In Lancaster County and its daughter settlements, many schools have traditionally used discarded public-school textbooks and workbooks from the 1950s. Now they tend to use texts and workbooks from the Amish-owned Gordonville Print Shop in Lancaster County, Pennsylvania, or curricular materials from the Schoolaid Publishing Company, another Lancaster County enterprise started by Old Order Mennonites. Among other items, Schoolaid produces textbooks on English, health, mathematics, German phonics, and reading. Another source of materials for plain schools is Study Time, a northern Indiana company that publishes a math series, a geography text, and even activity materials for preschoolers. Pathway Publishers in Aylmer, Ontario, is another Amish-owned curricular source. Founded in 1964, the firm publishes *Pathway Readers* and a host of other materials, providing Anabaptist themes and values-based curricula to their Old Order Amish and Mennonite constituencies. While not exclusively religious, their curricula emphasize basic education within a morality-based context. For example, the eighth-grade reader specifically recounts aspects of Anabaptist history, both in Europe and in North America.[19]

Just Call Me Teacher

Most teachers are rumspringa Amish women in their late teens or early twenties, "with a knack for learning and a flair for teaching."[20] Although men will sometimes teach, mostly in the Midwest, they often have difficulty supporting a family on a teacher's salary.[21] Men are usually paid more than women, especially if the former have a family, but in general the pay is still relatively low, since a teacher's work is seen more as a service to the community than as a way to earn a living. Because Amish teachers themselves are products of an Amish education, they rarely verbalize any frustration with local restrictions on their teaching. Most appear to be content with the curriculum and the structure of their system. After all, their students will not be spoiled by high school, with its godless curricula and teachers, permissive discipline, sex education, coed gym classes and immodest uniforms, computers, televised lessons, and the latest educational fads. Both the teachers and the community they represent believe that the primary key to success in Amish education is a carefully chosen curriculum, taught by a teacher who models for the children what it means to be a committed Amish woman or man. The teacher's preparation, style, and classroom management—although significant—are of secondary importance.

This does not mean that the Amish do not care about the quality of instruction. In most places they support both informal and formal teacher training. An Amish teacher's professional training generally consists of serving for at least a year as a teacher's helper. If this assistant teacher wishes to become a full-time teacher, she is generally offered a contract, but in Lancaster County, at least, she must take a two-week class on teaching phonics, plus a six-week summer workshop on classroom management, discipline, and other practical concerns. She will also probably read extensively from back issues of *Blackboard Bulletin*, a Pathway monthly publication dedicated to an improved curriculum and more effective instruction in Old Order schools. During the school year, at least in the larger settlements, teachers will also have periodic in-service days or meetings prior to and during their teaching careers, "for discussion and learning from each other." Here teachers and board members consider everyday issues and problem situations likely to be faced in the classroom. Also, groups of teachers and board` members customarily visit other schools and observe classes once or twice yearly. Some school boards periodically arrange for a group of their teachers to spend a day with an experienced teacher, studying and reviewing the teaching of some specific skill, such as vocabulary development or phonics instruction. In Lancaster County, Pennsylvania, a highly regarded Old Order Mennonite teacher has regularly offered in-service instructional classes in phonics for current and prospective teachers from settlements throughout the state. Other in-service discussions frequently center on preparation, classroom management, discipline, and how-to techniques for anything from improving handwriting to planning for the Christmas program. These meetings are in addition to the important annual school-board-sponsored meetings for interested teachers and board members.

Despite these efforts to provide growth opportunities for their teachers, not all of the Amish are pleased with the quality of the teaching and the commitment of their teachers. A respected retired teacher wrote: "With no testing required for one to become a teacher in an Amish school, it is REAL challenge to keep our education level up to a good, solid eighth-grade level. Anymore, most of our teachers were educated in our own schools, and we are losing a little here, a little there. The majority are young women [girls] who will soon be married; therefore their whole hearts are not in teaching. I fear that too many board members are somewhat blind to what is happening; also, they are not familiar with the curriculum used."[22]

The Pennsylvania Vocational-School Compromise

All states require Amish students to complete the eighth grade, but the details vary from state to state. In Pennsylvania, state law mandates that students stay in school until age fifteen, unlike many other states that simply require completion of the eighth grade or mandatory schooling until age fourteen. Since most students finish the eighth grade before they reach fifteen, the Pennsylvania Department of Education and Amish parents reached a compromise on this dilemma.[23] The Amish promised that they would require their eighth-grade graduates to attend an Amish-controlled vocational-education program until their fifteenth birthday. This schooling consists of a once-weekly three-hour class, often held at the teacher's house in the evening or on a Saturday morning during the school year. In some districts the fourteen-year-olds return to their own school building for instruction during the school day. In Lancaster County, a vocational class may have thirty or more fourteen-year-olds when the program opens in August. Both parents and teachers carefully monitor the children's attendance, because they do not want the community to jeopardize their good relations with state educational officials. In Lancaster County, students are required to bring to class a German songbook, a German-English New Testament, and a diary of their week's work activities.

Because of this language component, the Amish in some locales call this last year of education *Deutsch Schul* (German school). Most vocational classes begin with an opening exercise, often in German and with a distinctly Christian focus. Each student may take a turn reading a verse of the New Testament, first in German and then in English, until that day's chapter or chapters are completed. This reading is done without commentary by the teacher. At some point students recite the Lord's Prayer in German. Additionally, the class will sing several songs in German, some from songbooks and some from copies provided by the teacher. Frequently these are sung to the tunes of gospel songs, such as "Just a Closer Walk with Thee" or "I'll Fly Away." These devotional activities may sometimes take an hour.

In most vocational schools, teachers have the students take turns copying their diary entries from the previous week into their official classroom diary. "The reason pupils copy their work into the school diary," explained a former teacher, "is to encourage neat handwriting and correct spelling and punctuation." These entries record what each student did and how long he or she spent during the week performing farm-, shop-, or homemaking-related activities. A typical submission consists of one to six sentences, like the one below, written by a fourteen-year-old boy in Franklin County, Pennsylvania:

Feb. 24, Tues.

I did chores and worked up in the log house. Finished the hay racks for the calf and made a thing to hold the bottle while the calf sucks milk.

Matthew and me cleaned out the shop.

This afternoon we started getting the old chicken house ready for farrowing hogs. We hauled the chicken nests out and the slats.

We put a heifer down in the meadow and a dry cow up in the heifer pen.

While students copy their diary entries or translate German passages from the New Testament or hymnbooks, the teacher might call each one up to his or her desk to recite the German memory work for the week.

Many parents and students regard these weekly classes and requirements as busywork. Thinking back on his vocational-school experience, an
Amish man in his thirties declared: "Our vocational schools were useless.
They were a total waste!" He and other critics see German/vocational school
as either an intrusion that interferes with the "real" world of work in which
they are now engaged, or an absence of any substantive preparation for life.
Almost all students report that they look forward to the end of their formal
schooling. When asked if students who turn fifteen during the school year
ever stay on to the end, informants universally answered, "Never!" This
does not mean, however, that students abandon all school-related endeavors. From early childhood on, most Amish children and youth indicate that
they enjoy reading, and they almost certainly read more than their non-
Amish counterparts.[24] This should not be surprising in a culture that pro-
hibits radio, television, and computers.

Reading the Right Stuff

If an ongoing interest in reading after finishing school can be attributed
to schooling, Amish schools appear to be highly successful. Both secular
and religious histories are perennial favorites with readers of all ages everywhere. Small, Amish-owned bookstores do a brisk trade in books dealing
with Anabaptist history and issues.[25] Many Amish, young and old, also like
publications about Native Americans and pioneer life. Family bookshelves
often contain volumes on Revolutionary and Civil War history. Readers are
also often deeply curious about other lands and peoples. Except in the most
conservative settlements, they especially enjoy *National Geographic* magazines, which offer a chance to see sights and travel vicariously to other
places in the world.

    Librarians report that certain novels (such as *Heidi, Pollyanna*, and *Black
Beauty*) and books with Amish themes (such as Yoder's *Rosanna of the Amish*
and *Rosanna's Boys*) are popular among children and young teens. The *Little
House on the Prairie* series by Laura Ingalls Wilder has been another enduring favorite. Mrs. Gideon Byler, a well-known *Die Botschaft* "scribe" (community letter-writer) from Franklin County, Pennsylvania, self-published a
six-book Lizzie series, which some readers have dubbed "the Amish *Little*

House on the Prairie." Her volumes have been revised and picked up by Good Books, which has issued them in a new, flashier format.[26] In some settlements, teens and preteens also borrow adventure and mystery stories, such as those by Zane Grey and the Hardy Boys series. Westerns by Louis L'Amour are very popular in certain settlements. Teenage girls often read books that their grandmothers and mothers read when they were young, such as the Christian-based novels by Grace Livingston Hill or the Nancy Drew mysteries. Many girls read religious romance novels by Janette Oke. Both boys and girls frequently enjoy suspenseful classics like *Tom Sawyer*, *Treasure Island*, or *Kidnapped*. According to female Amish Facebook readers, Karen Kingsbury and the Bible take top honors among the rumspringa set.[27]

What are regarded as acceptable reading materials vary widely from settlement to settlement. Many families subscribe to at least one of the three Amish periodicals devoted to family, community, and church news throughout the settlements. The best known is the *Budget*, from Sugarcreek, Ohio, published weekly for well over a century. It is especially popular in Ohio and the Midwest. *Die Botschaft*, published in Lancaster County, Pennsylvania, began as a plain writers' alternative to the *Budget*, since the latter featured "too many letters from the Beachy Amish and other non-plain groups." The *Diary*, also from Lancaster County, prints monthly settlement news but also regularly features topics of special interest, such as greenhouse management, bird watching, astronomy, and many others. With the exception of an occasional High German or Pennsylvania German word or phrase, these three periodicals are written in English. Farming magazines also have been perennial favorites, and families frequently subscribe to local newspapers. Many teenage boys, and a surprising number of their fathers, faithfully read the sports section. In the more progressive settlements, families may get *Newsweek*, *Time*, or *U.S. News and World Report*, although some conservative affiliations discourage any kind of news magazine. In many circles, *Reader's Digest* seems to be the most popular secular magazine for a wide range of Amish readers.

Many parents freely monitor their children's or young teens' reading matter, and they do not hesitate to censor material that they believe promotes worldly thinking or living. A father succinctly expressed the sentiments of most Amish parents: "It is the responsibility of parents to provide decent reading material." Most parents routinely reject books or articles that mention evolution, dinosaurs, or an ice age, since virtually all Amish accept the young-earth theory espoused by the majority of conservative Christians. "How could dinosaurs have lived millions of years ago, when the Bible teaches that God created the earth only 6,000 years ago?" they ask rhetorically. Many Amish also consider books that feature fairy tales or talking animals, or have fantasy or science fiction themes, as foolish. "There are enough true things to write about without wasting your time reading stuff that is made up," they say. For this reason, many parents include fiction in the time-wasting category, since it, too, is invented. Referring to Ted Wojtasik's novel, *No Strange Fire*, centering around a rash of Amish barn fires started by an arsonist in the Big Valley of Pennsylvania in 1992, one parent objected, saying: "I wouldn't want my children reading this because the author spends too much time describing the sinful behavior of the world rather than what really happened. Besides, nobody actually died in the fire like he says in the book."[28] That attitude, however, seems to have changed for a significant number of large-settlement Amish readers who, according to Valerie Weaver-Zercher, admit to enjoying Amish romance fiction.[29]

Parents also try to prohibit books or magazines that use profanity or allude in any way to sexual or vulgar behavior. A minister criticized Levi Miller's *Ben's Wayne*, a novel portraying the struggles of an Amish young man coming of age in Ohio, "because the author made it look like it's common for all of the young men to leave the Sunday-morning church service and take a break during the reading of the scripture. Besides, he actually wrote that they went out and peed. This should not be written about in any book." A parent related that he routinely monitored his children's bookshelves, and even the mail, to check for "trashy ads and catalogs coming to our mailboxes, with very descriptive illustrations." Parents have sometimes based their decisions on the acceptability of a book from unofficial reviews in *Die Botschaft* or the *Budget* written by David Wagler, a well-known scribe from Iowa who is also a widely read Amish author and cofounder of the Amish-owned Pathway Publishers in Ontario.

Pathway Books and Periodicals

In many Amish homes, shelves contain books from Pathway Publishers, and magazine racks bulge with current issues of their monthly periodicals. Besides the well-known *Pathway Readers*, the company has published many other perennial favorites. An Amish teenager reported that he had read his favorite Pathway book, *One Way Street*, three times.[30] The story is a fictional account of an Amish youth who is led astray when he is attracted to a more liberal Anabaptist church that emphasizes expressiveness in worship and an outspoken assurance of salvation.[31] Another Pathway favorite is *Henry and the Great Society*, in which the protagonist loses his contented life by succumbing to materialism and change. Both books have been popular with youth and their parents for decades, and *Henry and the Great Society* was serialized in the 1980s in both the *Diary* and *Young Companion*.

Although the Amish editors of *Young Companion* aim at a youthful readership, most parents also peruse it. The magazine features carefully selected fiction, moral admonitions, and "Can You Help Me?," a question-and-answer forum that focuses on adolescent problems and concerns, such as "Is it all right for a couple to hold hands or touch lightly?" *Family Life*, which aims at a broader readership, also features a column, "The Problem Corner," that deals at times with adolescent worries or the concerns of their parents. Frequently, a panel of ministers responds anonymously to a potentially difficult situation, problem, or question. Some issues focus on troubling or embarrassing youth issues, such as questionable entertainment, dress standards among teenagers, dating behavior, rowdiness at singings, and vandalism. One topic that captured widespread attention dealt with "self-abuse" (masturbation), an issue acknowledged but rarely mentioned openly in Amish circles.[32] Children and parents often vie over who will be the first to read the latest issues, attesting to their popularity. Many families have their well-used copies of both periodicals bound annually and readily available.

Although *Family Life* is aimed at a broader audience, it seems to interest teenage readers as much as *Young Companion*, perhaps because it occasionally features adult issues rarely discussed by parents or ministers. A number of years ago, an editorial on Saturday-night partying in a large settlement provoked widespread comment and a flurry of letters to the editor. Articles or letters occasionally mention problems of alcohol abuse or drug use in certain unnamed settlements. Pathway's editorial stance consistently opposes alcohol, partying, and the cultivation and use of tobacco. This latter issue has resulted in some of the more traditional communities (such as the Huevelton, New York, Swartzentruber churches) rejecting Pathway's moral stand as being too similar to that of the Mennonites and therefore suspect.[33] Despite some opposition, however, the majority of Amish families subscribe to these two periodicals, and a number of Amish leaders believe that these magazines have had a salutary influence on both youth and adults by raising important moral issues and encouraging a more godly and consistent lifestyle.

The Lure of More Learning

Sometimes young people's love for reading or their curiosity about ideas or the outside world entice them to delve into reading materials that the community finds objectionable. Non-Amish coworkers or local librarians sometimes recommend and even provide books that promote critical thinking or encourage additional formal education.[34] For some readers, these ideas provoke a discontent with their limited education and stimulate a desire for more learning. Some of these Amish young people eventually leave the community to pursue further education. The most prominent example is the late John A. Hostetler, formerly a professor of sociology at Temple University and the author of a number of widely-read books on Amish life. In *American Scholar*, he reported that he had never joined the Amish church, because he knew from childhood that he wanted more education than the community permitted.[35] Other examples occur in the fields of medicine and law.

Another avid childhood reader who left the Swartzentruber Amish at the age of eighteen later returned, to become a minister and eventually a bishop. He explained, "Reading is probably what got me into trouble in the first place." He believes that this activity planted those thoughts and ideas which led to his dissatisfaction with the Amish way of life. After spending several years in the military, he came back from Japan, was discharged, and was accepted as an engineering major at a nearby university under the G.I. bill. As a result of a brief trip home to tell his parents of his college plans, he changed his mind and decided to return to his roots. "I realized that was where I belonged."[36]

For every reader who leaves the Amish, many more Old Order youth remain to become self-educated. They now function as successful draftsmen, veterinary technicians, midwives, unofficial chiropractors, mechanics, hydraulic and pneumatic technicians, inventors, tax accountants, founders of banks, writers, historians, and occasionally even computer programmers for outside businesses—almost always without the benefit of a high school education or college courses.[37] Most of these self-taught learners also demonstrate an ability to analyze both mainstream and Amish society. In articles, reviews, and letters to the editor appearing in Amish publications, readers can find carefully reasoned critiques of public education, consumerism, environmental practices, and even the Internet and electronic culture. Many Amish are not averse to self-scrutiny and trenchant criticism as they lament some of their own shortcomings and questionable assumptions. The depth of their analyses often belies their limited formal education.[38]

To mainstream educators and parents accustomed to the rhetoric of flexible curricula, interactive learning, student engagement, and responsive interventions, Amish education may appear to be sterile or stifling. But it has proven to be widely effective for the Amish, given their cultural context and goals. Hostetler has noted: "Today the Amish are quietly developing a school system that is integrated with their way of life. The Amish schools protect their youth from alienation inherent in the loss of community life and generally produce stable, dedicated adults who are productive members in both their faith community and in American society."[39] Hostetler himself grew up in an Amish family in Iowa and attended school in a simple rural schoolhouse. Despite the absence of curricular innovations or expensive learning resources, he, along with some other Amish children both then and now, embarked on their careers as lifetime learners. Unlike Hostetler, however, the majority of the Amish accept the communal limitations on education as an integral part of their heritage. Few appear to long for the freedom to seek more schooling or to challenge their cultural and religious values, their assumptions, and the status quo.

Rather than regarding their societal restrictions on education as arbitrary or harsh, most Amish believe that these are necessary to avoid the pitfalls and excesses of mainstream society, with its emphasis on individualism, materialism, and worldly concerns. They view too much education, especially secular education, as dangerous to the character development of their youth—a danger that they fear will corrupt their lifestyle of simplicity, obedience, and integrity. Thus they give careful and ongoing attention to the form, content, and scope of their children's education. They believe that what happens during these formative years will help establish an Amish core that will see these youth through the new challenges and temptations they face, both in the outside world and in the company of their peers. They believe that what happens during these formative years will help establish an Amish core that will see these youth through the new challenges and temptations they face, both in the outside world and in the company of their peers. Tacit confirmation that the Amish educational system is functioning as its leaders and as parents intend comes from the fact that their grown sons and daughters embrace the Amish faith, values, and culture, but education is not the sole factor that leads youth in that direction. We now turn to Amish parenting practices.

From the outside, parenting in Amish society may seem simpler than in mainstream America. Amish parents, however, face significant peer pressure to succeed in rearing children who are both well behaved and willing to choose the Amish way.

(Sean J. Hagins)

Chapter Five

Parenting
Holding On and Letting Go

*Letting children go unsupervised to watch the trash that comes
over the TV every day has to be the greatest form of child abuse.*
—Amish father

Parenting Paradise or Pressure Cooker?

Outsiders who are welcomed into an Amish community frequently
comment on the richness of family life there. These visitors often
report much interaction, conversation, and laughter between parents and
their children. A college professor who visited Amish families for many
years noted a comparative absence of open conflict among the generations.
She observed that in farming families, the children, youth, parents, and
grandparents frequently "chored" together. Even teenagers seemed to relate well to their younger brothers and sisters. Often the older children,
both male and female, cuddled, carried, or played with the infants, toddlers,
and other younger siblings.[1] She also noticed that when the youngsters lost
interest in adult-centered activities, they usually went elsewhere to play or
socialize, rather than disturbing their parents. Only once, amid hundreds
of hours of visiting, did the professor witness an angry outburst between

Amish parents and children or observe rebellion, disobedience, or physical punishment. "Perhaps," she acknowledged, "this was true in part because they knew they were being watched."

Nevertheless, if the professor's experience and impressions reflect typical parent-child relations, the parents' dedication to their task most likely is a key factor, if not the primary one, in the continuation of the culture. The Amish regard parenting as a profound and serious calling from God, to whom they are accountable. Virtually all of them believe that parents carry a heavy responsibility for the outcome of their children. After all, Amish leaders teach that faithful parents produce faithful children. The relevant Bible verse that preachers frequently quote in sermons is Proverbs 22:6: "Train up a child in the way he should go, and when he is old, he will not depart from it." The Amish retain nearly 85 percent of their youth, which suggests that parents are unusually successful in transmitting their way of life to their children.[2]

If social indicators are any measure of parenting success, Amish parents again appear to be doing well in both peer-centered and adult-centered settlements. Despite the fact that some youth in both kinds of settlements drink on the weekends, most abide by the law and behave responsibly within and outside the Amish community.[3] Relatively few are involved in serious deviance or criminal activity and, almost without exception, are reliable, hard workers. Typically, youth express deep respect for their parents and families, including many Youngie who never join the church, and even those who join but later leave. Such expressions of love, responsibility, and caring are hardly accidental. A quick perusal of the Amish periodicals *Family Life* and *Young Companion* reveals article after article focusing on both the challenges and the privileges of conscientious parenting and the obligations of children to respect and obey their parents. As Christians, these parents feel the responsibility of influencing the eternal destiny of their offspring by encouraging them to embrace the faith of their forebears, extended family, and community.

Finally, because they are a separatist group, the Amish know instinctively that the transmission of their culture to their children is a crucial task for the survival of their way of life. This is especially true because they do not seek converts. The Amish know that they are only a generation or two, at most, from the loss of their distinctiveness and culture. Therefore, the future of their society is wrapped up in the parents' ability to transmit their Amish heritage to their offspring—a sobering responsibility for any Amish father or mother.

The basic architecture of Amish society prepares parents for their task of rearing children who will choose the Amish way. Parents' and children's roles are clearly defined. Not surprisingly, Joe Wittmer found that Amish youth, when compared with their non-Amish counterparts, perceived their parents to be much more unified and congruous in their parenting roles and values.[4] Young and old alike believe that God has appointed parents, with their years of experiencing life and accumulating wisdom, to lovingly care for, nurture, and discipline their offspring. Parents teach children that they have a God-given responsibility to love, honor, and obey their parents "in the Lord."[5] Because the Amish consider the Bible to be the authority for parent-child relationships, everyone regards these roles as divine mandates.

Although children are cherished, Amish society is decidedly not child centered. With confidence, fathers and mothers allot work assignments around the house and determine the frequency and duration of family activities. Children and teenagers rarely challenge their parents' ways of parenting or their decisions. Many Amish look with surprise or quiet amusement at their non-Amish neighbors who read the latest books on child rearing or attend parenting workshops, although growing numbers of Amish in the large settlements are reading Christian books on parenting.[6]

For the Amish, success in child rearing can be found in the pool of social capital and wisdom residing in the extended family and the community. One Amish woman, noting the middle-class tendency toward child-centered homes, declared: "You English [non-Amish] spend far too much time explaining things to your young children. Just let them know what you expect and then have them do it."[7] A writer in the Amish periodical *Blackboard Bulletin* advised: "Never let your child say 'No' when you ask him to do something. Expect nothing short of prompt and complete obedience. Remember, delayed obedience is disobedience. Get the child's attention; assign the task, and expect it to be completed with *no* reminders. Repeating instructions develops irresponsible habits."[8] Most Amish parents also do not hesitate to spank their children. The Amish are not trying to rear assertive, critically thinking individualists. Instead, they value children who are obedient to their parents and, in the future, will find it natural to be obedient to God and the Ordnung.

Another feature of Amish living that helps parents is that their pace of life is generally slower than that in a typical middle-class home, thus allowing more quality interactions between parents and their children. Compared with many mainstream Americans, far fewer Amish parents must balance nearly impossible work schedules with endless family demands. Amish couples rarely face the problems of finding sitters or day care for their preschoolers or of juggling their job responsibilities to mesh with the busy extracurricular lives of their school-aged children. Amish mothers almost always work at home, and older siblings learn to care for their younger brothers and sisters. Nor do Amish parents need to taxi family members to and from Girl Scout cookie sales or Cub Scout campouts, 4-H exhibits or science fairs, music or ballet or karate lessons, gymnastics or swimming practice—in short, to the multitude of obligatory activities surrounding the daily life of typical middle-class households. In contrast to mainstream parents encouraging outside activities for their growing children and youth, Amish fathers and mothers prefer their younger children and those in their early teens to work and play at home.

Moreover, Amish parents in both traditional and New Order affiliations rarely encounter the dilemmas facing conscientious mainstream parents in a media-saturated society. They need not decide how much TV their children should watch or if they should block the MTV or HBO options on cable television. Whether they should give their twelve-year-old son the video game "Call of Duty: Black Ops II" for his birthday, or allow their fourteen-year-old to rent *Hangover* or *Hangover II* for her sleepover, are simply nonissues. In typical small settlements or conservative youth groups, most Amish parents need not worry either about the negative impact of the ads, images, and articles in teen magazines or the explicit lyrics by the latest rap singer. Nor are they upset when their children visit friends whose mother, father, or guardian they barely know. Few Amish parents are concerned that the latest sitcom or movie star will influence their children to come home with piercings, a tattoo, or a shaved head. Little wonder, then, that at least in the adult-centered settlements, Amish parenting appears to be simpler and less anxiety-producing than mainstream parenting.

The Quiet Years

The contrast between parenting difficulties that mainstream parents and Amish parents face shows up dramatically in their children's early teen years. Both cross-sectional (studying different groups at the same point in time) and longitudinal (studying the same group at different points in time) research findings indicate that in mainstream society, parent-teen conflicts most often peak when the child is around thirteen or fourteen.[9] Developmental psychologists believe that in these pubescent youth, this clash is triggered by the growing influence of peers and by society's pushing them toward independence. These forces contribute to an increase in the youngsters' need for more autonomy and the subsequent parent-teen conflicts. Most Amish, however, report that the years from thirteen through fifteen are relatively tranquil in their culture for both youngsters and their parents.[10] One reason for this difference may stem from the fact that, outside of school, Amish youth in the early teen years have comparatively little contact with their age-mates. An Amish fourteen-year-old will celebrate her birthday almost exclusively with immediate family members and relatives. Almost no organized activities or forms of group recreation exist for Amish youngsters prior to their joining the youth at age sixteen or seventeen. If a fifteen-year-old wants to play softball, he does so with his siblings, close neighbors, or age-mates that come visiting with their parents.

This relatively quiet period probably arises from a combination of factors, one being that Amish children complete their full-time schooling either at the end of the eighth grade or at age fifteen. Most students report that they look forward to being done with school, so they can start their life "in the real world." Initially, this real world consists of working full time at home or gradually transitioning into full-time employment away from the home when they reach the allowable legal age. They have been taught from childhood to value work, and for most Amish, work has traditionally meant manual, tangible, sweat-of-the-brow labor rather than studying books or dealing with abstractions. Now they can finally work with their hands, un-encumbered by the requirements of sitting in a classroom.

Contrast this slow pace and the limited contacts of a young Amish teenager with the situation for a typical mainstream middle school or junior high student. Many of them commonly pursue multiple activities with their peers at a frenetic pace. These activities, plus homework, often fill almost all of the out-of-school hours for these early adolescents. Except for school, most young Amish teens interact with their peers only on church Sundays every other week or at the occasional school sale, benefit sale, or farm auction.

Parental Perplexities

In observing these parenting differences in the two cultures, one might be tempted to conclude that Amish parenting is relatively stress-free. Amish parents, however, take their responsibility with utmost seriousness. As one parent wrote: "Remember that virtues can often be lost in a two-step, two-generation manner. The first generation fails to see the danger, and neglects to provide basic and sound teaching against sin. Naturally, the next generation will not have true convictions against it."[11] A minister expressed the sentiments of many parents: "We parents . . . have to be constantly vigilant if we are going to maintain high standards among the young ones in our community."

Not only do Amish parents fear a loss of standards, but they also recognize that they could lose their children to "the world." Even if only one child left the faith and subsequently became a successful and respected member of the outside world, most parents would feel a significant sense of failure and loss. A middle-aged Amish father lamented, "We have buried five children, but that has not given us as much grief as the one who has strayed." A mother wrote poignantly of her feelings on losing her children to the world: "How do parents feel when children leave home? It is so heartbreaking. At first I cried and cried, and when I got over that, it just made me sick. Still, I had to do my daily work. Sometimes I feel I didn't treat them right when they were growing up. I didn't show enough love, didn't talk nice and kind, didn't teach them enough about God and pray[er], and so on. Whenever I think about it, such as now when writing about it, it brings tears to my eyes. We can't change what already happened. I will keep praying for them as long as I live. Signed, A Lonely Mother."[12]

Parents' standing in the community directly relates to their success in rearing children who become committed, conscientious Amish adults. "You can judge the parents by looking at their children," a Nebraska Amish man asserted. In those communities where the official family directories list the membership status of each child in every home, the "failures" of parents with non-Amish children are published for all to read.[13] In some settlements, a minister will not be considered for the office of bishop unless all of his children are safely in the church, or at least preparing for membership.[14] Some Amish even evaluate parents on the outcome of their grandchildren, as did an older Amish man who maintained that "the real test of parents is to see how their grandchildren turn out." In the same vein, a young Amish man announced, "All of the grandchildren on my mother's side are still Amish, and only one grandchild on Dad's side left the Amish."

In some places, communities hold in high esteem those parents whose children are among the first to join the church when they become eligible. Conversely, parents lose status when their children delay membership beyond the specified age of joining. Such postponement puts stress on the parents, and the longer the delay, the greater the tensions that rise among them, their wavering sons or daughters, and the church. Although many parents tolerate the deviance and disobedience of the middle teen years, when a child reaches the expected time for joining the church, parents are less likely to be patient with their children's reluctance. In some areas, community tolerance also ends when the uncommitted son or daughter reaches a certain age (usually twenty-one). This especially holds true for children who are dressing or acting in objectionable ways. At that point, the community expects the child either to come into full compliance and join the church or else leave the home and the community. "Roy will be twenty-one this summer," reported a father. "If he doesn't give up baseball and join the instruction class this time around, we will come into trouble with the church if we let him live at home."

Parents who are regarded as lax or inconsistent in either their personal lives or parental responsibilities may be counseled, pressured, and disciplined if they fail to enforce church standards. This is most common in the smaller, plainer communities and in some New Order settlements. Both parents and their delaying children may be stigmatized. One minister's wife commented: "It's a disgrace that Amanda has still not become a member at twenty-one. But what can you expect, since her mother was also pretty wild when she was Amanda's age." Even if young people join the church but still fail to comply with community values, observers often attribute this to parental failure.[15]

In many places, behavioral expectations are high not only for parents, but also for the teenagers. In *Young Companion*, various parents listed the desired characteristics of a "normal" teenager. A father of sixteen children wrote, "A normal Christian youth should respect his parents, be friendly, and if reminded of any wrong on his part, should be ready to make amends." Another writer responded this way: "Christian youth should be Christlike, compassionate, humble, meek, full of love, and an example to the believers. They should respect their parents and obey them in the Lord. They should enjoy and cherish Christian fellowship, singing, helping others, and above all they should enjoy their time spent at home with their families." A third writer, however, returned to the theme of the parents' responsibility in nurturing these Christian traits in their children: "The concerned parent will watch to avoid bad habits, worldliness, laziness, wastefulness, intemperance, disrespect, pride, and other such traits that might show up in young folks. Also, the parents should encourage humbleness, love, respect, temperance, as well as learning to work and being a help in the home."[16]

Amish parents must constantly deal with the challenge of influencing their children, while at the same time allowing them the freedom to choose or reject their teachings and influence. Denise Reiling believes that in some settlements, parents are expected to allow, if not encourage, youthful deviance during Rumspringa so their teenagers will have a genuine choice to make in deciding whether to be baptized or leave the Amish.[17] In a cultural setting that promotes "parental complicity," to use Reiling's term, she believes that parents as well as their children experience considerable stress because of these conflicting expectations. If children perceive their parents as being abusive, too harsh, or unreasonable, the young person may become rebellious and later decide to leave home and, ultimately, the Amish way. At the other end of the spectrum, Amish parents who encourage too much creativity or intellectual exploration also run the risk of losing their children to the outside world, albeit for a different reason. Whatever the setting, Amish parents constantly face pressure to succeed in this high-stakes parenting task. Although they have considerable influence, it is nonetheless limited, especially during the rumspringa years, when their children face equally daunting and sometimes contradictory expectations from both their parents and their peers.

Conflicting Demands

Parents of teens may also feel caught between the conflicting pressures from their growing children and their own adult peers in the church. Some teenagers may coerce their parents into going away for the weekend, so the house will be available for unsupervised weekend partying. When teenagers host singings or parties, they may press their parents not to report group misbehavior to the church leaders, or not to call the police if some of the participants become overly boisterous, destructive, or out of control. Some parents claim that other parents also pressure them not to report illegal activities to the authorities. "They say they don't want to give the church and the Amish a bad name in the community. What's a person to do?" a father asked. A *Die Botschaft* writer suggested that in dealing with rowdiness, "to call out the law for help is again not letting our light shine. [If] the police have our sons' names on record, then what will it come to, if they are called to service as trying to go for C.O. [conscientious objector status] of which we don't know how soon it could come to such."[18]

Sometimes parents fear possible retribution from rebellious youth if they "crack down" (exert control) or call the authorities. A father said he disapproved of the carrying on, "but the boys would get down on me if I didn't allow it."[19] Occasionally parents may cave in to these pressures in order to please their children and their children's peers. One man recalled an after-singing party when the host father came out to the barn to check on the young people. Although he found that a number of teenage boys were drinking openly, he smiled and joked with them. During the conversation, one boy came up behind the father and poured a bottle of beer over his head. As everyone laughed, the father said, "Since I'm here, I might as well have a beer, too. Give me one of those things," and drank it along with the teenagers.

Although uncommon, bishops have occasionally threatened to discipline parents who allow their children to engage in forbidden activities, such as hosting a party or parking a car on the premises. According to one Amish informant, a Lancaster County bishop warned parents that if their children attended hoedowns "with antisocial behavior . . . their parents will have to answer to the church leaders."[20] Also, some of their bishops were said to have warned that parents who knowingly permitted gangs to party on their property would be brought before the church council. In one case, a father was held back from communion twice for allowing his wayward son to park his car behind their barn. "What can I do?" the father lamented. "If I make him quit parking at home, he'll just leave, but if I am held back the third time, I will be put in the *Bann* [excommunicated]."

Traversing the Minefields

In certain settlements, especially the larger ones, a significant minority of Amish youth are more likely to distance themselves from home and church by their behavior. Parents typically experience considerable stress if their sons or daughters socialize with non-Amish youth from another Anabaptist group or with the English. Even if these outsiders show interest in the Amish way of life, the adults fear that however sincere the seeker might be, he or she could unwittingly bring in deeply ingrained worldly influences, attitudes, and habits to contaminate their church and their youth. A parent explained: "Young people who sow their wild oats still have the basic Amish core that draws them back. Converts, however, do not have that same base." Parents know both intuitively and experientially that such friendships can threaten the fabric and integrity of their separatist society and the future of their children in continuing as members of the Amish.

Parents also know that if their children dally with English teenagers, they may become romantically or sexually involved with an outsider whom they will eventually marry. Parents especially worry if their daughters date non-Amish youth. A father explained, "Boys may fool around with English girls for a while and then 'tell them off' [break up], but girls naturally become more attached in a relationship." When Amish children marry outsiders, they almost never return. Unless the spouse converts to the Amish—an unlikely event—this "unequal yoking" in marriage spells the end of the parents' hopes for the child's return to the fold.[21] Furthermore, if the son or daughter should divorce, he or she would be disqualified from returning to the Amish as long as the former spouse lives.[22]

A Breach in the Wall

Separation between Amish youth and the world was seriously threatened during World War II, when nearly 800 young men received draft notices from the government. Draft boards required that Amish young men, along with other conscientious objectors, participate in Civilian Public Service (CPS) or its Canadian counterpart during World War II. Fifty of the young men decided to serve in the military, either as soldiers or in non-combatant roles. Virtually all of the others joined the CPS as conscientious objectors.[23] Officials often sent these conscripts hundreds of miles from home to work with non-Amish personnel. Parents and church leaders feared that such isolation from the community would lead to increased defections.[24]

During the 1950s and 1960s, parents worried even more about their sons who were sent to urban centers to fulfill their alternative-service obligations in hospitals and other nonprofit organizations. "This kind of voluntary service was a more dangerous environment for our boys than when they were working in remote areas as firefighters or on conservation projects," an Amish man explained. More than one young Amish man became smitten with a nurse or nurse's aide. Many Amish males admitted that they faced temptations at their workplace. A grandfather recalled that during his alternative service, about twenty new student nurses rotated into his hospital every thirteen weeks. Predictably, some Amish young men were attracted to these young women. Another Amish man recalled his experiences as an orderly in a hospital in the 1950s: "I am not proud of some things in those two years. Things were not always what they should have been. There were many temptations. Working in a hospital, we were working with women mostly as fellow workers. These hardworking, dependable boys were eye-catching to some of these girls. Some boys ended up getting hooked."[25] A grandfather declared that "many of these girls wanted a boy, and it didn't matter whether he was Amish or not."

To reduce these temptations, Amish parents and leaders sought ways to minimize the threats, whether imagined or real. During World War II, they appointed ministers who regularly visited CPS centers and work sites to provide worship, counsel, and a familiar presence from home to remind them of their accountability. Meanwhile, Amish leaders lobbied the government to allow more of their sons to stay at home. They sought farm deferments, rather than placements that would put their teenage boys in questionable surroundings and activities.[26] Parents and leaders, however, were less successful in the 1950s and 1960s at keeping in touch with their young men in urban settings, despite their apprehensions for their sons' welfare and future. Although the number of Amish young men who participated in alternate service was relatively small, the concern of Amish adults clearly showed their fears at having their youth mix with the world away from home.

Overall, relatively few conscripts were swept away by the pleasures of "the world, the flesh, and the devil." More often they were influenced by contact with members of more liberal Anabaptist groups. CPS inductees from "higher" denominations challenged their Old Order counterparts with reasons for adopting more evangelical beliefs and practices. At the same time, most of the more progressive Anabaptist volunteers were known for their conscientious, responsible, and devout lifestyle, without the trappings of Amish austerity. "I was working in Wooster and driving a car at the time, even though I was a member of the church," an Ohio Amish man recalled. "One of my Mennonite buddies asked me if I was going to go back to the church when I got out. I couldn't really tell him because I didn't know what I was going to do." Another young man had decided that he wanted to become an airline pilot after his alternate-service duties were over. Both eventually returned home. The first man confessed his wanderings and was taken up again in the church. The second returned to join the church and eventually became a bishop. Another who returned said that he was not sure what he would have done if he had not had a girlfriend waiting for him back home.

Worries at Home

Despite these stories of happy returns, a number of youth left the Amish during their voluntary-service experience, and some of those who returned became disenchanted with Amish traditions or restrictions.[27] Perhaps Amish parents are more bothered by local deviance than by their children's behaviors in unsupervised and distant circumstances. They know from experience that the combinations of peer influence, excessive drinking, and youthful inexperience can be a toxic mix, with the potential to drastically change their children's and their own lives.

Besides these continuing concerns, Amish parents worry for several other reasons. One is that many of them recall their own youthful excesses at home and hope and pray that their children will avoid making similar bad choices. As Dirk Eitzen has pointed out, Amish youth have been ill-prepared for life in the outside world, so it is not surprising if they make bad decisions that may profoundly affect themselves, their families, and their communities. At the least, extreme behaviors bring disgrace to the community and the potential for reproach to the parents. Finally, concerned parents regard such behavior as ungodly and worry that an untimely death could result in their sons or daughters being eternally lost. Most parents object to the excesses of their rumspringa children but often feel powerless to change a tradition that has existed long before they themselves were teenagers.

The Appeal of Other Christian Ways

Although parents understandably are disquieted by the attractions of the world, the flesh, and the devil, many Amish believe that the appeal of more liberal Anabaptist groups poses an even greater danger to their plain communities' continuation than worldly or fleshly lures. "When young people go out drinking and partying," an Amish man explained, "they know that they are acting wrong and need to stop it before they come back. When they start going with the Mennonites, they begin to question the whole Amish way of life. And that's dangerous." Another man who eventually left the Amish concurred: "My parents worried more about me visiting a Mennonite church than about my brother who was out partying and carrying on. I would be the one to come home with questions." In Elmo Stoll's novel, *One Way Street*, the winsomeness, warmth, and ostensible freedom of the local Mennonites attract the teenage Old Order protagonist. Although he initially finds these qualities appealing, the young man later decides that this one-way street too often ends in liberalism and eventual ruin.[28]

A more subtle but perhaps equally dangerous way to get onto the one-way street, according to the Amish, is through moral and spiritual drift. They see this as the gradual but ever-present tendency to abandon practices, beliefs, and behaviors that once characterized the Old Order Amish. The number of former Amish now on the membership roles of the "higher" Amish-Mennonite, Beachy Amish, Mennonite, and Charity churches provides them with ample evidence that drift leads to defection. They believe that drift within the church is dangerous, but they are especially troubled by its impact and influence on the upcoming generation.

Language Worries

With the exception of first-generation immigrants to America, a concern unique to the Amish is the possible decline of their mother tongue. Generally, successive generations of immigrants seek to learn their new country's language for practical reasons, and also to become integrated into the mainstream culture. Amish parents, on the other hand, do not want their children to be assimilated. Instead, they value their children learning and maintaining both the German of their ancestors and the Pennsylvania German or older Swiss dialects as a sign of their Amish distinctiveness. Over the years, many Amish adults have also worried about what they regarded as an apparent decline in the use of High German, the language of worship and of their Bible. They believed that facility in the sacred language of their fathers had been deteriorating, not only with adults, but especially among the young. "Many of the youth do not even know the German hymns anymore," lamented a minister. A young man from Franklin County, Pennsylvania, admitted that he understood very little of the German he heard in the worship services. A young woman from Daviess County, Indiana, claimed

that she did not understand what she was committing to in her membership vows, because she knew so little German.

Although these fears or tendencies still exist in some settlements, in
Lancaster County, Pennsylvania, most parents believe that their youth are
more functional and competent in church German than they or their parents were in the past. They attribute the change to better teaching and better
curricular materials, originating mostly from Pathway Publishers. Also, the
vocational schools in Pennsylvania are often called German *Schul*, probably
in recognition of the central role that the study of German has assumed.
When I visited a vocational school in Lancaster County, a significant portion
of the class time was devoted to translating German hymns into English.[29]

Many Amish adults, especially in the large settlements, complain that
too many youth rarely speak Pennsylvania German when they are at work
or when they gather with their peers. In Lancaster County, Amish softball
players and fans speak virtually no Pennsylvania German at their softball-
league games. An Amish waitress in Pinecraft, Florida, said: "I don't like
to speak in *Deitsch* [Pennsylvania German]. It's too hard. Hardly anybody
speaks *Deitsch* where we live in Daviess County [Indiana], adults or teenagers. We feel much more comfortable in English." An unmarried young man
from Franklin County, Pennsylvania, described his vacillating experience
and that of his peers with regard to the Pennsylvania German dialect. He
reported that the youth "begin to speak exclusively in English at about the
age of ten. Thenceforth, they will never use Dutch [Pennsylvania German]
amongst their peers. It makes them uncomfortable. Conversely, it is just as
unpleasant to speak to one's parents in English. Isn't that curious? . . . Parents decry the erosion of their maternal tongue for their children [but] when
unsure of the proper Dutch word, will immediately reach for the English."[30]

Many Amish parents believe that their German language and dialect
serve not only as symbols of their distinctiveness but also as a de facto barrier between the Amish and the world. A father stated that it was a very
good thing that Amish children typically do not speak English before entering first grade. "This acts as a shield against the influence of the outside
world," he explained. Similarly, a Michigan father thought that if teenagers
became too fluent in English, they would be able to make the transition to

"out there" too easily. In an anonymous article, the author admonished the readers of *Family Life* to use the Pennsylvania German dialect: "Anybody who speaks English around home when just family members are around, or while working or visiting with others who know Pennsylvania Dutch, is putting in a vote to drop a rich heritage that will never again be brought back if we lose it. The value of that heritage is so great that we can't afford to lose it."[31]

Thoughtful Old Order people can quickly cite what they regard as evidence that abandoning their language is a precursor to abandoning the Amish way. They know of Amish groups, such as a New Order church in North Carolina, that started an outreach in English to several families who were seekers "wanting to become Amish." That bishop stated, "We wanted it [our church] to be open to whoever wants to come, and we wanted English services for people who were not raised in the Amish church." It took only a short time, however, until the English-speaking group decided to become Mennonite, and most of the members purchased cars.[32]

On the other hand, virtually everyone in a thriving horse-and-buggy Mennonite settlement near Dayton, Virginia, speaks no Pennsylvania German, and most observers believe that this group has almost the same retention rate as their Amish, *Deitsch*-speaking counterparts. Although this Mennonite example may offer some hope that keeping the dialect is not essential to maintaining the Amish culture, most Old Order adults would probably echo the concerns that an Amish minister's rhetorical question expressed: "Can we still keep our Amish ways if we lose our language?" He had little doubt that as a group becomes more progressive, the use of both High German and Pennsylvania German diminishes, along with the group's Amish identity. Thus many thoughtful Old and New Order adults wonder if their youths' often careless language use reflects potential drift and the loss of a crucial cultural distinction, or whether it is merely a passing stage in their journey to Amish adulthood.[33]

The Lunch Pail Threat

Another frequently expressed concern voiced by parents and ministers is the potential impact on the majority of Amish children and youth who are now growing up off the farm. Like their predecessors (and most nineteenth-century Americans), the Amish have associated farming and a rural environment with wholesomeness and a rigorous work ethic. Conversely, they have linked an urban environment with worldliness, corruption, temptation, and sin. For most parents, "going into town," whether for work or play, symbolizes Lot's sojourn in the biblical city of Sodom, the prototypical urban image of wickedness and degradation described in Genesis 13:10–13. If the producers of the UPN reality series on Rumspringa had intentionally tried to reinforce that perceived dangerous connection and choose a title to upset Amish parents, they could have found nothing better than *Amish in the City*.

With the exponential growth of the Amish in the last several decades and the shrinking availability of affordable farmland, the old dream of fathers helping each son obtain a farm is just that—a dream.[34] Moreover, Amish leaders express dismay that growing numbers of their young people now show little interest in farming, traditionally the occupation of choice. Parents fear that the prospect of enormous mortgage payments, increased governmental regulations, and working countless hours for little profit has diminished farming's appeal for many youth, and even for adults. Also, finding meaningful work for each child in a large non-farm family poses a challenge for parents with a rigorous work ethic: garden and yard work are seasonal, and care of the horses used for driving the buggy requires only a limited amount of time. Family-run businesses may provide work for the older children, but most parents believe that nothing teaches self-sacrifice, perseverance, delayed gratification, and obedience as much as submitting to the never-ending chores of milking, feeding cattle, haying, and forking manure.[35]

This exodus from farming has raised a host of concerns. Not only are parents uneasy when their offspring find employment in town, but they are equally nervous when their teenagers and young adults work alongside non-Amish employees in factories or on construction crews. An Amish elder wrote: "Here in northern Indiana, with all the factories, and our boys and girls working there, they have more money than is good for them, to do and buy whatever they want. Many drift out in the world and get hooked with outside partners, never to come back."[36] A mother wrote: "Are we as parents fair to our children if we expect them to take an interest in our church hymns or in our singings if they have been exposed all week to radio music while going to and from their work? Or if they work in factories where the radio is blaring? Or babysitting, or cleaning homes where TV is waiting at the flip of a button?"[37]

A Nebraska Amish father felt that their group's working among the English has had a negative influence on attitudes toward sex and separation from the world. Because of outside employment, many Amish teenagers may be spending more time with non-Amish people than with their own kind. An informal examination of non-Amish Facebook "Friends" shows that many Amish youth do have a significant minority of English "Friends" from the market, the trailer factory, or the job site where they work.[38] Another worry related to the move off the farm and increased outside contact is Amish parents' concern that their young people will lose their dedication to hard work. Many Amish are troubled by what they perceive to be a dwindling work ethic among so many non-Amish employees. They fear the debilitating influence of too much contact with people "who work mostly for their paychecks and do as little as they can on the job."

Tourist Dollars: A Blessing or a Danger?

Similarly, many parents in large settlements worry about the possible negative impact of tourism on the youth in their communities. Although many Amish parents regard inquisitive, camera-toting tourists as more of an irritation than a threat, parents do worry about the influx of money, the dangers of materialism, and the growing dependency of the Amish on tourist dollars. Both a minister and an Amish mother from a Missouri community that has become a destination for Amish-based tourism declared that, for whatever reason, they could see a change: "Our young people seem to have developed a harder attitude since the tourists came." A parent from a small settlement said, "Even though it appears to you that we are isolated from the world, the trends that affect your children also affect ours because we have so much more contact with you than we used to."

Because the popular media continues to produce programs on the Amish, and because tourist bureaus in Amish areas often seek to capitalize on visitor interest in the Amish, such tourism is not likely to diminish.[39] Amish-themed reality shows continue to keep plain people in the public eye and help draw tourists into traditional Amish-based areas: over 7 million annually in Holmes/Wayne/Stark Counties, Ohio, and 11.5 million in Lancaster County, Pennsylvania. In May 2013, an Amish-tourism-based company in Lancaster County began "Amish Mafia" tours. Not surprisingly, many Amish, especially in these populous areas, admit that because of the enhanced economic opportunities, they have become, if not complicit with, at least dependent on the tourist industry.

With increased opportunities for the young to earn money from tourism or from factory work, parents worry that instead of their children learning the values of money and hard work, they will become slothful and self-indulgent. "In my generation," recalled one great-grandfather, "nobody had enough money to buy a car, or even go to town and buy drinks. What little we did earn went to our parents until we came of age at twenty-one. Now young people are making big money and many of them are keeping all of it for themselves." A father made a similar point: "When I was a boy, our parents kept what we earned until we were twenty-one and responsible enough to spend it wisely. They would save as much as they could on our behalf until we came of age. It was also a good way to be sure we didn't spend it on cars and such foolishness. My own son has worked in construction for the past three years, and he has nothing to show for it. I'm sure that he has wasted $45,000 on vehicles and other foolishness."

In 2005, a northern Indiana father lamented that "our boys working in factories can earn $1,000 or $1,200 a week. It's not good for them." For the Amish, more money, coupled with more leisure time, seems like a witch's brew, fraught with both financial and moral danger. An Amish market owner complained: "Nowadays, you can't get young people who want to work for us on Saturdays. We can't compete with carpentry or factory wages. There they make good money. Besides, they want their weekends free to go camping, tear off to the shore, or go on other out-of-town trips with their friends." Many adults wonder about what kind of church members the high-spending, pleasure-seeking youth will become, and whether getting large paychecks may indeed erode their traditionally strong work ethic.

Increasing Challenges

Whether their children encounter tourists or not, most Amish parents are convinced that being either an adolescent or being the parent of an adolescent are both more difficult today than when they themselves or their parents were young. They see the outside world as making constant inroads into their lifestyle, either subtly or directly. "When I was with the young people in the fifties," said a Lancaster County grandfather, "a few of the most rebellious boys had cars. Today all of the boys in some groups have them." Another grandfather recalled: "Back then if drinking went on, it was almost always the boys. Now some of the girls join in, and they are just about as bad as the boys."

As for drugs in the communities, an Amish mother maintained that drugs were unheard of among the Amish until the early 1970s. "Today if somebody wants to find drugs, he can," she said. In many settlements, especially the largest, parents worry about the accessibility and use of pornography. "It's available everywhere," lamented one father. "Our youngest son got involved with pornography through the influence of the van driver who hauled his carpentry crew to and from work." A bishop agreed that pornography was a growing problem. What especially bothers parents and ministers these days is the easy means of finding pornography afforded by Internet access, especially on smartphones. When I asked a counselor who worked closely with rebellious Amish males, and those court-ordered to seek treatment, how many of them were involved with pornography, he replied, "One hundred percent of those who have smartphones." Although this figure does not represent typical Amish phone users, it underscores the fact that significant numbers of young men struggle with pornography. As we shall see in chapter 11, the widespread perception among the Amish is that a growing use of the Internet and its attendant temptations and problems will continue to challenge both parents and the culture.

Tiptoeing a Fine Line

Considering these concerns and changes, how do Amish parents respond to their adolescent children? People who equate plainness with sternness might imagine these traditional parents to be harsh and authoritarian, demanding respect and instant obedience. Some do attempt to become more controlling with their teenage children. As a punishment for unacceptable behavior, they may keep their sixteen-year-old home from the next singing or two, or forbid him or her from getting together on a holiday with friends. Harsh punishments, however, are only infrequently meted out. Instead, many youth get a surprising amount of freedom, especially in the large settlements. Nevertheless, parents sometimes take desperate measures. Rhoda, a nineteen-year-old, recounted her entry into the youngie world: "It was quite a change and shock. In a weekend, I moved from being an innocent sixteen-year-old to becoming aware that the world was much more complicated than I realized." When she engaged in serious drinking at her first party, her parents found out and grounded her for three months. "I was utterly humiliated," she recalled. This severe punishment failed to stop her partying with peers, however, and she soon transferred from a relatively sedate, supervised youth group to one of the peer-centered party gangs.

Some youth spend entire weekends with their peers, totally absent from home and supervision. Their parents may not know where they are, who they are with, or what they are doing. When learning this, many outsiders react like the bus drivers who took three busloads of Amish youth to an Ascension Day get-together. According to a *Die Botschaft* scribe, when the drivers observed how little Amish parents monitored their children, "[they] were surprised the church doesn't require chaperones with the young people at such times, they said they would have [an] older person to [every] ten younger [ones] in a bus trip. It made us feel guilty as our youth have traveled the same way."[40]

In some places, Amish youth have enjoyed these freedoms from adult restrictions for generations. One commonly given reason is the major Anabaptist tenet of adult baptism. Because the church has limited control over the youth before they become members, parents stand back, knowing that their sons and daughters have the final say in a decision about whether to join the church. This reality gives young people considerable leverage during their rumspringa years. "Our parents don't push too hard," explained one young man, "for fear that they will make the children bitter." A Franklin

County, Pennsylvania, father concurred: "If I or the ministers push Roy too hard now to get rid of his truck, he will just leave for good."

Of course, the meaning of "pushing too hard" varies from affiliation to affiliation. In many settlements, what to do about an unbaptized son with a car requires careful judgment, because the church's expectations may be ambiguous. With the Andy Weaver group in Ohio, the decision is simple, because the Ordnung stipulates that sons must leave home if they purchase an automobile. On a different issue, however, an Ohio Old Order bishop did not "clamp down" on his son's having a television in his youngie hut, a small building rented or owned by one or more Ohio or Lancaster County youth for socializing and parties. The bishop confessed in a council meeting that he decided not to discipline his unbaptized son, for fear that his boy would simply "up and leave." The members, many of whom probably faced similar situations, accepted the bishop's decision. Many parents pray and anguish over where to draw the line. A young man who left his family to spend the winter in Florida agreed that parents have to walk a fine line: "My parents are not happy that I am down here, but they are afraid that pushing too hard will cause me to rebel." Perhaps these factors help explain the shift from the traditional Amish authoritarian parenting style to a more indulgent approach when their sixteen-year-olds formally begin attending singings with their peers.

Church leaders may also simply choose to ignore infractions rather than confront the Amish teenagers who are not yet baptized members. "Sometimes the church will just overlook some things," explained an independent-minded single male who had his picture taken for a passport. In many communities, "Don't ask, don't tell" seems to be an acceptable way to reduce confrontations and conflict. Although a few fathers will sometimes smash their teens' cell phones or guitars if they find them in the house, more often they will simply ignore the offensive item if their children are not flaunting their deviance. Similarly, if parents hear rumors that their daughter has been watching television while cleaning house for an English neighbor, or find evidence that their son is playing in a softball league, they may turn the proverbial deaf ear or blind eye.

Parents, however, are more likely to confront their children when they engage in flagrantly disrespectful or deviant behavior that will bring shame on the family or the church. In Pennsylvania, a local paper reported that an Amish youth doused a state policeman with beer as authorities attempted to break up a large party.[41] In another state, a news article reported that in an attempt to break up a Saturday-night party, "officers were greeted by several rocks, beer bottles, and beer cans, each thrown by persons in the group."[42] Sometimes inebriated youth do dangerous things that do not make the newspapers, actions they would never undertake when sober. A youth worker in a large settlement learned that a young man at a party climbed up into the rafters of the barn. When other partiers spotted him, they began to throw unopened beer cans up at him to "knock him down."[43] In situations when the offending youths can be identified, parents and church leaders will, in their words, "try to work with the offenders." The adults may hesitate, however, if they recall incidents where local youth re- taliated against those adults whom they regarded as being too punitive.[44]

Running to Extremes

Destructive acts by Amish youth toward other members of their commu- nity are nothing new. Nearly a century ago, an article in the *Budget* reported that Menno Graber and Bud Yoder were arraigned before Squire Lenacher and fined $4 for amputating the tail of Daniel Knepp's horse.[45] In the late 1990s, national media carried stories of a rampage directed against an Amish man in a small Iowa community. At least four young men were arrested for breaking forty-four windows, upsetting family carriages, and damaging household property.[46] A community in Missouri also has had a reputation for similar outbreaks over the years. Most of these youthful acts of vandalism share several characteristics. The perpetrators are invariably unmarried males who have not yet joined the church. They usually have been drinking, rarely act alone, and target a man or men in the community with whom they have real or imagined grievances. These targets have of- ten been parents, bishops, or ministers who have cracked down on youth behaving badly, who are regarded as harsh or unfair, or who have reported misbehaviors to the police or the miscreants' parents. In the Iowa rampage, the vandals believed that their victim had reported their underage drinking to local authorities. In another settlement, young men, upset with the strictness of their bishop, poured fly spray in the cattle feed, cut down and broke limbs off fruit trees, and damaged carriages.[47]

In Ohio, a Swartzentruber Amish minister was disturbed one night by a group of young men who were outside playing music on a forbidden radio. When the teenagers refused to stop or to cooperate, the minister tried to detain them by unhitching the horse of one of the offenders. One of them struck the minister on the arm with a jockey stick before they all fled. A passing milk-truck driver observed the boys and later identified them. The minister agreed that they were the offenders. Later, four of the teenagers returned, overpowered the minister, and in retaliation cut his hair short. This incident subsequently led to church problems and a serious breach, not only in the local church, but ultimately to a schism that resulted in dissatisfied members and the bishop forming a new Swartzentruber church.[48]

Occasionally, scribes in Amish newspapers allude to malicious acts and worry about possible resultant retaliations. A writer in *Die Botschaft* expressed such a concern: "Write-ups are in the daily papers about the wild drinking parties and hoedowns among our young folks etc. But it is NOT to be mentioned in our papers like *Die Botschaft* etc. And if any of the young folks get into trouble, whoever reports it will have some of their property damaged later on etc. So the people just more or less keep quiet about such things and 'look the other way as if they hadn't noticed.' Yes, we're too weak to stand up to persecution—from our OWN people."[49]

Such aggressive actions are rare in most communities, but a deacon from Pennsylvania who visited two of the settlements with a history of vandalism noted: "These problems will happen when the local adults check the young peoples' buggies for things, such as radios. When they find something forbidden, they'll break it up. Then the young folks will destroy the adults' property to get revenge. In the one settlement, quite a few of the ministers have moved away because of this." Some observers believe that the extensive migrations out of the Missouri community occurred because of fear of retaliation from disgruntled or angry youth. As an afterthought, the above-mentioned Pennsylvania deacon concluded: "You can't force the young. You have to sweet-talk [sic] them into joining the church."

Dealing with Deviance

Whether or not parents can sweet-talk their children into obedience and respect for people and property, they face the delicate task of acknowledging their offspring's freedom of choice. They must find just the right amount of pressure or accountability to restrain unwanted behavior without driving the young people into the world. When certain youth exhibit repeated destructive or rebellious tendencies beyond the control of their parents, the adults may resort to more serious attempts to bring the resistant child—usually a son—into compliance.[50]

When all efforts have failed, they may send the resistant teenager to a church- or faith-related rehabilitation center that specializes in working with rebellious or deviant youngsters. These organizations are generally run by more progressive Anabaptist affiliations, such as the Beachy Amish. The daily regimen is typically highly structured and disciplined, and Christian teaching and prayer are important components of the treatment. Although most Amish approve of the strict discipline in such centers, they worry about these non-Amish influences on their child. "When you have an organization run by former Amish, what is this saying to our son about where the leaders' hearts really are?" asked a father. Leaders in another settlement who initially sent some troubled youth to a Christian rehabilitation center in Alabama decided to withdraw from the program because of concerns about the distance from home and questions about the theology and leadership of those in charge.

A relatively new placement alternative that began in the late 1990s and continued to expand in the first decade of the twenty-first century has been the establishment of Amish or horse-and-buggy Mennonite-run mental health facilities in or near the three largest plain communities. Places such as Green Pasture (in Lebanon County, Pennsylvania), Whispering Hope (in several southcentral Pennsylvania locations), Spring Haven (in Wayne County, Ohio), and Rest Haven (in Goshen, Indiana) have provided treatment options not only for adults, but also for troubled or difficult youth. Some centers, such as Red Rock Refuge (in Perry County, Pennsylvania) limit their work to troubled boys. This latter organization is governed and operated totally by plain people and will sometimes work with struggling youth for five or six months.

Parents who believe that their children's peers are having a negative impact on their core values may move the family to an adult-oriented community, where the young people are kept in order and there is more control. One parent wrote in the "Letters to the Editor" section in *Family Life*: "If you don't want your children to grow up where they are out on Saturday night, play ball on Sundays, or date at age sixteen, then I think you had better move to a community where they don't do those things. And do it while your children are still in the lower grades at school. If you stay where you are, it is quite possible that your children will not heed your convictions. We found out that it is really hard on children to stay in the rules and convictions of their parents, because if all the others do it they will get very weak."[51] Parents who wish to move because of concerns about the youth typically try to relocate before their oldest child turns sixteen and begins going with the young folk.

Leaders in some of the settlements that have been formed to provide a more decent environment for their youth have resorted to writing their Ordnung and sending it to parents who are interested in the new settlements. In this way, they hope to attract only those families who will unreservedly support their goals and distinctiveness. Most of these settlements seek to be repositories and guardians of plain living and values for years to come. An example of this is the Parke County, Indiana, settlement, which originated in the early 1990s, mostly with families from Lancaster County, Pennsylvania. Although the settlement is nearly 700 miles from Lancaster, it is a full-fledged Lancaster County daughter settlement. All of the Parke County residents, youth and adults, dress and drive carriages following the Lancaster Ordnung. The founders, however, established rules that are considerably more conservative than those in the Pennsylvania mother settlement.[52]

In Parke County, singings were originally to be held only every other week and were to be monitored by adults. Organized sports, such as league softball, were forbidden, and softball itself was off-limits for everyone except school children. Midweek youth activities were discouraged unless planned ahead of time and approved. From the settlement's inception, young men did not own cars, and youth report that few, if any, of their peers smoke, drink, or party. "In a small settlement like this," a seventeen-year-old boy explained, "it's pretty hard to do those things without everyone knowing it." Volleyball is permitted when visitors come, but never on Sunday. After the singings, the youth get together for a time to play games.

Not all parents applaud this kind of strict control or migration to a new settlement, especially if the move is related to moral rather than economic concerns. An Amish parent whose daughter and husband were considering a move to Parke County criticized those who went there for being really more like Mennonites than Amish: "They are goodie-goodies, thinking they are better than we are back home." Actually, the majority of migrants to Parke County came from the most conservative southern part of Lancaster County.[53] Whatever the motivation for relocating to a new settlement, parents who choose to do so move away from loved ones, friends, and occupations at significant financial or emotional costs.

An Early Push to Reform

In response to rowdy singings, ministers or concerned parents have attempted to crack down to reduce "unwanted" or "ungodly" behavior. In Geauga County, Ohio, the fourth-largest Amish settlement, a group of eight bishops and eleven ministers gathered to answer the question "How we can change ways that our young folks have their gatherings?" years before any reform initiatives began in other settlements. They agreed to the following rules:

1. Singing to start around 8:00 [p.m.] and end around 10:00.
2. Youngie will be expected to leave soon after the singing is over.
3. No alcoholic beverages on the premises.
4. No music and no dancing at any time.
5. No smoking in house.
6. Late arrivals not welcome unless good reason.
7. Singing every Sunday night.
8. Home owner should not open shop or other buildings for Youngie after singing.
9. Unruly Youngie to be reported to church and parents.

They also discussed the possibility of changing the starting age to seventeen, of considering smaller allowances to teach the youth the value of money, of keeping the singing at a "reasonable size," and of having more singings in other districts on the same night if the crowds got too big. The person recording the minutes included a plaintive note: "Hopefully after singings boys and girls will go home, as many parents lie awake worrying where their children are."[54] Although it is not clear if their effort to change the behavior of their Youngie was successful, it was one of the first adult initiatives to intentionally reform youth gatherings.

Looking for Alternatives

Disturbed by rowdy gang activity, a Lancaster County couple tried unsuccessfully to print the following notice in a national Amish publication in the late 1970s: "If there are any young folks in Lancaster County that are tired of the standards of the groups they are in and would like to start a group with better standards, we would very much like to help."[55] At that time, parents taking such a proactive stand to change something as entrenched as the gang structure was highly unusual, and the letter was never printed. The only way of dealing with dissatisfaction with the local youth scene was to move the family to a new or smaller settlement.

Twenty years later, some Lancaster County parents again decided to try for a change. Persistent rumors of excessive drinking and increased drug use among some of the youth prompted them to take steps to organize an alternative group. In mid-1997, six months before the widely publicized drug bust, more than a dozen concerned couples began meeting to alert parents and ministers of alleged illegal and dangerous behaviors being reported among the young people. Several of the couples' sons were involved in the Antiques or other fast groups. The parents decided to write a letter of concern to the bishops of Lancaster County and its daughter settlements in three other Pennsylvania counties. The letter described signs of drug use and abuse that parents should look for. At the leaders' request, many bishops agreed to read the letter in their church districts prior to the fall communion. In part, the letter said: "Parents, beware of evil changes which your children could or might be going through. There are drugs out there easily available to our young people in the form of marijuana, heroin, cocaine, and other types that can be smoked."[56] Beyond disseminating their warnings, the parents decided to form an alternative, adult-supervised gang with a no drinking, no drugs, and a zero-tolerance policy. "We wanted a good Christian atmosphere, a wholesome place for our children to sing, and wholesome companions to socialize with," stated one of the founders.

Rebirth of the Quakers Gang

From these Lancaster County parents' efforts, a new group emerged and adopted the name of a former group, the Quakers. Most of the initial members in the new Quakers were young males, and many had come from the notorious Antiques. The majority had purportedly been involved to some degree in the drinking and drug scenes. A former Antiques member, who was interviewed later by a reporter for French television, stated that participants in this gang had been involved with marijuana and cocaine.[57] Besides having explicit guidelines for behavior, the Quakers were different from typical youth gangs in several other respects. First, the parents were highly involved from the start. Most of them attended the singings along with their children. "When people learned that us parents were involved," a mother recalled, "they accused us of acting like the Mennonites. Some also said that we thought we were better than others." Although the parents were not required to directly intervene in whatever happened, their presence provided accountability and restrained deviant activities. Second, the organizers asked two young married couples to serve as advisors. Since neither couple had children, they attended almost all of the singings and activities with the youth, and helped plan weekly or weekend activities for them. "It's not enough to tell kids not to drink and use drugs," said one of the mothers. "We need to provide them with good, clean alternatives." Eventually, the leaders crafted a written schedule of activities each month, including skiing weekends, work projects, and a service trip to the Bowery area of New York City.

From the beginning, this new group met with considerable resistance from more conservative leaders and parents in the Lancaster County communities. Some of the older people worried that the Quakers would become like the Goodies, a group from the 1960s that originated in part from a revivalist movement among the Amish and in part from indignation with some of the youthful behavior at that time. Among other things, the Goodies eschewed all drinking, partying, and any other form of ungodly behavior. They also had regular bible-study sessions, and these were criticized because they were not always led by a minister. One of the Quaker founders reported, "A bishop warned us to be careful of going ahead because he said there's pride involved in Bible studies." Like those in the Roman Catholic Church, most Amish are dubious about private interpretations of the scriptures. The majority of the youth in the Goodies eventually left the Old Order to join the New Order Amish or one of the Amish-Mennonite churches that emerged in the 1966 split. Some of these new churches permitted members to drive cars, use tractors in the fields, install electricity and telephones in their houses, and dress less plainly than their Old Order relatives.

Critics of the Quakers predicted that these young people would also defect from the Old Order Amish. Some anticipated that the Quakers would be a conduit into "car churches" like the Spring Garden congregation, a church that some Old Orders call a "pass-through" church for people on their way up to more liberal Mennonite circles. Disparagers believed that the adult Quaker leaders were taking a much-too-casual attitude toward vehicles, a mistake that would lead to mass defections. They also criticized the Quakers for their attire, especially the young women. "They look like Beachy Amish with their waved hair, shiny dresses, puffed sleeves, and short hems," said one observer.

Despite these critiques, the Quakers were well established by the beginning of the twenty-first century. They had forty-five members and regularly attracted interested families and their teenagers. "Besides that," explained one father, "several girls and boys are planning to join the Old Order church this fall. The biggest percent[age] of them will become Old Order." A year later the group had grown to more than sixty members. Both supporters and detractors recognized that the future of the Quakers depended on whether they joined the Old Order church or eventually defected to more liberal churches. In 2006, parents were still meeting to discuss the future of the Quakers but by 2013, the group had dissolved because not enough sixteen-year-olds were joining to replace the older ones who were leaving.

Supervised Gangs: A Monumental Shift

A major change in parent-youth relations occurred following the 1998 drug arrests. Concerned Lancaster County adults began to seek alternatives to the youthful party scenes commonly held on Saturday and even Sunday nights. Eventually, alternative groups with names such as the Eagles, the Hummingbirds, the Parakeets, and the Falcons emerged. Each one emphasized "decent, righteous behavior," and all adhered more closely to traditional Amish standards of dress and transportation than the Quakers. Many of these new gangs required all of the youth to wear Sunday church attire rather than informal garb to the singings. "Our youth are not permitted to carry on, laugh, or joke around during the singing itself, and boys with [sound] systems in their carriages will be talked to, even if they don't play them when they are with the gang," an eighteen-year-old reported.

From the inception of this alternative movement, the adult organizers met to decide what standards to expect and how to enforce them. They asked for advice and involvement from like-minded ministers and sympathetic bishops. Some of the Lancaster County leaders also "sought counsel" from a Holmes County, Ohio, minister who helped found an early alternative-singing movement labeled the Midway group. "At the time," a father explained, "things out there were so bad that they had almost no singings left among the Old Order group in Holmes County. Nobody was willing to host them. Their new group in Ohio began with only five youth, and it took a few years to see the changes take place. Now they have a number of decent singings going. The decision to change may be rapid, but real change may take years to happen. We can take our time in Lancaster County," he concluded.

David McConnell, an anthropology professor from Wooster College in Ohio, visited the minister whose concerns eventually led to the founding of the Midway alternative-group movement. The minister related an early experience on an Easter Sunday evening when the group was in its infancy:

We had about thirty young people downstairs and had finished supper and were preparing to sing, when just like that, the autos started pulling up in front of our house. It was mostly boys, but some girls, and they hauled the beer out and marched straight upstairs and started drinking. I'd say there were fifty upstairs and thirty downstairs, and then the ones drinking upstairs started rolling bottles down the stairs. So I went upstairs and one of the leaders, bein' as they were real brave, came right up to me and said, "And is there anything you want up here?" I said, "Yes, very much. Apparently you were never taught what this day represents." They were stunned and didn't know what to say. I said, "It's important that you understand [what Easter means] and repent." Then the leader demanded, "Are you trying to preach to us?" I said, "No, I'm just telling you the truth." The next day we found any number of bottles that were only half empty, and that was an eye-opener that we needed to talk with our young people. After that, the rowdy ones stopped coming to the singings. We always invite them, they are welcome, but they never come.[58]

"Starting a new group is not easy," confided a Lancaster County leader. "You have to go slow and get agreement from those who are interested. Of course, some people are always ready to criticize anything new. They ask, 'Why do we need another gang when we already have twenty-five to choose from? If parents want their child in a plain group, they can find them in the southern part of the county.' But we do what we have to do, not seeking to lead a cause or have a following, but just wanting to do the right thing." The leader of the reform movement in Ohio who confronted the rowdies on Easter evening worked hard to involve supportive parents when their group was being formed.

The adult leaders of the Eagles, one of the first supervised Lancaster County groups, took the unprecedented step of soliciting fifteen-year-olds as charter members. "We wanted them to get started out right," one of the leaders explained. "New youth need to learn standards and prohibitions so they can join and not bring prohibited items and wear them," wrote another. In these groups, written guidelines, which spelled out the requirements for the youth and the expectations for the parents, were distributed to interested families. The groups required total abstinence from smoking, drinking, and drugs. Members also had to agree to wear Amish clothing to group singings and activities, refrain from Saturday-night partying, and drive only horses and carriages.[59]

Leaders in another supervised group decided to have the singing and the "supper gang" at the same location. "Too much can happen from the time the Youngie leave from supper a few miles away till they arrive at the singing. It's much easier to get everybody together and start on time if they're already here," a parent explained. Other supervised groups followed their lead. Initially, the groups had also prohibited Saturday-night get-togethers, but one of the groups relented and permitted their youth to stay out until midnight. According to an observer, the same group lost several teenage boys in summer 2000, "because they wanted to play softball." "If the Youngie don't wish to follow the rules that are set up, they should find another group," said one of the founders. Some youth who felt coerced by parents or peers to join a group later resolved the issue of moving to a more compatible gang by deliberately breaking group rules and subsequently finding themselves expelled from the conservative group. Eric Wesner reported that one young Amish male who tried this was found out, however, and the adults did not permit him to change gangs.[60]

Not all parents who expressed an interest in the new movement found it to their liking. A couple who had attended one of these supervised gangs with their fifteen-year-old daughter decided to look elsewhere for their child's group. "We were involved for a while with the new gang," reported the father, "but we kinda dropped out because the youth were being policed too much. When she's sixteen, our daughter will start with the new offshoot from the Rangers, the Cherokees. Their attitude is simply, 'If you choose not to drink, take drugs, or have a vehicle, you are welcome.'"

Staying the Course, Maintaining the Hope

Even though most parents experience some disappointment or anxiety during their children's rumspringa years, in most settlements parent-child relationships appear to be strong and the parent-teen stresses temporary and manageable. One reason may be that most Amish grow up in stable families. Couples commit to each other and to the well-being of their family members for life. Parents writing in Amish publications frequently emphasize the importance of early training and the establishment of a strong parent-child attachment. One cannot read the articles, letters, and editorials in the Pathway periodicals without sensing the central position that family and parenting hold.

Some developmental psychologists might characterize Amish parents as coercive and oppressive. They might cite the Amish belief in corporal punishment for children; the parents' rigorous work demands; and, perhaps most of all, the requirement of strict, unquestioning obedience. Amish parents, however, feel that these expectations in and of themselves are not the problem; rather, it is these expectations in the absence of warmth and loving care that produce rebelliousness or emotional maladjustments. On the other hand, the parents also think that warmth without boundaries too often produces questioning, dissatisfied youth who tend to abandon the Amish faith.

Outsiders generally underestimate the amount of love and security that most Amish children feel. As a young man described as "independent minded" explained: "Most of us really respect our parents and do not want to hurt them. That's one of the main reasons we stay Amish." Parents, however, are not the only ones who offer a sense of acceptance and belonging to the youth. When it becomes apparent in the community that one of their own is on a seriously wayward trajectory, many relatives, friends, and ministers exert their considerable influence on the errant individual. Shachtman has shown how, if all else fails, the community can mobilize to try to bring the refractory one back.[61] Ultimately, however, the extent to which parents have succeeded in establishing a bond and a secure attachment with their children is most likely to be the critical factor in the child's decision. Amish parents believe with certainly that their influence is the key.

Despite the high personal and community expectations placed on rearing sons and daughters who will faithfully choose the Amish way, most adults do not appear to dread their children's teenage years. For one thing, many Amish parents take comfort in knowing that though many of them dabbled with worldliness and disobedience in their running-around years, most have become responsible, loyal Amish because of their own parents' patience and love. Moreover, they know that many leaders and pillars of the church had also crossed boundaries and broken rules, with parents and grandparents who did not lose heart or give up on their Youngie, either.

Through their confidence in the grace of God and the support of a united community, the Amish approach their children's adolescent years with hope and assurance. They believe that they have laid a firm foundation by rearing their children "in the nurture and admonition of the Lord" (Ephesians 6:4). They trust that they will reap what they have sown: responsible sons and daughters who will, in due season, choose to be instructed in the ways of the church and be baptized into the faith. These beliefs provide strength and sustenance for parents as they cope with the foolishness and vagaries of youth. We turn now to an important test of that training, in an Amish youth's teen years: their readiness to work hard and their willingness to stay within accepted boundaries in their leisure pursuits.

Camera use, restricted in the past, has become routine for growing numbers of Amish youth with cell phones. Many are taking and posting photos of themselves, their friends, and their activities on social media, such as Facebook and Twitter.

(Sean J. Hagins)

Chapter Six

Teen Culture
Working Hard and Having Fun

*When an Amish youth group comes to work on
a relief project, they accomplish about three times as
much as a non-Amish youth group.*
—Program director

Work as Virtue

More than thirty years ago, I was driving an Amish entrepreneur to our house to install a stove that we had bought from him. This was my first real conversation with a bona fide Amish person. In the course of our discussion, I asked the young father what he hoped for his two-year-old son. Among other things, he answered that he hoped Nathan, their firstborn, would become a hard worker. Not only did that happen, but his other six siblings have also developed the sterling Amish work ethic. Although hard work is not part of the Ordnung, all Amish parents want their children to be diligent workers. This virtue is regarded as a scriptural mandate and is a cultural distinction, as much as their plain clothes and horse-drawn transportation. The Amish regard work as a privilege and as an obligation to the family, the community, and God. They gain esteem and satisfaction not primarily from high-status or highly paid positions, but from meeting the financial needs of the family and working industriously and intelligently.

The Amish have traditionally understood work to be a vocation, or call-ing—a fulfilling end in itself, one that glorifies God and brings joy to the laborer and the community. Parents not only serve as examples of dedica-tion to work, but they also tirelessly instruct their offspring in developing a rigorous work ethic. As children and young people learn to work hard and take satisfaction in their accomplishments, they not only contribute to the family but also confirm their Amish identity and strengthen their ties with the community and the culture.

Parents expect children and teenagers, whatever their abilities, to make significant contributions to the family. John A. Hostetler has written, "The Amish ideal of work is not to get rid of it, but to utilize it in giving every member an opportunity to develop his faculties."[1] Children as young as three or four may begin learning how to work by "helping" their older sib-lings and parents. Rather than telling their three-year-olds that they are too young to do anything, parents encourage them to help pick strawberries, water the chicks, and feed the calves. "One of my earliest memories," a middle-aged grandparent recalled, "was having to dust down the stairs with a feather duster when I was three." The owner of a commercial orchard in Lancaster County, Pennsylvania, reports that when Amish families come to pick fruit, the contrast between their children and non-Amish children is dramatic. "Amish children usually keep to the task till the parents are satis-fied that the work is done or else they excuse the children," he said. "English children, on the other hand, may enthusiastically pick cherries for five to ten minutes till they get bored and end up in cherry fights, tree climbing, or sulking."

For Amish children, work and play often merge into one. Preschool-ers milk imaginary cows or rig up rope harnesses on stick horses to plow make-believe fields. Two young children told a visitor about their delight that morning in secretly sweeping the sidewalk and the porch to surprise their mother. When Hostetler and Gertrude Huntington asked a sample of elementary- and junior-high-age Amish and mainstream children to draw a picture of a happy time, many of the Amish drawings portrayed activities such as child care, yard work, cooking, and farm chores.[2] Not a single picture from the mainstream children was work related. The cover of an issue of the *Diary* featured a poem written by a nine-year-old Amish child entitled "Work Is Fun":

> *In the morning when I get up*
> *I make the bed so neat.*
> *Then quickly go downstairs*
> *And put stockings on my feet.*
>
> *I like to work with Mother*
> *And do the dirty dishes.*
> *I also like to set the table*
> *And clean the house as she wishes.*
> *I take good care of the baby*
> *And rock her to sleep*
> *Or just show her a book*
> *Which tells about a baby sheep.*
>
> *I like to sweep the kitchen*
> *And put the toys away*
> *So we don't have to fall*
> *And spoil this happy day!*[3]

Planting Fruitful Seeds

One reason Amish children learn to work at an early age is that most parents are skilled at assigning age-appropriate tasks to meet the emerging abilities and interests of their growing children. Tourists who stop at Amish roadside businesses often express amazement at how young children can tend the produce stand, make change, and assume responsibilities. Observers marvel that eleven- or twelve-year-old girls regularly cook, bake, and clean, and that boys, when they are scarcely middle-school age, milk cows, help with the haying, and even disk the fields by themselves. If the family owns a cottage industry, such as a chair or broom shop, children will often work there for a few hours daily when school is not in session.

When the children finish school at age fourteen or fifteen, they commonly work full time around the house or farm. Until state law permits them to accept full-time paid employment, they may "hire out" for a couple of days each week to do housecleaning or general farm work for nearby neighbors or relatives. A sixteen-year-old said he could manage the family dairy farm for several weeks, if necessary. "I know just what needs to be done, how to do it, and how to organize my younger brothers to get the work done," he announced. Few Amish would find his assertion surprising, since the community expects such competencies for boys this age. A father related that when he, his wife, and their younger children went to visit relatives for a weekend, he left the care of the farm and its forty milking cows in charge of their thirteen- and eleven-year-old sons. Another father reported that when he was away from home for several weeks helping a relative, his boys, under the direction of their seventeen-year-old brother, successfully ran their large dairy operation. A grandfather recalled that right after World War II, he was given foreman responsibilities on a relief ship transporting 700 horses to Poland as part of the reconstruction efforts in Europe. As a sixteen-year-old "sea-going cowboy," he was not only in charge of part of the herd but was also responsible for overseeing several older non-Amish volunteers.[4] The supervisors chose him, not simply because of his knowledge of horses, but because of his Amish work ethic. In communities where the Amish work in factories, employers actively seek Amish and ex-Amish youth, because they are hardworking and responsible employees: arriving on time, accepting responsibility, showing up every day unless they are sick, and not abusing break times and lunch hours.

These positive attributes do not make each family an Amish paradise, where the children and teenagers work without complaint, however.[5] Monday mornings may be difficult if the youth have been out with friends until the early hours. Given the choice, most Amish eighteen-year-olds getting home at 2:00 a.m. from their courting or 4:00 a.m. from a party would undoubtedly prefer to sleep in rather than get up before dawn for the 4:30 a.m. milking or their early morning van ride to the job site. Nevertheless, most manage to show up in the barn or at the job, with or without prodding. After breakfast on the farm, the father generally outlines the day's tasks for the boys, while the mother assigns chores for the daughters.

The Perks of Work

One reason work is so highly valued is that most Amish parents suspect that too much idle time impedes moral and spiritual development. After all, "An idle mind is the devil's workshop," and "Satan finds some mischief still for idle hands to do." A letter from a parent to the editor of Pathway Publishers expressed the concern of many parents: "We need to make work at home to keep the young boys and girls out of town after they're out of school."[6] Amish parents see work as the ideal solution for idleness and a God-given preventive against mischief making. When Amish parents look at neighboring English families, they are appalled that so many children idle away the summer in trivial or questionable pastimes. They cringe at the notion of sleeping until noon before spending the rest of the day scrapping over the remote control for the television. "Talk about child abuse," said an Amish father. "Letting children go unsupervised to watch the trash that comes over the TV every day has to be the greatest form of child abuse."

Although farm families do not need to invent meaningless chores for their children, they want sufficient work to keep all of them busy. Horses used for farming and transportation require year-round care. Growing produce and grain for the family and the market provides not only food but an abundance of field and garden work at just the right time for children who are out of school for the summer. And dairy farming requires morning and evening chores every day of the year. "[Dairy farming] is a great thing as it gives the children work . . . and keeps us from getting rich," a *Die Botschaft* scribe noted ruefully.[7] A minister admitted that one reason their church opposed piping milk directly through plastic tubing from the cows to the bulk storage tank was that it would eliminate the children's main jobs of carrying and dumping the milk by hand into the tank.

Work and Fun

In recent years, large numbers of Lancaster County Amish families have abandoned the cultivation of tobacco for health or moral reasons, and some parents have especially lamented the loss of labor-intensive work opportunities for their children. For a people who value hard work, tobacco-growing must have seemed like a gift from heaven. Transplanting the seedlings from the tobacco beds began shortly after school closed in May, and from then on, the plants needed almost constant attention. The children were mainly responsible for hoeing around each plant and eventually breaking off the stalk tops to promote better growth and curing. With nearly 6,000 plants per acre, tobacco demanded never-ending care through the long, hot days of summer.

When the humid days of August arrived, all of the family who were able to do so joined in the sweaty, sticky job of cutting the tobacco leaves, spearing them on four-foot lath sticks for drying, and hanging them in the curing sheds. Sometime after Christmas, the cured tobacco had to be cut from the stalks or stripped, a labor-intensive indoor job that could last through February. Stripping rooms were often cold, drafty, and invariably filled with acrid tobacco dust. The family eventually removed the leaves from all the stalks and then baled the entire leaf crop for the tobacco auction.[8] To outsiders, such long, tedious work, with everyone participating, could seem like a breeding place for family dissension. Yet many Amish adults recall these hours together as wonderful times of conversation, song, and storytelling among the generations.

Work and leisure are less compartmentalized for Amish young people than for their non-Amish counterparts. Most mainstream teenagers work primarily to obtain the possessions and pleasurable experiences that they otherwise could not afford.[9] Their labor is generally an unpleasant but necessary means to that end. In contrast, when I asked a seventeen-year-old worker in an Amish bakery what she did for fun, she appeared to be puzzled by the question. Her coworker answered that they had fun baking and waiting on customers, and this on a frightfully hot August day with no air conditioning or fans. Similarly, a twenty-year-old explained that on his annual seven-day vacation from the outdoor-furniture shop where he was employed for fifty hours weekly, he helped his family on the farm or worked with a neighbor filling silos.

In Amish society, work often combines recreation and socializing, as manifested in various frolics, or work bees: sewings, quiltings, and, in some communities, corn huskings.[10] Even today, if someone is disabled or alone and needs help husking corn or cutting firewood, community members, old and young, often pitch in to help out. Such needs also provide local youth with an excuse to get together on a designated afternoon or evening. They typically work together for several hours, after which they may eat, sing, play games, or dance, depending on the community. In the plainest groups, this may be the only social event for youth other than the Sunday singing. Work, service, and recreation also combine for the Ohio New Order youth, who plant and care for potato or peanut patches in their districts as fundraisers, usually for a local charity, but sometimes for Christian foreign-relief projects. After they plant the plots, the young people continue to gather periodically throughout the summer to tend them and then play volleyball and socialize. When they finally dig the potatoes, the youth celebrate with a huge supper featuring, among other foods, mashed potatoes prepared from the culls. In both New Order and Old Order settlements, young people may meet on a Saturday to plant or weed a garden, paint or roof a shed, or do a massive cleaning project for a widow or shut-in.

Certainly the most exciting shared-work project is the iconic community barn raising. Here young men from miles around assist the adult males in constructing the barn, while the young women help their mothers prepare and serve meals for all. Sometimes young men join their fathers to travel with the Mennonite Disaster Service, Christian Aid Ministries, or other relief groups in volunteer cleanup and rebuilding projects in the aftermath of natural disasters. A group of eleven young men from one of the youth groups in the Pennsylvania Amish valleys hired a van to take them to Arcadia, Florida, to help in relief efforts following the three hurricanes that devastated parts of the Sunshine State in fall 2004. Similar groups of young men went south again to help survivors of Hurricane Katrina the following year, and they returned periodically for several years. Many Amish responded quickly to Hurricane Sandy in 2012 by providing cleanup and rebuilding operations in coastal areas of New Jersey and New York. Part of the attraction of such efforts is the opportunity to travel and work with Amish from other settlements, but the relief work takes priority. In addition, new avenues of service have opened, as some Old Order communities are cooperating with other conservative Anabaptists and the federal draft board "to provide a government-approved option for alternative service for conscientious objectors if a military draft is renewed."[11]

Sometimes the work ethic of the Amish has put parents in conflict with local, state, or federal Occupational Safety and Health Administration (OSHA) regulations. In some areas of central Pennsylvania, parents allowed their thirteen- and fourteen-year-old sons to stack lumber all day in Amish-run saw mills. "When visitors or outsiders came to our mill, us boys ran and hid until they left," a nineteen-year-old recalled. On hearing such stories, several members of Congress sought legislation to curtail all involvement with dangerous machinery until the youth were eighteen. Supporters of the Amish countered by saying that non-Amish youth were allowed to operate very dangerous machines at age sixteen when they received their driving permits. The issue was finally resolved early in 2004, when President George W. Bush signed into a law a bill exempting Amish youth from a number of restrictions in the Child Labor Law.[12]

Take Me Out of the Ball Game

Although Amish adults want their children and teenagers to learn how to work hard, many are still ambivalent about play. One parent commented: "Young folk have a lot of energy, but I still think hoeing . . . for charity is a better way to work it off than softball or volleyball. But even hoeing gatherings can get too frequent until the young people are not contented to stay at home." Many more parents express concern if their sons are involved in organized sports. Through the years, many Amish young men in the large settlements have formed softball teams and joined summer softball leagues. They frequently play under the lights, both against each other and against non-Amish teams. In Lancaster County, various youth groups field their own teams, with names like the Warriors, Rebels, and Bandits. The level of play and competition is considerably higher than at picnic pickup games. One year, a Lancaster County team, the Routers, competed in California for the national title.[13]

To the amazement of their English neighbors, the bishops have continued to oppose the participation of their youth in a local softball league. They explain their reservations in terms of the Amish values of hard work, frugality, simplicity, and separation from the rest of the world. Their objections mirror those of the editor of *Young Companion*:

What if the players are no longer children, but young adults (or even adults that are not so very young)? What if the motive is no longer relaxation and diversion, but a spirit of competition? What if our plain clothes are left in the closet and the players don uniforms? What if these teams compete in tournaments and win the state championship in their class, and then go on to the nationals? . . . How unfortunate that so many people who claim the Christian name do not follow his [the apostle Paul's] example, nor grow up and put away childish things. It is even more unfortunate when batting and catching a ball becomes more than play—when it becomes serious competition between opposing teams, when it requires many hours of precious time, and when there is a great outlay of money for equipment, uniforms, and travel.[14]

In another issue of *Young Companion*, "A Fellow Pilgrim" wrote, "The greater the pleasure the world gets out of sports, the greater is the sin for us as Christians to follow or practice sports."[15] A bishop who moved from a large settlement to Canada declared, "Worldliness is creeping in through sports." Many adults worry that the players look anything but Amish with their barber haircuts, high fives, and form-fitting uniforms. Moreover, teams have to pay for lights, umpires, and the use of playing fields, all of which run counter to traditional Amish frugality. Besides that, a team in Indiana was actually sponsored by a local bar, Duke's Tavern, a sponsorship that offended many Amish. Stories occasionally surface about drinking and fighting among players on rival teams caught up in the heat of competition. One bishop likened these events to the circuses and games of the decadent Roman Empire. Parents also worry because away games require the use of motorized vehicles. On some game nights, virtually no Amish carriages can be found in the ball-field parking lots. The adults are also unhappy that triple-headers sometimes last until midnight, even though their children must rise early for work. An even greater concern is that league playoffs often occur on Sundays, thus competing with church and family gatherings. Perhaps the final straw in the Lancaster County settlement was a rumor that males and females were using the same restroom at one of the ball fields. A man who was a teen in the 1990s, before the 1998 drug bust in Lancaster County, also reported that youth could buy street drugs at softball games.

Growing numbers of parents felt that something had to be done, and be done quickly.

The Bishops' Edict

Because of such concerns, the Lancaster County bishops convened an unprecedented special meeting in the late 1990s to deal with the softball issue. This resulted in the release of an *Abschtelling* (official mandate) stating that church members were forbidden to play or even attend league games. It also noted that church authorities should discipline any mothers who washed their son's softball uniform.[16] The bishops believed that the wearing of team uniforms by the Youngie crossed the line between having fun and being of the world. The most controversial edict, however, was that all future softball games could only be played at school, and then under the supervision of a teacher. Sunday-afternoon games and picnic pickup games were officially out. Following the ruling, some young men delayed church membership so that they could continue to play. An exasperated bishop stated, "If softball playing is more important than following church guidelines, it is better that they go elsewhere." Despite the official ruling, a team captain reported that at least twenty Amish teams continued to compete in the local softball leagues. Another ten to fifteen organized teams, all made up of youthful non-members, played regularly on summer evenings or Sunday afternoons.[17] Church members who had been playing softball immediately dropped out, however, and Amish adults who had been spectators stopped attending.[18] In the following decade and a half, the softball ban was either relaxed or ignored by increasing numbers of youth, and, according to an informed observer, few bishops were taking an active stand against youthful participation in 2013.[19]

Parental reactions to the bishops' decision reveal the differing attitudes toward organized sports, at least in the largest Amish communities. Some Lancaster County parents complained to each other about the bishops' edict. "At least we know where our children are and what they're doing," said the parent of a player. "I would rather have my son playing softball than partying with his friends," a mother admitted. "It might help keep him out of trouble." A father declared: "If I would have had to give up softball as a sixteen-year-old or else leave home, I would have left home. The bishops don't understand how important sports are to these young boys." Most Amish parents from smaller communities, however, expressed relief that they did not have to worry about their teenage children being away from the family evening after evening because of playing or watching softball. An article in *Family Life* summarized some of the unease that many feel concerning organized sports: "Sports belong to the world. . . . Games promote a generation gap. . . . Sports break down our separation [from the world]. . . . Sports detract from worthwhile things."[20]

Acceptable Alternatives

Despite negative attitudes toward sponsored sports and large, competitive tournaments, most Amish have accepted informal local sports and recreation as legitimate. Traditionally, softball has been the most popular game at school. Children learn to play during their recesses and lunch hours. Both boys and girls participate, and most seem to enjoy the sport equally. Although Amish youth like to win, most games are social occasions, characterized by good-natured fun rather than cutthroat competitiveness. Players rarely criticize each other for ineptness or poor judgment, and most young people seem to win or lose with equanimity. According to Thomas Meyers, a sociologist who has taught in an Amish school, this cooperative behavior stems from the core values of caring and friendship that the entire community reinforces. He has related his firsthand observations: "Children play games with great gusto, but place little emphasis on winning or singling out the individual. I have been a teacher in an Amish school, and I was amazed that when we played softball in the fall or spring there was never an argument about who was out or safe at a base. Instead there was a quiet agreement on such matters and the game went on. The game was enjoyed as a communal activity, with frequent rotation of positions."[21] In the summer, children and youth often play softball with siblings and neighbors in the evening (once the chores are done), on holidays, and when visiting with friends.

The most popular game among the youth is volleyball, regarded by many observers as Amish youths' national sport. One reason is that both sexes can play and socialize, whatever their skill level. Many families have their own volleyball-net poles permanently fixed in concrete-filled tires. If young people, especially in the small communities, decide to play at a creekside park or in somebody's newly mowed field, they have been known to stretch the net between the upright shafts of two parked buggies. At summer singings, young men will sometimes hang Coleman lanterns or fire up generators to power electric lights, so the games can continue well past sunset. In one of the large youth groups that I visited in Lancaster County, the players had set up six nets to accommodate everyone. In the late spring, a local businessman hosted a benefit auction and also sponsored a volleyball tournament that featured forty-eight teams and twenty-four nets.

Nowadays, volleyball is not confined to the summer months or outdoor venues. In the large settlements, the Youngie rent indoor facilities, such as gymnasiums in public schools or community centers, so they can play year round. In the past, when Amish youth have gone to Florida in the winter, they have traditionally played under lights at Pinecraft Park in Sarasota on most nights except Sunday. Since the middle of the first decade of the twenty-first century, the sun- and fun-seeking youth are increasingly choosing to go to nearby Siesta Key on the Gulf of Mexico, where they take over most of the park's dozen nets and play for hours on the sandy courts. Most players there have acquired considerable skill in serving, setting, digging, and spiking. Just as with recess or pickup softball, however, the emphasis continues to focus on having fun together, rather than on winning.

"March Madness," Amish Style

When Amish elders in Lancaster County were young, the two most popular sports were softball and cornerball (*Eck Balle*). Volleyball was relatively unknown. Cornerball was the Lancaster plain people's equivalent of the NCAA's March Madness, except that it was played for most of the school year. This sports phenomenon is the Pennsylvania German version of dodgeball, and it was often played in barns when the weather was cold. With the advent of warmer weather, games often moved from inside to the fenced-in manure pen outside the barn, one of the first signs of spring to the rural southeastern Pennsylvania German people. Besides being a staple in most one-room schools, cornerball had been an essential element of farm sales and auctions held in late February and March.[22] Farm-sale announcements from the first half of the twentieth century often included the line "Ball players invited," a sure indication of cornerball. Until the 1950s, the game flourished among most of the Pennsylvania German communities.[23] Although the "fancy" or "church Dutch" eventually abandoned this pastime, it still thrives among the plainest Amish groups and most horse-and-buggy Mennonites in Lancaster County.

Unlike organized league sports, cornerball is the quintessential plain game, requiring nothing but a small ball, an empty cow pen or lot, and a dozen willing players. Cornerball calls for two teams of six players, who try to eliminate each opponent by hitting him with a leather-covered ball. In the past, these were often homemade by wrapping a quarter-sized steel nut in twine and covering it with black tire tape. Balls today resemble a slightly oversized hackysack firmly packed with leather scraps and sand. Participants prefer playing in barnyards, where the winter manure accumulation has softened in the sun. They scatter a thick layer of straw on the area, known as the *Mosch*. It provides them with a soft surface on which to duck, dive, and roll as they seek to avoid being hit.

A game consists of three rounds, or innings, in which one team takes its first turn by throwing the ball at members of the other team, and then takes a turn with its players being the targets for their opponents. The starting four players on the throwing team position themselves at each corner of a square about the size of a volleyball court, hence the name cornerball. Their first two opponents, who are their targets, crouch in the middle of the *Mosch*, as far from the thrower as possible. Players must throw only from the corners. They hurl the ball to their teammates from corner to corner, watching their opponents for a slip or momentary lapse in concentration. Each throw into the center is critical, since someone will be eliminated. Every time a corner player fires at an opponent, one or the other of them will be out, either the hit target or the errant thrower. A teammate replaces an eliminated player until all six players on one side have made an out. Teams then switch positions to finish the round. The winner of each round, and ultimately of the game, is the team that has the most surviving players and accumulated points.

Cornerball may be the most competitive of the plain peoples' sports. Experienced corner men and boys develop their skills to a high level. They become adept at faking throws and looking at one opponent while throwing at the other. Meanwhile, their most skilled opponents dash about and leap into the air with amazing agility and contortions. The best players combine speed, throwing accuracy, faking, and strategic ability. Some are widely known and applauded for their aerial acrobatics. They sometimes leap horizontally into the air like a high-jumper, presenting only the soles of their boots as a target. Occasionally, depending on the speed of the throw, the hardness of the ball, or the point of impact, throwers injure their opponents. One young player recounted how the cartilage in his outer ear crumpled from a direct hit. In another game, an older player was rushed to the hospital with a shattered cheekbone from an errant throw. Generally, however, these competitors would only suffer a loss of pride, especially when the married men defeated the Youngie.

In some locales, teams play for hours on end at auctions or farm sales. Hundreds of plain-clad spectators may pack the perimeters, cheering for their groups or for the underdogs. At a benefit auction for the local fire department near Gordonville, Pennsylvania, three games ran concurrently, one in the outside cow pen and two in barns. Black-garbed players, many wearing traditional hats and even glasses, kicked straw and chaff high into the air with their running and leaping. Traditionally, Old Order Mennonite teams compete against the Amish, or the married men challenge the unmarried. Cornerball players are typically from either the more conservative settlements or the Lancaster County "buggy gangs." Teenage males from "higher" gangs tend to regard cornerball with some disdain and have mocked the players with exaggerated motions and derogatory shouts. Nevertheless, such behavior is the exception, and even in the closest contests, players and fans alike relish the occasion and the fun. One observer stated, "Cornerball is the only place I have ever seen Amish grandfathers so excited they literally had to grab a hold of their hats when they cheered." Few outsiders, however, witness a cornerball contest today. Even in Lancaster County, the historic heartland of cornerball, the game has dwindled in most areas. It is still played at spring "mud sales," but otherwise cornerball has become all but a memory and relic of earlier times.

If interest in cornerball has declined or disappeared for most trendy Amish youth, either as players or spectators, it has been replaced for many with big-time professional and college spectator sports. Youthful Amish Facebook pages (overwhelmingly for males) feature postings, photos, and fan talk about their favorite teams. Many youth, again mostly males, post shots of themselves and their buddies at major league or NFL stadiums in Baltimore, Cleveland, Philadelphia, and Pittsburgh, cities within easy driving distance of the large settlements. One indication of their infatuation with professional football is that during the five-month NFL season, a significant number of large-settlement teenagers skip the Sunday-evening singings to watch the games on big-screen televisions in the various youngie huts. Although football and baseball capture the most interest and attention, professional hockey also ranks high for many teenage boys in Pennsylvania, as does professional basketball, especially in Indiana. Many boys also track college sports. Predictably, a sizeable number of Lancaster County boys follow Penn State football, Holmes County boys root for Ohio State, and Indiana Youngie list Indiana University and Notre Dame as their favorites in both football and basketball. As a result, young men who dress English with their favorite-team sports jackets, logo caps, and paraphernalia often look like high school or college students.

More Outdoor Activities

While participation in organized, highly competitive, or Sunday games causes concern among adults in some communities, virtually all of them regard nature-related or outdoor activities as acceptable. Hunting of all kinds is the most popular fall and winter outdoor pastime for males, from the most conservative Swartzentrubers to pickup truck–driving youth at the fast end of the spectrum. The males in this latter group smile broadly for their Facebook profile snapshots, dressed in the latest Cabela's camouflage (camo) outfits and proudly displaying the mule deer they stalked in Colorado or the trophy elk they shot in Montana. On the other hand, some Swartzentruber hunters have been fined for their refusal to wear "worldly" state-mandated, day-glow orange when they hunt deer or wild turkeys—and most have never even heard of Facebook, let alone taken or posted a single picture. Whether plain or fancy, however, twelve-year-old or even younger boys almost everywhere begin hunting under the supervision of older family members or relatives. Many youth transition beyond conventional rifles to bows and arrows or black-powder firearms. Girls are less likely to hunt, but it is not unheard of. In some communities, criticisms pertaining to wasted money or time periodically surface when adults and youth travel to distant hunting camps or take expensive trips out west to hunt bear, antelope, or moose.[24]

Fishing is another popular outdoor activity, especially for families. Some youth have their own rowboats or canoes, and occasionally a national news service will feature a photo of an Amish carriage with a rowboat or canoe strapped to the top. Sometimes teenage boys in the large settlements push the limits by owning or renting powerboats for fishing or waterskiing. In some Pennsylvania settlements, dating couples traditionally go fishing on the Ascension Day holiday, forty days after Easter. Amish teenagers and adults from the eastern states will sometimes charter boats to fish in the Atlantic Ocean or Chesapeake Bay. Fishing on the Great Lakes is popular with Amish youth and adults in the Midwest and in parts of Ohio and Pennsylvania.

Another established pastime among youth, especially among males in midwestern Amish communities, is birdwatching, or birding, as it is called by the dedicated hobbyists. These rural people typically notice and appreciate birds around their houses, gardens, and fields, as evidenced by the abundance of bird feeders, bluebird boxes, and purple-martin houses. Venturing out for the express purpose of identifying and listing birds, however, began in the large Indiana and Ohio Amish settlements. In Lancaster County, serious birding is a recent phenomenon among youth and relatively rare among either the Youngie or adults. In 2013 it had very few local adherents, compared with their midwestern counterparts, where scores of avid birders—adults, teenagers, and children—pursue their hobby in many communities.[25]

The Lancaster County–based monthly, the *Diary*, features "The Birdwatchers' Diary," a column written by a well-known Amish birder and author from Juniata County, Pennsylvania; in northern Indiana, a young man barely out of his teens took over the production of *Feathers and Friends* magazine, which highlights both articles and many photos of birds taken by plain birders.[26] The editor's family and many others post their annual listing of all bird species in a prominent place in the kitchen. Even teenagers record their life lists of all the birds they have ever seen. Several Amish circle letters (a round-robin packet of letters written by each member in turn) have been formed by birders who take turns writing about their bird sightings and the observations they noted since the last time the packet of letters arrived. Some birding circle letters are composed entirely of youth. In Juniata County, Pennsylvania, a fifteen-year-old claimed, "Every boy in our school is interested in birds." In some places, teachers will invite local birders to lead half-day bird hikes for their students.[27]

Except for Lancaster County settlements and a scattering of conservative communities, another popular outdoor activity for both recreation and transportation is bicycling. In the summer of 2006, two unmarried Amish men from southern Indiana rode their recumbent bicycles through British Columbia and the Yukon Territory to Alaska. In April and May 2012, five brothers, all birders from northern Indiana, ranging in age from seventeen to twenty-two, bicycled to Texas to witness the spring bird migration and identify birds native to the Lone Star State.[28] In Lancaster County and a few other settlements, scooters are permitted as an alternative to the prohibited bicycling, but few riders there do any long-distance scootering.

Since the mid-1990s, rollerblading has emerged as a means of both recreation and local travel, at least in the large settlements.[29] A young man said that he routinely skated fifty miles round trip from Penn's Valley, Pennsylvania, to see his girlfriend and claimed that it took him only two hours each way. "It's faster than a horse, and it's fun. You just feel free," he declared. As a precaution, he wore a vest equipped with battery-operated flasher lights while skating back at night. Meanwhile, with shoes in one hand and a lunch pail in the other, some Amish youth will routinely skate several miles to and from work. The sales manager at Roller Derby Skate Company, just outside of Lancaster County, said he had sold "a few thousand pairs of skates" to Amish customers, for up to $180 per pair.[30]

When the weather is too cold and snowy for inline skates, ice skating and sledding take over as the most common recreation in northern settlements. Many young men become adept at ice hockey, a popular sport for generations in the large settlements. In Lancaster County, a group of young hockey players formed a league of eight teams, with an estimated 50 percent of the players having grown up in Amish homes.[31] In recent years, snowboarding and downhill skiing have also gained prominence, as evidenced by many Facebook profile pictures or vacation photo albums.

During the summer, youth traditionally swim in nearby farm ponds and creeks, and young people will sometimes travel together for a weekend at the ocean or the nearest Great Lake for boating, fishing, and swimming. In a society that values modesty in one's attire, males and females were traditionally not expected to swim together. Today, youth from the more conservative settlements and New Order youth may wade close to the shore at the beach, fully garbed and with shoes in hand, or they may actually swim with their clothes on. In marked contrast to this are their more daring Amish counterparts. In 2012 these trendsetters were virtually indistinguishable from English youth, with the males wearing board shorts (longish, colorful, knee-length pants popularized by California and Australian surfers) and most females wearing two-piece tankini bathing suits or, more often, regular bikinis while swimming or playing beach volleyball. Their long hair on the top or in the back is the only visible clue that these teenagers might be from Amish homes. Besides their beach trips, many Amish youth enjoy water sports in their home area, especially the teenage boys. If Facebook photos are any indication, waterskiing continues to be a perennial favorite, with young skiers frequenting places such as Tappan Lake near Holmes County, the Susquehanna River or Raystown Lake for Lancaster County youth, or the numerous Indiana lakes for those from the Elkhart/LaGrange area.

The newest addition to the Amish panoply of sports became public with an article in *Runners World* in 2012.[32] A Mennonite dentist from Lancaster County, Pennsylvania, decided to expand his passion for running into a full-moon monthly run. A few young Amish men in the area heard of the event, were invited to run along, and decided to join their English neighbor. "The reason it took off with the Amish is because they could run without being seen," the founder explained. "Basically they wear their regular Amish clothes when running, but they run in brand-name running shoes." The group initially grew from four or five Amish runners to a dozen, but it then exploded as others heard of the ten-mile nighttime run. In fall 2013, as many as thirty Amish participated, most of them rumspringa males. The runners had to seek refuge from a thunderstorm in a barn once, and another time one of the nighttime runners stepped on a skunk. When an Amish father heard about this growing new sport, he was not surprised. "If I were young now, I'd be right there with them. I used to run around the block [farm perimeter] when I was their age. Sometimes my daughter and her friend will run the two miles home from the Sunday night singing." One outside observer thought that this might be a fitness replacement for the traditional after-singing "Walk-a-Mile" game.

Travel Fun

In all Amish communities, visiting friends and relatives within one's church district and settlement continues to be a favorite activity for all ages. In the not-too-distant past, travel between settlements was often limited to special occasions, such as weddings and funerals. Now, except for the most conservative affiliations, families routinely hire local drivers with vans to "haul" them to visit relatives and friends in distant settlements. In addition, many families will travel by Greyhound or Amtrak, or with one of the several companies offering guided bus tours to Amish clients. Both young and old enjoy excursions to historical destinations or national parks. They also visit Amish settlements in scenic or recreational areas, such as in Sarasota, Florida, or Rexford, Montana.[33]

As a result, many youth have also expanded their own travels to visit young friends or relatives in settlements hundreds of miles away. Often a small group of friends will organize a "load," as it is called, to share the expenses of hiring a "taxi," the common name for these locally owned vans.[34] Sometimes the youth are accompanied by a married couple or other Amish adults, and they may visit one or more settlements where they have relatives or friends. Even youth or adults from a Swartzentruber group in Stark County, Ohio, may go by bus to visit a sister group in nearby Medina County, Ohio, or to settlements as far away as St. Lawrence County in New York, Minnesota, Mississippi, Missouri, or Wisconsin. Ohio New Order youth routinely travel to other New Order settlements in Illinois, Kentucky, Michigan, North Carolina, and elsewhere. At times, youth from Lancaster County will make the 1,200-mile round trip to the northern Indiana settlements (or vice versa) when they are invited or hear about an upcoming party.

In all communities, both hosts and guests look forward to having visitors from other settlements. These occasions provide a change from their daily routine, a chance to visit again with distant relatives and friends, and an opportunity to socialize with those who potentially may become new friends and mates. Host communities will sometimes organize special singings and activities, such as volleyball games, while their young guests are there. Some observers believe that these intersettlement contacts have strengthened both the holding power and gene pool of Amish communities in recent years.

Fun and Friends in the Florida Sun

Facebook reveals much about the travel destinations and interests for those at the mobile, motorized end of the behavioral spectrum, especially for teens in the large settlements. A perennial favorite in the warm-weather months for many eastern Amish youth is a weekend or vacation trip to Atlantic shore locations, such as both Ocean Cities (New Jersey and Maryland, with the latter being very popular among the Lancaster County youth), and the Delaware beaches. In the winter, Siesta Key on Florida's Gulf Coast, only a short distance from Sarasota's Pinecraft enclave, is by far the most popular destination for hundreds of Amish youth, not only those in the big settlements, but many Youngie elsewhere. Facebook photos at the shore abound, especially from the public beaches that border the volleyball courts at Siesta Key Park.

Many Amish parents do not want their teenagers to vacation at distant points with an unchaperoned group of peers, whether for a weekend at the ocean or for two weeks in Florida. In the large communities, some younger parents will take their entire family for a Pinecraft vacation. They become decidedly wary, however, when their teenagers want to go to Pinecraft with their peers. Sometimes, from their own past experiences as Youngie in Pinecraft, parents worry about the lack of supervision and accountability, as well as the kinds of peers their children may encounter. They recall rumors of alleged drug use and occasional police raids made to investigate complaints of underage drinking, loitering, or disturbing the peace. These complaints generally centered on the small city park in Pinecraft that has traditionally been the hub of local nighttime activity, although longtime residents say that conditions improved greatly when the city banned alcohol at the park and established a closing time.

Nevertheless, many Amish youth have been journeying to this favored winter destination since the late 1920s. Beginning as a celery farm, Pinecraft was soon subdivided into many small building lots. The majority of winter residents originally were older people from the North, beset with cold-aggravated illnesses and discomfort. Most found that basking in the sunshine and warmth of the Gulf Coast boosted their spirits, even if it did not reduce their ailments. As time passed, more and more winter-weary Amish and Mennonites found their way to Pinecraft, bought or built a small place, and stayed until it was time to return north for the spring church council and communion. Some still came for health reasons, but many more simply sought the warmth of the sun, the relaxation of leisure activities, and the enjoyment of conversation with like-minded visitors.

Today, Pinecraft literally bursts with people and activity for most of the winter months. From just around Christmas through March, three bus companies serving Amish and Mennonite clientele fill weekly buses with mostly plain-garbed passengers. The two drivers on each bus spell each other, so that except for dinner and breakfast stops, they can drive straight through to Pinecraft from Illinois, Indiana, Ohio, and Pennsylvania. The majority of bus travelers are older adults. Most youthful Amish who come to Florida are likely to come in their own vehicles or catch a ride with friends who drive. Sometimes entire families will head south to join their parents and grandparents during the Christmas break. In January and February, the peak vacation months, local residents estimate that as many as 2,000 visitors per week squeeze into the 500 available apartments and rooms in Pinecraft's one square mile.[35]

Rather than being the party center that it was in the past, Pinecraft now serves mostly as the venue for nightly volleyball games under the lights. For a number of years, an elderly security officer arrived promptly at 10:00 p.m., shut off the court lights, got back into his vehicle with lights flashing, and made sure that everyone was out of the park before locking the gate. "In my eighteen months on this job, I have only had guff from one girl—the one in the red car over there," he reported. "She doesn't mouth off at me. She just won't move on when I tell her." Several of the Pinecraft residents with rooms or apartments worry about renting to unmarried youth. Although landlords rarely use the word "trashed," at times it appears to have been an apt description for their vacated properties. "One of the girls was skating around the kitchen with her rollerblades on," complained a housekeeper. "They left a terrible mess."

Another reason Pinecraft has been suspect is that people often view it as a refuge for alienated youth, and even adults, who have abandoned their moral and spiritual values. For dissatisfied Old Order church members, it can serve as a temporary stop on their way out of the Amish fold. "They can go to Pinecraft an Old Order member, transfer to the local Amish church for a while, and eventually move on to a conservative Mennonite church. That way they avoid being shunned when they join a more liberal Anabaptist church," an Old Order member explained. Some plain people relate stories of teenage family members or friends who came to Pinecraft, allegedly to waitress in a restaurant or work in construction for the winter, only to abandon all semblances of faith. They purportedly live outside of any Christian fellowship and are involved with drugs, sex, or divorce.

More commonly, however, people who leave the Amish and remain in Sarasota simply transfer their membership into a relatively plain Anabaptist group and may eventually make the move up to a more progressive Mennonite church. Former Amish constitute a significant minority in many of the plainer Mennonite churches in the Sarasota area.[36] Because of these circumstances, bishops in some conservative Amish districts forbid their members to visit Pinecraft for any reason, including health concerns. Even in progressive Lancaster County, "some bishops have decided to discourage people from going," according to one resident. A newly ordained minister there had to sell his house in Pinecraft. Some bishops will reluctantly allow older people to spend the winter months there if their physician or chiropractor recommends a change of climate, or if the members offer convincing health reasons.

One stumbling block has been that many Old Order communities view

Pinecraft as part of the technologically progressive New Order Amish—or, more recently, the New New Order, otherwise known as the New Order Christian Fellowship, the highest step on the Amish escalator. Because of the overflow crowds in the winter, the local Amish church gathers in a meetinghouse instead of members' homes, a departure from normal Amish practice.[37] More significantly, the resident Amish have electricity and telephones in their Florida homes, and most have air conditioning and microwaves. Adding to the skepticism on the part of some Old Order people back home is that the majority of men, single and married, routinely stroll or bicycle hatless around Pinecraft, an omission that in many communities would raise eyebrows, at the least, if not provoke severe criticism. One conservative winter resident, however, declared, "I'd rather go barefoot than hatless." Bishops fear that exposure to such luxuries, conveniences, and examples may cause not only the youth, but also baptized members, to return home dissatisfied with gas or kerosene lamps and the absence of power-line electricity. Finally, the bishops ask, how will young people ever learn to develop a respect for hard work, simplicity, and self-denial when they daily observe Amish elders wasting time at shuffleboard, checkers, and even golf? They wonder what kind of example that provides.

When the *Philadelphia Inquirer* and the *Boston Globe* ran front-page articles on Pinecraft as the ultimate Amish vacation destination, they focused on the shuffleboard generation.[38] An eighty-year-old who has been wintering in Pinecraft for years, however, complained that "too many young people are coming down here and spoiling it for everyone. In the past, people came for health reasons." Whether his assessment is accurate or not, everyone agrees that many youth, especially from the large settlements, make their way to Florida each winter. A mother from Pennsylvania reported that fourteen teenagers (ten boys and four girls) from their settlement went to Pinecraft for two weeks but spent most of their time on Siesta Key, playing beach volleyball every day. Siesta Key has become the undisputed destination of choice for pleasure-seeking Youngie.

According to one longtime resident, a possible reason for this shift from Pinecraft—with its tiny rental cottages, increased prices, and inquisitive neighbors from home—is that the youth can instead combine their resources to rent condos or vacation cottages on Siesta Key, a pleasant bus ride less than ten miles from the village. In Pinecraft proper, not only would loud music or open drinking raise Amish adults' eyebrows, but it most likely would bring a quick response from the Sarasota police and a citation for disturbing the peace. On the other hand, security officers on Siesta Key normally turn a blind eye to discreet drinking on the beach and also to discreet partying in the rented condos and cottages, unless things get too loud. "What happens in the condos and cottages stays in the condos and cottages" may be the new mantra. If Facebook postings, pictures, and "Likes" are valid indicators, most of the youth from the big three settlements, plus assorted Youngie from Illinois, Iowa, Michigan, and elsewhere, rate their Siesta Key experience highly for the action and the atmosphere. With its endless beach-volleyball games, Florida sunshine, white sand, ocean views, easy access to alcohol, like-minded peers, and lack of accountability, it is the popular choice for youth who prefer the party crowd to the decidedly adult or family-centered focus of Pinecraft.

Youngie from Indiana constitute the majority of Amish youth visiting Siesta Key during the two or three weeks around Christmas. This coincides with the winter vacation break in the trailer and RV factories where many of them work. Some teenage Indiana males estimated that between 100 and 200 youth from their state come for the sun and fun at that time, and they pointed out that their group constituted the majority of the volleyball players occupying the dozen or so permanent nets set up by the park. As the winter season progresses and the tanned Indiana youth return to their home towns and work, they are replaced by pale but equally animated youth from Ohio and Pennsylvania. By planning ahead, several youth in 2013 could rent a cabana behind the high-rise condos for about $165 per week each, a very affordable price for Youngie who work full time and may be paying minimal rent at home. And even for those who have to "cook" in a microwave or live on Domino's Pizza and wash their own clothes at a local coin-operated laundry, they consider these "hardships" well worth the costs.

Besides the lure of the climate, the beach, deep-sea or bay fishing, sports, and the company of other young people, some youth seek freedom from the demands of the church and accountability at home. A young Amish man from Pennsylvania who came to visit soon found Florida to his liking and decided to stay there permanently. He confessed: "My parents aren't real happy that I'm down here. And I admit that this can be a dangerous place for young people, without supervision and all." Nevertheless, many youth apparently consider it a small price to pay for this exciting time away from their bosses at work, their parents at home, or the preachers at church. Most long-term winter residents, however, believe that youngie behavior in Florida is much better now than it once was. Back home, a Lancaster County mother expressed relief that her seventeen-year-old was going to Pinecraft with a "good bunch of youth, not like some of them who come from other settlements. It's too easy for the youth to get out of control down there." Many youth and their parents would undoubtedly agree with her assessment.

Hostetler has reported that parents in the past worried not only about what their children did in Pinecraft, but also about the Florida Reunion, a back-home weekend bash held each summer by youth who had been to Sarasota.[39] Typically, the reunion rotated among Indiana, Ohio, or Pennsylvania sites, and hundreds of young people attended. In essence, it was the same as a Lancaster County band hop or an Indiana party, with the reunion held at an upscale campground, country club, or resort. According to informants, the atmosphere at a reunion was decidedly laid back, if not hedonistic. Attendees drank, danced, listened to live bands, and reminisced about the good times they had partying in Florida. Each participant paid an admission fee to cover the expenses of the site rental, musicians, food, and drink. Hostetler has stated that the nature of the reunion often resulted in strong sanctions on any church member who participated. Although the late Noah Gingerich believed the reunion to be a thing of the past, a young man who has lived year-round in Pinecraft for several years reports that the annual party is alive and well.

Despite the various articles on Pinecraft over the years, few outsiders actually wandered around Graber, Kauffman, and Yoder Streets, named for early Anabaptist residents. Today's tourists frequent Yoder's Restaurant and Der Dutchman, with their home-style, Pennsylvania German cooking, but they usually confine their meandering to Bahia Vista Street, the main east–west thoroughfare cutting through the center of Pinecraft. The filming of *Amish Mafia*'s second season there in 2013, however, may seriously change the numbers of curiosity-seekers entering this plain people's paradise. Perhaps enterprising opportunists will plan to do *Amish Mafia, Part II* tours through Pinecraft, similar to the ones being touted in Lancaster County in summer 2013. If they happen, life will go on in the neighborhoods, but most residents will long for their simpler, sun-drenched, protected past.

Cutting Capers Back Home

The truth, however, is that parents in large settlements worry more about the kinds of youth bashes that take place right around home than what happens in Florida or at some distant Florida Reunion. The get-togethers are called "hops" or "band hops" in some locales, and simply "parties" in others. They may be planned and sponsored by a gang or simply develop spontaneously at an opportune time, such as when someone's parents go away for the weekend. They may best be described as weekend drinking and dancing parties. In one settlement, these events occur most often during the warm months. Organizers prefer the main summer-holiday weekends of Memorial Day, the Fourth of July, and Labor Day, rather than in the weeks before spring and fall baptisms or during the winter.

In the past, news of the parties could be found at the local convenience store, ball field, or hitching rack, or even in a specially designated mailbox reserved for such announcements. Now, in the large settlements at least, youth text or call each other on their smartphones or send out the information on Facebook. These events may draw as many as 1,000 youth, and they have also attracted the attention of non-Amish neighbors, law enforcement officials, and the press. Local papers near the large communities often publish front-page accounts of parties, police raids, and arrests involving Amish youth.[40]

A lesser-known form of recreation—known as scouting, tomcatting, *Rowda*, or *Hounda*, depending on the community—has been common for many years for youth in the plainer settlements in Ohio and Pennsylvania. In Lancaster County, scouting continues to be most frequent among the conservative open-buggy gangs and their like-minded offshoots. It centers on hassling courting couples. Several youth, usually males, travel to the houses of young women who are entertaining suitors on Saturday nights or after the Sunday-night singings.[41] Where scouting is still practiced, it consists of playing pranks on the male, such as hiding his horse or dismantling the harness or the carriage. One suitor climbed into his buggy, only to find it sagging under the weight of a massive anvil that scouters had managed to hoist into it. Another young suitor, when he went to untie his horse in the dark, was startled to find that some intrepid scouters had hitched the farmer's bull to his buggy.

One young man described several scouting incidents that took place in his community. "It happened one time that a boy and girl were sharing a room in a courting way. Their window was forced open from the outside and a chicken was flung inside, followed by a goose, a cat, a sheep, and a calf." He continued, "I was too little to be a ringleader, but mind, I lent a spirited helping hand, and I got knocked around somewhat [by the boyfriend]. It is only because he lacked the main strength that I am not as bald as a peach today. As it was, he took a painful fistful of my hair. Perhaps he wanted them to paste in his scrapbook, I don't know—there is no way to find out; he never speaks to me much." In the same community, he related, "a newly courting couple was a prime target for scouting. The hapless young man who tied his rig by the barn on a Sunday night and accompanied his beloved into the house there to spend some quality time with her might come out again to find his horse gone and a harnessed cow in its stead and his carriage parked on a shed roof. Or, what was worse, sometimes the harness was dismantled, and the pieces scattered hither and yon, and the carriage parked in the creek, with the seats balanced atop the chimney."[42] Most scouters claim that such activities are carried out and accepted in a spirit of fun, or at least resignation. Whether or not this is true, scouting continues to thrive in certain conservative pockets, but it has all but disappeared among the supervised gangs or the car-driving Youngie.

Despite occasional forays into objectionable leisure-oriented or trifling activities, the Amish youths' work ethic and daily habits of self-discipline define them over time more than does their involvement in sports, parties, or scouting. They learn to work hard at an early age and will continue to do so until after they retire. For some youth in the large, peer-oriented settlements, the activities of their running-around years are simply a brief interlude in a culture of responsibility. Virtually all who return to be baptized into the faith will end their deviance. They will assume roles as faithful church members and responsible adults, for which their parents and grandparents will offer sincere praise to God. Their return is also a testimony to the effectiveness of their early socialization by their parents and the entire community. As one Amish father explained, "At the end of the day, chickens come home to roost." Although most of the Youngie will eventually come back to the nest, a significant number of them will take months or years to finally return, if they ever do. For many teens, these are the vulnerable years. They have far greater freedom to experiment with their gadgets and explore the allure of the outside world. Most of this will be done in the company of their peers. The most important venue for socializing in almost all communities is the Sunday-night singing, to which we now turn.

*In most communities, Sunday-night singings are the sanctioned settings for
youth to socialize with their peers. In Lancaster County, girls of the same age
sometimes wear identical colors as their "buddy bunch" friends when going to
the singings.*
(Photo © BlairSeitz.com)

Chapter Seven

Singings
The First Step to Independence

We all count the days till our sixteenth birthday.
—A teenager

Far More than Songs

Although few outsiders ever receive an invitation to an Amish youth singing, those who do may initially wonder what the big attraction is. A typical American teenager would almost certainly be bored attending a similar social activity: sitting on hard wooden benches around long tables for two hours; singing, among other songs, hymns in a language used mainly in church; and having limited spontaneous interaction with their friends. Few outsiders would recognize that this event is fraught with great significance for both the adolescents and their parents. For the first time in their lives, these young people are interacting in a setting that is not predominately adult-centered. When a young person reaches the "right age," which is sixteen in most settlements, Rumspringa opens the door for youth to shift their focus from family to peers. Donald B. Kraybill has said: "It is the key moment that ritually signals a rite of passage. . . . Youth are betwixt and between home and the church."[1] This shift may explain the ambivalent feelings that many Amish parents express as they release their children to the company of their peers. Intuitively and experientially, parents know that singings are much more than either a religious or a social event. They provide the first real testing ground to see if the values espoused by the adult community will be accepted or rejected by their children. Little wonder, then, that both adults and teens take a keen interest in this important tradition.

Ever since anyone can remember, a singing has been the community-sanctioned weekly or biweekly event in which the unmarried youth in a church district meet at a member's house on a Sunday evening to sing mostly German hymns.[2] It appears to have been part of Amish culture since their arrival in North America. Although much has been written about Amish worship services, little has been published about Sunday-night singings. One reason is that in many communities, singings are off-limits to observers. Outsiders may be invited to Sunday worship, weddings, and funerals, but few ever attend singings. In some communities, not even Amish adults are welcome. More than any other area of Amish society, singings have been the domain of the young. Having musical talent or enjoying music matters less than socializing with other youth in a setting with minimal adult control. The singings offer increased independence and an arena for developing relationships that will shape the youth for the rest of their lives. This is especially true in male-female relationships.

The Doorway to Rumspringa

It is not surprising, then, to find that singings are held in virtually all settlements.[3] Traditionally, youth attend until they marry—or until they and everyone else conclude that marriage is unlikely (by age thirty), at which time they drop out.[4] Nobody apparently knows why sixteen is the magic age to begin going with the young folk. But in most settlements it is a milestone, universally regarded by both adults and youth as a watershed event. It is undoubtedly a more important transition than obtaining one's driver's license or graduating from high school in mainstream society, because the change of status for Amish youth is so abrupt. In some settlements, especially the larger ones, teens move from highly regulated lives to exhilarating or scary freedom, and sometimes surprising excesses, in a single day.

Most of them excitedly anticipate their new status, although a few fifteen-year-olds experience some anxiety as their birthday approaches. Now, more than ever, they must establish their standing among their peers of both sexes. Such anxiety occasionally leads some youth to stay home on Sunday evenings instead of immediately joining the group. Referring to his grand-daughter, who had recently turned sixteen, an Amish man explained, "Sally is family oriented and hasn't been exposed to all that excitement." She concurred, "I'll miss my brothers and sisters at home." A fifteen-year-old boy who had not fully matured physically expressed doubts that he would join the youth when he reached his next birthday. In a few settlements, going with the youth happens gradually, and some youth may routinely delay their entry for several weeks or months. "We begin somewhere around sixteen and a half or seventeen—whenever we feel like starting," explained a seventeen-year-old.[5] Much more typical, however, is the response of a seventeen-year-old from a large settlement who was asked what would happen if some new sixteen-year-olds might not feel quite ready to start the social whirl. "It would never even happen," he grinned. "We all count the days till our sixteenth birthday." Obviously, attitudes toward beginning to attend the local singings vary greatly.

Stepping Out in Style

In most places, Amish tradition links a boy's ownership of his own horse and carriage to his involvement with his peers at the singings. In acknowledging their son's new rumspringa status, parents customarily give each boy his own carriage and horse at the age of sixteen, so he can drive himself, and often his sisters, to the weekly or biweekly singings.[6] In many communities, a young man's carriage is easily discernible from the family carriage. In certain conservative Lancaster County gangs, unmarried youth still drive open buggies year-round. Until the 1970s, all young couples traveled in these "courting buggies," completely exposed to the elements and to the eyes of the curious. A father who was a teenager at that time conjectured that the move to closed carriages began when some non-Amish youth began hassling courting couples by jumping in the back of the buggies as they passed. "Also, it was ridiculous riding around in an open buggy in the freezing winter," he added. When church districts began to permit closed carriages for the youth, some elders worried about a possible surge in sexual immorality. Others complained that it would be easier to hide radios or other forbidden things. Nevertheless, most adults soon accepted the change when they failed to detect any discernible moral decline.[7]

Amish teenagers do not alter the basic contours and configurations of the community's approved types of carriages. For example, they do not custom paint them, change the color, or embellish the wheels with chrome spokes.[8] A young person's carriage, however, often has its own accouterments that a knowledgeable outsider can quickly identify. In many places, the young owners customize them by adding auxiliary features to conform to the latest fads of their peers. In Lancaster County, young men's carriages may sport two dozen or more red reflectors around the rear perimeter, compared with the four or five reflectors on the family carriage. In addition, the trend-setting youth now attach a strip of blinking LED lights to the rear of their carriages, which serve to attract the attention of passing motorists and the young drivers' peers. Frequently, teenage boys dress up their slow-moving-vehicle triangle with a decal from the National Rifle Association or the NASCAR racing logo, and one carriage sported a Great Adventures Amusement Park bumper sticker. An article on carriage accouterments in the *Lancaster Sunday News* reported that boys' carriages sported a variety of decals and bumper-sticker messages, including "Single and Ready to Mingle" and "Get High on Milk: Our Cows Are on Grass."[9] Another visual clue to young men's transportation in Lancaster County is that many youth employ white or blue harness guides and keepers, rather than the traditional black accessories that characterize adult carriages.[10]

The main differences between adult-owned and youngie-owned carriages in many settlements may actually be their interior variations. One of my English friends in northern Indiana related the following: "I rode with a bishop on a hard bench with a piece of cloth covering it. On the other hand, I've ridden with a seventeen-year-old who had plush foam on seats covered in velvet, a sound system that rivaled my own son's sound system in his car at that age, and tricked out with lights on the inside as well. From the outside, however, they [the youth's carriages] tend to be reasonably nondescript."[11]

In central Pennsylvania's Big Valley, the Nebraska youth drive simple, white-topped, open-front buggies that are basically identical to their parents' carriages, inside and out. They are constructed at home or a neighbor's shop for half the cost of buggies belonging to teenage males in the nearby Renno or Byler affiliations. The Nebraska design is a plain brown, wooden riding box with friction foot brakes and two hard benches. It also features a kerosene lantern and a blanket for the benches, to protect the passengers from blowing horse hair, dirt, or cold air. On the other hand, youth from the valley's most progressive group, the Byler Amish, purchase yellow-topped carriages that look like their parents' buggies on the exterior but can differ significantly inside.

Riding in Style

Marvin, a personable nineteen-year-old Byler youth, expressed obvious pride as he showed me the inside of his newly purchased carriage, an incongruous juxtaposition of plain and fancy. "I went down to Lancaster County to buy this one because their carriages are a lot nicer than the ones sold here in the Big Valley. One thing, their buggies have nicer switch boxes, made out of oak with this glossy finish, and they have this ignition switch so that nobody can mess with my battery-operated lights," Marvin explained. "They also put these nice burnt edges on the trim with acetylene torches," he pointed out. The switch box also featured a toggle for his running lights (flashing lights used at night for safety) and another switch to control the two interior floor lights. Finally he showed us the cigarette lighter, "for my spotlight," he quickly added.

Everything in Marvin's carriage was color-coordinated in maroon, from the swirled, velvet-covered walls, ceilings, and carpets to the wine-colored dyed sheepskin on the front seat and the rabbit's foot hanging from one of the switches. Even the two theater-style inside lights glowed red. Artificial roses and apple blossoms decorated each corner, and a wreath of roses encircled the overhead dome light. A pair of fluffy dice, a car air-freshener, and a mini-flashlight inscribed with the name of the carriage shop dangled from the switch box. The box itself sported a decidedly non-Amish decal of a bald eagle clutching an American flag in its talons. Two more eagles graced both ends of a glossy shelf where he kept his *Liedersammlung*, the thin songbook used at their Sunday-night singings. "Indian feathers" hung from a tack in the ceiling, and more feathers intertwined with the roses in the wreath. A small stuffed teddy bear completed the plush decor. One observer described this kind of elaborate interior decoration as "neo-Vegas."[12] In the glove box Marvin stashed a bottle of musk cologne, and the polished dash featured a clock and a battery gauge. A second air-freshener dangled in the rear. He stored his horse blanket under the back seat.

Marvin had purchased the most luxurious carriage available. Unlike the bare-bones Nebraska Amish buggies, his carriage featured fiberglass shafts and hydraulic brakes; battery-operated yellow safety lights mounted on the front; and red flashers, reflector tape, and six reflectors mounted on the rear. "Dad and Mom gave me $2,500 toward the carriage. I had to pay the rest from what I saved from my job working for an English neighbor," he explained. At the time of his purchase, this high-end, Lancaster County–made buggy cost him $6,000, plus another $800 to have fiberglass wheels instead of wooden wheels. It would have been $1,000 more for aluminum wheels. In 2013, young men purchasing similar buggies in Lancaster County had to pay at least $8,000 or $9,000 for such glitzy transportation.

Only a few of the conservative communities will permit their youth to individualize their carriages. In Mercer County, Pennsylvania, a historically plain settlement, young people call their carriages "cozy-cabs," and the owners lovingly "fancy them up" with plush carpets and velvet. Nevertheless, most do not sport heaters, clocks, and speedometers, nor do they hide stereo speakers or battery-operated DVD players behind a curtain in the back, as do some of their large-settlement counterparts. Even young men from the more sedate New Order Amish occasionally succumb to carriage fads. Some years ago, according to one teenage girl, the then-current style was to sport a cracked windshield. To the consternation of their parents, her brothers and some of their peers reputedly cracked the glass in their own windshields to make the appropriate fashion statement.

Top-of-the-Line Horsepower

Besides having a fine carriage to drive to the singings, most young men seem to prefer fast, high-stepping horses, ones that can awe or intimidate their sisters or girlfriends. "I always hated to be stuck with the family horse," recalled one Amish man, "some old plug which my sisters had wore out going to town shopping Saturday morning. I wanted my own horse, fresh and raring to go, to head out on a date." "It's like in your society," explained an eighteen-year-old. "Young guys want to drive around in a sports car, not the family station wagon."

A spirited and well-proportioned horse adds status to its owner as the youth seeks to impress his male and female peers. In Lancaster County, young men usually prefer saddlebreds, but some like standardbreds best. Marvin, from the Byler group in Pennsylvania's Big Valley, chose a saddlebred horse to go with his affiliation's traditional yellow carriage. "Saddlebreds look good when you drive them," he explained. "They hold their heads up high and are also high steppers. They may not be as fast as standardbreds, but they are stronger in the long haul. The Nebraska boys' horses look so tired because the church won't let them use the rein that holds their head up. And some of their horses aren't very well cared for," he added. "Sometimes our boys will race our horses after the singing. One horse will break out of line and try to pass the horses in front. One time I went over the crest of a hill at night because my horse couldn't get past the others. But these back roads [in Mifflin County, Pennsylvania] are pretty quiet around 11:00 [p.m.] when we race. Another time I let my horse run like that, and he passed about fourteen carriages when I couldn't hold him back. Horses like to run once they get into it. But it's hard on the horses. I sprained one of our horse's legs six months ago, and it's still bad. You learn not to do that," he grinned.

For Marvin and many Amish young men, receiving their horse and carriage, a quintessential symbol of Amish culture, is one of the first of several steps into full-fledged Amish adulthood. Some males, however, mostly in the large settlements, put their horses out to pasture or leave them in the stable for most of their teenage years. Instead they opt for car keys and a driver's license and travel to singings or elsewhere with varying degrees of convenience and horsepower. A father complained, "I have to take Raymond's horse out every once in a while or he would never get exercise. Now that he is running around, he neglects his horse."

A Glimpse from the Past

No matter how routine or exhilarating the ride to the singing might be, the significance of the event itself, for both the participants and the community, cannot be overstated. Beneath the mundane appearance of a group of young people singing church songs churns the excitement and color of this major institution in the life of Amish youth. In a rare look at the past, writer and musician Joseph W. Yoder, who grew up Amish in the Big Valley of Mifflin County, Pennsylvania, was the first to capture the vitality of a traditional singing in the late nineteenth century in *Rosanna of the Amish*:

> At a singing two or three tables are set end to end along one side of the living room for the singers. The girls sit back of the table along the wall while the boys sit on the other side. . . . During the singing of any hymn all persons present are supposed to join in the singing or abstain from conversation. Sometimes it happens that boys forget and annoy the singers by talking too loudly, whereupon the man of the house says, "Let us have order. . . ."
>
> When the tables were filled, as others came they stood back of the young men, both boys and girls, until there were well onto a hundred voices singing. . . .
>
> There is no part singing; all voices sing in unison. Since the Amish do not have these chorales set to music, they must be passed on from generation to generation by rote. Consequently only boys and girls with a keen sense of pitch and sound can ever learn to sing them and many can never learn them well enough to "lead" singing. Little Crist and Ben Sharp wanted to learn to lead so they followed with great care. Yost turned to Little Crist and said, "Now, Cristly, you lead the next verse and if you 'stall,' I'll help you out." . . . After they had sung several of the slow chorales, one of the girls announced *Wo ist Jesus mein Verlangen*, to the tune of "What a Friend We Have in Jesus." The "fast" tunes are easily sung, but the chorales must be learned for preaching services; no fast tunes are ever sung there.[13]

Singings Today

Although Yoder's passage depicted life more than a century ago, his description still accurately portrays what parents in scores of settlements call "decent" singings. At the adult-centered end of the spectrum of settlement types, singings generally stay on task with a minimum of distractions, such as extended conversations or horseplay. At the extreme end of the peer-centered communities, singings, if they are held at all, often bear only a faint resemblance to the traditional event and may actually involve little or no singing. In those places, singings and parties may become synonymous with rowdiness and disrespect for the host parents and their property. Not surprisingly, parents in certain areas of the large settlements, such as parts of Holmes County, Ohio, and northern Indiana, eventually refused to host singings. If the parental and youthful estimates are correct in those two areas, as many as half of the youth today do not attend any singings, the likely fallout from the youthful excesses of their parents and even their grandparents.

Depending on the size of the young person's gang or church district, and whether youth from other districts are welcomed, a dozen to 200 young people may show up at a singing. In the past, as many as 400–500 youth attended these Sunday-night events. In the settlements where singings occur within the boundaries of a single church district, they almost always take place at the same home that hosted the district's house church that morning. This is a practical custom, since the church benches and songbooks are already there. In many settlements, the host family traditionally prepares a substantial presinging supper for the young people and the one or two dozen relatives and invited neighbors who will later "help sing."

In Lancaster County, where singings are generally large, the "supper gang," as it is called, and the singing occur in the same location. So that the host family for the supper gang does not have to provide all the food for as many as 200 people, various youth are assigned to bring additional food items, such as chips, salads, and desserts. The host family supplies the main dishes. In the past, some of the teenage girls would clean up and wash the dishes before the singing started, but as one mother said, "Nowadays, that's left to the host family to do." In Somerset County, Pennsylvania, no evening meal is provided, and there and in a few other places, only youth who attended the morning church service are permitted to go to the singing that evening.

Although the basic format of singings in most settlements is similar to the one described in *Rosanna of the Amish*, other aspects vary. Today, in the four or five largest settlements, some youth arrive at the singings in cars or pickup trucks instead of carriages. Also, whatever the weather, singings are rarely held outdoors, even on the longest June evening.[14] Shortly before the singing is to begin, males and females gather in separate groups, just as they do for the morning church service. At the appointed hour, they file into the house, barn, or shop and seat themselves on benches along the longish row of tables, boys on one side, girls on the other, as in Rosanna's days.[15] The singings may begin as early as 7:00 p.m. and last until 9:00 p.m. or later, depending on the local custom, the time of year, and the available light for outdoor activities.

In various settlements, getting the youth to break off their games or socializing to start the singing can be a challenge to the host family. Youth report that sometimes singings have started an hour and a half late. To combat this late start and subsequent late finish, an adult leader in a supervised group promised the children of the host family that they could quit fifteen minutes early if they started on time, a challenge they readily accepted. This helped the host family's teenagers and the more mature young form the lines and proceed inside. In some settlements, the young women always go first, and the young males file in only after the singing has started. In settlements where parents, relatives, and children are invited, these guests take their seats in the back or on the periphery, usually before the youth enter.

The Plain Repertoire

Once the youth are seated, well-worn songbooks—traditionally from the German songbooks, plus *Heartland Hymns* in many Lancaster County singings—are passed out to each person, just as in the Sunday-morning church service.[16] The singing is now ready to begin. In Old Order circles, no one welcomes the group, leads in an invocation, or takes charge. Yet everyone from the newest sixteen-year-old to the oldest visiting grandparent knows the precise script for that community. In some places, the youth may quietly leaf through their hymnals for a couple of minutes even though the songs are well known. Finally someone breaks the ice and calls out the number of a hymn. "They don't want to appear too forward in getting their song sung," explained an Amish elder. Throughout the evening, youth may wait two or three minutes before calling out the name or number of the next song. The boy or girl who chooses the hymn also starts it. In other settlements, the singing begins immediately since a teenager from the host family is expected to choose and lead the first selection. In some places, that person calls out the page number for the requested song, but in other venues, the person simply begins singing his or her chosen song. Occasionally, two people will start different hymns simultaneously. "In our gang, it was a competition to sing," one father remembered. The other singers quickly join in singing while turning to the appropriate place in the book, since they know virtually all of the page numbers by heart.

Although each settlement has its own repertoire of songs and tunes, the first songs usually consist of the slower tunes. In some plain as well as progressive settlements, these first hymns almost always come from the traditional *Ausbund* song book. Many of these songs recount the persecution of the Anabaptist martyrs. In a Sunday-morning worship service, there are *Vorsingers* who, alone, sing the first few words of each line before the group joins in. This still happens in some of the most conservative singings, but in most places no "lining" is done, and the andante tempo of the songs is similar to that of Protestant hymns like "A Mighty Fortress Is Our God" or "Rock of Ages." In many settlements, the youth never sing from the *Ausbund*. In Indiana, youth in some of the Amish settlements of Swiss extraction use the *Schwartzs' Song Book*, a compilation of German hymns, gospel songs in English, secular folksongs, country-and-western songs, and even romantic songs.[17] The book also includes several Swiss and English yodeling songs, favorites among some of the Swiss Amish people. The youth reportedly do not select the secular songs until near the end of their singing.

When singing German songs, young people sing all of the melodies from memory, since there are no musical notations. Because nobody uses a pitch pipe at singings, the person starting the hymn may begin the melody too low or, more frequently, too high. At this point, singers with a better musical ear immediately "take over and get the tune on track." In the plainest groups, such as the Swartzentruber and Nebraska Amish, all songs are in German and come from the *Ausbund* or the *Unpartheyisches Gesang-Buch*. Youth in the plain settlements and youth groups still sing in unison, since part, or harmony, singing has traditionally been regarded as showy and worldly. In the more progressive areas, however, part singing is not only permitted, but embraced by most youth and their parents.[18] This relatively recent change has affected many New Order youth and has even spread more broadly to the more progressive Old Order Amish circles. A Lancaster County mother reported that virtually all supervised youth groups now sing four-part harmony in their Sunday-night singings. These youth have learned the songs at week-night music classes taught by knowledgeable Amish or Mennonite adults with a love of music. Depending on the teacher, youth may learn to sing harmony from old-fashioned shaped-note songbooks or from standard musical notation. Pitch pipes are allowed in the week-night "practice singings" but are not permitted at the Sunday night events.

Over the years, non-traditional songs from the outside occasionally slip into the Sunday-night singing repertoire. The country gospel song from the 1960s, "We Need a Whole Lot More of Jesus and a Lot Less Rock and Roll" became popular in several singings in Lancaster County during that period. Occasionally groups add a secular English chorus to German religious verses. Since the early 1950s, scattered youth groups in Illinois, Indiana, Ohio, and Pennsylvania juxtaposed the chorus from "Bluebird on Your Window Sill" with the end of a German hymn.[19] A sixty-year-old recalled, "From the first time I heard the song, I liked the thought." A middle-aged Amish father from Holmes County, Ohio, reminisced, "When I was young, it was the top song on country station WWVA in Wheeling, West Virginia, where they had the Saturday-night Wheeling Jamboree." And since many Amish youth in Ohio and Pennsylvania listened to the Jamboree on clandestine battery-powered radios in their buggies or at their Saturday-night gatherings, "maybe that's how it caught on," the grandfather conjectured. Another Amish man stated, "Back then, it took only a week for a song that reached the 'Hit Parade' [a popular weekly radio program] to get into the Amish community."

Upping the Tempo

About midway through many singings, the traditional songbooks are collected and different ones are distributed. From here on in, the tempo of the music quickens noticeably. Most songs are sung to approximations of gospel tunes, such as "Amazing Grace," "When the Roll Is Called Up Yonder," and "Will the Circle Be Unbroken?," depending on the group. In the past, outsiders who attended singings noted that in more traditional settlements, many tunes seemed to be pitched uncomfortably high on the scale, and some described the singing style as nasal or even hillbilly.[20] These same observers, however, found that in recent years, the quality of the music has increased noticeably, a likely outcome of the growing numbers of youth involved in the music classes.

A custom that has persisted through the years in many settlements is that near the midway point of the singing, family members (usually young teenage girls) suddenly appear carrying water pitchers and glasses, to fortify the singers for the duration of the singing. When youth from Somerset County, Pennsylvania, visited a singing in the Big Valley, they were startled to see that these young people customarily drank directly from the pitchers. "Since we also watched everyone drink from the pitchers at the noon meal, we had already decided that we were not thirsty!" the visitors reported. In Lancaster County, hosts always place filled water pitchers and glasses on each table. In Ohio and elsewhere, some of the Swartzentruber groups still set out small containers of salt on the tables, "because it helps the youth to sing better by opening their throats." Grandparents from Indiana and Pennsylvania recall that sixty years ago, the hosts would always place salt shakers on the tables for the same purpose. This tradition persists in a few scattered settlements even today, but in most places salt has given way to mints or throat lozenges.

In the last half of the singing, many Old and New Order groups regularly sing gospel songs in English from mimeographed sheets, standard hymnbooks, or custom-printed settlement songbooks that consist of songs the community has selected and approved.[21] A recent trend in some Old Order groups, however, has been to print High German translations of English gospel songs learned in Amish private schools.[22] This practice has resulted

in a significant increase in the number of new songs in the accepted repertoire, which have even slipped into the traditional afternoon or evening
singings at wedding receptions. Teenagers in Lancaster County reported
that one new song became so popular that it was sung at every wedding
reception they attended the previous fall. These changes have not occurred
without some uneasy attention or concerns, however. A thirty-something
single male from Lancaster County wrote: "Today's groups with *Heartland
Hymns* and other English songbooks tend to reject reliable songs of worship
in favor of temporarily 'feel-good,' self-pleasing songs. I would say these
songs rob the youth of their understanding of God's order and handicap
them . . . from true Godly order."[23]

In some Old and New Order settlements, many young males regard the
actual singing part as a female domain. "My brother doesn't sing because
he wants to be cool," explained his teenage sister. The young women there
assumed the responsibility of requesting songs and singing, while most of
the young men, according to a visiting teenager at the youth-only singing,
"cut up." "Some of their boys were throwing popcorn or corn curls at other
singers, and some of them were actually smoking during the singing," he
recounted. Observers have also reported that the teenage boys typically tire
of singing more quickly than the girls. An elderly minister and his wife recalled that at their singings sixty years ago, some boys would occasionally
try to lighten up the evening by singing their own version of the "Loblied,"
the only hymn sung in every Sunday worship service by Amish everywhere.
"They sang it to the tune of 'Yankee Doodle,'" reported the couple ruefully,
"and they could make the words fit!" A woman from a large settlement re-
members: "When I was a teenager, it was often only three of us girls who
would be inside singing. The rest of the youth were outside doing whatever." A bishop's wife in a rural Pennsylvania settlement declared: "It's hard
to take church [at your place] when you know the young folks will descend
on you and bring drinks and music. Often not much singing is done. Sometimes as many as half a barrel of bottles will be picked up."[24]

In contrast to the peer-centered communities, the Ohio New Order
Amish and a number of the supervised youth groups in Lancaster County
regard the singing more as a religious exercise than a social occasion. In the
New Order groups, a minister, relative, or even a young man designated by

the host family may lead a short bible-study session at the midpoint. Predictably, the behavior at their singings is more churchlike. Usually everyone sings, limited conversations take place between songs, and most attendees (both male and female) participate and request their favorite songs.

In a few of the plain as well as the progressive communities, the youth do not expect or welcome parents and other adults to the singings. A visiting Amish parent from Somerset County, Pennsylvania, who asked to attend a singing at one of the Amish affiliations in the Big Valley with his teenagers, was told by his host: "We have never done it that way around here. Only the young folk go to the singings." "I was not surprised," the father reported later, "to find out why their singings had more of a reputation for rowdiness than for good singing." An informant from one of those groups claimed that youth often smoked, drank, and played Rook instead of singing. According to participants at another youth-only singing, however, the absence of adults does not automatically equate with teenage rowdiness. "Except for some teasing and talking between songs, our singings are decent," they reported.

In one settlement, a ploy to end things early centered on the traditional farewell and blessing song that signals the close of the singing portion of the evening. Parents have complained that when some of the young men tired of singing, one would prematurely start their farewell song, such as "*Ich sage gut Nacht*" ("I Say Goodnight"), and, as the final note died, all the boys would leap to their feet and file out, effectively ending the singing. One mother reported, however, that when the teenage boys in her group tried that back in the 1970s, the girls would interrupt them with shouts of "Be quiet, it ain't over yet!" and would continue to sing until the designated ending time arrived.

Closing Customs

Today, as soon as the farewell song is sung, host family members in many settlements typically appear with light refreshments (such as chips, popcorn, pretzels, apples, and cheese) and seasonal beverages (mint tea, cider, or hot chocolate). In most places, soft drinks are not served, but at least one Swiss Amish settlement reportedly provides a glass of homemade wine to all youth who attend. In Mifflin County, Pennsylvania, host families customarily set out bean soup and other leftovers from the shared noon meal, plus the traditional half-moon pies—baked, crescent-shaped turnovers made of pie dough and filled with stewed *Schnitz* (dried apples). In some settlements, such as in Mercer County, Pennsylvania, hosts serve no refreshments at all.

A generation ago, a unique custom developed at some singings in Lancaster County. Near the end, host-family singers and some of their friends would leave the room and return shortly thereafter, bearing trays of the locally popular figure-eight-shaped hard pretzels, signaling to everyone that the current song would be the last of the evening. Next, the singers would break into a traditional "Thank-You-for-Having-the-Singing" song—origin unknown. Then everyone would sing "Happy Birthday" in English to those celebrating a birthday within the next week. During the latter song, many of the singers would pelt all those being "honored" with a barrage of pretzels. One boy admitted: "It's not always fun. Getting hit with hard pretzels in the face and head really stings." In some groups, this pretzel shower was also directed at youth whose boyfriend's or girlfriend's parents attended the singing that night. Elam explained: "You know how hard it is to meet your girlfriend's parents when your friends are around. Well, everybody sings the song 'Cheer up, Elam; cheer up, Elam; don't be sad; don't be sad' [sung to the tune of 'Frère Jacques'] while they bombard you with pretzels."

A *Die Botschaft* scribe who had recently hosted a singing expressed her predictable sentiments on pretzel showers: "Pretzel throwing at the 'birthday ones' was new to us. What a waste! Pretzels are not cheap. Next time you young folks are tempted to throw food think of the poor children who go to bed 'hungry' daily."[25] A mother claimed that such a barrage wasted at least three bags of pretzels a night and wished "the adults could find a way to end such waste!" That mother is obviously pleased that such pretzel showers in Lancaster County have all but disappeared from the scene, along with other vestiges of the past.

Another *Die Botschaft* scribe from that generation expressed her displeasure at some of the youthful antics at a singing she had recently attended: "I was quite disappointed and ashamed with the behavior of many of the young girls and boys at the singing at Mike Lapps. Young folks, WHERE is our RESPECT for others?? Especially to those who give us a place for our gatherings? The girls seemed to be quite fussy [rowdy] and much water was being splashed at the time they should've been singing. Also, I wonder to whom we sing? Singings should always be quiet like at church and the songs should be sung *onstlich* [in earnest], so that we would not be mocking God, who sees and hears all."[26]

Most Amish parents, however, would probably consider throwing pretzels or popcorn and splashing water to be a fairly benign rumspringa expression among the Youngie. Adults in non-supervised settings worry more about those couples or cliques scattered around the premises who may continue their pre-singing socializing or game playing. They know that in some areas, even after most of the young people have already entered the singing venue, a sizable number—more often the sixteen-year-old boys—may linger outside or gather in other parts of the building, coming in twenty minutes or more late. Others may stay out until the last few minutes of the singing or never come in at all. In one unsupervised Lancaster County gang, most of the sixteen-year-olds customarily stayed outside or elsewhere in the house until the last ten or fifteen minutes. "They usually sit in their buggies and listen to music and then show up for the last few minutes so they can tell their parents they actually attended," reported a disgusted eighteen-year-old. A parent commented on those who entered late in his letter to *Die Botschaft*: "Along Hershey Church Road they had a . . . youth singing. Oh! it was so wonderful—about the first thirty boys wore a kinda satisfied and happy look on their faces, Oh! so respectful, those boys gave us pappies a hearty handshake, my feelings were to give each boy a deserved pat on the back. Of course those fellows helped sing even lead some slow tunes from the [thick] book. Then came the last twenty or thirty boys when the singing was almost over and [a] few of those were under influence of strong drink, Oh! what were the feelings of us pappies now??"[27]

Nevertheless, whether decent or rowdy, commended or criticized, supervised or free, the singing remains at the center of social life for Amish youth in the strongest communities or church districts. The singing of religious songs in German helps strengthen and reinforce the religious and cultural distinctiveness of the Amish. Thus this often low-key event provides far more than a setting for social interactions and mate selection. Even for

the rowdiest of youth, the venue provides a safe haven that minimizes social interactions and intimate relationships with non-Amish youth. It is
little wonder that adults hope and pray that their Youngie's singings will
be "upbuilding." By blending increased freedom with songs of the church,
Sunday-night singings help confirm the youths' Amish heritage and may
ultimately help prevent or reduce some of the excesses that have often accompanied Rumspringa, that experience to which we now turn.

Rumspringa illustrates the wide range of experiences available to youth in various Amish settlements and affiliations. In this photo posted on Facebook, these teenagers are watching a movie on their laptop on the way to their Sunday-night singing.
(Courtesy of an Amish Youngie)

Chapter Eight

Rumspringa
Stepping Out and Running About

We don't give our young folks leave to go out and sin just to
get it out of their system. We give them a little space so they can
be with people their own age and find a life partner.
—An Amish minister

A New Stage

U ntil the two young men from Lancaster County, Pennsylvania, were
charged by federal agents in summer 1998 with trafficking in cocaine,
the word Rumspringa was known only to Pennsylvania German speakers
and a few academics who studied the Amish. Since then, it has been crop-
ping up on talk shows, television advertisements, and t-shirts (one logo
reads, "What happens in Rumspringa stays in Rumspringa"). An alternative music group from Los Angeles calls itself Rumspringa, and a number
of bands (including Nits, an art-rock group from Holland) have featured a
song by that name. There is even the musical, *Rumspringa*. UPN's reality
series, *Amish in the City*, brought the term into pop culture by using the
word in every episode. Likewise, several American television series, including *ER* and *Judging Amy*, featured an Amish rumspringa-based plot. Oprah

Winfrey devoted a program to the Rumspringa of young adults who grew up in Amish families, which also helped to popularize the term and give it a place in mainstream culture and thought. Although entrepreneurs have yet to invent "Rumspringa Rum," a small company in Bird-in-Hand, Pennsylvania, calls itself the Rumspringa Brewing Company. British filmmaker Lucy Walker's documentary, *Devil's Playground*, focuses on the extreme end of the rumspringa experience.

The main focus of *Devil's Playground* was Faron Yoder, a young man from LaGrange County, Indiana, who had spent time in reform school and who claimed gangster rapper Tupac Shakur as his idol. Yoder, the son of an Amish minister, was a likeable eighteen-year-old who dealt drugs to support a $100-a-day methamphetamine habit.[1] In fear for his life, he went into hiding after allowing law enforcement authorities to plant a wire on him to obtain incriminating evidence on other local drug dealers. Although not as deeply involved as Faron, the other main characters also indulged in various self-destructive behaviors—or, at the least, atypical practices for Amish adolescents. One teenager bragged, "If I were living at home, then I couldn't have 200 different channels of DirectTV, stereo, Nintendo, and a fridge full of beer."[2]

Critics of *Devil's Playground* generally acknowledged Walker's persistence and skill in filming this previously undocumented aspect of Amish life. Most were surprised that she was able to penetrate the Amish community in amassing over 300 hours of highly unusual footage. What many failed to recognize, however, is that she was dealing with an extreme end of the behavioral spectrum, and that the experiences of Yoder and the others were not the norm. Typical Amish adolescents, even in their rumspringa years, would not permit anyone to photograph them in the way that Walker did. Not only would day-to-day rumspringa behavior have been unavailable to her and her camera crew, but most viewers would have undoubtedly lost interest in the mundane world of weekly singings and Amish teenage friendships that would have filled her documentary.

The partying and drug use that Walker has captured occurs not only in the northern Indiana settlement featured in the film, but also in the other large settlements. As we have seen earlier, drinking occurs in some small settlements too, but drug use there is typically uncommon. If Rumspringa signifies more freedom for teenagers to choose their friends and activities, however, then it occurs among the Amish everywhere.[3] Although nobody knows when such a practice began, it probably relates to the Amish beliefs in adult choice and the baptism of believers. *Devil's Playground* viewers learn that being born into an Amish family is not enough to qualify one for church membership. Only a teenager or adult, choosing freely, is qualified to become a full-fledged part of this believers' community.

A Mennonite writer whose parents grew up Amish presents a more nuanced portrayal of the rumspringa years, at least as they occur among many Old Order communities in Ohio's Holmes, Wayne, Stark, and Geauga Counties. In his novel *Ben's Wayne*, the author Levi Miller describes typical rumspringa behavior during the running-around years of the mid-twentieth century.[4] In it, one family member leaves his Amish family; some of the *Bouve* (young men) drink and smoke; and carloads of youth drive to nearby Wheeling, West Virginia, to see the live Saturday-night Jamboree radio broadcast. In addition, the eighteen-year-old protagonist, Wayne Weaver, experiences sexual temptations with his girlfriend and later with a nurse at a hospital where he does his volunteer service. At no time do the main characters hook up, get involved in drugs, deliberately shame their parents, or disgrace their community. Nevertheless, Miller's realistic description reputedly offended some family members, who felt certain scenes were too personal or explicit. Most reviewers thought *Ben's Wayne* accurately portrayed Rumspringa for most youth at that time. The 2012 film, *The Amish*, also gives a balanced depiction of compliant youth pondering their future, playing volleyball on a Sunday afternoon, or remembering their baptismal experience.[5]

Finding One's Place

The rumspringa experience arrives about halfway through the teenage years, however, when life shifts suddenly from a relatively tranquil home and a parent-centered existence to a much more exciting and emotionally charged environment. Now, singings, peer relationships, dating, and eventually finding one's life partner take center stage. In both traditional and smaller settlements, the transition is generally smooth and manageable. Youth continue friendships and relationships that go back to their earliest memories: associations developed in school, at church, and in community activities. Their Sunday-night singings may broaden to include youth who live in the adjacent church districts, but through activities, such as visiting relatives, benefit sales, local markets, or auctions, small-settlement teens know virtually every young person and the families they come from. In rural Juniata County, Pennsylvania, a typical seventeen-year-old can name each of the 120 teenagers who attend one of the two Sunday night singings held in their nine-district settlement. Proximity and geography helps shape the setting and the youthful landscape.

The story is often different, however, in settlements with scores or even a hundred or more church districts, as we will see later in this chapter. In places like northern Indiana and Allen County Indiana, some of the youth interact with peers whom they have chosen on the basis of similar interests and values, more than on their locality. In Elkhart and LaGrange Counties, Indiana, these youth groups are called crowds, each reflecting varying degrees of conformity to or rejection of adult behavioral standards.[6] In the latter situation, the change for a sixteen-year-old may be precipitous, dramatic, and often out of control. Whatever the setting or local customs, and whatever degree of rowdiness or obedience occurs, Rumspringa is the time for youth to prove themselves among their peers and establish their future trajectories.

When Amish young people turn sixteen or seventeen in a large settlement, they may choose from a variety of peers with whom to socialize as they navigate their rumspringa years—from compliant to rowdy, and all shades in between. Lancaster County, however, has evolved into a system that enables youth to find like-minded peers from a variety of youth groups. These gangs, as we have seen in chapter 5, cover the spectrum from the plainest open-buggy groups and the adult-supervised ones to the motorized and partying youth, who post Facebook and Twitter descriptions of their most recent drinking bashes. Few outsiders knew anything about this Amish gang structure until the 1998 drug arrests for the youth caught trafficking in cocaine. The association of Amish gangs with the Pagans motorcycle gang simply added to the public's misperceptions that Amish gangs meant Amish deviance.

In the parlance of the Lancaster County Amish, a gang simply denotes a local youth group of fifty to a hundred or so self-chosen peers.[7] At age sixteen, Lancaster youth choose to join one of the scores of gangs. In December 1993, many non-local Amish and horse and buggy Mennonite readers of the newspaper *Die Botschaft* first learned about the gangs when a well-known Lancaster "scribe" revealed the names and membership count for all of the fifteen gangs in the county at that time.[8] For the most part, the names of the gangs appeared to be innocuous, if not quaint: Antiques, Bluebirds, Canaries, Cardinals, Crickets, Chickadees, Happy Jacks, Orioles, Pilgrims, Pinecones, Pioneers, and Souvenirs, among others. Over time, virtually all of these names disappeared as the groups disbanded, only to be replaced with an assortment of new gang names, chosen by the youth in the upcoming generation. In 2013, new group names, such as Avalanche, Black-hawks, Falcons, Ravens, Penguins, Sea Gulls, Icebergs, Mustangs, Sea-hawks, and Wrens, among others, appeared on the scene.[9] As of late 2013, the estimated number of gangs in Lancaster County and its daughter settle-ments was seventy-eight.

When word of the gang phenomenon first reached *Die Botschaft* readers in other settlements, many were surprised to learn that some of the gangs actually had nearly 200 members. Their reactions ranged from disbelief to amazement. They wondered what was happening when large groups of youth spent long periods of unsupervised time together. Many Amish from distant settlements puzzled over how such a non-Amish phenom-enon originated in Lancaster County, since Amish everywhere tradition-ally value small, decentralized structures. They also wondered when all of this began, and why the ministers and parents would allow such a thing to happen.

Historically, identifiable gangs in Lancaster County were relatively un-known until the first half of the 1940s. Early in the twentieth century, when the Amish population there was small and districts were few, most Lan-caster County families knew each other. Many youth were related and often attended school or church together. They socialized at a work frolic or at the fall weddings, and youth across the settlement got together at the Sunday-night singings. As the settlement grew, however, the youth population rapidly expanded. An Amish historian related that increasing numbers of youth would converge in the town of Intercourse, Pennsylvania, on a Sun-day night, instead of attending a singing or staying home on evenings when there were none. To curb this practice, in 1929 church leaders decided that any youth who were already church members and "found guilty of stopping in Intercourse on a Sunday evening would be asked to make a confession before the church council."[10] The ministers and elders continued to struggle with the problem of having many youth congregating in town or driving around the back roads in large numbers.

A middle-aged Amish man related that, according to his father, a group of concerned parents in the late 1940s pushed for the formation of a new breakoff group as an alternative to the traditional large get-together. As a result, the one large group eventually separated into smaller ones. Some formed primarily on the basis of proximity, such as youth from the densely populated Groffdale area (in the center of the county) who formed a group that became known as the Groffies. Young people, however, were free to join the group of their choice, regardless of where they lived.

By 1950, at least three groups had emerged. According to John A. Hostetler, these original gangs were the Groffies, the Ammies, and the Trailers.[11] Elderly informants remember that the Groffies were the "fastest, wildest, and most liberal"; the Ammies were the moderates; and the Trailers were the most conservative. Young men in the Groffies were more likely to drive cars and party on the weekends. The Trailers, on the other hand, originated in the more sparsely populated and conservative southern part of the settlement. They drove only buggies, dressed mostly like their parents, and generally avoided the party excesses of their faster cousins. Over time, the gangs grew to 100 or more members and then divided, generally with the older youth splitting off from the younger, less mature members to form a new gang. Thus the three original groups split into six, and then twelve. By the beginning of the twenty-first century, more than thirty gangs reflected various positions on the traditional–progressive spectrum.

Amish adults from distant settlements have wondered, "Aren't these Lancaster County gangs bound to have problems?" Inquirers soon learned that the behavior of youth in the current gangs varied as much as youthful behavior in the early gangs of the 1950s. One church leader explained that of the approximately 2,200 youth in Lancaster County in the mid-1990s, almost 10 percent belonged to the Antiques, a peer-centered gang in which all of the males drove cars and dressed English. This group had few singings, sponsored notorious drinking parties, and was later identified as the gang to which two of the young men convicted of selling cocaine belonged.[12] Several other fast groups followed less excessive but similar behaviors to the Antiques, in that most of their male members also drank, drove vehicles, and owned their own cars or trucks.[13] The half-dozen smaller buggy gangs, such as the Bluebirds, Canaries, Chickadees, and Pequea, were at the plain end of the youth spectrum—more adult-oriented and tradition-centered. Members dressed conservatively, rode in old-fashioned open buggies, and generally conformed to the dress and transportation standards of their elders. The young women in the buggy groups were the only ones in Lancaster County who consistently wore large black bonnets over their *Kapps* to singings. The middle groups reflected aspects of both ends of the spectrum.

The Critical Choice

In contrast to the way large-settlement gangs have evolved, youth in small settlements have the choice of who will become their close friends, but not in what kind of group to join. Geography determines their peers. The majority of these small-settlement Amish youth would feel most at home with one of the Lancaster County buggy gangs.[14] Because most of these more isolated Youngie attend singings exclusively with peers and friends from their home-church district, they would be surprised to find that in Lancaster County, gangs contain a mixture of youth coming from all parts of the settlement. Small-settlement teens might also be astounded to learn that some Lancaster gang members come from adjacent and even distant counties for singings, fun, and special friendships.[15] A smattering of youth have traveled nearly 200 miles one way on weekends, and some young people whose families have moved to distant settlements have commuted from as far away as western Pennsylvania, New York State, or even eastern Indiana to join their friends for the weekend activities.[16] Each person may pay $100 or more as their share in hiring a van and driver for the weekend.[17]

One result of self-selected gangs is that members from a half-dozen or more different youth groups may attend the same church, and brothers and sisters from the same family may belong to three or four different gangs. Non-Amish visitors to an Amish church service most likely would be oblivious to this. When they observe the young men filing in to worship, dressed in identical hats, white shirts, black vests, suspenders, and broadfall pants, these rows of youth probably look more or less like black-and-white facsimiles. Likewise, the young women, with their long parted hair, organdy head coverings, plain-colored dresses, and dark stockings may appear to be cookie-cutter copies of modesty, humility, and sobriety, despite their membership in different gangs.[18] Although the nuances may be subtle to outsiders, Amish adults can quickly identify the kind of gang to which each young person belongs by their haircuts, the tilt of their hats, suspender styles and colors, and the kind of shirt buttons for teenage boys, as well as by hem length, the brightness of dress materials, the use of straight pins or buttons, and the thickness of the stockings for teenage girls.[19] Even without such indicators, the local youth, ministers, and parents all know each young person's group membership and where it fits into the larger constellation of gangs.

Long before they join, most preteens learn from older siblings or friends about many of the gangs and their place on the plain–wild continuum. In the late 1990s, when asked to describe the Lancaster County gang scene, a ten-year-old girl promptly identified and described each of them in detail. While compliant youth generally choose a reputable gang preferred by their parents, some Youngie choose a wild group, often launching themselves into conflict with their parents, especially if the adults were never rebellious. Many Amish adolescents are torn between not wanting to be a goodie-goodie, yet not wishing to disappoint their parents and grandparents or incur their displeasure. By any measure, an Amish teenager's choice of gangs is as momentous as the important peer decisions that any English youth might make. An Amish gang will influence how members spend their free time and money; how they dress and style their hair; how they use technology, what mode of transportation they choose; if they use or reject tobacco, alcohol, and drugs; how they relate to the other sex; and if or when they join the church. Finally, if they do become church members, their mates most often will come from the same gang.

Buddy Bunches: Those Oh-So-Special Friends

In good Anabaptist fashion, gang members are not drafted or picked for desirable qualities, as are candidates for an exclusive fraternity or sorority. Basically, anyone who shows up may join a gang. Within most Lancaster County gangs, new members automatically become part of a smaller, more intimate unit known as a "buddy bunch."[20] This cohort consists of as many as fifteen to twenty age-mates who join the gang at about the same time. Another buddy bunch forms as soon as the next fifteen to twenty newcomers come along, and so forth. Traditionally, each person in a buddy bunch has a special friend, or "sidekick." In some of the adult-supervised gangs, however, there has been an intentional effort to downplay or even eliminate the sidekick component, in an effort to break up cliques or avoid outliers or isolates. If a sixteen-year-old does not find a sidekick, he or she could feel alone and vulnerable. One young woman poignantly recalled her sense of rejection when she failed to find a buddy: "I still remember how painful it was when a girl who promised to be my sidekick changed her mind and dropped me. I didn't have anybody to be my special friend. Finally, my cousin and another girl agreed to let me be with them, but I always felt like the outsider—like they were saying, 'It's a privilege for you to be running with us.' Eventually, I just stopped going and dropped out of the gang for three years. I finally started with a different group, a fairly common reason for changing gangs."[21]

When asked what determines the size of the particular buddy bunches in his gang, a seventeen-year-old explained, "We like each group to have at least eight boys and eight girls, just the right size to play volleyball." In some gangs, buddy bunches may consist of only eight to ten members, with an unequal number of males and females, but a group rarely exceeds twenty people. Most teens interact with their buddies throughout their dating years, and they find their most intimate and enduring friendships in the bunch.[22] The main reason for this lifetime bonding may relate to the sheer amount of time buddy members spend together. On Sunday afternoons, members typically socialize throughout the entire day and evening. Depending on the season, they play volleyball, go sledding or ice skating, or have indoor activities, such as table tennis or board games. Softball is still a popular warm-weather choice with some buddy bunches in Lancaster County. All the buddy bunches in a particular gang eat together in a large supper gang before a combined evening singing, but even there, they socialize mostly with their own age-mates.

In many gangs, the young women in each buddy bunch wear "buddy colors" (identically colored dresses) to singings and other events. Traditionally, they bring their changes of clothes to church in bags and switch to their matching attire right after the morning service. "The boys aren't very cooperative, and they don't really get into wearing the same colors. Besides, they don't have as many clothes as we do," explained one sixteen-year-old girl.[23] When a singing occurs at the home of a buddy bunch member, the buddies have the choice seats at the tables. Buddy bunch members in Lancaster County will also either get together by themselves or join with the entire gang on appropriate holidays (such as Ascension Day in May, the Monday after Easter, or the Monday following Pentecost Sunday) for day trips, picnics, hikes, sports, or parties.

Because buddies run around together and are highly involved with each other, most teens usually take membership instruction and join the church at the same time. Although the importance of the buddy bunch may decline somewhat when youth begin seriously dating, these ties usually remain strong throughout their lives. Even after members marry or move away, they keep in touch through visits, buddy get-togethers, and circle letters. Few high school or college classes in mainstream society maintain such close ties over the years as Amish buddies do.

Addition and Division

Occasionally teenagers do not like either the gang they originally chose or their particular buddy bunch. Anyone may change gangs, but switching is not common, since friendship patterns in the new gang are already in place. Males are more likely to change gangs than females are, and the most common reason is that a young man's "special friend" (girlfriend) is in another gang. Teenage girls are more likely to change if they fail to find close friendships. In general, however, individuals are reluctant to change gangs unless their buddy members or their sidekick (best friend) goes along with them. Traditionally, changes occurred more frequently when a number of gang members—usually the older buddy groups—decided to form a new gang. This typically happened when a gang approached 100 members or when the eighteen- or nineteen-year-olds increasingly found the behavior of the younger members irritating, immature, or morally objectionable. Such splits were common. Some years back, a gang split when thirty-five of the older Rangers broke away to form the more conservative Pinecones. A less common division occurred when the entire seventeen-year-old buddy bunch led a split from the Diamonds to form a new gang, the Sparkies. This, too, was a conservative split, but it was unusual in that it was initiated by younger members rather than the oldest ones. In Lancaster County currently, only the unsupervised gangs split in the traditional manner. In the supervised gangs, the advisory board decides when gangs are getting too big and need to divide.

A bishop observed that splits occur under certain predictable conditions: "Most gangs naturally evolve from slow to fast in Lancaster County. Groups may start out with conservative ideals and practices, but they soon move toward behavior that is unacceptable and ungodly." When asked why this sequence of change moves from slow to fast, a twenty-year-old explained, "When it's time for your younger brothers and sisters to join a gang, Mom and Dad want them to pick a slower group. Even if they [the younger siblings] agree to that, they will still want the same kind of fun and freedoms that their older brothers and sisters have, so they bring that desire right along with them to the gang. Usually the younger ones bring in the faster ways." A minister offered another explanation: "Most parents appreciate a plain group and want their children to be in one. Because of parents' pressure, however, too many young folk who are 'pushing the fences' end up in a decent gang, and, like bad apples, sooner or later spoil the barrel." He, along with others, believes that at the present time, newly formed gangs in Lancaster County typically lose their conservative bent in about three years.

Unless they are seriously dating, youth in the adult-centered settlements typically stay at home on Saturday nights, because their only approved social activity is the Sunday-night singing or the planned midweek singing practice. On the other hand, many youth at the peer-centered end of the spectrum usually meet not only during the week, but also spend most of the weekend together unsupervised. In some areas this is called an "overnight," when teens will often be gone from Saturday afternoon until the predawn hours of Monday morning.[24] Thus, on a typical Lancaster County Saturday night, some youth interact with their families in ways reminiscent of small-settlement life, while, a mile or two away, their more liberal counterparts behave in ways similar to mainstream youth bent on having a good time. In some settlements and groups, however, good times are not limited to Saturday nights.

Sunday-Night Shenanigans

Except for parts of the large settlements in Indiana and Ohio, almost all Amish youth attend weekly or biweekly singings on Sunday nights. As we have seen in chapter 7, this is the traditional door to the rumspringa experience and the venue for social interactions with peers. Depending on the settlement or group, adult supervision or control ranges from hands-on in the supervised groups to virtually nonexistent in some of the most traditional communities. Following the farewell song at the Sunday-night singings, courting couples everywhere customarily depart immediately for the girl's house, refreshments, privacy, or socializing with other courting couples. In some places, all of the unattached youth remain for another hour or more after the singing to socialize, sometimes in same-sex groups, but often with the sexes mixing. If some youth fail to join in or actually leave the main group at this time, they are usually the sixteen-year-olds, who tend to arrive, leave, or create mischief with their excitement-seeking age-mates. In one community, some sixteen-year-old boys brought whiskey to their singing and dumped it in the chickens' water supply to see the effects of alcohol on thirsty birds. During summers in a large Illinois settlement, a sizeable number of youth would leave as soon as the singing ended to go to the local drive-in movie theater outside of town.

After-singing activities vary considerably, however, depending on the settlement or group. In communities where tobacco is tolerated, some teenage youth, usually boys, may immediately begin smoking, but in sectors of the large settlements, girls also smoke, albeit usually more privately. If drinking occurs, it is most commonly a minority of the males who stay outside and drink behind the barn or shop. In some of the peer-centered gangs or settlements, however, observers report that half or more of the unsupervised youth participate in drinking and partying. Such behavior is rare in many Old Order circles, especially in the supervised groups, and almost never occurs among the New Order youth.

In some settlements the non-courting youth customarily stay in the house or barn to play board or card games such as Parcheesi, Monopoly, Settlers of Catan, Uno, Phase 10, checkers, chess, Dutch Blitz, Old Maid, and even Masterpiece, a game where players bid on famous paintings. In most places, games using standard playing cards are forbidden, although a conservative boy visiting a large settlement expressed surprise that teenagers there openly played poker. In the plainest settlements, they more often play their traditional "barn games": activities such as Six Old Maids, Swat, and Steal the Bacon.[25] In other settlements, following the singing the youth may clear away the benches or move to a nearby location to dance. In some places the dancing may last only half an hour, but elsewhere where the youth might continue dancing into the early hours of the morning. The style of music and dancing depends on the nature of the group. Today, unsupervised groups may dance to downloaded music on an iPod, the sound blasting from a high-end sound system from somebody's pickup truck or SUV. In the meantime, their conservative or open-buggy cousins may be dancing to the strains of a harmonica or simply to the unaccompanied singing of the young people, with or without a caller or leader to direct the songs or sequences. In some settlements, this kind of activity has been called "four-square" dancing. In the most conservative Lancaster County gangs, it is still called *Ring Spiele*, a kind of prescribed square dance. A seventeen-year-old exclaimed: "You should see it, dancing outside together under the stars. It's wonderful!" For him, at least, music was incidental to the excitement of being together with his young male and female peers.

At times, as the night wanes, Sunday-night drinking becomes the main activity in certain gangs or areas. Neighbors may call local law enforcement officers to complain of excessive noise, reckless driving, or presumed underage drinking. Sometimes even the Amish host families have been known to call the police when they felt that the activities were "getting out of hand."[26] This has usually been the choice of last resort, however. "There's a lot of pressure from our children not to do anything. And there's even pressure from some of the other parents to look away," reported a frustrated father. "We might get bad publicity in the news. So we're just supposed to let it go and clean up the next day."

Band Hops and Parties: The Extreme Rumspringa Experience

Someone driving along the back roads of a large Amish settlement on a summer Saturday night would never happen on a hand-painted sign proclaiming "Amish party—next lane right" or "Amish band hop here tonight—BYOB!" Few English passersby would even realize that the growing crowd at the end of a Lancaster County farm lane or a Holmes County, Ohio, gravel road that ended at a secluded field or reclaimed strip mine is actually an Amish youth gathering, which they refer to as a "band hop." Rather than seeing horses and buggies, the observer would probably encounter a line of "muscle" (high-performance) cars, late-model diesel pickup trucks, or an assortment of "beaters" (older-model vehicles), depending on the age and discretionary wealth of the young person. Many cars would sport "mag" (custom alloy) wheels and booming sound systems. One might see the occasional telltale buggy, but in most venues the party set overwhelmingly arrives in motorized vehicles. The twang of electric guitars and an electric bass tuning up reverberate over the normally quiet countryside and pinpoint the location of the band hop. Loudspeakers crackle and boom with the background rattle of drums, and somebody's voice tests a highly amplified sound system powered by a gasoline or diesel generator. A band hop is ready to begin, an event that can easily run through the night until the young men on dairy farms must leave for the next morning's milking. Although these gatherings have been a part of large communities for as long as anyone can remember, their continued appeal lies in providing the excitement of a totally unsupervised activity for these otherwise hardworking rural youth.

Band hops may be planned or may simply be spur-of-the-moment occasions, seized on by opportunistic youthful gangs when somebody's parents leave town to visit distant relatives or friends for a weekend.[27] News of the party travels quickly and widely over the Amish youth grapevine in the plain areas or via texting, Twitter, and Facebook among the faster-track youth. Band hops usually take place in an Amish shop building, a local park, a rented picnic ground, or a clearing in an accessible but relatively hidden patch of woods. If the event is planned, organizers sometimes notify friends and relatives from neighboring states, and carloads of youth may drive hundreds of miles to attend parties. In previous years, the more rowdy gangs invariably sponsored the band hops, but today it can be anyone with some organizational skills and a yearning for excitement. As many as 500 youth may attend, although 250 may be more typical. In Indiana, local newspapers have reported 1,000 youth in attendance.[28]

Outsiders rarely attend band hops, but some Amish youth occasionally invite non-Amish relatives or English friends. In summer 1996, a college student—who grew up in an Old Order River Brethren home and attended a one-room Amish school, but had not joined the church—was invited by his former schoolmates to come with them to a band hop.[29] When he arrived, he discovered that most of the Amish males were virtually indistinguishable from him and his college friends. He reported that they dressed in the styles in vogue at the time. A smattering of teenage boys wore the traditional suspenders, and most donned baseball-type caps with the bills turned sideways or backward. Haircuts were mostly barber cuts, roughly mirroring the hairstyles popular in mainstream culture. On the other hand, only a few of the rowdiest sported body piercings, and nobody displayed tattoos. The most extreme fashion statements for the males were an occasional earring and moustache. Most females also dressed in the current English clothing styles, and very few wore the traditional head covering. In describing a party, one Amish teenager expressed her displeasure and seeing females drinking and partying while wearing a head covering.[30] Although most of the young women did not literally let their hair down, at this particular event those who were smoking or drinking replaced their head coverings with baseball caps. Males outnumbered females three to one.

On the makeshift stage, two of then-popular local Amish bands, the Roamers and the Renegades, played classic rock songs from the 1960s and 1970s. During the 1980s, some Amish bands played heavy metal and even disco music. By the late 1990s and the early years of the twenty-first century, country-and-western music had regained its earlier popularity, both at Saturday-night hops and Sunday-night parties. Even when bands were playing country-and-western music, the Amish style of dancing was not the usual square dancing or round dancing. Teenage boys and girls would face each other, bump hips, kick under the other's legs, and embrace from time to time. In 2013, dancing among the most daring youth included hip-hop and rap. At the 1996 band hop, the Roamers generally played with two six-string guitars (rhythm and lead), a bass guitar, drums, and a keyboard. The musicians, a group of self-taught Amish youth, performed with $1,000 electric instruments and, reputedly, a $14,000 Peavy sound system. Partiers periodically rewarded their favorite musician with cups of beer. At some point during the night, the musicians passed the hat to help pay their expenses. One former band member from the Roamers reported that their group earned $16,000 in contributions over the four years they played.

Drinking was the other major activity. Although a few brought coolers full of hard liquor and other forms of alcohol, Miller Lite was the drink of choice. Most males carried two cans stacked in one hand while drinking from the third can. On this particular night there were no kegs in sight. A number of teenage boys eventually became inebriated, and some passed out. The student visitor reported that the smell of urine permeated the area immediately adjacent to the shop where the band hop was held, since the celebrants continually went outside to relieve themselves. Most of the young men were smoking Marlboros or Marlboro Lights rather than the traditional cigarette-sized Winchester cigars permitted in some settlements.[31] "It is definitely not cool to be smoking anything other than cigarettes," one of them declared. At this particular event, a knot of teenage males gathered outside around a bong, and the visiting student estimated that at least 10 percent of the young men went outside to "smoke weed or snort cocaine," albeit somewhat discreetly. In the past, fights would occasionally break out between individuals who had had too much to drink; none did at this event, however, and partygoers say that rumbles are less frequent today than in the past.[32]

Conversations among the males centered on drinking, cars, occasionally on drugs ("Think how easy it would be to grow marijuana in these cornfields"), and girls. At this particular band hop, some young men claimed that the local law enforcement officials were lax about underage drinking among the Amish, compared with police in the next township. Nevertheless, as a precaution before they left, many celebrants bequeathed their unopened six-packs to those who remained. The hop continued into the early hours of the morning, and the last to leave poured out the rest of the leftover beer.

Over the years, a few other outsiders have occasionally attended youth parties. A young English man, who eventually became a respected Mennonite minister, attended an Amish party in the 1960s when an Amish friend invited him. His friend met him at the barn around 10:00 p.m. As the visitor entered, he observed cases of beer stacked high along a wall. Up front, an Amish band played on acoustic instruments. Most of the males in the crowd were drinking, smoking, and playing cards for money. The card players lounged around "tables" formed from hay bales that they had shoved together. Several times he heard players admonish each other to be careful not to start a barn fire with their cigarettes. After a few hours, some card players left the games to be with their girlfriends. The visitor reported that the couples then scattered throughout the haymow "to make out"; although he observed caressing and kissing, he saw nothing more intimate. The band continued to play, while some of the card players persisted in their games, apparently oblivious to the music or the couples around them.[33]

Amish adults who attended hops or parties in their youth say that although the names of the bands have changed, the basic script for today's gatherings remains remarkably similar. Shops or outdoor sites, such as picnic groves, have generally replaced barns as preferred party venues. In most places, Amish youth still exclude the non-Amish from these social events—occasionally by force, if reports are accurate. Harmonicas and jaw harps continue to hold sway in the small, conservative settlements. Elsewhere, these have given way to electric guitars, keyboards, and drums. As one young man said, "All Amish youth like music, and they like it loud." Amish parents who long ago put aside their musical instruments, amplifiers, and loudspeakers in exchange for church hymnals may sometimes allow themselves a grin as they reminisce with their peers about the bands of their youth. "We had several bands in the sixties. Two of them were actually invited to come and play at the Grand Ole Opry, they were so good," an Amish grandfather told me with obvious pride. "In 1967, some of us went to Sunset Park in Rising Sun, Maryland, to an Osborne Brothers [bluegrass] concert. After it was over, we invited them to come back with us to Lancaster [County] and play in one of our barns, and they accepted. Their big bus pulled into the farm about midnight. It was wonderful. Our banjo picker, who is now a minister, played right along with their lead picker, and they played for most of the night."

For many Amish youth, behaving in ways that the adults would find unacceptable may add an extra bit of excitement to the experience. For parents, however, music is often the least of their concerns. Some families have reported spending half of Monday morning loading trash bags with bottles, cans, broken glass, and other refuse scattered about from the previous night. Amish parents in these settlements frequently express their frustration and helplessness: "What can we do?" asked a father. "How do you stop something like this that has been going on for years? You can't do it alone."[34] Actually, many respected parents, honored grandparents, and even ministers who worry about today's youth behaved similarly during and after the singings they attended in the past. A description of what some from that generation were up to came from an Amish writer who sent an anonymous letter to *Family Life* in 1969:

> Not all our youth are involved in these [rowdy] happenings. No, not half. But too many are. Sometimes such parties bring in young people from different states and communities. When I actually saw what took place, I was shocked.
>
> There is still a vivid picture in my mind of a boy and girl walking hand in hand down the lane, the girl carrying a beer bottle and talking boisterously. It made me think, "And this is a Christian community known far and wide for its plain people." Yes, it happened at one of their farms.
>
> As another car approached, the couple slipped over the grassy bank. I stood watching them. Paris hairdo, miniskirt, sheer hose, college haircut, checkered shirt—surely it had to be a dream. It was hard to believe that only hours before the couple had attended a plain church.
>
> Knowing nothing of the planned party, some friends and I had spent that evening in a nearby home. Since we had tied our horse where later they parked their cars, we suddenly found ourselves in the center of the activity.

As the shadows lengthened over the scene, cars were lining up, one after the other, five, ten, fifteen, up to a total of twenty-five cars. Dirty talk filled the evening air. The roar of stationary racing motors became louder as dusk shed its blanket over this shame. At the very moment, Mom and Dad were probably lighting a lamp.

Some people will be saying, "Such things are not for the public to know about." I wish, too, the public didn't know, but in this case, they knew all too well. A local paper had a write-up on these doings. . . . With cigarettes in one hand and beer in the other, these young people could hardly be imagined as the future church. Now and then, religion was heard mentioned—in mockery.[35]

Some non-Amish residents, especially those who live in communities with large Amish populations, have not hesitated to advise Amish parents about improving the behavior of their teenage children. In the "Letters" section of the local newspaper, a disturbed resident offered a number of pointed suggestions in a "Letter to Amish Parents" after learning that a local convenience store had to hire a security guard on weekends to reduce shoplifting and "harassment of customers," and that four Amish youth were apprehended by the police for "public drunkenness."

May I suggest you as a group care for your young people by giving them something constructive to do with their time on the weekends? They dress in English clothes, drive cars and drink beer as if to pretend they are not Amish. Give them pride. . . . The young people need a place to gather. I'm talking about baseball games, volleyball games, homemade ice cream parties, picnics, chicken barbecues, or even a well-chaperoned hoedown.

Parents could sit in the barn with the kids and show them they will tolerate clean fun only. Open your homes to the kids. It is extra work and bother, but wouldn't it be worth the effort? . . .

Please take time to find a way. Haven't you turned your backs long enough? Someone will be killed again. How many highway deaths involving Amish does it take in this area to get your attention?

At this point, I only say at least I tried.

—An Intercourse Resident[36]

If some parents talk only infrequently to their children about the youths' behavior during or after the singings, it is even less likely that these adults would relate their own past antics to them. Sitting in a Sunday-morning service, one would be hard pressed to picture any of these scrubbed young men and demure-looking young women dancing and drinking the night away. It is even harder visualizing their staid and serious-minded parents or grandparents, some of whom are now pillars of the church, swinging with their partners or downing beers with their peers. "I hate to say it," admitted a minister, "but I gave my parents a much harder time than my children give me. Truthfully, my wife and I have a lot to be thankful for."

The Electronic Rumspringa

Although most of the wild rumspringa behaviors of the past persist primarily in the memories of Amish adults, many of today's teenage excesses are widely accessible to a significant minority of Amish youth and to the hundreds of millions of others who have access to the Internet. Most Amish adults worry that the rumspringa extremes of the past posed less of a threat to Amish youth and the Amish way of life than does today's option of 24/7 access to the Internet. In 2006, when I finished my research for the original edition of this book, I did not even mention the Internet as a challenge to the Amish. I devoted only eight words to cell phones, explaining that instead of having to check a designated mail box to learn if a party was in the offing, Amish "youth call each other on their cell phones"—just a handful of words to cover phones and the young. Now—except for some of the plainer affiliations, most New Order Amish, and the majority of youth in the conservative wing of the supervised groups—cell phones not only are used by many in the large settlements, but they have also opened the door to the Internet. Cell phones have even infiltrated many rural Amish settlements, such as Hazeltown, Iowa; Clymer, New York; and Lawrence, Mifflin, and Juniata Counties, Pennsylvania. In my research for this revision, I have identified youthful phone users in many of the thirty states where Amish reside.

Ever since Alexander Graham Bell first patented the telephone in 1876, the Amish and the telephone have experienced a conflicted relationship.

From the start, most Amish, or at least most Amish ministers, regarded telephone use with skepticism, if not outright rejection. Even without a well-articulated position, they intuitively realized that telephones reduced face-to-face communication, could disrupt family life, and most likely would lead to time wasting and gossiping—hence the grudging compromise of restricting telephones to small, uncomfortable phone shanties.[37] The advent of cell phones not only added another level of complexity to their plain and simple lifestyle concerns but may also have introduced more serious issues than wasting time or gossiping.

Several things bother both traditional and progressive Amish adults about cell phones. First, for various reasons, the leaders dislike the practice of texting. When I asked an Amish bishop about this, he immediately mentioned sexting, an answer that surprised me, since I assumed he would not know about sending sexually explicit photos of oneself or others to someone via a phone. He next pointed to the appeal that texting seems to have for the youth, citing a young man texting in church until he realized that the bishop had stopped talking and was waiting for him to put his phone away. Many, if not most, Amish still prefer the act of writing letters by hand; anticipating, opening, and reading them; and often preserving these handwritten records as cherished mementos in a designated shoebox or desk drawer. As writer Erik Wesner has pointed out, texting involves no voice, uses little-understood symbols and truncations, and is not even written by hand, which qualifies texting as "the most 'un-Amish' form of modern communication."[38] Another predictable objection is that virtually all of these phones include electronic games and other time-wasters. Finally, cell phones are easily concealed from parents or ministers, thus reducing accountability for their use or misuse.

Of course, concerns about cell-phone use apply equally to Amish adults. Many contractors, carpenters, business owners, and market-stand Amish feel that they need a cell phone to stay in business in an increasingly difficult and competitive financial climate. So, despite the church's oft-stated reservations or objections, growing numbers of Amish church members either reluctantly or willingly sign on for open or secretive cell-phone ownership. Affiliations, and even church districts, vary significantly over cell-phone issues. Leaders' reactions range from tacit and even open acceptance of these phones, at least in the workplace, to a mandate to excommunicate disobedient members. Perhaps because of their awareness of the disagreements among adults on this issue, many rumspringa youth, even those who have joined the church, see no problem or feel no dissonance in owning and using cell phones themselves.

Smartphone Challenges

The simple, no-frills cell phone, however, may be the least of the technological challenges facing the Amish. Since the beginning of this century, ministers have been speaking regularly about the dangers of computers. In those earlier days, they were probably thinking of desktop computers at the local library and laptops they saw being used by McDonald's customers or by coffee-sipping tourists outside the local Starbucks. When *Family Life* published its first extensive article on the dangers of cell phones in 2010, smartphones had already invaded the large Amish communities, especially among the youth.[39] What sparked even greater concerns were the persistent warnings about the sleaze available on the Internet, especially pornography. This particular threat was the main reason most Amish bishops had immediately rejected computers when they first began showing up in Amish workplaces. Imagine the ministers' surprise and consternation those clergymen experienced when they learned that most of the newest cell phones, easily accessed and easily concealed, were much more than a phone—that they actually provided the same dangers and capabilities that had caused the leaders to reject computers. Thoughtful adults realized that the range of options just a click or two away on a smartphone was exponentially more powerful and dangerous than simple cell phones to their traditional way of life, the health of the community, and the well-being of its users.

With the introduction of smartphones, many of their children have now transitioned in record time from simple, one-to-one conversations with friends into a previously unknown and mostly uncensored link to virtually everything the worldwide web has to offer. Amish youth, with their glitzy iPhones, Androids, or Blackberries, have quickly learned the nuances of various phone options, provider contracts, benefits, gigabytes, memory chips, downloading, uploading, and Internet services and pleasures. Phone ownership among the fast-track youth has exploded. In 2012 and 2013, some youthful Amish phone owners from the fast circles in northern Indiana and Pennsylvania's Lancaster County estimated that more than 75 percent of their friends and acquaintances owned cell phones, and they thought that at least half or more of those phones were smartphones. Although their figures were just guesses, they do show that these sophisticated phones are not a rare occurrence.[40]

Discovering the Internet was a heady experience for many of these young people who had spent their first sixteen years surrounded by friends and family within a protective, separatist, conservative, culture. They have quickly learned that they can access the same Internet sites as mainstream teenagers or their older siblings, usually with little or no restraint or direction from parents. Not surprisingly, they have been captivated by the potential of their newly acquired electronic device. They and their friends have now found that prior to an upcoming beach or mountain weekend excursion, they can check not only the local weather, but also the three-day forecast for Ocean City, Maryland, or Stowe, Vermont. Once at their destination, they can navigate flawlessly to the nearest fast-food restaurants, local sports bars, campsites, or cheap lodging, utilizing the built-in GPS on their smartphones.

Moreover, these youth—who grew up in a parent-controlled, photo-restricted environment—have traditionally been expected to reject posing and picture taking. Most, however, have found their built-in phone cameras to be a novelty offering great excitement and entertainment. They have quickly mastered not only the art of digital picture taking, but also the ability to download, transmit, and tag any number of photos or videos. To add to the fun, they have found that they can then print their photos at a nearby Rite Aid pharmacy or Walmart, with directions to the stores' locations, courtesy of the GPS on their smartphones.[41] They have also learned how to upload their photos to various venues on the web. In fall 2012, a young Amish teacher was summarily fired when her community learned that she had taken pictures of her students in the classroom and had posted them on her Facebook page. Although Amish techies have even figured out how to upload their recorded video footage to YouTube, nobody has yet posted live classroom scenes from one-room schools. On the other hand, if these youth are capturing an evening volleyball tournament in Mount Hope, Ohio, or Youngie at Amish parties in Shipshewana, Indiana, or Lancaster County, Pennsylvania, these previously private and local activities, whether wholesome or questionable, literally have become instantly accessible and permanently available to millions of viewers worldwide.

Predictably, these youthful Amish users have not limited their Internet access to their weekend excursions or to playing Uno, solitaire, or Tetris on their smartphones. With Amazon.com or Barnes & Noble, Amish bookworms can browse or buy from a selection of a million book or magazine titles on virtually any subject, whether wholesome or questionable. Just as easily, they have found that they can renew borrowed books or DVDs from their local library. Contrary to their parents' wishes or their church's Ordnung, ambitious youth can now find and take the necessary steps to enroll in an online GED program—and even follow up with free online undergraduate classes on subjects ranging from accounting to evolutionary biology—available from dozens of colleges and universities.

Although the likelihood of a typical Amish young person pursuing these educational choices has been admittedly small to date, large numbers of Internet-using Amish youth wholeheartedly embrace an array of exciting options easily available from the previously forbidden world of popular culture, such as movies, fashions, music, and much more. With the right apps, sports-minded youth can follow their favorite teams or watch sporting events streaming live on ESPN. Smartphone owners with a credit card can rent virtually any classic Hollywood film or new release, ranging from *The Sound of Music* to *Django Unchained*. If they are at least twenty-one, they can even order any X-rated materials available; if they are under twenty-one, they can get a sympathetic friend to order for them. In terms of free online entertainment, they can access hundreds of excerpts or complete soundtracks from full-length Hollywood or international films, past television programs, movie trailers, amateur or professional videos, and thousands of musical groups or solo performers—all available at their fingertips.

When it comes to music, today's Amish youth have an unparalleled and unlimited number of selections from which to choose. Most of their grandparents who ventured into the popular music scene in the 1950s favored country-and-western songs—Johnny Cash was a favorite—with a sizeable group also listening to "Your Hit Parade" on Saturday nights with the old tube-type radios or, a few years later, diminutive and easy-to-hide transistor radios. Many of their children, the parents of today's youth, also preferred country-and-western tunes, but in the 1970s and 1980s, a significant number of them ventured into Top Forty music and classic rock, such as the Rolling Stones, John Mellencamp, Tom Petty, and Fleetwood Mac. These youth listened on their boom boxes, which were often hidden behind a curtain or blanket in the back of their carriages. Those who adopted the new technology first, and those who had the biggest boom boxes and best sound, were regarded as being cool by their peers.

In contrast, today's music-loving young people can listen far beyond the boundaries of country-and-western songs and the classic rock of their parents. Their phones afford instant access to a virtually unlimited world of music, past and present. Hundreds of these plain youth, reared without electronic technology in their houses and steeped in singing Christian songs learned by their older siblings at the Sunday-night singings, have developed an immediate fondness for the alluring world of secular music, whether it is Britney Spears or rapper Eminem. When they hit sixteen, many youth become high-tech listeners of whatever music emanates from their smartphones or iPods. They can transfer an unlimited amount of music to their iPods from computer-owning friends, who will download hundreds of iTunes songs—sometimes for a price, but often *fer frei* (for free). From their smartphones, they can listen to thousands of free songs from Pandora or, for $9.95 a month, can get their music from Spotify, two Internet options that offer every genre from contemporary religious music to rap. In an unpublished study of Facebook profile pages, the researcher concluded that hip-hop music appeared more frequently on the "Like" list among northern Indiana Amish Youngie than youthful listeners in the other big settlements.[42] Country-and-western, however, still ranks high with music-loving Amish youth today, although their tastes reach far beyond that genre. Classic rock continues to be checked in the "Like" category on Facebook. A popular musical group from Pennsylvania, Noiz Boyz, composed mostly of youth growing up in Amish homes, has a wide following, especially in Lancaster County.

But parental concerns reach for beyond their children's musical preferences or their listening habits. In the past, parents often expressed worries about their teenage daughters acquiring a taste for soap operas or talk
shows by having easy access to television while working as housecleaners or
babysitters for English families. Today, opportunities for television watching have expanded exponentially for any youth with a smartphone, not just
those working for the English. Now these teens know how to find an almost
unlimited and uncensored number of past and current programs through
Hulu or other online entertainment services. They can call up anything
from *Leave It to Beaver* to *Friends, Hawaii Five-O,* and *Breaking Amish,* the
last two being favorites in 2012. Hulu will even keep subscribers informed
weekly as to what the currently hot TV offerings are, from *Saturday Night
Live* to Ellen DeGeneres, and all for just under $100 per year.

Not all aspects of youthful Amish preferences, however, mirror mainstream tastes and interests. In 2012 and 2013, *Dancing with the Stars, American Idol,* and most reality shows did not appear to have any significant
Amish following, except for the two well-known shows *Breaking Amish* and
Amish Mafia. Even so, young Amish viewers derided the first as laughable
and the second as a pathetic mass-entertainment hoax having no connection to Amish reality and no interest in portraying the truth. The one reality
show mentioned by a number of Amish males was A&E's *Duck Dynasty.* It
follows the members of the Robertson family, who have made a fortune by
providing duck calls and other paraphernalia to duck hunters. The family is
outspokenly Christian and committed to Christian and family values. The
television version of *Friday Night Lights,* a sports drama about teen football,
was frequently mentioned by males as a Facebook "Like." *One Tree Hill,* an
ongoing saga of two half brothers competing in high school and college
basketball, also placed high on the list of male favorites. *Two and a Half
Men,* a show about two males and the growing son of one of them, was also
popular, albeit criticized by one of the show's stars for its "filth."[43] Other
programs that rumspringa males mentioned frequently were *Family Guy,*
a Fox-produced animated sitcom series lampooning modern society; *Prison
Break,* a drama reminiscent of the 1960s program *The Fugitive;* and *Chicago
Fire,* a natural choice for young men involved as volunteers in their local fire
departments. Past episodes of these and other programs are easily located

and watched on smartphones. A commonly "Liked" set of films for males was the *Fast and Furious* series, with plots centering on car racing. Besides dramas, mysteries, and sitcoms, Amish males rated sports, hunting, and other outdoors-related offerings among their favorites.

Teenage girls, on the other hand, listed favorite movies more than they did TV shows. Frequently mentioned films were dance related, such as the *Step Up* movies and *Footloose*. In the romance category, *Dear John* tells the story of a girl who breaks up with a soldier and then falls in love with a student from a conservative college. Another film in that genre is *The Last Song*, featuring Miley Cyrus as a product of a broken home who eventually falls in love with a young man with a similar past. In the process, the female protagonist finds a new relationship with her dying father. Another highly rated film was *Like Dandelion Dust*, adapted from a Karen Kingsbury novel by the same name that centers on pain and ultimate redemption. One more preferred movie with the same theme is *Soul Surfer*, the true story of a Christian young woman who lost an arm from a shark attack and subsequently journeyed back to wholeness. Knowing the kinds of films that many adolescents watch today, mainstream parents would undoubtedly be happy to have their teenage children listing these as their favorites. Most Amish parents, however, fear that anything Hollywood has to offer might very well endanger their children's commitment to Amish and Christian values.

Discovering the Heady Whirl of Social Media

Although many large-settlement Amish parents were acquainted with movies from their clandestine rumspringa visits to local theaters in the 1970s and 1980s, relatively few knew anything about social media and Facebook until they were already entrenched among significant numbers of their youth. Even if parents had happened to hear the term "social media," most had almost no information or experience to evaluate its possible impact. But many Amish teens, especially those with a penchant for exploring the outside world and an interest in technology, had already jumped headfirst into social media. "Amish youth have always been interested in new technology," declared a father who grew up in the 1980s. When this technology combined music, mass media, instant messaging, and links with peers, it caught on with the daring end of the youth spectrum.

The general public first learned of the involvement of Amish youth on Facebook in mid-2011, when Gil Smart, a writer for newspapers in Lancaster, Pennsylvania, surprised his readers with a front-page article on this topic. Not only were most English readers probably taken aback by the juxtaposition of the two subjects, but most Amish parents would have heard about Facebook for the first time. Shortly thereafter, Johns Hopkins University Press contacted me about writing a revision of *Growing Up Amish* to address this new development. I accepted, and was subsequently surprised by many things that I learned.

Amish teens have never needed encouragement to experiment with new technologies, nor have they needed electronic assistance to locate outside pursuits or find like-minded peers. The Internet, however, has made both of these possibilities captivating and much easier. With the availability and growth of smartphones, these young users know how to post messages, share photos, and keep current through Twitter, Instagram, or Facebook by seeing what their "Friends" are posting, viewing, doing, and "Like"-ing. A few of the older youth and young marrieds had ventured into Myspace in the first decade of this century, but the advent of user-friendly and widely publicized Facebook and its competitors proved to be an attraction that many English and Amish youth could not resist.

With relatively few exceptions, I would not have known from their Facebook profile pictures or their photo albums that most of these youth came from Amish families. The majority of Amish Facebook photos for both sexes were basically indistinguishable from those of their mainstream high school and college age-mates. Almost no Amish males posed with their trademark broad-brimmed hats or suspenders. Instead, hat-wearing teenage boys chose baseball caps with the bills facing in any direction but to the front. They overwhelmingly sported barber haircuts, with a few, mostly from northern Indiana, displaying spiked or dyed hair. A small number even wore their hair in a close-cropped military style. "It is one less thing to worry about jumping out of bed in the morning," one of them explained.

Many of the males posed at their friends' requests or did their own "selfies," the almost compulsory pictures of themselves that smartphone users take at arm's length. They were attired in sports-related t-shirts, sweatshirts, or team jackets in these photos, depending on the time of year. Hunting attire, especially camo, was also popular. When out with their friends during the spring and summer months, the young men often wore board shorts and t-shirts or tight-fitting tank tops, the latter known as "muscle shirts" or "wife-beaters." In hot weather, many males simply posed shirtless in their photos. Teenage boys from northern Indiana were more likely to wear earrings than either Lancaster County males or Amish females in general. Although many big-settlement males sported necklaces and the Livestrong-type gel or rubber bracelets popularized by bicycle racer Lance Armstrong, I never observed visible tattoos. When dressing up for a formal occasion, such as eating out with several couples or with their peers at an upscale steak house, trendsetting teenage Amish boys generally wore whatever attire was currently popular with their English male counterparts.[44]

When dressed in English garb for their Facebook photos, fashion-forward females adorned themselves with an assortment of jewelry, such as necklaces, bracelets, and rings, and a few even displayed diamond-studded earrings. Also, most young women appeared to use some combination of eye and facial makeup, and many wore colorful nail polish. One Indiana observer reported: "It is very subdued. A little foundation, a light shade of lip gloss, one bracelet, one ring—that kind of thing." Occasional style-setting females even sported ankle bracelets when out with their peers. On more formal-occasion dates, such as for a limousine party in Indiana's largest settlement, teenage Amish girls wore the same kind of evening wear as non-Amish girls, often appearing in sleeveless, strapless, or spaghetti-strap gowns. Most young women in 2013 had long hair, although some had obviously trimmed it, but relatively few combed and parted it according to community standards when with their peers. Although proportionately more teenage girls than boys dressed Amish, fewer than 20 percent of the girls on Facebook wore traditional garb and head coverings of any type in their photos.[45] Of course, their Facebook pages, just like those for the males, displayed more than a smattering of selfies. Unlike the males, however, a surprising number of the young women featured pictures taken by professional photographers. Some were close-up portraits, and others were staged with luxurious props and professional backdrops. Occasionally, several teenage girls dressed up and posed together for a group portrait. Everyone dressed in the same style for the photographer, with equal numbers of portraits featuring the young women all wearing traditional Amish garb or all wearing their English clothing.[46]

Besides following mainstream dress and grooming standards, Amish Facebook users often imitated the kind of self-presentations common among their English counterparts. Many male and female rumspringa youth copied urban-ghetto or gang-related hand signs in their own Facebook pictures. Varieties abounded. Some displayed scissor-type signals on both hands; others flashed a pistol-like pointing, with the thumb raised above the outthrust index and middle fingers; and some extended their index and little fingers while they held their hand either vertically or pointing downward.[47] Most youth were probably unaware of the origin of these gestures or their meanings. The sign with index and ring fingers pointing up is called the "devil's horns" or the "devil's head" and identifies members of the notorious Mara Salvatrucha, a violent street gang whose adherents migrated from El Salvador to the United States. Upside down, the same sign forms an M-shape and is most commonly associated with heavy-metal groups, such as Black Sabbath.[48] A common pose for Amish young women was a deliberately raised chin and puckered lips. Nicknamed "Duck Face," it may or may not have been intended or even regarded as any kind of intimate invitation, but few females probably gave it any serious thought. Many Amish adults, however, would label such an expression "bold," a pejorative term used by the Amish to describe insolence or the absence of modesty or humility.

Not surprisingly, another mainstream cultural influence on young Amish Internet and Facebook users shows up in the abbreviated form of writing that has emerged with texting. In entering this domain, I had to learn a variety of acronyms (expressions that use the first letter of every word in a phrase). Texters and Internet users share generally agreed-upon acronyms. LOL is probably the most common, generally translated as "Laughing out loud," rather than my multiple interpretations as "Lots of love," "Lots of luck," or "Lots of laughs." OMG stands for "Oh my God," or perhaps "Oh my gosh" among its plain users. IMHO may be the most culturally appropriate acronym for Amish Youngie—"In my humble opinion." I was surprised to learn that some Amish youth employ the F-word expletive, commonly written as WTF, or alternatively as "What the f**k" or STFU ("Shut the f**k up"). The majority who use the F-word are male, but a few females will also employ it. Occasionally, one can find the latest slang terms for intercourse, homosexuality, masturbation, and prostitution. Although the use of these words may not equate with actual behavior, adults pray that their youth will not be either subtly or directly corrupted by them, and consequently introduce worldly attitudes and expressions into their lives, not to mention transmitting them to their younger siblings and into the Amish culture. Most certainly, no Amish ministers or parents would be ROTFL ("Rolling on the floor laughing"), an acronym that many youth would undoubtedly label "cool."

Many Amish Facebook users, like their mainstream counterparts, continue to pay close attention to what is popular among their peers. As we have seen in chapter 1, Amish youth typically have not needed to expend much time, money, or emotional energy worrying about dressing like the trendsetters. One style fitted all. In the past, those youth who were style conscious usually lagged a step or two behind what was currently in vogue with English youth. This may still be true for the sixteen-year-olds entering their Rumspringa today. Abercrombie and Fitch t-shirts and Aeropostale jackets were popular among sixteen-year-old females in 2011 and 2012, but an eighteen-year-old trendsetter in one of the fastest Lancaster County youth groups remarked dismissively, "I wore those brands two years ago, and now they are definitely out with us older ones."[49]

Today, however, since many, if not most, Amish Facebook users interact in an environment intentionally mirroring mainstream fashion values and trends, it appears to be more important and challenging to them to discern and acquire the current "in" fashions. With sufficient money, fashion-conscious Amish youth can now be stylish by English standards, since they view the same websites and ads that model, reflect, and promote the latest mainstream clothing fashions. The one setting where being stylish appears to be especially important to the faster Amish crowd is that of the perennially popular youngie beach excursions, which are the most commonly photographed destinations in their Facebook photo albums.

Besides revealing the Amish fast-track youths' tastes in popular culture,

Facebook shows their interactions with each other, especially on the weekends. In addition to describing previous parties, some Amish Facebook users will post about an upcoming or proposed party, informing all of his or her Facebook "Friends," sometimes numbering as many as 1,000, with a simple keystroke or two. "That's what we hope for," a young man from northern Indiana reported with a grin, "for news of our party to go viral" (being picked up and passed from his "Friends" to their "Friends," ad infinitum). Of course, party announcements are not unique to the Amish rumspringa culture, but a notice about an Amish party will often reach the Youngie's English Facebook "Friends," with the possibility of outsiders coming to join the party, something that troubles even those parents most tolerant of the "let-them-get-it-out-of-their-system" approach.

The social pursuits of many of the youth reflect activities far removed from popping corn, pulling taffy, and sipping hot chocolate, the typical pastimes in traditional settlements or families. Much more common are photos of Youngie displaying or imbibing their favorite party drinks. Although hard data on the drinking behavior of Amish youth is difficult to find, James A. Cates, a professional with long experience working with alcohol abusers, has estimated that probably 70–80 percent of the youth in his area "have become drunk at least once during their rumspringa years, . . . to see what it's like."[50] Others have written about the teens' attraction to beer pong, a popular drinking game in college fraternities and at Amish parties. Participants stand side by side at both ends of a ping-pong-sized table. Players throw or bounce ping-pong balls at their opponents' sixteen-ounce red Solo cups, fifteen of which are arranged in a triangle at either end of the table. Whenever the thrower lands his or her ping-pong ball in a cup, the opponent must drink some or all of that cup's contents. A Franklin County, Pennsylvania, Amish girl received dozens of "Likes" after posting a picture of a beer-pong table set up for action. Another picture showed Amish boys playing beer-pong outdoors, shielded from public view by a wall of hay bales.

In many settlements, especially the largest, Amish Youngie have historically had a subculture of alcohol use and partying with a number of youthful imbibers. Social networks undoubtedly contribute to its maintenance today. Mostly the males, but also some females, tout their love of Amish parties and frequently post pictures of drinking activities, imbibers in various stages of inebriation, drinking games, and favorite beverages. Beer is the most common drink, but pictures of youth posing with vodka or whiskey bottles also appear with regularity. A significant minority of Facebook users, especially males, flaunt their drinking excesses. Revelers from the large Amish settlements claim that at most parties, various youth become sick and throw up because of overindulgence, and it is not uncommon for some to eventually will pass out. Youth who post photos of parties or their alcohol-fueled escapades usually receive kudos for their drinking prowess or their party excesses. I have yet to see any of their Facebook "Friends" question their immoderation or challenge their behaviors or values, which most likely is a reflection of how strongly drinking is accepted by many youth as the norm for rumspringa parties.

With hundreds or even thousands of Amish youth on the Internet, one is bound to find evidence of lawbreaking or other deviances from time to time. In states where the legal drinking age is twenty-one, the most frequent illegal activity by far is underage drinking. The second is driving under the influence, whether in a carriage or, more generally, in a car. A less common but recurrent infraction is resisting arrest, usually at a party and often by fleeing the scene, primarily on foot but occasionally by vehicle.[51] From time to time, newspapers will report partiers (almost always male) harassing the arresting officers. At one such event in Indiana, revelers attempted to overturn one of the police cars at the scene. In another incident, some youth climbed a tree and dumped water on an officer below. I have never seen Amish Facebook writers urging violence against the police or anyone else, however.[52]

Although the Amish eschew violence, youth who are drinking sometimes do destructive or dangerous things. As mentioned earlier, the most potentially harmful drinking-related incident that I have heard about was related to me by a counselor who worked with Amish youth in a large settlement. He reported that a drunken young man at a barn party climbed up onto the rafters, and soon other inebriated young men were throwing unopened beer cans at him "to knock him down." Fortunately, he escaped unscathed from a possible fatality caused by a direct hit to the head or by being knocked off the beams.[53]

The most serious illegal activity—one that is less common and occurs most among the fast fringe of the big-settlement youth—is the sporadic or regular use of drugs. Cates, the founder of the Amish Youth Vision Project, believes that marijuana is the most commonly used illegal drug, but that the percentage of Amish teens smoking it is small.[54] A relatively minor handful admit to illegally using certain prescription drugs, such as Xanax, the opiates, and Adderall (or "addys"), an amphetamine employed in the treatment of attention deficit hyperactivity disorders. Although I have never seen any reference to drug activities on Amish Facebook pages, today's frequent Internet users undoubtedly know far more about drugs and drug use via the web. They can easily find portrayals of drug paraphernalia, drug deals, usage, and users' reactions in music videos, television programs, and movies. Parents worry that such exposure might provoke curiosity and tempt their offspring to experiment. Drugs are beyond the pale for most Amish youth, even the heaviest partiers, but, as the FBI's 1998 Lancaster County drug bust and a more recent arrest in Ohio over Amish drug trafficking have revealed, a serious problem exists for a small but persistently troubled minority.[55] All large communities can name some of their youth who have served or continue to serve prison time for consuming or selling illegal drugs. Most youth in the faster circles know who has tried drugs, which individuals are addicted, and who the sellers are, and at least a few can identify the suppliers. Although the number of Amish youth engaged in this level of illegal behavior is small, that provides slight consolation for the parents and families of those who have strayed so far from cherished Amish values.

A different Internet danger that may worry Amish parents as much as drugs is the possibility of their children developing intimate relationships with non-Amish youth and adults, especially if they have partied together. Parents may have more concerns about those "Friends" who could entice their offspring away from the fold than fears about Internet stalkers and seducers. Moreover, parents sense that many of those new online male or female "Friends" may have dubious or nefarious interests in striking up a "relationship" with an Amish person. An attractive eighteen-year-old, dressed for her Facebook profile photo in traditional Amish garb, told me that she had eighteen "friendship requests" the previous day. "I don't know what it is. For some reason, some people out there want to be 'Friends' with an Amish person," she said.[56] "Friendships" can also work the other way. Any curious Amish youth can initiate contacts with attractive or otherwise appealing English youth or adults on Facebook or even on commercial dating sites, including Christian ones. Parents fear that those who appear to be wholesome and upright youth may really be seeking to obtain or provide sexual services or images, either for money or for pleasure. The opportunities for derailment and disaster are ever present, especially in the rumspringa years.

As we have seen in chapter 5, Amish parenting is a much higher-stakes endeavor than it would initially appear. All parents know that their standing in the community is greatly affected by the outcome of their children, and that children who fail to "turn out right" and reject the Amish way will ultimately result in a serious loss of status among the parents' peers. Consequently, both Amish parents and the Amish community have a deep and vested interest in these transitional years, an interest that transcends the shallow curiosity or titillation expressed by outsiders. The quality and fabric of Amish society is clearly bound up in the warp and woof of Rumspringa.

Although the parents' role is primary, a number of other cultural aspects combine to strengthen the gravitational pull toward following the Amish way. The possibility of a fulfilling lifetime relationship and children to love and nurture is an extremely persuasive incentive for most Amish youth to pursue an Amish lifestyle. Following the choice of whether to be Amish or not, the most important decisions and task for Amish youth is finding a lifetime mate. It is to this important subject that we now turn.

Although courtship always took place secretly in the past, today this covertness happens only in the plainest communities. Males always initiate the dating and courtship that traditionally surround Sunday's afternoon or evening activities.
(Sean J. Hagins)

Chapter Nine

Courtship

Looking for Love

When Eli asked to take me home after the next singing,
you can be sure that I went all out to impress him.
—Eli's wife

Getting Together

Although mate selection occurs naturally in every viable society, in a separatist religious group such as the Amish, both the community and the parents are especially invested in their children's quest to find a mate. Not only do they hope that their children will marry, but all Amish parents fervently desire that their sons and daughters will find a spouse among the faithful and establish a committed lifetime relationship. Parents realize that the future of their society depends on the formation of stable family units within the Amish faith. Despite their substantial investment, however, these Anabaptist parents allow their offspring the freedom to choose or reject potential dates and mates, in contrast to traditional societies that arrange marriages in order to maintain cultural separation.[1] Such liberty carries risks, but it is consistent with their culture's belief in adult choices. On the other hand, the Amish realize that failing to place any limits on young people's dating and marriage choices can also result in a loss of members or of commitment. The community has resolved this by allowing their youth to choose whom they will marry, as long as that person is a baptized church member. They permit no exceptions to this practice, which anthropologists call "endogamy" (marriage within one's group).

No matter how much parents and leaders worry about these issues, typical sixteen-year-olds give little thought to the cultural complexities involved in mate selection. Rather, they are elated with the exciting possibilities that are emerging and are absorbed in the jitters and joys of developing a "special friendship," as they call it. Many of them worry about their inexperience and whether they will find that special friend or be found. "Others take life as it comes," declared a mother of four young children. As youth mature, they become increasingly aware that dating or courtship will eventually lead to a lifetime relationship. To be Amish almost always means being married. Indeed, remaining unmarried is usually considered to be living in an incomplete state. Community members often feel sorry for females who were "never asked" and worry about males who never marry. Singles sometimes feel that they lack the respect, status, and power that their married counterparts enjoy. Unmarried men will never be placed in the pool to be candidates for the ministry, and unmarried women are often called "girls" well into middle age and beyond.

Youth feel the pressure to join the church, settle down, and marry. "We have two sons in their twenties who aren't married yet," worried an Amish deacon. "We wish they'd hurry up and find a wife." On the other hand, an Amish woman said: "In recent years it is changing, with the girls being more content even in their upper twenties. Jobs are more available to support themselves." Although teenagers may not be thinking about power, status, financial stability, and cultural viability when they enter the dating arena, they see a clear connection between dating and marriage.

Courting, Then and Now

In the past, virtually all dating and courting relations were concealed. In *Rosanna of the Amish*, Joseph Yoder's description of a Sunday night in cen-

tral Pennsylvania during the late 1800s captures the traditional air of secrecy:[2]

> Soon after the early autumn sunset, the buggies began coming over the hill.
> The boys were bringing their sisters and maybe a sister's friend, but not
> their own girlfriends. Boys are rarely if ever seen driving in daytime with
> their own girlfriends. The greatest possible secrecy surrounds their social
> relations. The one time when prevarication is permissible is when a boy is
> charged with having a "girl" or when a girl is charged with having a beau.
> Both will deny the accusation to the last even though they know it is true,
> and that is why they are never seen together alone in daytime. They do not
> take their "girls" to singing, but they do take them home after singing. A boy
> never goes to his girl's home in daytime alone, and he does not enter the
> house in the evening when he calls on her till after her parents have retired.

A little later, Rosanna's suitor, Crist, decides to visit her for the first time:

> He had put a few grains of corn in his pocket, and when he reached the
> house he made sure that the parents were in bed. He then went to Rosanna's
> bedroom window, tossed a few grains of corn up against the window, and
> waited. In a moment he heard the window raised very quietly and Rosanna
> whispered, "Who's there?" He whispered back, "Crist Yoder." They sat in the
> kitchen by a very dim tallow candlelight, because the kitchen was farthest
> away from the bedroom where the old folks slept, and the old folks must not
> know. Secrecy was the important thing.

In some smaller, more isolated settlements, or in conservative affiliations, present practices still resemble Yoder's description. There, courting
couples still do not disclose information about their boyfriend or girlfriend,
and parents often distance themselves from their children's romantic relationships. Although parents usually learn the identity of their child's special
friend in these traditional communities, young people still try to keep their
relationships a secret from family members, sometimes not revealing or
even mentioning the name of their boyfriend or girlfriend. Some couples

had not told their parents their partner's name until they were ready to seek permission to marry.[3]

But secrecy is now the exception in most communities. Although engagements may still be kept secret, dating itself has become characteristically much more open today in most Amish communities. Young couples now routinely discuss their boyfriends or girlfriends with their families and peers. Also, once the couple has established a special friendship, the young man may appear for meals, conversation, and family activities, depending on the settlement's customs. In the Big Valley of Pennsylvania, a conservative Amish area, a young man from the more progressive Byler affiliation claimed that almost everyone in their group already knows about an upcoming wedding, even before it is formally announced in church. "Nobody around here is surprised when a couple gets published," he asserted. In the nearby Nebraska affiliation, couples keep this information much more private.

Waiting for Dating

Amish youth rarely, if ever, begin dating before age sixteen. Nobody seems to know how this became the magic age. Perhaps it relates to European or colonial American practices, or perhaps parents have intuitively recognized that early dating tends to result in premature commitments or early sexual activity.[4] Whatever the reasons, young Amish adolescents have few sanctioned opportunities to mingle with members of the opposite sex. They are always sex-segregated in church, and elsewhere (with few exceptions) they stay with their own sex to play or socialize. Age-mates and older siblings would unmercifully tease any fourteen- or fifteen-year-old boy and girl who paired off. If social pressure were not sufficient, parents would directly intervene to stop the relationship. Since everyone in each community knows when dating is supposed to begin, however, early dating is not an issue. The actual age when youth begin pairing off varies by settlement and by sex. In some communities, young males are expected to postpone dating for six months to two years from the time they begin attending the singings, even if they receive their own carriages at age sixteen. Elsewhere, all sixteen-year-olds may begin dating immediately, if they wish. In certain settlements, sixteen-year-old girls may accept a date with a seventeen- or eighteen-year-old boy, but sixteen-year-old males customarily delay their dating activities. A sixteen-year-old boy who would attempt to date in such a settlement would be regarded by everyone as presumptuous and "acting too 'high,'" according to an eighteen-year-old.[5]

Just as teenage boys receive a carriage and horse from their families to denote their passage into a new stage in life, a teenage girl's new status is often acknowledged with a gift from her family. In Mifflin County, Pennsylvania, a girl's parents may give her a corner cupboard when she starts attending the singings. In other communities, parents give their daughters hope chests. In some parts of Lancaster County, as a father explained: "Every girl around here gets a bureau while running around. A girl is proud of things in her bureau. There are embroidered pillowcases, bed sheets, tablecloths, hand towels, wash clothes, dish clothes, [and] crocheted dresser doilies."[6] In some New Order settlements, the parents of a sixteen-year-old provide her with practical gifts, such as quilts, cookware, and a treadle sewing machine. These tacitly acknowledge her new status and portend her future role as a housewife. If she marries, she will have a well-stocked trousseau and gifts from her family that she will take to her marriage.

Getting to Know You

Before a first date ever takes place, Amish young people have had ample opportunity to get to know their age-mates in the surrounding area and form opinions about them. They have interacted with their immediate peers— although with limited contact between the sexes—all their lives at church and school. In some larger settlements, their peer contacts expand rapidly when they turn sixteen and begin attending the singings. Elsewhere, they are able to interact with the opposite sex at work frolics and weddings. New Order Amish youth typically see each other weekly at their Wednesday-night youth meetings, and also at their work projects.

In some of the more conservative settlements, teenage boys and girls still play Walk-a-Mile, a traditional game that their grandparents enjoyed when they were the same age. After the singing, all of the unattached youth stroll hand-in-hand or arm-in-arm along the back roads in the vicinity, with the boys walking closest to traffic. Invariably, the males do the choosing. Traditionally, the boy who is "it" selects the girl he wishes to walk with by replacing the boy who is walking with her. The one who is "it" taps the other on the shoulder and orders him to move forward or backward so many places in the line. That boy now becomes "it," and the activity continues. In some areas, girls also choose whom they will walk with. Sometimes the activity will last an hour or more as boys and girls interact with many different young people in an informal setting.[7]

In certain parts of northern Indiana, teens get to know each other on Saturday nights when the boys go "cruising." Groups of five or six eligible girls will get together at one of their houses to await the arrival of different groups of boys who will drop in during the course of the evening. The boys may stay for an hour or two, playing games such as Uno or Rook. The girls have prepared snacks of chips, pretzels, and sodas for their visitors. "This is the way our grandchildren who are with the youth folk get to know each other," a grandfather explained. Most parents believe that this is a better setting for their teenage children to meet other youth than what they experienced during their teenage years. All of these opportunities pave the way for the young people's eventual pairing.

Dating Traditions

In small settlements, among conservative youth groups, and in New Order settlements, couples almost always begin dating or courting in the context of Sunday-night singings, the most important event for these youth. They may first meet before the singing, when the boy goes to pick up the girl he has asked out, or their meeting may occur afterward, when he takes her home, depending on the local tradition. In all settlements, however, the boy takes the initiative in dating or courtship. He may show his interest by writing a letter, or by going through a mutual friend instead of directly asking the girl for a date. She will typically respond through a third person. Having a mutual friend who prepares the way or relays the response to the invitation reduces the likelihood of public rejection, shame, or teasing.[8]

The script for the first date varies considerably from settlement to settlement. In some plainer Lancaster County groups, when a teenage boy wants to establish a special friendship with a girl, he invites her to take a walk with him after a singing. Two boys may pair up for moral support, and each asks a girl to join them at a designated time and place, somewhere away from the crowd. A young man from the conservative Lancaster County Pequea gang recalled his first experience: "A couple of my friends had walked with Ruth before, but she turned them down when they asked her to go steady. . . . I was nervous with Ruth—wow, was I ever—and had no idea what to say. You put your arms around each other and just walk for a while. Oh, we talked about the weather, small talk. After maybe ten minutes we were discovered, and a whole bunch of sixteen-year-olds chased after us, at least ten of them. I was completely red—you can't talk or visit at that point, you're so embarrassed."[9] Presenting the girl's perspective, a mother wrote, "Some [girls] have this shy feeling to a certain boy and the boy to the girl." A young man from a conservative group explained: "When the boy asks the girl to walk a second or a third time, the other youth take special notice. If anyone sees her going to his buggy after the singing without his invitation, we all know that they have become special friends." "Then when they start down the lane together in our settlement," he continued, "everyone begins to whoop and scream and shine flashlights on them. Sometimes the guys even run alongside the buggy and rock it. I don't know how this got started, but it often happens."

Even if he has not personally contacted her before, a girl often knows of a boy's interest through her friends or siblings, before he asks her to walk with him. But one woman declared, "Some girls are totally surprised when asked for a date by a certain boy." In other groups, a boy shows his interest by inviting the girl to ride with him to or from the singing. In some places in Lancaster County, a girl will typically accept the boy's initial invitation but will demonstrate her level of interest in him by the amount of care she takes in preparing the customary after-singing snack. One newlywed recalled her first date with her future husband: "When Eli asked to take me home after the next singing, you can be sure that I went all out to impress him. If I hadn't been interested, he would have gotten just the bare minimum."

At this point, in most settlements the couple begins seeing each other every other Saturday night, on the weekend that the girl's district does not have church. Sylvan, a young man in a conservative Lancaster County gang, described a typical date: "I might arrive at her house around 7:00 [p.m.]; she'll come out and help me unharness my horse. We'll play Monopoly or Scrabble or cards with the brothers and sisters or other dating couples. Around 9, the boys will go out to the barn, have a smoke, feed the horse, take a leak. Ruth fixes a snack for everybody, a Sloppy Joe maybe, some applesauce. We're sort of intent on a clean courtship. Especially Ruth. She didn't really want to, but I have kissed her a few times."[10]

In these conservative settlements or groups, courting youth still start and maintain their courtship through letter writing, even if they live only a mile or two away. Samuel, an eighteen-year-old from a conservative Lancaster County daughter settlement, explained: "Three weeks before I wanted to take Sarah home from the singing, I wrote her about my intentions. I wanted to give her a chance to think about being my special friend. Also I wanted her to talk to her parents to see how they felt. She wrote back, saying yes, I could take her home after the singing." Beyond getting acquainted, the small talk and descriptions of family events in these letters help confirm their status as special friends. They also provide a means of cementing relationships when there are restraints on their face-to-face contacts. For the most traditional youth, the arrival of the daily mail is often a time of great anticipation and teasing. Even after couples begin dating steadily, personal contacts during the week have typically been limited, and telephone conversations have traditionally been restricted and sometimes difficult to arrange. With the widespread availability of cell phones, however, a more independent youth in one of the large settlements will probably have his or her own phone and have much more contact with that special friend. In general, phones allow couples not only to talk much more frequently, but to arrange to be together more, a mother reported.

Dating in the Fast Circles

Dating among youth in the faster crowds resembles the dating practices of mainstream youth in several ways. For one thing, fast-track youth are less likely to begin dating as seriously as their traditionally minded cohorts. One older teen described it more as "hanging out with a bunch of friends," rather than settling down with that special friend. The cars and trucks of these youth make it far easier to do things with others on short notice or in more distant settings. Thus these teens interact with each other with much greater frequency, in many more settings, and probably with less seriousness and intensity than those youth who are buggy bound.

Formal dating is much less common overall among older teens in these faster crowds. Also, they are slower in joining the church, beginning serious courting, and giving up their youthful pleasures. Many of these youth would regard the kind of courtship described earlier in this chapter as quaint, if not amusing. For many, their goal is to extend the relative freedom of their rumspringa period, so they can expand rather than restrict their worldly experiences. Few of these things lend themselves to the traditional view of courtship, where a young man seeks to find God's will in choosing who will become his lifetime partner.

Dating by the Rules

Acceptable norms for dating behavior vary widely in different settlements. In all New Order groups and in several Old Order groups (such as in Kalona, Iowa, and Somerset County, Pennsylvania), young people must either be church members or candidates for membership before they can date. In groups like these, dating and courtship are synonymous, so that when a young man and a young woman finally appear together publicly, everyone assumes that they will marry. Playing the field is either discouraged or forbidden. Having to be a church member first can indirectly or directly act as an incentive to join the church. Critics of the New Order churches often point out that their youths' tendency to join the church when they are a year or two younger than their Old Order counterparts may have more to do with wanting to date than with some kind of spiritual maturity and discipline.

Both Old Order and New Order members often disparage those settlements in which the youth "date around." "We believe that courting should be that time for a couple to be sure that it is the Lord's will for them to marry," an Old Order father explained. "Finding one's life mate should be a matter of prayer." A minister was incredulous when he heard that some young men in a neighboring state had dated as many as five different young women during the previous year. He would have undoubtedly been shocked to learn that in some settlements, young men report having dated as many as forty different females before settling down, and a Swartzentruber deacon recalled one of his buddies claiming that he "went to bed with 100 girls." Whether or not this statement was an example of youthful exaggeration, "bedding" does not automatically equate with promiscuous sex in that culture, as we shall see later in this chapter.

New Order churches, besides objecting to casual dating, disapprove of long courtships, because of the increased temptation toward physical intimacy. A New Order parent explained: "We discourage dating for an overly long time, like one or two years. You do not ask for a date just for a date. You have to have a goal of searching for a lifetime companion."[11] In general, their young people do not even begin going out until they are eighteen or nineteen. Because of these factors, New Order couples tend to marry at least a year later than do most of their Old Order neighbors. All New Order groups, and many morally conservative Old Order ones, consistently advocate "pure courtships" that require totally hands-off behavior between the sexes. A well-known admonition to these youth is "Lips off, laps off, hands off." Most supervised singings, organized by parents in the large settlements to reduce rowdiness and immorality, also require prospective members to agree to these prohibitions before they are permitted to join the group.

Recognizing the danger of their children's establishing friendships with non-Amish youth, Amish communities and parents vigorously combat their offspring dating outsiders. When mixed dating occurs, the teenage Amish boys are more likely than the girls to get involved with the English. "Boys have more outside contacts and opportunities, and girls are more obedient," an Amish father explained. These separatist parents and elders overwhelmingly view dating outsiders as a violation of the New Testament teaching, "Be not unequally yoked together with unbelievers" (2 Corinthians 6:14). Based on this biblical admonition, they regard such unions as entering into an unholy alliance with the world. A concerned father asked me to pray for his nineteen-year-old son, whom the parent thought was attracted to English young women he met first at a local grocery store and later at a sales stable. Some parents require their children to either give up dating the non-Amish or else leave home. Others prefer to give their wayward son or daughter time. "Let the fire go out by itself. As they get to know each other, they will see how mismatched their ways are," a father explained.

If two young people from non-affiliated groups (those which do not share the communion service or visiting ministers, and thus are not "in full fellowship") begin dating, the person who is from the more progressive affiliation will generally face fewer objections from his or her family and church than the person from the more conservative affiliation. In general, it is more acceptable to date someone who is more conservative than somebody who is more liberal. "In the Big Valley," a young Mifflin County, Pennsylvania, man reported, "You're okay as long as you go with someone whose church still practices strict shunning." This concession was essential for Pennsylvania's Nebraska Amish, because by 2013, they were splintered into five non-fellowshipping factions. One church consisted of only one family. Consequently, all Nebraska leaders granted permission for any of their youth to date someone from a different Nebraska affiliation, a necessary compromise in reducing the chances of genetic problems from inbreeding. Some members from plain groups like theirs often worry that marrying into a more liberal affiliation will introduce new ideas and dissatisfaction with the status quo, and may even influence the member to leave for the spouse's more liberal group. Either outcome threatens the integrity of the community. Thus, in the plainest groups, adults try to keep a careful eye on budding relationships. In these communities, church members who date someone from a more progressive settlement may be warned first and then excommunicated and shunned if they persist.

The Ideal Date

What constitutes an ideal date depends on the age, sex, and settlement of the Amish youth. The one common denominator is that the person must be Amish. Many progressive Amish believe that young men in plainer communities place more value on young women whose proclivities will be useful in their roles of housewife, helpmeet, and mother—traditional traits such as hard work, perseverance, and submissiveness. In one large settlement in Ohio, teenage girls described as "plain-looking" have boosted their dating prospects by dropping from a "higher" to a more conservative group, with its greater emphasis on role fulfillment and lesser emphasis on physical attractiveness. *Family Life* and *Young Companion* regularly feature articles and stories extolling character over appearance and substance over showiness. Nevertheless, in the progressive communities at least, many teenagers of both sexes admit that a girl's looks and personality are highly valued commodities in seeking a date and a mate. And some more-progressive Amish with contacts among the plainest groups believe that even these latter young men increasingly choose dates on the basis of "pretty."

In describing the characteristics teenage girls desired in boys, writers for Pathway Publishers claimed that females admired males who embodied traditional Amish values, such as industry, strength, responsibility, and humility—in short, those that would help make good husbands, fathers, providers, and responsible church members. A nineteen-year-old in a small Amish community described the most popular boys as "kind, soft-spoken, neatly dressed, as well as outgoing and friendly." A mother of five in her midthirties, however, reported, "I always wanted a good-looking husband, and as you can see, I found one." So for at least some Amish youth, love is not always blind.

Sex, the Sacred Subject

As in virtually all morally conservative Christian groups, the Amish unequivocally advocate sexual abstinence before marriage. Because the Amish are very private, they rarely disclose anything about their sexual attitudes or behaviors to outsiders, researchers, or even to each other. Although parents know very little about this aspect of their children's lives, they are very concerned about the sexual temptations and possible intimate activities of their youth. A parent from Indiana may have expressed the sentiments of many adults in a letter to *Family Life*: "We remember when sex education was started in public schools with disastrous results. Parents need to be educated in this, but children don't need any suggestions. Maybe this would be a good time to recommend the 'Sacred Subjects' booklets, which can be parent controlled."[12] These are advertised as "a set of six booklets written by an Amish minister to help parents talk to their children about life, growing up, and keeping themselves pure." The titles are "I Wish I Could Have Confided in My Parents," "Ignorance Is Not Bliss," "To a Girl of Eleven," "To a Boy of Twelve," "Before You Date," and "Before You Marry." The set has been discreetly advertised for several years and "is available to married couples," who, one might assume, will broach these topics with their children at "the right time."

Many adults admit that they grew up with little or no overt teaching at home about sex. A middle-aged mother from one settlement said: "Our parents believed that with regard to sex, we would learn what we needed to know when the time came. I can't believe how little I knew." A mother from a very plain Amish settlement in western Pennsylvania considers that fewer than half the girls in that settlement had been told about menstruation. A researcher who developed close relationships with several Swartzentruber women over the years thinks that at least some of her plain friends knew almost nothing about sexual matters going into marriage. She reported that one bride was "shocked" on her wedding night, totally unprepared for a sexual encounter. When the researcher then asked this woman if she would teach her daughters about such matters, the mother replied emphatically, "No, I wouldn't want to scare her to death." A younger mother from a "higher" affiliation recommended that parents have "the talk" with their sons and daughters "sometime before they marry," advocating that mothers speak with daughters and fathers with sons. An Ohio Amish man felt parents should be much more proactive in providing information to their offspring regarding sexual intimacy in marriage. "If we don't do our duty and teach our kids what intimate love between man and woman is all about, they'll find out about it in a way that is dirty and lustful."[13]

To respond to this perceived omission, concerned ministers and laypersons from a New Order Amish affiliation in Ohio wrote and distributed a four-page brief entitled "Christian Courtship." Their stated purpose was to establish courtship practices based on scriptural principles. The booklet consisted of twenty-five questions and answers. For example, question fifteen asked, "Should body caresses be permitted?" The written answer advised the following:

In the earliest stage of courtship a strict "hands off" is an ideal policy. Then as mutual affections continue to grow, an affectionate handclasp becomes in order, and in maturer courtships (especially after engagement) a hand resting on the shoulder should not be objectionable. The sacred "first kiss" should be strictly reserved for sealing the engagement, and from then on a farewell kiss with a moderate embrace may be sanctioned. Caressing, such as embracing, hugging, necking, petting, or any bodily contact for the purpose of gaining any unchristian liberties, or that stimulate immoral thinking should never be permitted, before or after engagement. "Can a man take fire in his bosom and his clothes not burn? Can one go upon hot coals and his feet not be burned?" (Proverbs 6:27–28).

Ignoring Limits

Rumors of youthful sexual behavior crop up among the Amish more frequently for communities or affiliations outside one's own. Referring to a large community in another state, an older Amish man declared, "With the kind of things that go on there, either lots of the youth are using birth control or lots of girls are having abortions." He based his suspicions on the party reputation of the settlement, coupled with its low premarital pregnancy rate. When asked how he knew this, he could not support any of his allegations of premarital sex, birth control use, or abortions, however, and many adults in that large community report that they have never heard of abortions there. That does not mean, however, that none occur. "If one Amish girl had an abortion," said a mother, "you can be sure it would be the best-kept secret in the world."

Although most settlements have relatively few premarital pregnancies, among the Amish at least three of them have a reputation for "moral looseness" in their courtship. Curious about whether the rumors of premarital pregnancies were true in two of these settlements, an Amish parent examined the wedding dates from the community directories to see on which day of the week couples were married. "Couples who have to get married are wed on Sunday instead of on the traditional weekday," he explained. Using Sunday weddings as his standard, the statistics revealed that over a three-year period, between 20 and 30 percent of the weddings occurred on Sunday rather than the traditional days. An analysis of Sunday weddings and first births, however, failed to confirm his suspicions. A former resident of one of those communities declared that Sunday marriage ceremonies did not necessarily indicate premarital sexual relationships, but could instead result from other forms of unacceptable physical intimacy.

An Ohio New Order Amish minister alleged that in another settlement in his state, "at least half of the girls are pregnant on their wedding day."[14] His source was a Mennonite minister who lived in that community, and other Amish adults and youth in nearby settlements concurred with his assessment. A nineteen-year-old from a neighboring community declared: "I don't know why they have this problem. But they have always been different." Checking the community directory to determine the relationship between wedding dates and birth dates for the first child, however, revealed that premarital pregnancies accounted for 20 percent of those births, rather than the purported 50 percent. Moreover, a survey of a more recent directory indicated that early births had dropped to 10 percent. When asked how he would explain such a decline, a father in that settlement attributed it to the community's having changed the age for going with the Youngie from sixteen to seventeen, and to the ministers having begun speaking out more for pure courtships and against parents who didn't emphasize these things sufficiently. In another community with a reputation for extensive premarital sexual activity, Amish informants claimed that out-of-wedlock pregnancies there dropped significantly in the two previous years: "The ministry finally decided to do something about it by pressuring the wayward youth— and also their parents." Many Amish regard these "problem settlements" to be among the plainest or most traditional, although not as plain as the Swartzentruber or Nebraska groups.

Joseph F. Donnermeyer and Elizabeth C. Cooksey did the best-documented study on the timing of marriages in relation to first births.[15] They examined Amish directories listing all of the Old Order and New Order groups in Holmes/Wayne/Stark Counties in Ohio, with the exception of the conservative Swartzentruber Amish, who refused to participate in directories. Analyzing data on mothers who had been born between 1940 and 1969, they found that 10 percent of all couples gave birth to their first child within the first seven months of marriage. An additional 12 percent gave birth within the eighth or ninth months of marriage. "Our estimate of pre-marital conceptions is likely a conservative one," they concluded. They also compared early births among the New Order, Old Order, and Andy Weaver Amish, a very conservative group. They found that "the percent[age] of pre-marital conceptions occurring among the New Order youth was less than half the level of the Old Order youth and less than one-third of the level of the Andy Weaver youth." Many Amish and non-Amish await the results of their ongoing data analyses for those who were born in the 1970s and early 1980s.

Although the actual premarital pregnancy rate in any settlement has turned out to be considerably lower than the alleged 50 percent referred to earlier in this section, most Amish would undoubtedly consider settlements with a 20 percent premarital pregnancy rate to reflect serious moral problems. When individuals tried to explain why some places struggled with higher incidences of premarital sexual behavior, the reasons varied widely. A common explanation was, "Moral problems simply reflect problems and dissension in the church." Others speculated that parental laxness and bad examples, alcohol use, and bed courtship were to blame. Referring to the relatively high premarital pregnancy rates in certain communities, some Amish reported: "These problems have existed there for generations. The youth have simply adopted the permissive attitudes from their parents and others." A deacon explained: "If only the boys are drinking, the girls will likely keep things under control. But if both boys and girls are drinking, couples are much more apt to be involved in sex." "Yes, this was the probably the case in ―――― County," a father concurred.

Violators and Consequences

If an unmarried Amish girl becomes pregnant, the outcome is predictable. She almost always marries the baby's father, unless he is not Amish. In the Lancaster County settlements, a first wedding announced for any time other than the community-sanctioned months means that the couple "had to get married."[16] These weddings will still be held on the traditional Tuesday or Thursday, but couples are expected to restrict the guest list to relatives and close friends. Also, they are to curtail the afternoon and evening festivities. An Amish man from western Pennsylvania described a similar practice: "The wedding size is smaller and [the couple] usually has what is called a 'day-only' wedding, meaning you are invited for the wedding ceremony and dinner and expected to leave by 5 or 6 o'clock. Aunts, uncles, and other close relatives, [plus] table waiters and cooks are invited for supper and they will leave by 8 or 9 o'clock. The ceremony will be carried out in the usual manner." Festivities at emergency weddings in some settlements, such as the Renno and Byler Amish in the Big Valley of Pennsylvania, must be over by 4:00 p.m.

A deacon in a large settlement reported that young women who are in the first trimester of pregnancy will occasionally slip by with a more elaborate wedding. "When the deacon and the bishop ask the couple whether they have had a pure courtship, they lie just so they can have a big wedding," he complained. Several other informants made the same comment about couples dissembling. In some communities, urgent weddings are simply conducted at the close of the regular Sunday church service. Among Pennsylvania's Nebraska Amish, some bishops have simply refused to perform the wedding ceremony for erring couples. The pair were instead directed to seek the services of a justice of the peace to be married.

Traditionally, when word gets out that an Amish couple has been sexually involved, the church expects them to marry as soon as possible, although an Indiana mother stated that the couple would not be pressured to marry if they were unwilling or unsuited for each other. Even so, the offending couple must immediately drop out of the Sunday singing socials and all other youth activities and begin sitting in church with the married men or women. If they already belong to the church, they are temporarily excommunicated—usually for six weeks—and then married. If they are not church members but wish to be married, the ministers provide emergency membership-instruction classes for them so that they can be baptized and taken up into the church. The bishop may combine and condense the nine sessions, or allow them to go to other churches for instruction on the off-Sundays, so the couple will not have to wait to complete the full eighteen-week instruction period. The wedding will occur shortly after the couple complete the membership classes and are baptized and taken into the church. When a scribe from the *Budget* reports that a person or a couple has been baptized and married on the same day, Amish readers assume that the bride was already pregnant.

In one of the large communities, some of the single members who have been sexually involved in any way during their dating or courtship relationships confess their misdeeds before the bishop and the church and ask to be placed in the *Bann* for six weeks if they are planning to marry in the fall. When a deacon was asked why this period lasted six weeks, he responded that since Peter denied the Lord three times, the offending party is to be excluded from membership for three consecutive Sunday services. Since church meets every other week, this means that these individuals will attend church on the three Sundays but will not participate in any after-church members' meeting or stay to eat with the church members. The Amish regard Christ's admonitions to forgive as applying to anyone who repents and changes, however, so at the end of the six weeks, the erring ones are restored to full fellowship with the church.[17] Observers report that the entire community genuinely accepts the erring couple. For most Amish, sins of the flesh are not considered to be worse than other transgressions. Thus, rather than being lost to the world for their fleshly failings, those who have strayed are fully restored into the community.

One violation that seems to be conspicuous in its absence is physical or sexual aggression by Amish young men, committed against their dates or special friends. In my nearly twenty-five years of studying Amish adolescents, I have never personally encountered or even heard of a single case of an Amish young man hitting or beating up his girlfriend. I have asked numerous older and younger Amish friends if they know of such events, and, to a person, nobody to whom I have talked has reported or even heard of a single instance of date violence. I have never heard of date rape among Amish youth, either. Even though such an event must happen occasionally, I am still convinced that they occur far less frequently with Amish Youngie than with mainstream American youth. Although the possible reasons for such actions are beyond the scope of this chapter, I would hypothesize that consistent teachings and examples of *Gelassenheit*, coupled with minimal exposure to violent media and violence in the home, contribute greatly to this dearth of unacceptably aggressive behavior.

An Old Courting Custom

An alleged cause for premarital sex is *Uneheliche beischlof*, commonly known as bed courtship, bedding, or bundling, depending on the locale. In Pennsylvania German, the term literally means "unmarried sleeping together." According to Beachy, European emigrants apparently brought bundling with them to North America,[18] and it existed among the Lutheran and Reformed Churches as well as the Amish.[19] The common explanation for its origins is that premarital bedding stemmed from couples courting in unheated houses. Also, those early dwellings usually lacked privacy for the young woman to entertain her suitor. In settlements where youth practice bed courtship today, they appear to follow the same script used by their parents, grandparents, and great-grandparents. Typically, the couple retires to the girl's upstairs bedroom or to a bedroom vacated by a sibling, where they lie down together. Historically, couples reputedly used a bundling board (a rough plank separating the partners), and, as one bishop described it, each was literally tucked firmly in a separate side of the bed. The bundling board and tucking routine, however, disappeared long ago. Nonetheless, the Amish expect that when their courting youth "go to bed," they are to refrain from sexual activity of any kind.

In most places where bundling is still practiced, the teenage girls also wear a special garment, the *Nacht Ruch* or *Unna Ruch* (nightdress or underdress) for the occasion.[20] "In our settlement," a young man related, "my sister and her boyfriend had to delay because she had not yet finished sewing her dress." The nightdress often consists of fancier materials or has attractive colors that are not allowed in public or in daily apparel. In one of the plainest settlements, the girls may use pink in their underdresses, a color never acceptable in any other context. In another settlement, courting dresses are white. In one other plain settlement, the girls may wear knee-length rather than full-length dresses. Teenage girls from the Swartzentruber Amish wear underdresses and simply remove their outer dress.

Courting dresses are never sheer, low cut, or otherwise suggestive. Before lying down, the boys typically take off their shoes and may also remove their shirts, depending on the weather. In some places, couples go to bed after the other family members have retired, and the boy may stay until 4:00

or 4:30 a.m., depending on when the family arises, the community's standards, and the strictness of the girl's parents. The degree of physical activity that takes place varies from community to community and from couple to couple. In her book, Saloma Miller Furlong describes hugging and kissing (*shmunzing* activities) as being the norm in Geauga County, Ohio, several decades ago.[21] A great-grandfather from Indiana claimed to have kissed all of the forty-plus young women he bundled with, but had no other overt sexual involvement with them.

A Controversial Practice

From the beginning, however, bed courtship was criticized, both from within and outside the Amish community. The rejection of bundling was one of the major issues that led to the formation of new settlements in Illinois, Indiana, Kansas, the province of Ontario, and elsewhere. As early as 1837, the Ordnung of Somerset County, Pennsylvania, condemned any of the youth who slept or lay together before marriage. Evidently the custom still persisted, because, according to one historian, the practice of bundling in Somerset County in 1851 was one of the chief reasons for members leaving to establish a church in Johnson County, Iowa.[22] Two years later, George Jutzi, an Amish writer from Stark County, Ohio, condemned the practice; and in 1870 David A. Troyer, a highly respected Amish bishop from Holmes County, Ohio, wrote against the dangers of *uneheliche Zusammenliegen* (lying together without marriage).[23]

Almost a century later, opposition to bundling helped give rise to the New Order Amish breakaway in Ohio. They unequivocally equated bundling with immoral courtship practices. While the majority of Old Order and all New Order leaders speak out against it on moral grounds today, scattered settlements in Indiana, Michigan, Minnesota, Ohio, New York, western and central Pennsylvania, and Wisconsin still condone bed courtship. Even in those communities, however, a few parents may refuse to allow their daughters to go to bed with suitors.

An Ongoing Custom

Despite the persistence of bundling in these conservative strongholds, it is no longer standard practice in most Amish settlements. The affiliations that still accept bundling are among those that are the plainest in dress and lifestyle.[24] These groups typically seek to uphold traditional behavior in every aspect of life. Since they usually have a higher retention rate than the progressive groups, the latter sometimes charge that the traditionalists use bundling as an enticement to retain their young people. In some settlements, the practice is actually regulated by the Ordnung. Community standards for bed courtship specify the frequency, place, and behavior permitted: the couple may begin going to bed on the fifth date, bundling is allowed only in the young women's bedroom, the young man may remove only his shirt and shoes, dating must never occur on Saturday nights prior to church in the young woman's district, the couple must always keep a light burning, and the young man must be gone before daylight. The specifics vary from place to place. In some settlements, young women are permitted to remove their head covering, and in others they are not. A Swartzentruber bishop in an Ohio community where bundling occurs admitted that this practice was not a good thing, but he thought that it would be impossible for him to eliminate bed courtship. "Our people would say, 'It's always been this way.' The only way I could see a change is if someone would start a new settlement and prohibit it, like those people did in Ethridge, Tennessee, or Sonora, Kentucky."

Scholars have criticized the accuracy of many early-twentieth-century writings on bundling, but two books published in the latter part of that century provided a non-sensationalized but authentic description of bed courtship. One recounted the actual events on the occasion of a sixteen-year-old Big Valley girl's first bed courtship; the second, a novel written by an author with an Amish background, portrayed a couple's bundling experiences from the young man's perspective.[25] Both writers described the respective couples as spending most of the night together, with the young man leaving just before the parents got up in the morning. Neither book mentioned any overt sexual involvement. Nevertheless, many Amish find the intimacy of the first account, and the sexual thoughts of the protagonist in the second, to be offensive.[26]

Stories from the Past

Outsiders and critics often assume that a young man's furtive escape in the predawn hours reflects the couple's shame over questionable or immoral practices. Members of the traditional communities that practice bundling, however, explain those actions quite differently. They say that when couples try to keep their courting a secret, the discovery of a suitor's entering or leaving his girlfriend's house provides relatives and friends with a splendid occasion for teasing and for entertaining relatives and friends with the story.

An older Amish adult recalled that during his courting days, he once overslept at his girlfriend's house. Hearing her mother approaching the room early in the morning, he quickly sprang from bed, grabbed his shoes, climbed out of the bedroom window, and ran barefoot through the cornfields to avoid discovery. A middle-aged man from Pennsylvania laughingly described a similar incident. His best friend also fell asleep on a Sunday night, which necessitated an early-morning exit. He needed to cross a barley field to get home, however. Not wishing to dirty his Sunday trousers, he decided to take them off and carry them through the field. Unfortunately, as the story goes, bull thistles were growing profusely among the barley, and by the time his friend reached the other side, the thorny plants had scratched his bare legs raw.

Numerous middle-aged adults from both the New Order and Old Order Amish who are now opponents of the practice concede that their having gone to bed never resulted in sexual activity. Many assert that their bed courtship was "pure," that is, without any sexual involvement. One elderly Amish man described his courtship experiences of bundling with dozens of young women on Saturday or Sunday nights over half a century ago. He affirmed that although he hugged and kissed almost all of his dates, they never engaged in petting or intercourse. Since their community attached no shame or secrecy to bed courtship, he often greeted the girl's parents before the couple went upstairs. If bedrooms were scarce, siblings would often give up a room for the couple, or if an older sister left home to teach or get married, the mother might help the next-in-line move in and take over the vacated room.

At times friends, who would drop by to visit the courting couple as they reclined together, would sit on the edge of the bed and talk. "Sometimes their friends drank and ate a snack in the couple's room," a visitor from a non-bundling settlement reported. "When I was there," he recalled, "the girl had a pumpkin pie and a bag of potato chips for the snack." On occasion, two couples would bundle together in the same bed, with the males on the outside and the females in the middle. A grandfather recalled a time when he and his buddy bundled with their girlfriends in the same bed: "I was in the center with a girl on each side. The thing I remember most," he exclaimed, "is how hot it was with the four of us together in one bed!" A second grandfather remembered as many as six youth crowded into the same bed. Another member of his generation observed that "six in a bed is really hard on the bed." An Amish man from Lancaster County recalled going to another settlement and sitting on the edge of the bed where his friend and his friend's girlfriend were lying. "I didn't know what to expect," he reported. His host asked him whom he wanted to bundle with. "I can't," the young man exclaimed. "If our ministers found out, I'd be disciplined. You'd be excommunicated with that!"

In many settlements that have since rejected the practice, going to bed together was regarded as the normal way to begin courting. In Lancaster County, a grandfather remembered his mother telling him, "You'll be too far away to return home tonight so you should plan to stay all night with her." She then gave him instructions on bundling etiquette. Another adult recalled that his mother's advice was short and plain: "There should be absolutely no touching. Don't act like a dog." A grandfather related that he never felt that his parents wondered about whether his bed courtship involved any sexual activity. He admitted to temptation as his relationship with his wife-to-be deepened, but she would remind him of their need to remain chaste. "The more she said we had to wait," he recalled, "the more respect I had for her." Many Amish realize that moderns would find such descriptions difficult to believe. A young Swartzentruber man who left the Amish and joined the U.S. Air Force related that his barracks buddies roared in disbelief when he told them that young men in his community went to bed with young women but did not have sex. "But we didn't," he insisted.

In that same community, rumors surfaced for a time that a number of teenage girls were on the "woman's pill" or that young males carried contraceptives in their carriages.[27] The bishop was so concerned about the youth in his church that he asked the local doctor if he was providing birth control pills for the girls in his district. The bishop was relieved when the physician assured him that his medical office was not offering such services to the area's young single women. Many Amish critics of bed courtship concede that relatively few teenage girls become pregnant today in most of the plain settlements where bundling persists. A Swartzentruber Amish bishop recalled that in their settlement, only five young women over a thirty-year span became pregnant before marriage. "Our group does better than those who don't go to bed together," he declared, adding that "our young people are taught self-discipline." A retired Mennonite physician who worked with that same affiliation for more than three decades reported that he did not encounter a single premarital pregnancy from that group. A young man from an Amish community in western Pennsylvania that practices bed courtship reported that in the sixty-year history of their settlement, he also knew of only five couples "that had to get married."

"Because the plainest groups are so isolated from mainstream society," a New Order father speculated, "bed courtship might not have the same sexual meaning and temptations that it does for most Amish."[28] An Amish man who engaged in bundling before he joined the New Order, however, recalls that bed courtship led to sexual temptation for him and his fiancée. A Canadian minister who strongly opposes the custom today does so from his experience as a young man fifty years ago, when a girl from Lancaster County introduced him to the practice. "It's not lying in bed together that is the problem," said a midwestern minister. "It's when they start touching."

None of the light-hearted anecdotes or more serious explanations satisfies the critics of bed courtship, however. They interpret a community's acceptance of bundling as evidence of "moral looseness and corruption." Their strongest argument comes from Romans 13:13, in which Paul condemns, among other things, "chambering and wantonness." Opponents of the practice equate chambering with bundling and bundling with sex.

"And even if no sex is involved, it causes lustful thoughts and is a terrible witness to outsiders," they point out.[29] An Amish father who practiced bed courtship in his youth came to adamantly oppose the custom and eventually moved to another state to join an Old Order affiliation that forbade the practice. He stated: "You needn't worry about sensationalizing it. I've not yet read any accounts that truly capture the custom. If anything, most accounts make it sound rather innocent and quaint. It is not. . . . This custom may have been innocent enough when it started, but it has become a very immoral practice. As parents we shudder to think of our children falling into this."[30] An unmarried young man from a settlement in western Pennsylvania wrote: "[My girlfriend] and I have quit the practice of bed courtship in January. Since then we both feel we know each other, and can communicate better than we ever did in the previous two years we practiced bed courtship. I would not go back to practicing it again, as courtship now has a new and deeper meaning."[31] A New Order father declared, "We want to see more communication in daylight, not at night, and we want them to be downstairs, not upstairs in a bedroom."[32] He undoubtedly would applaud the decision of the Pennsylvania couple.

A Waning Custom

One by one, Amish groups have condemned and abandoned bed courtship, and churches discipline unmarried members caught in the practice. Even Swartzentruber settlements in Kentucky and Tennessee have rejected it. By my best estimates, probably fewer than 10 percent of Amish communities support or condone bundling today, far less than in the 1940s or 1950s, when it was practiced in many more settlements.[33] The decline in Illinois, Ohio, Pennsylvania, and even horse-and-buggy Mennonite enclaves in Canada generally occurred because one or two influential men spoke out against the practice. Eventually they gained a critical mass and garnered enough support to change their community's attitudes and its Ordnung. Some Amish grandparents in Lancaster County, however, believe that youth with misgivings about the practice actually initiated the rejection of bed courtship. A grandmother thought that part of the opposition came from single young women who had moral qualms about the practice. When they told their boyfriends about their convictions, "some of them dropped the girls," the woman reported.[34] "The older folk thought that it was all right because it had always been done this way, but a lot of us realized that it was wrong. The young folk eventually brought about the change," insisted a grandfather. "And we wouldn't let any of our children go to bed either."

Nevertheless, reactions in many plain communities to the critics of bed courtship reveal how deeply ingrained the practice has been. A Swartzen-truber bishop asked, "What would a couple do if they didn't go to bed? Often a boy is shy and they don't know what to say. They feel more at ease laying in bed." He also decried the traditional courting custom of the girl sitting on the boy's lap in a rocking chair, which occurs in some of the plainer communities, such as one outside Bowling Green, Kentucky.[35] "That's more of a temptation than going to bed together," he insisted. A young husband agreed: "A lot worse things have happened sitting up on the couch than laying in bed. What's all the fuss about? Our ancestors have gone to bed for generations." Another proponent of bundling concurred: "We have always done it this way. If it was good enough for our grandparents and parents, it is good enough for us. If we're not careful, we are going to drift into liberalism." Those who hold on to the custom accuse the critics of being proud and divisive, while opponents of bed courtship claim to have been ostracized and treated like pariahs by the guardians of traditional practices.[36]

Many Old Order people concede that the influence of antibundling groups like the Mennonites or the New Order Amish fostered the demise of bundling in many Old Order communities. One Indiana Amish man recalls that as early as the 1940s, his girlfriend's mother refused to let him and her daughter go to bed, explaining to her, "Your brother Aaron will be home tonight, and you know that since he has joined the Mennonites, he doesn't approve of the unmarrieds going to bed anymore." Among the Amish, the most influential treatise against bed courtship, *Ein Risz in der Maurer* (A Break in the Wall) was written and published by the late Ohio New Order Amish minister, Rob Schlabach, in the 1970s. In the opening pages, written in High German and in the Fraktur script (a practice sometimes used when the author or editorial staff judged the content to be too private or too provocative for outsiders or children to read), he claimed (somewhat erroneously, as we have seen earlier in this chapter) that up to half of the young women in some Amish communities were already pregnant on their wedding day. He attributed part of this to various causes: corrupting contact with the outside world, apathy and indifference on the part of parents and church leaders, the influence of the automobile, and the use of drugs. Most of all, however, he blamed the practice of bed courtship. After tracing its history from early Europe to the present, this New Order author, to nobody's surprise, advocated a non-physical courtship:[37]

> It may seem frigid to some but the best and most scriptural boy-girl conduct is a complete "hands-off" policy. Paul wrote Timothy to treat "the younger sisters with all purity." "With all purity" would mean to abstain from anything that gives illicit pleasure sensations and arouses the baser nature. Only after marriage is the "cleave to the wife" in its proper place. Sitting on separate chairs or a fair length couch would be in order to help maintain this. . . . Is it right for us to pray "Lead us not into temptation" when we are not zealous in avoiding temptations whenever we can? How can parents pray the evening prayer on Saturday and Sunday evening and yet have open doors to rowdy, lusty boys or allow weekly boy-girl sleeping in the home? Jesus said, "Thou shalt not tempt the Lord thy God."

Dozens of Amish bookstores sold the treatise, and many believe that this book, along with the influence of Pathway Publishers, was instrumental in contributing to change in many Amish communities.[38]

In 1999 Pathway Publishers again picked up the courtship theme by reprinting an article that had originally appeared nearly thirty years earlier. The piece did not mention bed courtship by name, but it emphasized the danger of any kind of physical intimacy before marriage. In the same issue, the editor reiterated his concern over "impure courtship standards," warning youth and their parents about the ever-present lusts of the flesh.[39] This has been a recurrent theme for Pathway editors and writers since the earliest days of *Family Life* magazine.

One warning that the editors have apparently not felt a need to write about over the years concerns homosexuality. Although most Amish are well aware of homosexuality in mainstream society, most profess to know few, if any, youth or adults in their communities who are practicing homosexuals. The Amish consistently regard homosexual behavior as aberrant, shameful, and sinful. One ex-Amish writer described, with great mortification, bestiality and homosexual behavior among early adolescents in his community.[40] In a tragic case, a homosexual pedophile who attempted to molest one of the boys in a settlement in western Pennsylvania committed suicide after he was discovered. Although outsiders may debate the reasons for so few reports of Amish homosexuals, most Amish are confident that homosexuality in their communities is rare. They simply do not consider it a pressing issue.[41]

Of much greater concern for parents in virtually all communities is their unease that their rumspringa youth's need for emotional intimacy may combine with their emerging sexuality to draw the young people into what the Amish call "carnal relations." Despite these concerns, most Amish believe that their youth are considerably less involved in sex than mainstream youth. One father asked rhetorically, "Are all Amish girls virgins when they marry? Is everybody absolutely innocent? No. But overall, I believe our youth do better than the society at large." An eighteen-year-old from one of the fastest gangs in a large settlement adamantly claims that despite heavy drinking and partying in her social circle, she personally knows nobody who is sexually active.[42]

A French reporter flew to Lancaster County in summer 1998 after the story broke about the drug arrests there for cocaine and marijuana dealing. He wanted to research and write his own story, "Drugs, Rock-and-Roll, and Sex among Amish Youth." "I found enough to write about the drugs and rock-and-roll part," he related, "but as hard as I tried, I just didn't find much evidence on sex. I still don't know what is really going on."[43] Amish parents often say the same. Most work hard to imbue their children and youth with traditional Christian values that will foster sexual integrity before and after they marry.[44] They also promote courtship practices that avoid entanglements with worldly youth, since the future of Amish society depends on their separation from the mainstream. Other than having their children receiving baptism and joining the church, nothing brings more joy to an Amish couple than having their sons and daughters find Amish mates, enter into marriage, and establish strong and lifetime unions, a topic to which we now turn.

Although the origin of this custom is unknown, in almost all Amish communities the bride, groom, and their attendants sit in the Eck (corner) during the afternoon and evening wedding-day activities to dine, receive best wishes, and celebrate.

(Doyle Yoder)

Chapter Ten

Weddings
High Times in Plain Places

Marriage is really the time when Amish youth settle down once and for all and leave their foolish, youthful ways behind.
—A young bachelor

A Homespun High Time

*H*ochzeit, the German word for wedding, literally means "high time" and reflects both the importance and the celebration that surround a central event in Amish life. This quintessential Amish experience combines all the elements of life that they value most: faith, family, friends, and community. Not only do weddings join two young people and their families in a lifetime relationship, but they reaffirm the health and continuity of the culture. They also mark the end of the couple's rumspringa experience. Adults, especially, rejoice in the knowledge that a new family unit is being formed, children will soon follow, and another generation of Amish will be launched. In an important departure from other ceremonies, the local community honors the couple and their young friends by giving them the featured place throughout much of the day's festivities. The wedding preparations and rituals serve to sustain and strengthen the values of the Amish community.[1]

Because Amish families sometimes invite English friends to their weddings, more has been written in magazines and newspapers about this event than any other aspect of Amish life.[2] In some of the most traditional communities in Pennsylvania, however, such as those in Lawrence County and the Big Valley's Nebraska Amish, as well as some Swartzentruber affiliations in various locales, English people are not invited to the actual "wedding church," although they are occasionally guests at the afternoon or evening festivities.[3]

In neighboring communities or different affiliations, most of the non-sacred events, such as preparations and afternoon and evening wedding-day traditions, vary widely and continue to evolve. In many settlements, couples marry at almost any time throughout the year except summer, but in Geauga County, Ohio, and Dover, Delaware, weddings are held even during the hottest months. Until recently, Lancaster County, Pennsylvania, weddings typically occurred only from late October to early December, on Tuesdays or Thursdays. The marriage season is not specified in the Ordnung, but the traditional fall season surely derives from farming rhythms, coming between the end of the fall harvest and the onset of bad weather.

Restricting these ceremonies to a narrow time period has not been without its problems, however, especially in large settlements. In Lancaster County, Pennsylvania, in the 1990s, 144 weddings took place in the traditional twenty-one eligible days, with seventeen weddings occurring on a single day. A nineteen-year-old girl was invited to five weddings in one day, and a bishop and his wife sighed as they related that they were invited to twenty-five weddings in the six-week period. In such situations, families reported considerable stress in trying to decide which weddings to attend and which to omit.[4] In contrast to the traditional compressed wedding season in Lancaster County, the Amish in Lawrence County, Pennsylvania, routinely extend the fall wedding season through the winter, with January being a common wedding month.

Within each particular church district, all the activities of the day are basically identical, thus minimizing individuality, choice, and differences in wealth. The Lancaster County Amish hold both wedding church and the subsequent activities at the bride's home, while in other settlements, the two events are in different houses or in a shop belonging to the family or an obliging neighbor. In some settlements, the parents of the couples have no assigned duties on the wedding day, while in others, the parents tradition- ally prepare the wedding feast and even miss the entire service.[5] Whatever the local customs, however, family, church members, and the local Amish community are invested in every aspect of this significant occasion.

Getting Published, Amish Style

Although Amish couples traditionally did not announce formal engage- ments, as English couples do, all settlements have their own script for be- coming engaged. In Lancaster County, it was commonly understood that a young man would ask the girl to marry him when the strawberry blossoms were in bloom, usually in May. "By the time the strawberries are on the bushes and the girl hasn't been asked," a father observed, "she realizes that she'll probably have to wait for another year to get married."[6] The reality today for most couples in the large settlements is that the young man must propose long before May, if not a year in advance of the upcoming wed- ding season. Otherwise relatives and friends most likely will have conflicts on that day with other weddings that have already been scheduled for that same date.

In the past, only parents and close friends knew far ahead of time about the couple's intentions to marry. The rest of the community would find out when the official announcement was made by the deacon at the close of a Sunday service. This is still the most common procedure in the small, more conservative communities or affiliations. The deacon or bishop waits to publicly announce (publish) a couple's intention to marry until one to six weeks before the wedding day. This custom originated in the sixteenth century in Europe, with the Roman Catholic Council of Trent. Initially known as the publishing of the banns, it was a formal announcement by a priest that a couple intended to marry. Later, Anglicans and other Protes- tant groups adopted the practice and brought it to the British colonies. In the past, the banns were announced in three successive Sunday services or feast days before the wedding, in order to permit church members or other citizens to disclose problems or irregularities, such as bigamy or the impending marriage of first cousins. Today Amish couples must still be published, and once the announcement is made on the Sunday after communion, they may marry as early as the following Tuesday.[7]

Permission to Marry

Depending on community or family tradition, a young man may or may not choose to ask the girl's father for permission to marry his daughter. "I was close to my daughters. They were my little girls. They all knew that they would have to get Dad's approval for the boy they wanted to marry," a father explained. Other couples simply inform their parents of their plans to marry. Because marriage and family play such a crucial role in Amish society, parents would never give their blessing to a son or daughter contemplating marriage with a non–church member. Any youths intending to marry must both be church members in good standing. Before the wedding is announced, the ministers or deacon in the bride's and groom's home districts must certify that both member of the pair are "in order" with their local congregations, meaning that they are accepting and abiding by the requirements of their respective community's Ordnung.

Typically, the young man goes privately to the deacon or bishop in his home district, states his intentions to marry, and discloses the name of his future wife and her desire to marry him. He then requests a letter signed by the bishop and the rest of the ministry, affirming that he is indeed a church member in good standing. The deacon or bishop asks him if he has been free of fornication, a sin that would result in an immediate six-week excommunication. If he is "pushing the fences" in other ways (dressing or behaving outside of the Ordnung), the minister expects the young man to immediately come into full compliance. At this stage, however, such admonitions are rarely necessary. For anyone who had been dabbling in the world, marriage is the final step into responsible adulthood. By now the wayward individual almost certainly has conformed to church standards. In some settlements, the ministers prepare a letter of endorsement, sometimes written in the ornate German Fraktur script and signed by each one of them. Finally, the suitor delivers the letter, known as the *Zeugnis* (testimonial), to the appropriate minister in the young woman's home district.[8]

In many settlements, the girl's deacon has traditionally served as the intermediary between the family and the church after receiving this *Zeugnis*, or witness. First, the young woman confirms her desire to marry her suitor. Then the deacon asks her if she has "remained pure" during their courtship. If she should say no, both she and her suitor would be temporarily excommunicated and placed "under the *Bann*" for six weeks. This not only would necessitate a change in their wedding date, but would also change the format of the wedding. The bride would not be permitted to wear a white wedding cape and apron over her dress at the wedding. Also, the couple would be required to scale down their wedding, with no evening celebrations, the same consequences for what happens if a girl becomes pregnant before marriage. Since couples rarely report sexual involvement, however, they routinely receive the church's blessing to marry.[9]

Following this conversation, in most affiliations the bride's deacon announces in her home congregation that the couple intends to marry. In the same service, the girl's father commonly invites every member of the local congregation to the wedding, depending on the settlement.[10] In Lancaster County, unless the announcement is made on council Sunday, the bride-to-be does not attend church when her wedding is published. If the young man is from the same district, he either leaves before the wedding announcement is made or else stays home to help prepare supper for the family.[11] The same night that the wedding is officially published, the couple attends the youth singing for the final time and invites either all the youth or just a select group of friends to the wedding, depending on their friendships and the space limitations at home.[12] In the past, the young man would drive his carriage to adjacent districts to invite close friends and relatives outside of the church district, but in this age of instant communication, that has been dropped in all but the most conservative affiliations. In the brief time period between the announcement and the wedding day, the couple appears together in public and begins to identify with the young married couples.

Festive Preparations

Some non-Amish writers emphasize that Amish couples do not have to worry about many of the wedding details that concern typical middle-class mainstream couples. There are no rings, wedding gowns, tuxedo rentals, bridal bouquets, organists, soloists, photographers, or reception-site rentals; no DJs or bands to hire; and usually no elaborate honeymoon plans to make. These are simply not part of the Amish high time.[13] As one observer has noted, the simplicity of their weddings reinforces the Amish values of close relationships, community, and faith, rather than calling attention to the couple's particular tastes, the sophistication of the arrangements, or the lavish expenditures that are typical of English weddings.[14] Plainness does not necessarily equate with smallness, however, since some couples invite 400 or more guests to the wedding and the subsequent afternoon and evening activities. Consequently, they can spend more than $5,000 for the day's event. In practice, however, the activities of the wedding and the wedding day are still scripted to minimize ostentatious display, so that the focus is more on the meaning and importance of the new family unit.[15]

Nevertheless, at least in the larger communities, planning a wedding is a major undertaking, one that begins months before the couple is published. One reason is that with large families, scores of relatives and close friends, local church members, and coworkers, the couple will typically invite hundreds of guests. An English friend of a couple in St. Mary's County, Maryland, counted four chartered buses, ten vans, and scores of buggies, wagons, and carts at the wedding site.[16] In addition to the local Amish, the couple invited friends and families from Indiana, Michigan, New York, Ohio, Pennsylvania, Virginia, and Wisconsin. "Nowadays," said an Amish mother ruefully, "months before the couple is published we often have to invite distant friends and relatives so that they can reserve a van and driver. Otherwise, all the drivers are already hired out long before the wedding." Because the Amish rarely employ outside caterers, preparing for this event and its many guests involves similar organizational and management skills to those required for a barn raising. Consequently, some communities have compiled a wedding-planner notebook that outlines tasks to be done, the sequence of events, recipes and quantities of food needed, and who is responsible for what. This guidebook is often passed from family to family as the need arises.[17]

How far ahead couples must plan varies, depending on the community and its customs. In parts of Iowa and Pennsylvania, the bride's parents have typically have bought and transplanted hundreds of celery plants into their garden in the late spring, in preparation for a fall wedding. This vegetable will not only be the base for the traditional hot creamed-celery main dish ("cooked with pure cream," an Amish elder informed me), but will also provide the edible centerpieces on each table—stalks of crisp, white celery hearts arranged in glasses, vases, or mason jars. Months in advance, many families will also buy dozens of chicks to raise and fatten. These will eventually provide the traditional main course that features chicken in some form.[18]

Changing Realities

Some wedding traditions, however, have given way to the realities of modern life, such as the method of inviting guests. In the past, before distant daughter settlements sprang up and phones were so readily available, custom required the groom to personally invite most of the guests. In the most traditional settlements, the couple may still send postcards to distant relatives and friends, often written with a single sentence, "Come to our wedding," giving the day and place.[19] "After all," a young man explained, "if you have lots of invitations to send out, you don't have time to write anything else." A more recent innovation, especially in larger settlements, is the use of printed invitations to the wedding and napkins embossed with the couple's names. Nonetheless, an Amish businessman in Indiana who provides this service was initially criticized for promoting formality and *Hochmut* ("high-mindedness," or pride).

In parts of Holmes County, Ohio, another non-traditional arrangement, made months ahead, is to reserve the "wedding trailers" (or "wedding wagons") built to refrigerate food, cook for large numbers of people, and provide the necessary accouterments for feeding hundreds of people.[20] Because some food preparation starts days in advance, the trailers are equipped with a walk-in cooler, a kitchen section with several propane stoves, and a sink with hot running water. They may also be stocked with folding tables and chairs, place settings, and linens. Providing this equipment and these services for Amish weddings has sparked a growing business opportunity. While Old Order Amish entrepreneurs hire pickup trucks to pull the wedding trailers to and from the sites, New Order businessmen pull their trailers with tractors.[21] Each rental unit typically costs the wedding hosts several hundred dollars. In more conservative settings, such as in Mifflin County, Pennsylvania, a few relatives or friends may lend the bride's family up to half-a-dozen kerosene or wood cook stoves for roasting the chickens, boiling the potatoes, and cooking the vegetables.

Moving toward the Big Day

In some settlements (such as Kalona, Iowa, or Lawrence County, Pennsylvania), the future groom lives with the family of the bride until the wedding day, so he can get to know the family better, help out around the home, and assist with the multitude of tasks required for the coming event. A married couple in Pennsylvania reported that in the past, "one of the traditional tasks assigned to the future groom was to clean out the manure from his father-in-law's barn or horse stable before the wedding day." In most places, the groom also begins growing his beard at that time. Meanwhile, the bride-to-be must be ready to assume many of the ongoing tasks that spring up because of uncertain communications and changing guest lists. Arranging these details reminds the couple that weddings are a communal and a family event, as well as a personal one. It provides an important and decisive entrance for the couple into full-blown Amish life and responsibilities.

By tradition and for practical reasons, the bride and her parents enlist many "wedding helpers" to assist in the preparations, serving, and cleanup. In Amish society, being asked to help with the preparations and wedding day festivities is a high honor, one taken seriously by family, relatives, and friends. Local church members often help ahead of time with food and site preparations, and afterwards with cleaning up and packing the bench wagons, or preparing the portable toilets for removal. Members routinely do this for the families of all the young women from the district when the daughters marry.[22] Early on, the bride's parents may choose a head couple to oversee all the activities, with the husband in charge of the men's tasks and the wife overseeing the women's. Cooking duties usually begin a day or two prior to the actual wedding day.

As the day approaches, the local helpers tackle the many tasks associated with site and food preparations. Often a family must build an extension to the house or shop where the wedding will occur, another cost for the bride's parents and a project that will employ many men, both young and old. It may serve as a cooking space or as a place to seat guests at the wedding. A crew of local Amish men and relatives frames the extension—which may be 2,000 square feet or more—with two-by-fours, plywood, particle board, and long rolls of heavy plastic to keep the temporary addition warm and dry. This building project may be the miniversion of a barn raising, because, with adequate preparation, the crew will often have the entire addition framed, roofed, floored, heated, and lighted in a single day.[23]

Preparing for the Feast

In all communities, the bride and her mother are free from the worry and responsibility of actually planning the menu for the wedding feast, since it is the same throughout the community. In Lancaster County, the three main dishes for the noon meal are chicken that has been roasted and removed from the bones and combined with bread stuffing and celery; heaping bowls of mashed potatoes and chicken gravy; and the traditional creamed-celery dish. Additionally, the family serves pickled cabbage; homemade applesauce; bread; traditional sweets and sours; and, for dessert, home-canned fruit, tapioca pudding, cookies, pies, and doughnuts. Although the specifics of the meals vary from settlement to settlement, the wedding dinner in almost all communities features some form of chicken and mashed potatoes with gravy.[24]

To accomplish all of the above, on the day before the wedding, the cooks and helpers work inside the house, shop, or newly built addition, plucking and preparing dozens of chickens, scrubbing potatoes taken from potato cellars or fifty-pound bags, and dicing bread for the stuffing. In Lancaster County, Pennsylvania, friends and relatives—often the grandparents and their cohorts—choose celery stalks for the centerpieces, dice gallons of celery, and fill dozens of roasting pans with plucked and cleaned chickens.[25] Nearby, or outside if the weather is clear, a team of four men spread out new plastic tarps or even bed sheets to blend the ingredients for the famous Lancaster County *Roascht* (consisting of stuffing bread, celery, and spices) that will be mixed with the roast chicken morsels.

In Lancaster County on a typical wedding morning, three or four men help their wives prepare the *Roascht* for baking, and three or four couples boil and mash the potatoes.[26] Additionally, pairs of local church women are assigned to take charge of other cooking details: two women to cook the creamed celery, two to prepare the pickled cabbage, two to make the gravy, and two to insure a constant supply of fresh-brewed coffee. These same women later oversee some of the afternoon cleanup. Other couples are assigned to set the tables and serve the guests.

Meanwhile, the *Vorgeher* (those who go before), or ushers, are honored family members or relatives who are charged with the layout of the dining area and are also responsible for supervising setting up the tables and benches immediately following the end of the service. For large weddings, the local church's bench wagon, and others from nearby church districts, have been dropped off at the house. These horse-drawn wagons, approximately the size of three carriages lined up end to end, transport the benches, hymnbooks, dishes, and several folding chairs for the elderly to use in church services throughout the district.

In settlements where the wedding church and wedding reception are held in the same location, the ushers meet on the morning prior to the wedding to survey the space available for the reception and "draw up a map" to show the layout of the tables and benches. Each table consists of three church benches, the legs of which slip into slots in a pair of plywood trusses, one at either end of the benches, and then clamped. The trusses elevate the three benches to table height and hold the tops flat and parallel with each other. All benches are marked with chalk, so they will be accounted for and quick to put together. The ushers typically assemble the tables and mark the floor in a trial run the day before, so that on the wedding day they will know exactly where every table belongs. As soon as the service ends, the ushers are responsible for making sure that volunteers place each set of three benches into its trusses, place all the tables in their preassigned spots, and set benches on both sides of every table. This transformation from church benches to wedding tables takes only a few minutes. As soon as the tables are in place, the servers place a white covering on each one. In those settlements where wedding church and the reception are held separately, the tables will have been set up ahead of time.

Volunteers report that they find working together at a wedding, whatever their assigned tasks—both in advance and on the wedding day itself—is remarkably stress free and energizing. Their labors will insure that at the wedding feast and the evening meal, the food will have been lovingly prepared, abundant, and, if all goes well, timed to be served hot and fresh. Meanwhile, what could be more satisfying than enjoying fine fellowship while creating a special feast honoring the union of a new couple and celebrating the formation of another Amish family? When the relatives and volunteers finally finish the preparations for the big day and have savored their evening meal together, those who have traveled from a distance will typically spend the night in church members' homes, in order to continue the fellowship and be close by and ready for the big day's activities. It is not by accident that working together to provide a smooth-running and joyous experience strengthens long-standing family and friendship ties.

The High Time Wedding Day

For all of those directly involved, the wedding day actually starts in the predawn hours. If the bride lives on a farm, the family will want all the cows to be milked and all chores completed long before the first horse-drawn carriages rattle down the lane. The hostlers, often young teenage boys who are relatives of the bride, care for the dozens of horses and carriages.[27] In some settlements, such as in Kalona, Iowa, the wedding party will be seated upstairs until the wedding begins. In the large Lancaster County and Holmes County settlements, the bride and groom sit down together on a bench or in chairs—either inside or outdoors, depending on the weather and local custom—with each flanked by their two *Newesitzer* (side-sitters, or attendants), who serve as witnesses for the wedding.[28] Arriving guests file past the seated wedding party to shake hands and offer their greetings and well-wishes. The bride and groom always wear new clothing, but they dress the same as they would for any regular church service. Their garments are indistinguishable from their side-sitters' clothing.

Each community has its own customs for acceptable wedding apparel. In most places, the bride and her two side-sitters wear the same color dresses, sewed either by themselves or by their mothers. In Lancaster County, tradition calls for navy blue, teal blue, or purple wedding dresses.[29] In some western Pennsylvania settlements, tradition, or even the Ordnung, requires brides and their attendants to wear robin's-egg blue dresses. In other settlements, the three young women arrive in their traditional black head coverings, denoting their unmarried status, but shortly after the ceremony the bride will exchange her black *Kapp* for the traditional white covering worn by married women. The groom and his two attendants also dress in their typical Sunday black and white. Among the most conservative gangs in Lancaster County, they, and sometimes the fathers of the bride and groom, wear black bow ties, a curious anomaly for otherwise plain attire. For the ceremony, the Lancaster bride and groom are shod in old-fashioned high-top shoes, normally worn only by older church members and by ministers and their wives. That day, the groom also adopts a broader-brimmed black hat, denoting his new status as a married man.[30] After the wedding, the couple will wear their wedding clothes as normal Sunday garb, although in Lancaster County and elsewhere, the bride puts away her new white cape and apron, which will be saved for her burial.[31]

When the appointed hour finally arrives, parents and grandparents typically enter the building first, followed by the ministers and other members of the *Freindschaft* (extended family). Some traditions call for the unmarried siblings of the groom to lead the procession of the young people, followed by the wedding couple's newly married or soon-to-be-married friends. The ushers show the guests where to sit, arranged by age and sex. Typically, these ushers are brothers or sisters of the couple and are regarded as important participants, not only in planning the seating, but also for following traditional protocol in where the guests are placed. Once they are settled in, everyone except the very old (who have chairs) and the wedding party sits through the three-hour service on the regular Sunday backless benches. English guests generally sit on chairs in the back.

The wedding service and ceremony are simple and have changed little over the years. Virtually everything is prescribed, and everyone knows the script. A description of an Amish wedding service in the 1950s seems remarkably comparable to a contemporary Amish wedding. In all settlements, the wedding church is similar to a regular Sunday church service in both format and duration. The proceedings are always conducted in a mixture of High German and Pennsylvania German, and the songs and sermons pertain to marriage. An English-type wedding rehearsal is never necessary or held, although the designated overseer may have taken a few minutes to walk the couple through their seating and standing protocol. Since the couple has already observed many weddings of family members and friends, however, this walk-through is mostly to allay jitters. Unlike some mainstream weddings, where the church service and ceremony appear to be secondary to the conspicuous attention paid to the bride, the groom, and the aesthetics of the setting, Amish weddings are solemn occasions, and, as such, all couples comport themselves with restraint and reserve. The sacredness of the event takes precedence over the preferences, personalities, and tastes of the individuals being married.[32]

Premarital Counseling

As the congregation begins singing the first traditional wedding hymn in German, the participating ministers rise and file out of the service, followed by the couple, who go with them into the adjoining upstairs or basement "counsel room" for the *Abroth*, a time of admonition and encouragement. Everyone is seated, with the bride and groom sitting together, facing the ministers, who are in a semicircle. The couple is first asked by the bishop why they are there, if they are free from sexual relations with others, and, finally, if they are free of fornication with each other, the last being the same question asked earlier when they first expressed their desire to be married.[33] If they should answer no to this last query, the bishop would immediately terminate the wedding. The ministers would then discipline the couple by temporarily excommunicating and shunning them for six weeks.[34] At the end of that time, they would be restored to fellowship and duly married, usually at the end of the Sunday church service. Both a deacon and a minister told me that they had never heard of such a last-minute, pre-wedding confession in their lifetimes. "I wouldn't want to say that a lot of couples lie," the minister declared. "Let's just say they couldn't face up to telling the truth." A bishop's wife added that erring couples generally have confessed such transgressions beforehand, rather than on their wedding day, to resolve those problems.

After the couple answers the questions satisfactorily, the ministers and bishops in attendance, often numbering a dozen or more, give counsel and encouragement to the couple. A minister described the kinds of admonitions that couples receive in his affiliation: "Try and prevent the first argument, forgiveness, be helpful in church matters as well as in the neighborhood. The groom is admonished to make his wife's life easier during the pregnancy, etc. They are told that husband and wife need to be *best friends* as well as lovers. . . . This is considered a *serious* lifelong project."[35] A young mother recalled that she was admonished, when "sewing clothes for our family, to stay decent and not [add] so many little fancy extras."[36] Depending on the bishop, the couple may be instructed that marital relations are acceptable any time except during menstruation, the wife's "monthly sickness." Some have told the couple that "this is the time for the woman's body to cleanse itself." "Not having relations during that time of month comes from one of the books of Moses," a minister explained.[37]

Also, in many areas the couple is advised to follow the example in the apocryphal book of Tobit, in which Tobias and his bride, Sara, fasted and prayed on their wedding night instead of engaging immediately in conjugal relations.[38] A young mother stated that she and her husband-to-be were admonished "to not come together as the *dumme Vieh* [dumb animals]." She reported, however, that the bishop did not elaborate as to what he meant by that. When asked if ministers ever counsel couples about birth control, a bishop responded, "Seldom, if ever, because children and large families are considered a blessing." In some affiliations, bishops tell the couple that they should not attempt to prevent pregnancies. In almost all settlements, this twenty- to thirty-minute session with the ministers is the only formal premarital counseling that the couple receives, although in at least one area in northern Indiana, the couple is expected to meet with the ministers for three such sessions before their wedding day.[39]

Wedding Songs and Sermons

While the ministers are counseling with the couple, the congregants are singing the opening hymn.[40] In Lancaster County, this first piece is a song that describes the church as Christ's bride. The assembly then turns to the "Loblied," the sacred hymn of praise sung at Amish worship services everywhere. Near the end of that song, which may last for nearly twenty minutes, the bride and groom return from their instruction period, rejoin their attendants, and the six of them take their places on the special benches or chairs in front of the ministers. The groom, flanked by his two attendants, usually sits facing the bride, who, with her two attendants, is seated about four feet away. In most places, at this point the congregation sings a third hymn emphasizing the relationship of the church as Christ's bride.

Then the minister, often a relative of the groom, rises to deliver the first sermon, focusing on Old Testament examples of good and bad marriages, from Adam and Eve through Noah and his sons who found wives. This opening sermon may last for a half hour or more. At its conclusion, everyone kneels in silent prayer, and then rises and stands for the reading from Matthew 19:1–12, a passage in which Jesus teaches about divorce. This is the only time in the first two hours that the congregation stands. Next the presiding bishop, frequently either a relative of the bride or groom or else the bride's home bishop, delivers the main sermon.[41] He resumes the biblical narrative with Abraham and the experience of the patriarchs, as recorded in Genesis. The bishop recounts their relationships, strong or flawed, and eventually mentions King Solomon and his disobedience in choosing many wives. Finally, the bishop reads from the Apostle Paul's instruction on marriage in 1 Corinthians 7 and Ephesians 5:22–33.

Based on the bishop's understanding of these scriptures and his life experiences, he instructs the couple on how to begin a godly home of their own and how to treat each other with love and respect. He admonishes them to be faithful members of the church and urges them to help others in need. Traditionally, he then moves to the story of Tobias and Sara from the intertestamental book of Tobit. The bishop emphasizes youthful Tobias's good works, the young couple's fasting and prayers, and the active intervention of Raphael, an angel sent from God, on their behalf.[42] The Tobias narrative precedes the wedding vows and may last for forty-five minutes. In many settlements, the kitchen helpers leave their tasks and come in to hear at least part of the main sermon and witness the marriage ceremony.[43]

Securing the Lifetime Knot

As the bishop ends this part of the sermon, he says, "Now here are two in one faith," using their full names or referring to them as "this brother and sister." He then asks those assembled to speak if they know of any scriptural reason why the two young people seated before them cannot be married. "You should let yourself be heard now," he intones. Some bishops have been known to pause as long as half a minute before proceeding.[44] The bishop then invites the couple to stand before him, saying, "If it is still your desire to be married, you may in the name of the Lord come forth." The groom then rises, takes the bride's hand, and they stand before the bishop to take their vows. He asks the following questions, calling each by name the first time he addresses them:

1. Do you believe and confess that it is scriptural order for one man and one woman to be one, and state that you have been led thus far?
2. Can you, brother, state that the Lord directs you to take this sister as your wife?
3. Can you, sister, state that the Lord directs you to take this brother as your husband?
4. Do you promise to support your wife when she is in weakness, sickness, what trials may befall you, and stand as a Christian husband?
5. Do you promise to support your husband when he is in weakness, sickness, what trials may befall you, and stand as a Christian wife?
6. Can you vow to remain together and have love, compassion, and patience for one another and not to part from one another until the beloved God shall part you in death?[45]

After the couple has assented to each of these questions, the bishop may read, "A Prayer for Those About to Be Married" from the *Christenpflicht* prayer book. This prayer states that the Amish understanding of marriage is "for the procreation of the human race and to avoid impurity."[46] Then the bishop, quoting from Tobit, joins the couple's right hands and holds them together in his own hands. He says, "So Raguel took the hand of his daughter, and placed it in Tobias's hand and said, 'May the God of Abraham, and the God of Isaac, and the God of Jacob be with you and help you together and give his blessings richly to you, and this through Jesus Christ. Amen.'" He concludes: "Go forth in the name of the Lord. You are now man and wife." Although the entire service might last more than three hours, the ceremony itself takes less than five minutes.[47] With no trace of emotion, the newly married couple returns to their seats. The bride and groom do not kiss, nor does the audience break the solemnity of the occasion with nods or affirming smiles. The Amish would regard such actions as frivolous and see them as a serious breach of decorum for such a momentous occasion.

In most Old Order churches, the bishop then resumes his sermon, and for the next ten or fifteen minutes picks up on the theme of the day, often recounting the rest of the Tobit story. When he finally concludes, he calls on five or six ministers to comment on the message or add thoughts of their own. In many places, these individuals will be the bride's bishop and the groom's bishop (if they did not preach), then ministers who are relatives of the bride and groom, and, in some places, the groom's father and the bride's father. These *Zeugnis* (testimonies) usually add about twenty more minutes to the service. In many areas, the congregation kneels while the presiding bishop reads again from the *Christenpflicht* prayer book, which includes a sober petition: "May they also enjoy the benefit of Thy divine comfort in all the affliction, suffering, and forthcoming troubles they meet in their married life." After the bishop recites the Lord's Prayer, the congregation rises from their knees and sits again to sing the final wedding song.

Center Stage in a Corner: The Festivities Begin

The three-hour wedding church service follows essentially the same script in virtually all settlements. Part of what subsequently happens is also standard everywhere, such as serving the wedding dinner to all guests, followed by an afternoon singing. The mood, pacing, and later events vary considerably from settlement to settlement, however, depending on the affiliation and the local customs that have developed over the years. In more progressive circles, the mood and focus shift rapidly from the solemnity of the wedding church to the newlyweds and the invited youth. The afternoon and evening events may range from being restrained (more likely in small or conservative settlements) to light and even jovial (in the large settlements).

In most places, the center for the wedding-day festivities is in the *Eck* (corner), a designated corner in the house or shop where two long rows of tables and benches converge in a right angle. The bride and groom sit at that convergence, flanked by their attendants, peers, and soon-to-be-married relatives. Nobody seems to know how this unique seating arrangement started, but until this century, virtually all Amish receptions featured the *Eck*. By 2013, a few scattered couples were following the mainstream custom of having a central table at the front of the room. Lancaster County Amish reputedly lavish more attention on the *Eck* and the new couple than do most Amish elsewhere. Lancaster couples appoint at least three married siblings or close relatives and their spouses to meticulously prepare and oversee the head tables in this corner. They set out and display the new china service for the wedding party, the groom's traditional gift to the bride. They also load the table with the special wedding-day presents of sweets-filled bowls, called *Eck Schissle* or *Eck Sach*. These gift bowls are covered with clear plastic wrap, bedecked with ribbons, and accompanied by a card showing the givers' names and a message of congratulations and blessing. Most other settlements have no close equivalent to these *Eck Sach*.

When the servers indicate that the meal is ready, the wedding party enters the dining area first, followed by the unmarried youth. In many settlements, the young men and women divide at the ends of the tables as they enter, with the males filling in one side and the females sitting across from them on the other. Once the youth are seated at the tables, the *Ecktender*, or wedding-corner helpers, serve these young people. At this meal, unlike the normal practice at any other occasion, the servers attend to the youth first, while the adults converse and watch the Youngie. The *Ecktender* in Lancaster County are often the aunts and uncles of the bride. The helpers may also treat the bride and groom to special snacks or their favorite foods.[48] In Lancaster settlements, the couple is often served rice pudding or tapioca pudding in wine glasses. During the meal, the bride shares many of her gift bowls of sweets from the *Eck*, sending them down the tables to designated friends or relatives who sample the contents. The dishes themselves, however, are to be gifts for the couple, and the bride will display and use many of them in her own home in the years to come.

Depending on the couple's church affiliation or district, families may serve wine to wedding guests, or, in parts of Indiana, Ohio, and Pennsylvania, to the wedding party. Wine was traditionally served at weddings in most settlements, at least to the wedding party, but that custom has diminished over the years. An Amish elder opined, "I think it died out in many places because it was abused." Instead of wine, in some areas of Lancaster County the *Ecktender* serve the wedding party and their close friends ginger ale or punch laced with ginger ale as an alternative to wine. Wine is making a comeback in some areas, however, at least for the wedding party. In parts of Lancaster County, the newlyweds and their side-sitters are served wine in the evening.

In Lancaster County today, relatives may wait on tables for the adults after the youth at the "first sitting" finish eating. Following the noon dinner, the rest of the young guests have several hours free for various activities while the adults eat, often in two more shifts, depending on the size of the wedding.[49] During that time, the *Ecktender* may sit at the *Eck* on behalf of the bride and groom while the couple leave the dining area to receive and open gifts. Often, unmarried sisters or cousins have been appointed to record all gifts and those who visited.

Gift-Giving: Housewares and Hardware

Gift-giving traditions for invited guests vary among the settlements. In Holmes County, Ohio, and many other locales, all guests bring their gifts to the wedding. In Lancaster County and parts of the Big Valley in Pennsylvania, however, only distant visitors and English guests arrive with their wedding offerings. The others will present their gifts when the newlyweds visit their homes in the next months following the wedding. The bride and groom may open their gifts later in the day, but in some places, the bride will appoint friends or relatives open and display the presents in another room or even outside, depending on the settlement and the time of year.

Typically, most items reflect the Amish values of practicality and simplicity. One English visitor described the display as a combination hardware store and housewares department. Male guests normally bring gifts for the husband, and females bring presents for the wife. Besides the traditional dishes, pots, pans, cutlery, canners and canning jars, and roasters that the bride will use, guests may give push or power lawn mowers, weed whackers, garden hoses, hoes, rakes, and watering cans—tools appropriate for the lawn and garden caretakers, usually females in most settlements. The husband often receives carpentry tools or work-related equipment, such as hammers, screwdrivers, tape measures, shovels, and wheelbarrows. A non-Amish visitor counted twenty super-size cans of the lubricant WD-40 and a pair of heavy-duty wire cutters in the wedding display. An Amish groom admitted: "I liked it when someone took a $20 bill from his pocket and gave it to me. Then I could get what I really wanted." In Lancaster County, women often give the bride presents in her favorite color. Sometimes friends will give family gifts, such as a picnic table or lawn furniture, or even some that are simply for fun, such as a croquet set, jigsaw puzzles, and board games. "There's no competition or status symbols involved," a man declared, "but people do think about how these gifts compared to their own wedding."[50]

In the past, the parents of the bride provided a cow for the couple to help them get started, and this practice continues in some of the more conservative and rural settlements. Today, however, with increased prosperity, the bride's parents usually give the newlywed the essentials for housekeeping, and the groom's family provides the couple's first lodging—fixing up an adjacent building or preparing a separate part of the house for them. The gifts from the bride's family consist of the furniture, housewares, quilts, linens, and clothing that she brings to the marriage. Most likely this is a remnant from the early practice of providing a dowry, although few use that term today.[51] The household gifts from the bride's parents may easily exceed $5,000, an amount equivalent to what they have invested in the wedding. A young housewife pointed out to visitors the things that her parents had given her when she was married. They included the dining-room table and chairs, the corner cupboard, a dry sink, a china cupboard, a hutch, a bureau, their bedroom suite, a gas stove, a stainless steel cooking set, and a sewing machine. Her husband explained, "My dad helped us get on our farm by selling it to us at a very low price." A great-grandmother from southern Indiana received a farm from her family when she married during the Great Depression.

Festivities and Song

By midafternoon, when the last guests have finished eating and the dishes have been cleared, benches are set around the main dining area in preparation for the afternoon singing. One of the men from the couples in charge goes outside to call in as many youth as he can to come back for the afternoon singing. Songbooks from the local church districts are then distributed. Traditionally, everyone knows what songs will be sung first. In some communities, adults do most of the singing, and the music serves mainly as a backdrop for youthful conversation and gaiety. The bride may send more of her gift packages of sweets down the tables for the couple's special friends and guests to sample. From time to time, people will leave the singing to look at the gifts, the candy dishes, or the cakes. This singing lasts until late in the afternoon in parts of Pennsylvania, or ends as early as 3:30 p.m. in Ohio New Order groups.

"How many [youth] come back in depends pretty much on how fast a gang the [bridal] couple was running with. The faster the gang, the fewer come in for the afternoon singing," a young Amish man explained. In some large settlements, a portion of the young people, against the wishes of their parents, will leave the wedding grounds for a time and gather at a nearby house to be away from the adults and with their peers. Some of them may amuse themselves with card games, either with regular playing cards or a special Rook deck, depending on the settlement or gang. They may also join in recreational activities, such as ping-pong, pickup volleyball, or other on-site options. If the youth are accustomed to drinking alcohol with their peers at weddings, it generally starts during this unsupervised time.

At some point in the afternoon's activities the groom's unmarried peers follow the old custom of capturing him and pitching him over a fence into the waiting arms of the young married men. This symbolizes his change of status. An English visitor observed a variation of this custom at the Maryland wedding mentioned earlier in this chapter:

Some of the young, newly married men were horsin' around near the pasture. I am not sure what it is called that they were doing, but as Omer explained, he said, "There is an old saying that you are not truly married until you are 'thrown over the fence.' . . . So the young men were taking this year's newly married men—all except Raymond [the new groom]—and tossing them over the pasture fence. There were so many men on both sides of the fence it looked like they were playing volleyball with the young men. My husband said it looked like a rock concert. Every time they were successful at sending a newly married over the fence, you would hear the crowd yell out "Yeah." Likewise, the young women entice the bride to unwittingly step over a broomstick in her symbolic rite of passage into marriage. This custom is still practiced with high energy and enthusiasm in many areas.[52]

Pairing Off

At most weddings, the second meal, or wedding supper, is served late in the afternoon. Local custom dictates who is in charge of preparing this meal, which has its own traditional menu. Although it varies by settlement, the supper usually features chicken again, with some kind of potatoes, vegetables, and more desserts, including ice cream. In traditional and progressive settlements alike, the events surrounding the wedding supper and the subsequent singing are the most exciting part of the day. After the adults have eaten first, the youth are paired up and enter as couples, and they will eat and remain together for the evening singing. At the wedding in St. Mary's County, Maryland, the English guest captured the excitement and mixed emotions that many youth experience prior to the pairings. "Emma and Raymond [the newlyweds] emerged from the house with a notebook and were immediately surrounded by young men. I asked Solly Jr. what that was all about. . . . He said that if a young man has a steady date, they are paired to sit with each other at the evening meal. Those who do not have steady dates give their requests of whom they would like to be paired with to the bride and groom. The bride and groom then turn the list over to the seaters, and they will be paired for the evening meal. He said a lot of young people are shy, and this is a good way to break the ice and get to sit with a girl you have your eye on."

For many youth, especially the youngest teenagers, this part of the wedding is both stressful and exhilarating because it will be their first occasion to be paired up with someone of the opposite sex. Sixteen-year-old boys may worry about whether they will know the girl they get assigned to or whether she is somebody they like. Until they gain enough courage, many of the younger males will request a cousin as their partner to avoid embarrassment. "At my age," a twenty-year-old explained, "you just learn to take it as it comes and don't get all excited or upset." Girls often have a different concern. In many settlements, single females outnumber single males, so the fear of not being chosen by a boy and having to file in with a female peer may cast a pall on the day's festivities. If boys outnumber girls at a wedding, however, they apparently accept being paired up with another boy better than girls who have not been chosen. As one young mother recalled, "I'd say that girls in general don't want to be left over."

Typically, the bride has already worked on compiling the list of couples who will sit together at the evening meal.[53] If someone fails to show up, she must rearrange the seating on the spot. "If the boys have a preference," a father in Lancaster County explained, "they tell the bride. The girls have no choice." The bride may try to accommodate the young men's wishes, but she has the final say.[54] "Her closest friends get their choices first, her family next, and the church youth get whoever is left over," an unmarried man grumbled. A twenty-one-year-old single male from Pennsylvania's Big Valley complained, "Out here it may take more than two hours to get all of the couples together. Lots of youth don't want to go with the person that they were assigned to, so there's lots of requests and changes. Here the *Newehocke* [side-sitters] will help the bride arrange things."

The Grand Entrance

After the couple's list is completed to the bride's satisfaction, all of the youth assemble outside (weather permitting), with the males in one group and the females in the other. In an atmosphere charged with suspense, one of the groom's attendants begins reading off the names of each couple, calling out the young man's name first, then his partner's name. The two young people leave their respective groups, join hands, and form a waiting line.

Once everyone is paired, the bride, groom, and their attendants lead the procession into the dining room. In some settlements, they are followed by those couples who were recently married, then by those who will be married later in the fall, next by those who are seriously dating, and, finally, by everyone else. In settlements where this arranged pairing occurs, the older guests anticipate the Youngie's entrance to the wedding supper. In some places, curious adults—especially women, according to one report—crowd around both sides of the entrance. One Amish man declared that these avid spectators are looking for potentially budding romances and hoping to obtain grist for future gossip, speculation, and teasing. Even an Amish father declared, "It's interesting to see who's dating and who might marry sometime in the future."

Sometimes parents find out for the first time whom their children are interested in. The English visitor reported the onlookers' reactions at the wedding in St. Mary's County, Maryland: "One of my adult friends, Simeon, said that the adults ALL watch the entrance of the young folks . . . see who is sweet on who. And they do! When the young folks were called to the table, a hush fell over the crowds and everyone moved close to see who was paired with who. It was quite cute to watch these nervous young men walk in with their dinner dates. . . . It had to be especially unnerving for them knowing ALL eyes were on them. The crowds were quiet except for whispers and giggles." A New Order mother noted that at their weddings, "we try not to have 'gazing lines' watching the young people." More recently, some weddings, notably in northern Indiana, have dropped the custom of pairing off for a grand entrance, thus reducing stress for both the planners and for youth who fear being left without a partner or find themselves placed in an awkward or undesirable arrangement.

More Feasting and Festivities

Most Amish settlements have not yet picked up on the mainstream custom of the newlyweds cutting their wedding cake. In Lancaster County, after the meal is finished the servers cut the cakes, which are home-baked gifts from a score of close friends and relatives that are on display at the *Eck* table. In settlements where the bride's family is responsible for providing the cakes, one participant reported spending an entire day baking angel-food cakes.[55] In Lancaster County, many friends decorate their gift cakes with themes commemorating events in the couple's lives together, their occupations, or a hobby. If the bride was a teacher, the couple might get cakes with a school-house or school-bell theme; if the couple liked to ice skate, they might get skaters on a mirror pond; or if the groom was an avid softball player, the cake might be shaped and decorated like a baseball diamond. Cakes at New Order weddings have traditionally been decorated only with icing flowers or a small Bible on top.

In various settlements, cake with ice cream is still considered an important traditional dessert, especially in Lancaster County, where young couples share from the same dish. In parts of the Big Valley in Pennsylvania, the bride usually sends plates of cake, along with other sweets from the gift dishes, as her thank-you to the cooks and helpers. Most northern Indiana weddings feature a large wedding cake, sometimes baked by a local Amish person who does this as a part-time business.

Meanwhile, the bride and groom preside at the *Eck* and receive the best wishes and farewells from early-departing guests. In the past in Lancaster County, the groom and his attendants passed out cigars to the men, but that custom has disappeared in all but the most traditional Amish circles. Now the groom may distribute cigar-sized beef sticks for the guests, and the couple often gives mugs with their names and the wedding date, or perhaps pens featuring their first names, the wedding date, and the couple's favorite inscription on love or marriage.[56] In the more progressive circles, the couple's names and the date of the wedding appear on the table napkins, although some settlements regard this as being "too high," especially since paper napkins are rarely used anywhere among the Amish.

More Singing and More Fun

Because the supper at large weddings may take more than two hours before everyone is served, the traditional evening singing might not begin until 8:30 p.m. and may last until 10:30 p.m. or later. Guests sometimes sing from a different book than they did in the afternoon singing, such as the "thin book," the *Unpartheyisches Gesang-Buch.* Also, it is not uncommon to

use fast tempos, similar to those of hymns sung in Sunday-morning worship services in mainline Protestant churches. In some locales, guests even
sing gospel songs or choruses in English.

Among groups such as the Swartzentruber, Nebraska, and Lawrence
County Amish, the youth may remain until midnight or later, square dancing or playing games, and then eating once again.[57] In Lawrence County,
Pennsylvania, dancing in the evening is the highlight of the day's activities.
Their youth follow a prescribed repertoire of dances that most likely have
their roots in early Americana folk customs. Beginning with "Four Lads"
and "Shoot the Buffalo," they proceed through ten dances in a row, ending
with a break immediately after "Sally Got Drunk." Following a short pause
for a snack and a drink, they resume with "John Brown" through ten final
dances, ending with "Little Red Wagon.[58] Observers could easily imagine
that they were watching a slice of history from the late nineteenth century.
"It's really like square dancing, except the couples go in circles instead,"
a young man who attended a wedding in one of the small settlements reported. "They would have ring games. There would be as many as twenty
couples involved. They girls would be singing as they skipped around."
Often a boy would pick up the tunes as the leader, and all would join in
the singing. In some conservative settlements, the youth would pair off for
Walk-a-Mile (see chapter 9).

Among the Swartzentruber and some Nebraska Amish youth, the Youngie meet around 9:00 p.m. to play their traditional game, Snap and Catch—
a kind of tag with an exciting twist. For the participants, it must surely be
the most stimulating part of the day's activities, since it is also a kissing
game. The teenage boys stand together on one side of the room, with the
girls on the other. A boy approaches the huddle of girls, slowly circles them,
and suddenly snaps his fingers at his choice. Her ostensible task is to keep
from getting caught, but once he catches her, he is allowed to kiss her. Then
it is her turn to "snap" a boy. When I asked if the kisses were passionate or
perfunctory, a young Nebraska Amish friend claimed that most kisses were
usually token or dutiful, but occasionally a kiss would be more ardent for a
favorite. When asked what keeps a boy from repeatedly snapping and kissing the same girl, a deacon reported that it would not happen because of

peer pressure. Not surprisingly, participants traditionally play this game for two hours or more, in a room separate from the adults.

Following the dancing or the game, the youth gather round the *Halb Nacht Dish* (midnight table). It is laden with warmed-up dishes and left-overs from the two wedding meals. This time each girl sits with a boy as-signed by the hostlers. In at least one settlement, a father reported that the youth turn over the plates from the previous meal and eat off the back sides. "It works," he reported. "Our plates have a rim around the bottom."[59] The Lawrence County *Halb Nacht Dish* is a bit more spartan than that of their Swartzentruber cousins and features chips, candy, store-bought ice cream, and canned peaches. Not surprisingly, however, this fun-filled evening and the pairing up with a potential date or mate provides these conservative youth with an exciting contrast to a chore- or work-filled life.

Wedding Mischief

In some settlements, young friends or family members traditionally play tricks on the newlyweds. Stephen E. Scott recounted stories of celebrants putting rubber spiders in the couple's gravy or chewing gum in their food.[60] A traditional prank among some Swartzentrubers is to thread a string through the prunes in their customary side dish, so that when somebody attempts to help themselves, they lift out the entire connected contents of the bowl. In Lancaster County, some youth play tricks on the newlyweds at the end of the day's festivities.[61] Pranksters have hoisted the groom's car-riage onto the roof of an outbuilding or powered up their chainsaws outside the couple's bedroom window after the newlyweds have retired. Sometimes they have scattered cornstarch, pepper, flour, and even doughnuts between the sheets. Others have set an alarm clock to go off in the middle of the night. Many practical jokes center on hiding or disassembling things: the horse's harness, the bedroom door, or even the bed. Some new couples have left the wedding festivities, only to find their bed in the middle of the cornfield or assembled on the top of the house. As a final touch, some pranksters even included a kerosene nightlight on a nightstand next to the purloined bed.

In Lancaster County, mischief-makers might try to remove the washing machine that the couple will need next day when they do the obligatory chore of washing wedding-related linens and other laundry. The *Lancaster Intelligencer Journal* featured a photo of an Amish man climbing a sixty-foot silo, where the agitator from a washing machine had been tied by the couple's young friends the night before.[62] In a similar incident, the following notice and letter appeared in *Die Botschaft* at the end of the wedding season: "To Whom It May Concern: If your boys were at the wedding at Aaron Ebersol's, will you ask them if they hid their washing machine. They cannot find it since the wedding. Please let them know. Thank you. Signed, A Neighbor." The next week, this follow-up letter appeared in *Die Botschaft*: "Attention: To the people who were at the wedding at Aaron Ebersol's. They had hidden their washing machine. It was found and hidden again at about 9:30 [p.m.] or 15 of 10:00. It was found in the evening and hid again and put in the haymow. They know who hid it there. Then it was removed from the haymow again and they haven't found it yet. Their wedding date was Nov. 13, this is now Dec. 10. Let's help them find it. If you had boys there at the wedding, would you please ask them if they helped remove it out of the haymow. And if they did would you please let Aaron know where it is. Thank you."[63] Because newlyweds know about these traditions, they make special efforts to hide the washing machine and their horse and carriage from potential jokesters.

Many adults complain that too many of the pranksters get carried away. A *Die Botschaft* scribe inveighed: "There was mischief going on Tuesday evening with uninvited guests. It is such a shame to ruin someone's day by such dirty and unruly things. It is too bad when we as Amish must get the police out to keep things under control at an Amish wedding."[64] In settlements where adults have concluded that wedding pranks or partying have "gotten out of hand" over time, they have sometimes abolished the evening meal and nighttime festivities. Some New Order Amish, and even some Old Order groups, have now instituted "day weddings," in which all activities are concluded in the afternoon. A New Order father wrote, "Our bishops frequently remark that we have received great blessings by having 'day weddings.' This eliminated much of the questionable activity, 'belling' [noise-making], drinking, barn games, etc., which was common. . . . The youth seem not to want to come for the ceremony and noon meal and will show up only for the evening activity."[65]

Amish Honeymoon

In Lancaster County, the newlyweds usually spend their first night together at the bride's home. The next morning, tradition calls for them to be up by 5:00 a.m. for breakfast, and then to help the family with the cleanup from the wedding's aftermath. This serves as a tacit reminder that although one may be entering the joy and excitement of young married love, dishes and clothes must still be washed, houses cleaned, and duties performed. After breakfast, the pair's first task is to scrub the floors and wash the tablecloths and linens from the previous day—if they can find the washing machine. The bride's parents, siblings, nearby aunts, and sometimes even church members living close by also show up to help load the benches, pack away the dishes and songbooks, and even send back the portable toilets, a practical addition in recent years in the large settlements.

Although weddings are officially observed for only a day, rather than the two weeks in the time of Tobias and Sara, some Amish, such as those in Lancaster and Mifflin Counties in Pennsylvania, celebrate the newlyweds' status for several weeks, until the pair moves into their own place, typically in late winter or early spring.[66] During the week, the couple usually stays with the bride's parents. On weekends, however, they routinely visit all of their local relatives, and then Amish friends who attended their wedding (even some who were not invited). In Lancaster County, they first call on the parents of the groom, followed by both sets of grandparents. After those visits to immediate family are completed, the couple may join two or three other newlyweds, usually cousins or close friends, and travel together on successive weekends to see uncles, aunts, and other wedding guests, "as it suits best," explained a mother. Not only do the small groups of newlyweds enjoy journeying with each other, thus reducing the number of separate visits for which host families must prepare, but this practice helps establish the couples' new identity as "young marrieds." The touring generally begins on a Friday night and ends on Sunday night. With careful planning, couples can visit nine or ten homes in one weekend. A young man described the well-crafted itinerary: "Friday evening they can go to supper at one house, stay for a couple hours, and then go for an overnight at a different place. Next morning they can have breakfast at a third home, dinner at someone else's, supper at a different place, and if they do it right, get in two more families that night." All the while, they are being assimilated as a married couple into the adult community.

Making the Rounds

Families anticipate the visits from these new couples and like to see them arrive in their carriages. Since the host families are told approximately when the couple will arrive, they are prepared, not only with their wedding gifts, but with ample supplies of snacks or a full meal, depending on the time of their young guests' arrival. Sometimes host families will lend a horse and carriage to the newlyweds, so they can make other nearby visits, if the pair had to come in a van. In Lancaster County, the groom traditionally prepares a game, story, prank, or riddles to entertain the host family. The children especially look forward to these *Yung-g'heierditricks*, as they are called. The groom might do sleight-of-hand tricks or use scissors to cut folded paper in unexpected ways. Or he might ask the children a perennial riddle, such as "Where was Moses when the light went out?" (Answer: "In the dark.") Host families may also offer entertainment, such as mini-shuffleboard and other table games. Sometimes the host father will provide tricks or riddles of his own to challenge and entertain the visiting newlyweds.

An Amish grandfather described a prank from his generation where the host father was asked to put as much of his hand as he could through the crack in an open door and then had to grasp a raw egg in the shell that was placed in his fingers. Everyone understood his predicament, since any true Amish man "dare not" drop and break a perfectly good egg. The host would be trapped in that dilemma until he either figured a way out or broke the egg. One father chuckled as he recalled a prank that he and his newlywed peers played on their host families. Sometime during the conversation, games, or festivities, "one of the visiting young married couples would prowl around the house of the host and hide the gifts which the host intended to present to them at their departure. . . . When we would be ready to leave, the hosts would be frantically searching for the gifts to give." The newlyweds enjoyed seeing both the reaction of their hosts and how long it took them to figure out what had happened. Even if many of the *Yung-g'heierditricks* are well known, these visits are highly anticipated and later provide wonderful stories for regaling family and friends, both old and young.

After visiting two or three hours at one place, the couple or couples move on to the next home, where they are similarly greeted and feted. "It's easy to gain weight during those visiting weeks," one young Amish man reported. "Everyone wants to give you food." Newlyweds stay over at the last home they visit on Saturday night and either go to church with their host family in the morning or continue their rounds with families who have an off-Sunday. Finally, they return home with the carriage or van laden with gifts and treats. An exhausted bride and groom, on their way back from visiting distant relatives in late January, concluded that they would have to be satisfied with the fifty visits that they had already completed. "We still have a hundred families to go, but it's just too much. We have too much to do getting our house fixed up." A young Nebraska husband from the Big Valley in Pennsylvania said that sometimes couples took a year to get around to all of their relatives and invited guests.

Securing the Bonds

Several weeks after a Lancaster County wedding, the family of the groom sponsors the traditional last official event for the couple, the *Infair*.[67] Before the pair moves into their new dwelling, tradition calls for the family of the groom to invite the newlyweds and the bride's family to the home of the groom's parents on a Saturday. The guests arrive at about 9:00 a.m. and talk, play games, and feast until midafternoon. John A. Hostetler has stated that the purpose of this occasion is to acknowledge that two kinship systems have joined to form a new, lifetime union.[68] If one were to devise an effective transition strategy to incorporate and establish newlyweds as full participants into the adult community, it would probably look very much like what happens every year in the settlements in Lancaster and Lawrence Counties, Pennsylvania.

Amish newlyweds everywhere, however, appear to adjust to marriage and adult responsibilities and expectations equally well in communities that do not practice the post-wedding tradition of extended visiting and the *Infair*. The ability of the new couples to quickly assume their adult and matrimonial responsibilities is a testimony to the strength of the parents and the community in preparing the couple for their lifetime commitment. From childhood, they have learned the importance of working hard, "giving themselves up" for the sake of others, and obeying God's commandments instead of following their own will or whims. All their lives they have been taught and have watched the distinct roles of husbands and wives, and fathers and mothers, being played out. They have realistic expectations of what constitutes marriage and parenthood in the Amish community. Thus it is no surprise that they adjust so quickly and so well.

Except for baptisms or ordinations, weddings are the most important events in the life of the Amish community. The Amish regard the union between a man and woman to be as sacred and as permanent as the union between an Amish individual and the church. Marriage is never an experiment, as it often is in mainstream culture, since divorce is not an option. The Amish point out that Christ sanctioned marriage, comparing himself to a bridegroom and the church to his bride, thus validating both the importance of the church and of marriage. The sanctity of marriage and the lifetime union that is required demand the constant attention of the entire society. Thus the church service, the ceremony, and the activities of the wedding day must always be under the sponsorship and control of the church. The stakes are too important to allow for the personal whims, preferences, or shortcomings of any couple or family. A strong union is the culmination of the harmonious working of every aspect of the community. Their society not only celebrates the union of two of their beloved Youngie, but also recognizes that each wedding bodes well for the future of Amish society. We now turn to speculations on what that future might be.

Many Amish wonder what effects changes, such as those introduced by smartphones and Internet access, will have not only on the youth, but also on the future direction of Amish life and culture.
(Daniel Rodriguez)

-⟶꩜⟵ Chapter Eleven ⟶꩜⟵

The Future
Keeping Faith in a World of Change

*For hundreds of years we have tried our best to keep
separate from the world, but now it comes full force to
us through something we can hold in our hand.*
—Amish father

An Unpredictable Future

Not many Amish, old or young, spend much time ruminating about the abstractions of successful identity formation or cultural viability. Although the older generations may be concerned with the eventual outcome of the young, the Youngie are certainly more focused on the upcoming weekend than on thoughts about the future of Amish society. Riding with one's friends to a Saturday-night party or deciding whom to take home after the Sunday-night singing most likely are uppermost in the minds of Amish youth. But their parents and grandparents intuitively know that their society's survival will ultimately depend on the degree to which their youth absorb an authentic Amish identity and make a lifetime commitment to God, their church, and the community.

The last Amish community in Europe disappeared in 1937, almost 200 years after the ship *Charming Nancy* docked in Philadelphia with its first recorded contingent of Amish. Subsequently, the history of the Amish in North America includes thousands of people from Amish backgrounds who never joined the church, members who abandoned the Amish way, and scores of failed settlements.[1] Some communities collapsed under the weight of economic hardships or natural disasters, and others because of strife within the church. On occasion, entire congregations abandoned their Amish heritage for a more comfortable, "progressive," or evangelical vision of Anabaptist Christianity. Despite the robust growth in the number of Amish today, these failures remind them that their future existence is not guaranteed. During the crucial rumspringa years, most youth will effortlessly move into Amish adulthood, but some will be tempted to leave for more expressive or liberal churches and lifestyles.[2] If most of the youth refuse to embrace the Amish way, however, then the strands that form the fabric of their society will unravel.

Few among the Amish predict a sudden demise for their culture, but many wonder how long they can maintain traditional Amish values and practices in the face of modern and postmodern society. Many elders in the large settlements worry that creeping change will eventually destroy the essential core of Amish life. Furthermore, they fear that the "true Amish" may be migrating out to the smaller settlements, leaving behind those who look the part but have lost their core of simplicity, community, and faithfulness. "How much of our tradition can we give up and still be Amish?" an elder asked. "When will we have become worldly on the inside and simply look Amish on the outside?" Leaders struggle with knowing how much and when to change. Amish at either end of the conservative–progressive spectrum agree that change, whether prompted by economic or by moral issues, is inevitable, and they know that it can ultimately contribute to either the survival or the destruction of their culture.

Perennial Preoccupations

As we have seen in chapter 1, a serious concern among many Amish is that the majority of the families can no longer make a living by farming. In the large settlements, most of the available farmland is either already un-

der cultivation or has been turned into shopping malls, industrial develop-
ments, or housing tracts. Even among most small settlements, few of them
have even a third of their families who farm full time.[3] Many Amish fear
that the loss of a farm livelihood or home diminishes their future viability.
Until the mid-twentieth century, the Amish and farming were practically
synonymous. Although the Amish never declared that farming was next to
godliness, most equated the two. Traditionally, almost all children learned
to be Amish in the context of the farm. Farming reinforced the Amish core
values of hard work, simplicity, and separation from the world. "Time will
tell how we Amish will do as a society," said a young business owner. "The
present generations are the first in which most of the children and youth
have grown up off the farm." Donald B. Kraybill has contended that the
occupational shift to business poses a most serious challenge to historic
Amish values and viability.[4]

Despite these concerns, farming may not be the most crucial ingredient
for socialization into the Amish way of life. The majority of non-farming
Amish appears to be successfully transmitting their heritage and rearing
their children as faithful Amish adults. As of this writing, however, the results from research on this issue are contradictory. Lawrence P. Greska and
Jill E. Korbin found that 23 percent of the non-farming families in Geauga
County, Ohio, had at least one child who was no longer Amish, versus only
15 percent of the farming families.[5] Thomas J. Meyers found no differences
between farming and non-farming families in children leaving the faith,
but Julia A. Eriksen and colleagues found that non-farming families were
nearly six times more likely to have at least one non-Amish child than farming families.[6] Many Amish think that the presence or absence of fathers
at home is the more critical retention factor.[7] They worry that increased
numbers of Amish fathers who work on construction crews or in factories
are away far more than fathers who farm. Researchers have yet to study the
influence of father-absence on Amish children, but its negative impact is
well documented in mainstream society.[8]

Besides paying attention to these economic and societal factors, parents
continue to worry about peer influences that affect their children as the
youth decide whether to follow Amish traditions. "Will our Youngie remain
true, or will they walk or fall away?" parents wonder. This peer issue be-

comes much more salient as their children move into and through their rumspringa years. The Amish know that there will always be individual casualties within the group, but the impact and loss will be more far-reaching on the community if critical masses of youth begin abandoning the culture.

The movement toward supervised groups for the Youngie has been a great encouragement to many Old Order Amish parents and leaders in the large settlements. Since this movement had its start in Ohio in the 1980s, it has since spread to parts of the large settlements in Indiana and Pennsylvania. Adults express their relief that the youth and their parents now have a choice for a "decent Rumspringa," one that resembles the lifestyle and values espoused by the church. This movement, initially suspect and stigmatized as being too restrictive, is now experiencing widespread acceptance by parents and ministers. Thus the one area that was generally troublesome and out of control for years is increasingly becoming an integral part of a seamless society. Although some Amish wonder if the youth are being so channeled and scrutinized that they lack any real choice and may later become dissatisfied, most adults believe that the new groups are strengthening moral behavior, church values, and righteous living.

On the other hand, Old Order leaders have watched the gradual change being played out in the more theologically progressive groups around them, such as in the New Orders and the Beachy Amish that share some of the same theological and behavioral tendencies. The New Order churches started out with concerns for the spiritual and moral well-being of their youth and for their society in general. Now the Old Orders note the New Order's widespread acceptance of telephones and electricity in their homes. Several members in the "highest" sectors of the "electric" New Order settlements may own microwaves, hairdryers, and even computers. In other settlements, many members routinely use their modified tractors to drive to town or go for picnics, causing observers to speculate about how long it will be until their people switch from gasoline-powered farming vehicles to automobiles or pickup trucks. Some Old Order neighbors also wonder if televisions and DVD players will infiltrate the New Orders.

Furthermore, all of the New Order settlements that decided to regularly conduct their church services in English have abandoned their Amish connections.[9] In Lancaster County, the horse-and-buggy New Order churches declined precipitously in the latter decades of the past century. In 2001 an Old Order minister reported: "Of their two [New Order] districts around here, all of the youth in the one have left. The other one is struggling to keep their few young people who are still there. Almost all of their youth have moved into the Beachy church or other more-progressive Anabaptist groups. Once they move up, they rarely come back." His observations proved to be prophetic because by 2006, Lancaster County's New Order church had virtually disappeared.

Predictors of Defection

Those who study the Amish (or the transmission of culture in general) also examine other factors that relate to the retention or the defection of the young. Two research studies of Indiana youth found that the fewer contacts they had with outsiders, the more likely they were to remain Amish. "If we want our children to remain pure, we have to reduce the dangers of the secular, corrupt world," say the parents. In many of the plainest settlements, such as the Swartzentrubers, adults intentionally seek to limit close contact between their children and "worldly youth" or "higher" Amish with their liberal ideas, wayward pastimes, and alluring gadgets. One reason that the Amish do not actively seek converts is their intuitive sense that seekers, however sincere, could infect the church and the youth with their deeply ingrained worldly influences, attitudes, and habits.

Meyers's study has suggested that the simple factor of rural isolation is related to the retention or attrition of youth.[10] He examined family records from the Amish directory in northern Indiana and found that the highest level of defection occurred in families residing closest to towns.[11] If these results are typical of other settlements, they confirm the Amish suspicion that "going to town" is where their members encounter worldly contacts, activities, and temptations that are inherently corrupting to youth. An Amish farmer declared: "Cities are dangerous and destructive. After Cain killed Abel, the Bible says that he went and founded a city."[12] In certain Swartzentruber settlements, once their children learn English, parents intentionally leave their school-age children at home when the parents go to town. In this way, they minimize contact with worldly influences that might lead their children astray. They are resolute in their belief that rural areas are the only settings in which to live and rear a family.

Similarly, no Swartzentruber children go to public schools. This practice, along with the Swartzentrubers' significant retention rate, supports Meyers's finding that Amish children who attended public schools are almost twice as likely to defect as children who attended private schools. Denise M. Reiling has noted that in the area of Indiana where she conducted her study on the Amish, 80 percent of the children attended public school, and their then-current attrition rate was 20–25 percent, significantly higher than that reported in almost any other Old Order community.[13] John A. Hostetler and Gertrude Huntington concluded, "For an individual to become Amish, the person must be kept within the Amish have community, physically and emotionally, during the crucial adolescent years."[14]

Their degree of isolation may help explain why the most conservative affiliations, including the Nebraska Amish in Pennsylvania and the Andy Weaver or Swartzentruber groups in Ohio, have higher retention rates than their more progressive counterparts in the Old and New Orders. Most Amish informants believe that the ultraconservative groups lose fewer than 5 percent of their youth, one-third the loss reported for many Old Order groups. In the greater Holmes County, Ohio, area, only 3.7 percent of the conservative Andy Weaver group chose not to be baptized, compared with 15.3 percent of the Old Order youth.[15] These statistics confirm Laurence R. Iannaccone's research findings that religious groups that are more conservative, separatist, and demanding retain adherents better than more accommodating religious groups.[16]

On the other hand, the most progressive New New Order churches, by virtually everyone's estimations, have the highest defection rate of all. In the past, a few districts had lost 50 percent or more of their youth to even-less-conservative Anabaptist groups, especially to the Beachy Amish. Lora Friedrich and Joseph F. Donnermeyer have reported that 43 percent of New Order youth chose not to be baptized into the Amish Church.[17] More recently, Kraybill and colleagues reported defection data obtained by Stephen Scott from the Holmes County, Ohio, community directory. The two New Order groups, the New Order Christian Fellowship and the regular New Order church districts, showed dropout rates of 68.5 and 40.4 percent, respectively.[18] "We are like mules," declared a New Order elder ruefully. "We work hard in our generation, but we don't reproduce."[19] A New Order father, seeking to understand this loss of their youth to more liberal Anabaptist groups, speculated: "Our emphasis on evangelical teaching, such as the new birth, personal holiness, and sharing our faith puts less importance on keeping traditional forms. It also makes our people more congenial [*sic*] and comfortable with the religious activities and services of more-liberal Anabaptists, such as Beachy Amish and conservative Mennonites." Many New Order Amish admit to feeling a kinship with those "higher" Anabaptist groups that emphasize adult baptism, non-resistance, an assurance of salvation, evangelism, and foreign missions. Although the gap between typical Old Order Amish and Beachy Amish remains relatively large, the step up from New Order Amish to Beachy Amish is much smaller. "After all," observed an Old Order man, "New Order Amish are basically Beachy Amish without the cars."

Some Old Order people claim that the problem lies more in the example set by New Order parents. One Old Order deacon commented: "It's because the parents and their churches are change minded and compromising. When the youth see the parents taking steps away from their traditions, they figure, 'If Dad and Mom can make a change, so can I.' But, of course, they keep going further." A New Order member mused that the youth leave primarily when they observe adults living by a list of rules, rather than by a deeply held conviction.

In his study of Old Order Amish defection, Meyers has found birth order to be another predictive family variable for leaving the Amish faith, with defection among the first three children occurring much more frequently than among the rest of the siblings. Particularly when compared with the first two children, the likelihood of later-born children leaving declined almost linearly: "Those most likely to reject the values of their parents appear to be in early sibling positions, and those who conserve the tradition come later in the family."[20] Meyers has not speculated about why the oldest child is more likely to defect. Greska and Korbin, however, have found that in Geauga County, Ohio, the fourth-largest Amish settlement, if the oldest child leaves the church, a younger sibling is four times more likely to leave than in families where the firstborn joins the church and stays Amish.[21]

In both Old Order and New Order settlements, males are dispropor-tionately more at risk to defect than females. Ministers' reports and Amish community directories both reveal that women joining the church typically outnumber men by more than the expected male-female birth ratio.[22] Nor is this tendency limited to the Amish. It reflects the fact that in religious groups, at least in Western society, females tend to be more faithful and deeply committed to their religious beliefs and practices.[23] When asked why this might be so among the Amish, one young man remarked, "Boys find it harder to be obedient and submissive to the rules than girls." His father added, "Boys generally have more contact with the world, have more op-portunities, and are more confident that they can make it out there than the girls," further evidence of the importance of separation from the world for the Amish.

Meyers's summary of defections in northern Indiana probably reflects the tendencies in other Amish settlements, as well: "The profile of likely defectors would include males who are in early sibling positions, did not attend an Amish school, grew up in communities that to some extent have relaxed the Ordnung, or were in close proximity to urban areas and hence in more frequent contact with the dominant culture during the childhood years. Furthermore, if these males remain single and opt to leave the farm and begin their occupational lives in industry, they may have a tendency to become even more involved in 'English' society."[24] Steven M. Nolt and Mey-ers have reported that after examining church districts in the Shipshewana area of northern Indiana, the locale that showed the highest level of defec-tion, between 54 and 62 percent of adult children from those families either never joined the Amish church or joined later than others and then left.[25] The authors have attributed these surprisingly high defection rates to the factors mentioned earlier. Since youth in small settlements generally remain more isolated from surrounding society, and, if Nolt and Meyers's obser-vations are correct, they are much more likely to choose the Amish way.

Dynamics of Amish Retention

One factor that promotes retention in the communal society of the Amish is that their young people are not simply leaving a church. Instead, they are abandoning an all-pervasive way of life, one reinforced by the entire community, and especially by their parents and extended families. As a young Amish man struggling with the decision of whether to leave explained: "The thing that keeps many of us from leaving is knowing that we will deeply hurt our parents if we go. Most Amish youth have great respect for their parents." On the other hand, some Amish believe that a disproportionate number of defectors experienced some kind of psychological, physical, or sexual abuse in their families, although no systematic studies on this subject have been carried out.[26]

Since parents keenly fear for their wayward children's salvation and eternal destiny, most youth recoil from inflicting this kind of heartbreak and pain on them. In addition, many youth, especially in the most traditional circles, believe that if they join the church but later break their membership vows and leave, they will go to hell when they die. An Amish man explained, "We're taught that if we leave, if you don't stay with what you were raised in, and honor your parents, which they say is 'doing exactly as I tell you to,' 'if you're not honoring me, then you'll go to hell.' "[27] Reiling has reported that in her sample of twenty ex-Amish that she interviewed, "almost every one of the defected co-ethnics [former Amish] reported still fearing for their salvation, even though they had subsequently joined a Christian church that did accept John 3:16 as the plan of salvation."[28] In another state, a young man who left the church for theological reasons found his confidence in that decision profoundly shaken two years later, after hearing the Amish bishop at an Old Order funeral declare that this former member was going to hell for breaking his membership vows. So for some, at least, fear of damnation most likely motivates them to "stay with the church and keep my vows."

Not only can fear be a factor, but the community is also structured in ways that tangibly benefit those who choose to join the church and stay. Young couples generally receive financial support from their families when establishing their own homes. Children who become members often receive part of their family inheritance, even before the parents die. As a further incentive, some parents have promised their sons state-of-the-art carriages or other possessions if they will join the church. In more extreme cases, parents have offered a wayward child a house or a farm if he will accept the Amish way.

A more immediate enticement for remaining is that in some Old Order and New Order settlements, youth must first become church members before they are permitted to court, and all settlements require church membership as a condition for marriage. Many Amish men admit that an Amish sweetheart was a powerful motivator in making their decision. Someone asked a Lancaster County Amish man widely known for his independent tendencies why, despite serious reservations as a young man, he decided to join the church. "I had found this cute little thing at a singing, and she wanted to be Amish," he acknowledged. "I ended up marrying her at twenty-two, since I was afraid somebody else would get her." Girls generally become church members at an earlier age than boys, so a female's membership status provides additional motivation for a young man to eventually join. An Amish woman whose husband had lived the "fast life" for more than ten years before he joined the church explained, "If the boy is leading a very worldly life, the girl will be more conservative and he won't be able talk her into leaving." Her own experience convinced her that an Amish suitor would probably be more successful in winning the girl's hand by his joining the church than by insisting that she break her membership vows and marry outside the church.

Another possible reason for young men joining the church or staying Amish relates to their status as conscientious objectors. Historically, only Amish church members in good standing have been automatically exempted from military service. To the embarrassment of church leaders and the satisfaction of Amish critics, baptisms and church memberships among young males rise disproportionately during times of national conscription or military action. One writer reported that in his community in the summer of 1942, "many joined during that period because the country had entered World War II, and it was hard to get a non-resistant status if you did not belong to a church."[29] An Amish grandfather recounted that he joined the church in the 1950s to avoid the draft.

Some young people remain Amish because they fear that they are neither educationally nor emotionally prepared for life in the outside world, although this is probably most common among groups that seek to reduce their contact with mainstream society. Some defectors report that they delayed leaving for fear that their eighth-grade education and limited use of the English language would hinder them from making a living in the English world. Finally, some youth apparently remain Amish because of inertia. They find it less stressful to stay than to face the inevitable changes and the significant stresses and turmoil that generally accompany one's leaving.

Signs of Hope

Thoughtful Amish adults realize that youth join the church for many reasons, and they worry that those doing so for the wrong reasons can negatively impact the overall level of life and commitment in their communities. Despite such concerns, many Amish adults discount the predictions that the Amish, especially the younger generation, are drifting away from their cherished values and behaviors. Many believe that they see signs of a moral or spiritual renewal, especially in portions of the large settlements. As evidence, they point to the growth of the large settlements' alternative adult-supervised singings as a healthy sign. An Amish grandfather who attended a supervised-gang singing in Lancaster County remarked: "I could hardly believe what I was seeing. The young folk came in, sat down, behaved, sang well all evening—it was amazing to know that this kind of singing was possible."

Growing numbers of youth are joining groups that require an alcohol- and drug-free environment for young people who want "a more decent way." In Lancaster County, two of the original supervised groups, the Hummingbirds and the Eagles, both organized in the late 1990s, had grown so fast that the initial gangs had divided into a dozen regional groups by 2013. Altogether, in 2013 the alternative groups involved nearly two-thirds of the estimated 4,800 rumspringa-aged Youngie in Lancaster County.[30] In other large settlements, these alternative gangs are also among the fastest growing. Observers maintain that in many communities, young people in general are drinking, smoking, and partying less than their grandparents and parents did in the 1950s, 1960s, and 1970s. Some adults report, "We had band hops and hoedowns way more often in our day than youth do today." Some Amish observers contend that many of these youth are actually held to higher standards of behavior than are their parents. A highly regarded minister's comment is typical: "I am thankful but sort of ashamed to say that my own children have been much easier for me to handle than I was for my parents." Finally, in many church districts, parents indicate that the age at which youth are joining the church is again going down. In Lancaster County, this is widely regarded as a direct result of the supervised-gang movement.

Nevertheless, in other areas, adults wonder whether times really are better or worse today with regard to the young. Certainly many young people continue to stray for a time and sow their wild oats during their Rumspringa. And most Amish parents decry the worldly excesses of the fast-track youth. Many adults, however, may still speculate privately that "it really might be a good idea for the Youngie to go on and get it out of their system so that they will be contented church members when they do join." In her extensive study done in the 1990s in a rural midwestern community, Reiling concluded that their youth overwhelmingly believed that the adults in that settlement expected the Youngie to experiment with worldly behavior for a time, in order for the weak and unworthy to "be 'weeded out early lest they infect the rest of the group.' . . . For this selection process to be fully effective, the individual must have the opportunity to deny the profane by being exposed to temptation. This belief prevents Amish parents from acting against, and in many cases causes them to condone and even encourage, the more serious forms of deviance, such as the consumption of alcohol."[31] Whether or not one can generalize Reiling's findings to other settlements, it is still true that Amish youth are very aware of their parents' verbalized or tacit expectations. It is also true that one's peer group is a primary reference group, whether wayward or obedient. Not only can an individual's peers pull him or her away from acceptable Amish practices and values, but youth can also exert a potent influence on each other to identify with and become part of the fold. There is both safety and danger in numbers, and peer-group influence can act as a two-edged sword.

All who would become part of the Amish community must ultimately choose to accept the requirements of the Ordnung. Kraybill has argued that this very act of choosing whether to join or leave is a key to Amish viability and retention, theorizing that such an action serves a strong sociological and psychological function by giving each youth a sense of having chosen his or her destiny. In whatever kind of community, perceived choice can solidify and strengthen one's commitment and satisfaction. Kraybill also has posited that this freedom to choose is what helps bring vacillating youth back. Although they may taste and test the mainstream world, the majority opt to return and become upstanding, responsible members of the Amish community. In his judgment, this ability to choose acts as the linchpin for increasing an individual's future adult loyalty. If Kraybill is correct, those youth we are now describing will have a significant choice to make prior to baptism.[32]

The Growing Challenge of the Internet

Besides dealing with sociological and cultural factors over the centuries, the Amish have faced myriad decisions on what to do about technological innovations. Kraybill has carefully enumerated the various struggles and outcomes surrounding new technologies, from automobiles to inline skates, from telephones to cell phones, from milking machines to artificial insemination, plus dozens of other challenges.[33] Depending on the issue, the typical reaction of Amish adults may range from a cautious, wait-and-see approach by the ministers, to pockets of individual or family experimentation, to a widespread movement to permit the new technology or practice. Sometimes the extensive use of a technological development, combined with pressure exerted by members, will provide the impetus to legitimize the change. Past disagreements over issues, however, have often produced turmoil in churches, migrations by certain members, the establishment of new settlements, or historic schisms that divided the church and its members. Nevertheless, whatever the technology or issue, those Amish who are most thoughtful and committed will evaluate its impact on individuals and families and also on the stability, well-being, and economic survival of their culture. The ideal, however, may lose out if a persuasive or powerful critical mass forms to counter whatever proposals are put forth.

For the past decade, the most important technology-related issue facing the Amish has involved smartphones and the Internet, and nobody professes to know how that issue will be resolved. In many places the youth—with their smartphones and, occasionally, laptops—are at the forefront among the Amish. Typically, most Amish adults have known little about the Internet, so in attempting to counsel their children they feel confused and hampered by their lack of technological knowledge or skills. Parental concerns are twofold. Will Internet contact corrupt their youth? And does growing Internet usage have the potential to contaminate, dilute, and erode their cherished practices and, eventually, their entire Amish way of life?

Those Amish who see or use computers in the workplace, learn about them through their teenage children, or go online in their local library do not doubt that the Internet, like most technologies, offers advantages for its users. Those who work in non-Amish venues, such as markets or factories, recognize immediately that the Internet can provide help for small businesses, farmers, homeowners, and homemakers. With a smartphone or laptop, a business owner can locate potential customers, products, resources, vendors, and venues almost instantly. Farmers can check the latest weather forecast, commodity prices, innovations in grass farming, new fertilizers, or the most effective treatment for outbreaks of cow mastitis. Mothers can shop online for a new canner or a Victorio food mill / strainer from Lehman's Hardware in Kidron, Ohio, and have it delivered to their door. Meanwhile, their sons can order the latest tree stand for hunting or camo boots from Cabela's while getting the same home delivery.

The Internet Cornucopia

Although adults may be uneasy with their teenage children's online involvement, venturesome Youngie may be excited to dabble in Spanish, try a website's "introduction to algebra" lesson, play chess or Scrabble online, or, best of all (for many males, at least), follow their favorite sports teams. Another definite attraction is the instant access to information through sites like Wikipedia. The allure of finding immediate answers to questions on virtually any topic appeals to curious learners at any age or stage. Nonetheless, an Amish friend told me that "a middle-aged Amish woman sighed to me just recently that it is so hard to have an argument at a family gathering anymore, because whenever discussion questions arise the kids whip out their cellies and Google it." The Amish would never use their word "upbuilding" to describe these options, but many of them are undeniably attracted to such features.

As Amish parents learn more about the kinds of websites and options available to their children, their anxieties are likely to rise. These parents are naturally concerned when learning that their children can watch an abundance of PG-13, R, and even NC-17 rated films displaying "worldly" values and sexual conduct that could undermine the Amish core attributes, such as modesty, stability, non-violence, and contentment—the traditional hallmarks of Amish life. If upset or discontented teenagers should Google "ex-Amish" or "former Amish," they will locate people such as Mose Gingerich, an ex-Amish man of *Amish in the City* and *Amish: Out of Order* fame. For a time, Gingerich provided runaway or transient youth from Amish households with a place to stay, help in finding employment, assistance in obtaining their GED, and information on getting a driver's license, as well as offering a support group of like-minded peers, church connections, and a listening ear. Although his services may have been helpful and well intentioned, most Amish parents would instantly reject them. The same computer search by an inquisitive or dissatisfied youth might also turn up the name of Saloma Miller Furlong, author, blogger, and founder of her organization to financially help people from Amish homes who, like her, have left and are seeking a college education.[34]

More searching on the same topic might produce the name of Joe Keim, another former Amish man whose organization, Mission to Amish People, offers, among other things, spiritual counsel, conversion to a more evangelical form of Christianity, and rebaptism after a conversion experience.[35] The Internet also provides opportunities for dissatisfied Amish youth to explore more expressive forms of Christianity that have no connections to Anabaptist teachings or Amish life. Disaffected or venturesome Amish can peruse the websites of thousands of churches—Anabaptist, mainstream, Pentecostal, evangelical, or fundamentalist—that will gladly welcome and integrate former Amish into their midst. Although those leaving the Amish could find comfort in the support, counsel, and services offered, their parents would consider such "help" to be antithetical to Amish culture, since it would not be aimed at encouraging their sons or daughters to return and be reconciled with their families, church, and community. Equally disturbing to Amish parents would be a website for gay Amish, two words that virtually no traditional Amish person would ever think of using together.

Despite most Amish parents' concern about their children's Internet involvement, online activities could provide the youth with such pleasure, satisfaction, or benefits that some parents might be lulled into lowering their guard and moderating their unqualified rejection of computers. A psychologist who has specialized in working with the Amish noted the frequency with which many Amish fathers ask their rumspringa children to check the weather forecast on their smartphones, missing the irony that they are encouraging use of the very technology that they, themselves, will not employ. Moreover, Internet addiction is especially worrisome to many parents, who fear that that a disproportionate number of youthful—and adult—users may find it hard to forego. They fear that the information, entertainment, or stimulation available online will interfere with their giving themselves up to a plain and simple lifestyle.

All of these things give pause to thoughtful Amish adults as they observe the encroachment of smartphones into daily Amish life, affecting both teenagers and their parents. Relatively few, however, claim to know what to do to stop the flow, or at least to reduce the inherent dangers associated with the Internet. "The Internet is here to stay and we will have to deal with it," said a Lancaster County father who spoke to a youth group on the possible risks in using the web. If change is to come, it is highly likely that teenage users will be the agents of such change. "They have already decided for the Internet," concluded the same bishop. In my contact with hundreds of Amish Facebook profiles, I have yet to find any teenagers expressing second thoughts, concerns, or regrets about their involvement with it.

Another factor that is undoubtedly encouraging change is the potential for economic benefits. "Can you imagine where we would be economically if the computer or smartphone is totally prohibited? Our businesses would not be able to compete today," a young Amish entrepreneur declared. A bishop expressed a similar idea when he stated, "Economics is the driving force and making it necessary for us to have it [the Internet] in the workplace." One potential resolution could come from the Ohio New Order Amish, who, in 2013, were seeking to refine a technology that blocked the Internet while still enabling their people to use basic computer functions for business. In this way, they sought to establish a firm line between using the computer for entertainment and using it for work. An Ohio New

Order friend described some of the complexities in trying to balance all of the conflicting needs and divergent ideas. Thus far, the leaders have agreed that computers capable of producing spreadsheets probably will be allowed, but any system that includes a mouse, a built-in camera, computer games, and, most importantly, any access to the Internet, will be prohibited. My New Order friend was optimistic that their churches would find a workable, effective alternative to an all-or-nothing impasse.

Also, since simple cell phones have been so widespread in the large settlements for a number of years, leaders most likely would face serious opposition in clamping down on all mobile-phone use. The same businessman mentioned in the above paragraph declared that "most ministers will never initially embrace change, for the simple fact that they oppose something that is new. But once a practice or technology works its way in, it is much harder to get rid of it." Some observers believe that the effort in the 1960s to ban technology that had already gained a foothold in Lancaster County ultimately resulted in the church's split in 1966, which then gave birth to the Lancaster New Order church. And in fall 2013, the Horning Mennonite Church, a conservative Anabaptist group whose members only drive black cars, vans, and trucks, experienced a church split over the issue of smartphones. Few want to experience another division like that, which deeply sunders families and church districts.

A Growing Concern

In an unsigned article in *Family Life*, the late Rob Schlabach, the respected New Order Amish minister from Ohio, wrote extensively on the dangers and evils associated with computer use.[36] *Family Life* subsequently featured an article entitled "Celling our Heritage: Cell Phones, Plain People, and the Electronic Age" in its "Insights and Ideals" section. The article cautioned against the addictive nature of smartphones, as well as the perils of accepting this new technology without considering the inherent dangers Internet technology poses to plain communities and values.[37]

By 2012, more parents, at least in the large settlements, were seriously seeking information on electronic media and gadgetry, such as smartphones, iPods and iPads, Facebook, and other devices or programs. At

about that time, a sympathetic and knowledgeable outsider was occasionally invited to provide informational sessions with some of the supervised
Lancaster County youth gangs.[38] The speaker offered a range of topics, including the basics of the Internet and social networks, their availability and
attractiveness, and the intrinsic risks of being connected to the outside
world. Depending on the audience, he discussed the potential impact that
Internet use could have on both the individual and the Amish community.
Eventually, the Amish in Lancaster County turned to some of their own respected leaders to address the issue of smartphones, and of Internet temptations and choices, with some of the supervised youth groups.[39]

On their own, some parents became proactive in creative ways. A friend
of mine from the conservative Lawrence County, Pennsylvania, settlement
related to me that one of his friends, whose son had a cell phone, brought
him that phone and asked if it should be destroyed. His baffled neighbor
did not even know how to turn on the phone. My friend showed him how,
as well as how to find out whom the man's son had been calling. Finally, the
two men checked all the existing text messages to determine if the boy was
involved in illegal or otherwise dangerous activities. My friend reported that
his neighbor not only found out who his son's companions were, but also
who had been providing alcohol to the teenagers in the local community
and where the transactions were taking place. My friend concluded by telling me that parents could indeed smash their children's phones, but doing
so would destroy useful information. A few fathers in large settlements told
me that they had registered their children's phones in the parents' names
and regularly checked the monthly itemized phone bills to determine if
their children were involved with strangers or with pornography sites. Another parent of two teenage boys related to me that he would occasionally
do random checks of the phone bills and phone numbers, despite the fact
that savvy teens could hide their tracks by erasing their calls as soon as they
hung up. None of the parents I talked to appeared to be troubled by confi-
dentiality or privacy issues.

While certain issues are being addressed, some crucial questions still
remain, ones that thoughtful Amish adults may not always vocalize but are
of definite concern to them. Is their teenagers' youthful dalliance with the
Internet qualitatively different, or any more dangerous, than past technolo-

gies, or is it just another rumspringa blip on their way to adulthood? Will the Internet be as easy to give up as their parents' own youthful but temporary love affair with automobiles or their fling with parties, movies, or professional sporting events, thus leaving the core of the community strong? Or could it be that youth will join the church and marry but continue to be attracted by the Internet, finding difficulty in rejecting the gratification of instant information, secret pleasures, or titillating stimulation found online? These questions are obviously as important as the answers to them are difficult to predict.

Coming Home

One source of hope and encouragement to Amish parents and leaders are stories of faithfulness and of successes from the past. As these incidents are recounted, for many listeners they confirm their belief that God will use the power of parents' and preachers' early teachings and experiences to bring many wanderers safely back to the Amish fold. Pauline Stevick has relates the story of Andy, an Amish prodigal son who left home to live with English acquaintances, returning home months later, "filthy and penniless."[40] Andy did not immediately repent or change his ways, but he eventually took instruction for baptism, sold his truck, and quit drinking. Today he is "with the church," and his parents confided to us that they would not be surprised if Andy were to become a minister.

Another man who grew up in Lancaster County rejected the Amish way in his youth and lived "in the world" for more than sixty years. He would spend his winters in Pinecraft, Florida, and most people there regarded him as an eccentric troublemaker. "Jakie was loud, obnoxious, and aggressive—not very loveable," recalled an Amish grandfather who had known him for years. "I always felt sad when people talked about him and treated him badly. He needed to be loved, just as all the rest of us sinners." In 1999, when Jakie was eighty-six, he returned to Lancaster County and asked if he could be taken back into the church. Not everyone was convinced that this was a good idea, but when he repented his unfaithfulness, he was fully restored. The following spring he took communion, died less than a week later, and was buried in the Amish cemetery. Everyone believed that even though he had lived a wayward and tragic life, God was merciful, and the church could be no less so.

Another example of mercy and forgiveness occurred about a year before Jakie's return, this time in the way the Lancaster Amish community responded to the two young men arrested for trafficking in cocaine. Parents universally expressed both shock and sadness that such events had transpired among their youth. The fact that the offenders were not church members but "in the world" at the time of their arrest did little to diminish the pain. A minister who sought to distance the Amish community from the two offenders by pointing out that they were not really baptized Amish was roundly criticized for his statements. Although everyone was relieved that the two were discovered and apprehended, the community grieved that their own offspring had become caught up in such illegal, destructive, and ungodly practices. Adults were shocked to learn that the culprits bought the cocaine from members of the Pagans motorcycle gang. They were even more dismayed to learn that these connections developed when the defendants hired some of the Pagans to work for them on their roofing crews. The two Amish youths evidently began to use drugs with the Pagans, then buy drugs from them, and eventually sell drugs to their Amish peers.

When the pair were finally arrested, they were charged in federal court with buying, using, and distributing cocaine that had a street value of $100,000. They initially pleaded not guilty, on the advice of their attorney. This strategy met with universal disapproval by the Lancaster County Amish, and most Amish agreed: "If they're guilty, they should plead guilty, even if their lawyer says that this is not the best strategy." The Amish ideal has always been to tell the truth, confess one's wrongdoing, and accept the consequences. Many Amish hoped that the court would make an example of these young men. "They should be found guilty and serve time in jail for what they did," some elders explained. "It will be a lesson to all of the Youngie who have been doing wrong," said a grandmother. Few, however, hoped they would be sentenced to the forty-year maximum prison term. More than three months after their arrest, the two defendants changed their plea to guilty of conspiracy to deliver cocaine. The community regarded this shift as a hopeful sign for the Youngie: they had indeed done wrong, but they were willing to repent.

The offenders had actually been cooperating as informants for the FBI for months, ever since the police discovered their dealings with the Pagans. After their arrest, the FBI required that as part of their community service, the two males should speak at a series of meetings to inform and warn Amish and plain Mennonite youth and parents about the dangers of drug use. The eight public meetings, which reached several thousand individuals and sometimes lasted for four hours, consisted of testimonials from the two convicted youths and warnings from the FBI, the Pennsylvania State Police, defense and prosecuting attorneys, and drug experts. Those in charge knew that if the press found out and wrote about these meetings, many plain people would shy away from the events. Therefore the organizers charged the parents and the youth to keep news of what was happening totally confidential. At times they even asked all in attendance to look at the person on either side of them and immediately report to those in charge the presence of anybody they did not know. Despite the thousands in attendance, not one person leaked any information to the press. Consequently, the media never learned about the meetings until after they were completed. One Amish man said: "We feel this was inspired by a higher power, like it was just orchestrated by the good Lord. It seemed that as soon as one meeting was over, the leaders thought there should be more. It's ironic that a conservative group like ours needed help, but we needed help."[41] Skeptics, both within and outside the Amish community, expressed doubts about the two culprits' motivation. "Sure they're willing to speak out about drugs now, since it certainly won't hurt them when it comes time for sentencing."

On the day of sentencing at the U.S. Federal Court in Philadelphia, dozens of reporters and photographers from state and national news services thronged the courthouse, awaiting the outcome for these Amish young men who had shamed their community, saddened their families, and grabbed unwanted national and international attention. But, unlike many confessed or convicted felons, this pair did not have to face the judge and their sentencing alone. As the two youths waited inside the courthouse, more than a hundred solemn relatives, friends, and supporters, together with the errant sons' attorney, strode somberly to the judge's chamber. Their Youngie had done wrong—terribly wrong—and nobody knew this better than those who accompanied the offenders. But, like the prodigal son, these two sons had also come to their senses and confessed their wrongdoing. At their sentencing, each expressed his apologies to the community for what he had done. "When I was a teenager, I got into the wrong crowd," Abner Stoltzfus, of Ronks, Pennsylvania, said. "It was a miserable life I led. I didn't know it then, but I know it now. I apologize from the bottom of my heart to my family for the embarrassment and pain I've caused." Abner King Stoltzfus, pausing several times to collect himself, also expressed remorse. "We lived a terrible life for awhile," he said, stopping to wipe his eyes, as many others in the gallery did. "We want to make it better."[42]

Everyone agreed that after they had completed their obligations to the state, they would be welcomed back to be reconciled with their families and their community. The Amish would be ready to receive their fallen ones— their precious fallen ones—back into the fold.[43] What was required of them to be fully taken up was the same as for other wayward youth: repentance for their sins, a desire to be part of the church, instruction in the beliefs and practices of the church, baptism, church membership, and a willingness to submit to the Ordnung for the rest of their lives. Despite their past offenses, they would be accepted as full-fledged Amish. Since that time, one joined the Old Order church and subsequently married an Amish girl in 2001. The other joined the conservative Spring Garden Church, a church with Anabaptist roots, and later transferred to a local charismatic bible church.

Not all Amish are forgiving, nor do all stories end happily or redemptively. Sometimes when their children leave the faith, parents harbor bitterness, along with their sorrow and shame, and the relationship is never restored. In most situations, however, the Amish are realists in their view of human shortcomings and sins. "We are human just like everybody else," they often say, "and we struggle with sin and must be forgiven." As members of a communal group, however, they may worry less about personal sins than about losing their collective soul, their core, their distinctiveness, and their identity. Whatever the outcome, they believe that only God knows the future and that he will be with the faithful, even if the way is perilous. What they know with certainty is that they have been called to obedience to God and to vigilance in their duties.

As the Swartzentruber bishop who had joined the U.S. Air Force as a teenager explained: "I don't think that the Amish are the only ones who will get to heaven. But I do believe that if you have been born Amish, you should stay Amish and be a good Amish member." Thus both Old Order and New Order parents labor to impart their faith and a faithful lifestyle to their children and youth, so that when the Youngie arrive at their time of decision, they will choose the Amish way, just as their parents and ancestors have done for more than 300 years. Parents believe that in remaining faithful, they can confidently entrust the future of their children and their society to God. This was the hope that prompted the mother of her straying Swartzentruber son to frequently set his place at the family table during those years when he was in the armed forces.

His homecoming, and others like it, serve as a reminder to Amish parents of God's loving faithfulness and help provide them with a sense of comfort and purpose amid the inevitable uncertainties, disappointments, and vicissitudes of life. Stories like this also remind wayward Amish youth, including those living amid the temptations in the city or those who are captured by Internet pornography, that they can return to the church, their families, and their Christian community if they repent, renounce their worldly ways and ideas, and commit themselves to the requirements of the church and the Amish faith.

Parents regard themselves as co-laborers with God, both to shape the direction of the lives of their children and to cultivate and nurture their growth into the next generation of Amish adults. Although parents believe that God will surely help them, they also believe in the adage that "God helps those who help themselves." Thus, as part of the Amish community and as individual couples, parents realize that they must diligently and intentionally work to construct for themselves and their children a social world that includes extended family, schooling, work, positive peer relationships, courtship, and marriage. All of these exert a robust and pervasive gravitational pull that keep the majority of youth in the Amish orbit and provide strong forces to help draw the wayward ones back from their rumspringa wanderings. This careful attention, along with intense parental and community involvement with their sons and daughters, all provide a strong Amish identity and help explain the remarkable retention, growth, and persistence of the Amish. The Amish also sense the dual responsibility of living lives of integrity and maintaining God's edifice. They believe that as long as they persist in their vigilance, God will help them sustain their future viability through the generations to come.

Epilogue

Anyone who has studied the history of the Amish knows that they have been out of step and out of favor with the dominant culture far more than they have been accepted or admired. Most Amish adults know the history of the years of scorn and even severe persecution they have had to endure. Yet many fret that all the positive attention and esteem that currently surrounds them may lead to their undoing, or at least to a false sense of their importance and ultimately to pride. As evidence of their present popularity, virtually anything Amish sells, whether produce at a roadside stand, exquisite hardwood furniture crafted in Holmes County, Ohio, or advertising time slots on *Amish Mafia* or other Amish-themed television programs. Despite occasional aberrant behavior—such as the widely-publicized beard-cutting incidents with the Sam Mullett Ohio group, allegations of Amish-owned puppy mills in Pennsylvania, or ongoing sexual abuse in a Wisconsin community—Amish credibility and status is at an all-time high. By every outward indicator, their future looks strong.

The continued success of the Amish in transmitting their culture to the upcoming generations has been at the heart of my ongoing interest in studying Amish life and adolescence for the past quarter of a century: How have they not only survived but continue to thrive and grow more than three centuries after their founding? My interest in their viability and longevity only deepened as I studied other cultural groups. In the past three decades, I have taught cross-cultural courses in Alaskan villages, the Caribbean Islands, Central America, South America, Africa, Asia, and the Pacific Islands. In my interactions with groups ranging from Alaska natives in Point Hope and Barrow, to the Maya in Belize, the native peoples in Samoa, and the Maori in the South Pacific, I have mostly encountered fragments of their traditional cultures, along with scattered efforts among once-esteemed elders to revive and restore the old ways and languages among the young.

My overall experience, however, is that the younger set has little interest in studying or returning to the old ways. Rather, they are interested in adopting Western habits, technology, and popular culture as quickly as they can. When my students and I sought to experience the "authentic culture," our hosts would designate an evening, or occasionally an entire day, where they showcased traditional dances, costumes, foods, and stories. As soon as the festivities ended, however, the youth quickly reverted to their cutoff jeans, t-shirts, ball caps, and iPods. One of my iconic images was of our primary Samoan cultural guide and interpreter, tending the smoking fire pit where a suckling pig was roasting for our traditional feast. He was bare chested, clad only in his lava-lava wrap, and heavily tattooed from waist to knees in the authentic style of his forbears. Nevertheless, when he turned away from us to tend the heap of burning coconut shells, I saw that his cell phone was hanging from a leather cord, a safe place to protect the device from the heat and the flames over which he was bending. In virtually all of the above settings, most of their cultural manifestations are no longer a part of everyday life and are only exhibited for special events or visitors like us.

The salient question for me is whether, or if, the day will come when the remnants of Amish culture will be trotted out to be remembered and reenacted for the benefit of curious tourists—perhaps the reenactment of a wedding, followed by a traditional wedding feast and songs in German. In light of their present growth and successes today, it is hard to even visualize such a scenario. But as I visited many Amish communities and talked with scores of teenagers and adults while researching and writing this revision, I found many Amish adults concerned about their future. None saw an imminent ending of Amish society as they have known it, but many worried about the nature of Amish life in the years to come, especially in light of the technological challenges they face today. When I asked dozens of parents and ministers to tell me what they perceived to be the biggest challenge they face, they overwhelmingly raised the issues related to cell phones, smartphones, computers, and the Internet. These concerns were not restricted only to those in the large settlements, but also surfaced in smaller Amish settlements scattered from Michigan to Missouri, from New York to Maryland, and points in between. At the same time, most adults admitted that they knew little about the intricacies and capabilities of this technology—for harm or for good. Nor did most of them profess to know how to monitor their children's phone and Internet use, let alone how to advise their offspring regarding these areas.

The Amish parents' uneasiness only intensifies when they realize that their children's smartphones enable these youth to view movies, television, and music videos, activities that the adults instinctively know pose a threat to their core values. The parents' main concern, by far, is that their off-spring, especially their sons with smartphones, laptops, or iPads, will find it easy to move from the risqué elements in mass entertainment to the corruption of Internet pornography, even from their increasingly sophisticated devices that can access the internet from anywhere in the barn or from the "back forty." In light of these fears and the parents' unfamiliarity with this ever-changing technology, it is no surprise that many Amish adults have taken a fatalistic approach to the problem. They can easily find themselves immobilized by their lack of knowledge and sense of powerlessness, hoping perhaps that the problem will go away or somehow resolve itself. Or they may simply choose to abdicate their involvement and trust that their ordained leaders will somehow work it out. I find that most leaders, however, struggle with the same feelings of impotence and inadequacy that stymie the lay members as they contemplate this intractable problem that seemingly has no apparent resolution.

Yet the Amish fear that if nobody acts decisively, the number of youth attracted to the Internet will continue to grow, and more and more adults will feel that they must be online for economic reasons. The situation appears to parallel mainstream society, where the young are in the electronic forefront, venturing into new territory and opening the way for the adults. This was one of minister Rob Schlabach's main objections to the Amish adopting simple word processors. He believed that not only have these de-vices desensitized Amish adults and youth and prepared them to move into a computer mindset, but, most importantly, they have reversed God's order of children learning from their parents and other adults. Schlabach insisted that this reversal created a non-scriptural precedent in which youth teach the adults.[1]

In light of these powerful and pervasive new changes, what options ex-ist, especially if the leaders feel divided, confused, and powerless to act? Certain events in the last half century may provide a hopeful alternative, in the form of Amish grassroots movements that provoked thoughtful action from the ground up. An instructive example of one such transformation is that of the Midway singing reform movement in Holmes County, Ohio, in the 1980s. Changes there came about despite the initial opposition of influential clergy members. It began with one concerned minister and a few laypersons that united with him to offer a wholesome alternative to the partying and rowdiness that had led local parents to refuse to host singings for several years. This determined group recognized their common prob-lem, developed a plan, spread the word, absorbed the innuendos and criti-cisms, and answered opponents' arguments as they emerged, whether from bishops and ministers or from parents who saw no reason to change the status quo.

A similar movement emerged in Pennsylvania's Lancaster County in the late 1990s, when two mothers were troubled by the lack of accountability for youth or their parents in what these women regarded as ungodly teen-age behavior. Seeking help and counsel from other parents and sympa-thetic clergy, they organized a group of their concerned peers to address a very similar set of problems to those in Ohio, again involving rowdy youth and unsupervised activities. Predictably, these founding pioneers also ex-perienced the same kinds of opposition and ridicule in their attempt to change practices that had existed for as long as anybody could remember.[2] Nevertheless, other parent-founded organizations began to emerge almost simultaneously in several other geographic areas. Negative publicity from the widely known Lancaster County drug bust of 1998 worked to soften the opposition to such reforms, since the secret of drug use within the Amish youth scene could no longer be hidden. These actions were not initiated by the bishops, but instead were started from the bottom up by groups whose conviction, zeal, and strategies ultimately changed Amish culture in significant ways.

One can find other examples of grassroots changes that developed over the years, such as the movement in the 1960s in Lancaster County to abolish bed courtship. Another was the gradual acceptance of professional treatment for mental health needs in the large settlements. This development began with a group of men who felt that the traditional "treatment" for those Amish suffering from mental and emotional problems needed serious attention. In 1995, those concerns led to the emergence of People Helpers, a group that sensitized and educated the Amish community toward a proactive and informed response to such problems. Both of these examples illustrate the importance of having a committed, confident, and thoughtful core group prepared to meet opposition gracefully but not compromise on high-moral-ground issues.

In retrospect, one might assume that the rightness of the causes and the passion of the leaders would assure the eventual acceptance of these new ideas or reforms, but histories, such as *Unser Leit: The Story of the Amish*, reveal that over the years, myriad other worthy causes failed in one way or another.[3] Even as recently as 2011, a well-intentioned attempt to provide recreation "in a clean environment," rather than rowdy parties, failed to gain sufficient supporters, and Chupp Field Park in northern Indiana fell under the auctioneer's gavel.[4] In neighboring Ohio in 2012 and 2013, another effort to provide wholesome activities for that half of the area's Old Order youth who did not attend traditional singings appeared to be in jeopardy. A small group of Youngie who were not involved in either the singings or the party scene approached some respected Amish adults and asked for help in organizing a drama enacting scenes from the Bible. The adults agreed to provide moral and financial support for this effort, and in its two years of existence, 20,000 people, almost all of them Amish, attended the programs. Not unexpectedly, however, the sponsoring group faced significant criticism for presenting such a non-Amish alternative. "After all, they [the youth] have singings that they can attend. Besides, we don't need more entertainment," declared an Amish elder. When approached for his counsel and support, a senior bishop rejected the idea, "because it does not fit into

God's scriptural order." The final outcome for this biblical drama movement was not yet clear at the time the present volume was published. Although change from the ground up can happen, these examples illustrate that it is by no means certain.

As for resisting unhealthy changes, the Amish have several things in their favor. First, a countercultural society like theirs could not have succeeded for more than 300 years without exceptional perseverance, insights, wisdom, and commitment, although they would give all honor to God's protecting and almighty hand in their lives. Another strength arises from their clearly defined boundaries and attainable expectations for anyone who is willing "to give himself up to God and to the community." Their well-defined identity helps them know who they are and what they are all about. Finally, they expect and practice accountability to each other and to God. In the midst of change and disagreements, most choose to stay with the community and work through these issues.

The Amish, at least in Western societies, are arguably the masters of transmitting their culture to their sons and daughters. The parents' clarity of vision and their successes through the generations have imbued them with confidence that they can rear the next generation in ways that will result in their offspring making God- and culture-affirming decisions. Amish children bond first with their parents and then with their immediate and extended families. Despite differences in temperaments and personalities, most parents throughout the Amish communities successfully provide the same set of core values and requisite degrees of warmth, correction, example, and accountability to their youth. Amish children benefit greatly from having intact families and from receiving prompt intervention and help when illness or death sunders family bonds. Relatively few families struggle in isolation with issues of abuse, desertion, or financial ruin. All of these factors combine to provide a rich cultural soil that produces the expected yield: the next generation of youth embracing the Amish way. These manifestations impress me most about Amish culture and seem to me to underline the secret of their viability and endurance.

When people ask me about the future of the Amish, especially in light of the Internet and technology concerns, I remind them that these are a hardy people with a proven record for meeting and overcoming many challenges.

I express optimism that they have the requisite skills to survive. Almost daily, I observe growing numbers of Amish adults grappling with the problems of the Internet. As my colleague and friend, David McConnell, has observed, the computer, the Internet, and smartphones infiltrated Holmes County, Ohio, without warning or adequate scrutiny. But now many responsible Amish leaders and adults there are stepping back to take a careful look and decide where and how to draw lines.

This awareness and action is also happening elsewhere. For example, the Groffdale Conference Mennonites, or Team Mennonites (meaning horse-and-buggy Mennonites), have been far more proactive in seeking alternatives to the all-or-nothing options regarding computers and smartphones that exist in numerous large-settlement Amish church districts. Their approach is similar to the Ohio New Order Amish: a carefully modified computer for work and communication, but rejection of recreational or "trivial" Internet use. Just before this book went to press in late 2013, word from the Lancaster County fall bishops' meeting surfaced with news that this body had unanimously agreed that smartphones would no longer be tolerated among church members. Any member found in violation of this *Abschtelling* (authoritative edict) would be excluded from the fall communion, and if he or she failed to comply within the next year, that person would be excommunicated and put in the *Bann* (shunned).[5]

Like my thoughtful Amish friend in Lancaster County, I trust that a majority of the Youngie with smartphones have both the integrity and an internal set of core values that will make them responsible users. Most will not need parents or the church to constantly monitor their phone bills to see if they are venturing into questionable areas. Nevertheless, it is likely that an increasing number of youth will yield to worldly enticements, especially in Amish communities where the Internet is already widely established. Amish elders recall their own rumspringa days and their susceptibility to temptation and peer pressure. They know all too well how easy it is for human beings of any age to fall far short of Amish teachings and ideals. Their word for it is "sin." They fear that the widespread availability of all kinds of temptation, coupled with the ability to avoid accountability, will undoubtedly combine to entrap those Youngie with half-hearted commitments. A professional living outside of an Amish community mentioned having young Amish friends who confessed to him that "they felt awful but helpless with their addiction to porn."

The larger and more sinister danger, however, may come not from individual casualties, however disturbing they may be, but rather from the spread of non-Amish attitudes and behaviors. Many fear that such predilections and "ungodly tastes" will be born and fostered by undisciplined, undisclosed, unrestricted, or unmonitored Internet use. Most Amish would undoubtedly describe such a breakdown as a combination of the "enemy within" (one's tendency to sin), coupled with the "occasions to sin" provided by the Internet. Beyond worrying about nudity and portrayals of sexual activity, thoughtful Amish adults believe that extended contact with the Internet may ultimately undermine the entire Amish value system that they, their schools, and the church have worked so hard together to nurture.

In examining the Amish perception of Jesus's teachings and example, one can understand the nature of their Internet concerns. The table on the next page contrasts the Amish understanding of biblical standards with what they regard as the form and content of the "worldly" agenda rampant on the Internet. The contrast is unmistakable to the Amish: the values, behaviors, and assumptions evident on much of the web are in direct opposition to Jesus's teachings of simplicity, separation from the world, and non-resistance. This helps explain why Amish uneasiness has often turned into a categorical rejection of the Internet.

Beyond the obvious concerns of the Amish have regarding the impact of the worldwide web, their worries will only increase when they consider the many possibilities for unanticipated collateral damage. Those who become involved with Internet pornography might find difficulty in remaining content in a monogamous, committed relationship. Fantasy sex may impinge on normal sexual satisfaction or faithfulness. The Amish might also legitimately worry about the dangers of distorted body images and lowered self-esteem for Amish young women if they are now comparing themselves with the air-brushed females populating the entertainment venues on the Internet and in the media. If problems such as these do occur, they need not become fatal errors that corrupt or bring down their culture. It is possible that discerning Amish youth could recognize what is happening and actually become agents for change. By joining together with like-minded peers

Worldly versus Amish Values

Extravagance	Simplicity
Self-promotion	Humility
Wastefulness	Frugality
Vindictiveness	Forgiveness
Competition	Cooperation
Expediency	Integrity
Secularism	Godliness
Self-indulgence	Self-discipline
Sexual freedom	Sexual control
Independence	Accountability
Selfishness	Generosity
Excess	Moderation
Instant gratification	Patience
Sense of entitlement	Non-resistance
Individualism	Community
Force	Non-violence

and church members, they could start their own grassroots movement to combat further damage to their core values and practices.

My ominous but uninformed predictions in the 1960s about the demise of the Amish turned out to be, in Mark Twain's words, "greatly exaggerated," Thanks to years of studying Amish culture and the advantage of hindsight, I am now offering a more modest but admittedly speculative assessment. If Internet use should eventually erode traditional Amish values, a different type of critical mass could conceivably take shape around the growing numbers of those dissatisfied or disenchanted with the old ways. These individuals would probably seek to join or form a more "welcoming, inclusive, and tolerant group" as an alternative to what they would regard as an overly strict or legalistic church. Amish history is replete with this kind of *Spaulding* (rift) that not only splits the church, but either dissolves the church's bonds with the dissenters or else morphs the group into a non-Amish alternative.[6] A possible outcome of such a rupture, however unwelcome and disruptive initially, may turn out to be beneficial in the end. The Amish remnant most likely will be strengthened, since such separations serve as a purifier by reducing internal pressures for unhealthy change and removing dissenters from their midst. Nonetheless, virtually all Amish, individually and collectively, view such splits with heavy hearts.

Even if the worst case scenario—massive defections or serious changes in traditional values in the larger settlements—should happen, I believe that numerous pockets of traditional Amish life will continue to thrive for years in the most conservative affiliations, such as the Swartzentrubers or the majority of the Nebraska Amish in Pennsylvania. The intentional separation that they maintain from the more liberal Amish, with their electronic temptations, will almost certainly delay the conservatives' acceptance of more modern technology and ways of thinking. Still, no group's future in remaining Amish is guaranteed. Even relatively conservative affiliations, such as the Andy Weaver Amish in Holmes County, Ohio, and the Lawrence County Amish in Pennsylvania, have reported the infiltration of cell phones among some youth in 2013. Nevertheless, my opinion mirrors that of Karen Johnson-Weiner, who believes that whatever happens elsewhere among the Amish, the plainest groups will continue to be the repository and remnant of Amish culture.[7] They will be much less likely to follow any Amish movement that could result in an Anabaptist group similar to the technology-selecting, car-owning Beachy Amish.

My sense is that if any culture, anywhere, can control whatever technology they encounter, it will be the Amish. They have had considerable practice over the centuries, and they have been taking definite steps, however belated, to keep the Internet "under control." Nevertheless, as Donald B. Kraybill has pointed out, the Internet differs qualitatively from anything the Amish have dealt with in the past.[8] It is far more invasive, interactive, and private than anything they have ever experienced. This electronic conduit will undoubtedly produce casualties—and perhaps even widespread defections—among Amish Internet users, especially for those who embrace all that accompanies this technology. It is conceivable that an unfiltered and unmonitored exposure to the world via the Internet could prove to be the proverbial Achilles' heel for individuals or a Trojan horse for their society. Nobody can know for sure, but the attraction, retention, and attrition rates of heavy Internet users among the Amish will certainly be a focus of interest not only for academics, but much more so for parents and leaders.

Will the Internet be a game-changer for the Amish? I am sure that they will continue to change, but I am also hopeful that with their considerable social capital, self-discipline, and faith in God, they and their separatist and peaceful culture will remain viable for years to come. If or when the Amish vanish, like the Shakers and so many other past religious groups, most of us in mainstream society, amid the pursuit of pleasure, affluence, status, and power, may scarcely notice their demise. But future generations would be the poorer for the disappearance of the Amish. They have and continue to gift our mainstream American culture with a people endeavoring to live by values based on deeply held religious and ethical principles, rather than on expediency, entitlement, and hedonism. We are both enriched by and indebted to the example and witness of these people who are the faithful in the land. Of this I am certain.

Notes

Preface

1. Smart (2011).

2. See V. Weaver-Zercher (2013), an excellent book.

3. Of the several books written on the subject, Kraybill et al. (2007) is the most complete.

4. See, for example, Carr (2010); and Subrahmanyam and Smahel (2011).

5. Dillard (2000) intrigues me with its treatment of humans as limited "time beings" on this planet. I only wish I would live long enough to see and chart the upcoming trajectories of Amish life and culture.

Chapter 1. Amish Life

1. As we will see in chapter 10, weddings provide an exciting venue for Amish youth, but English (non-Amish) guests rarely see or understand the youthful excitement and dynamics taking place in the afternoon and evening.

2. V. Weaver-Zercher (2013), xii.

3. Ibid., 253.

4. Graney (2003).

5. "Calgary Film Festival Guide," www.sharbean.ca [site discontinued].

6. See Eitzen (2008b) for an excellent essay on *Devil's Playground*.

7. Eitzen (2008a), 135. Also, Kraybill et al. (2013), 213, 396, offer a comprehensive summary and analysis of the spate of the various so-called reality shows featuring youthful participants, all with tenuous connections to their Amish past.

8. A notable exception to these shallow and sensationalized programs is *The Amish* (2012), the highly regarded PBS production in the *American Experience* series. It captured the largest viewing audience of any *American Experience* offering.

9. Eitzen (2008a).

10. *Amish in the City* did not become the 2004 reality-series hit that its producers might have wished for, although it did attract its share of media attention. UPN reported that this show was its most watched (by young-adult viewers) Wednesday-night program in three years, with an audience of 5.4 million its first night. It also attracted more viewers than any of the three major networks in that specific Wednesday-night time slot. Its achievements spawned the succession of other so-called Amish reality shows that followed, many of which garnered notoriety as well as commercial success.

11. All scripture in this volume is quoted from the King James Version of the Bible, the preferred version of the Amish when they refer to an English-language translation.

12. Six months after the series was over, thousands who attended the Gordonville, Pennsylvania, fire department's annual fund-raising auction and sale saw four non-Amish teenage girls carrying a placard with a picture of Mose Gingerich that read, "Have you seen this man?" As ardent fans, they were evidently hoping to get information on his current whereabouts from one of the many Amish who were at the sale. Mose did not return to the Amish fold ("Mose J. Gingerich" 2013). In 2005 he started a construction business in Missouri, which Mose later closed, due to health reasons. In 2010 he began his current occupation (using the name Moses), selling cars at a Toyota franchise in Columbia, Missouri. By 2012, Mose had been featured on the National Geographic Channel's *Amish: Out of Order* and had organized and briefly run a type of halfway house and related services for youth and adults leaving the Amish. According to Wikipedia (2013a), of the five participants in *Amish in the City*, only Ruth returned to the Amish.

13. If an Amish person is divorced by his or her spouse, he or she can still be a church member in good standing. That person may not remarry, however, until the divorcing spouse dies.

14. Kraybill (1994b, 1994c).

15. See P. Yoder (2003) for an excellent discussion of the Amish view of the state.

16. See Dyck (1993) for his treatment of the formative years of Anabaptism.

17. In a marked departure from their commitment to non-resistance, a group of zealots from Germany opted to establish an Anabaptist state by force. These radicals captured Münster in 1534 but were decisively defeated by a makeshift local army of Catholics and Reformed Protestants. This incident further incited resentment and hostility against the Anabaptists, who were already widely persecuted. See Nolt (2003), 15–18.

18. This tome, first published in 1660, is nearly 1,200 pages long and includes more than 100 graphic illustrations of Anabaptist persecutions and deaths (Braght 2002). Oyer and Kreider (1990) is a good introduction to *Martyrs Mirror*. Also see books on *Martyrs Mirror* by Luthy (2013), an Amish convert and director of the Amish Historical Library in Aylmer, Ontario; and D. Weaver-Zercher (forthcoming in 2014, from Johns Hopkins University Press).

19. Some of this historical material originally appeared in R. Stevick (2001).

Clasen (1972) provided a detailed account of this turbulent period in Anabaptist history. Nolt (2003) has the most comprehensive treatment of Amish history.

20. The major biblical passages used to support this belief are 1 Corinthians 5:9–11; 2 Thessalonians 3:14; Titus 3:10–11; and Romans 16:17.

21. Some Amish are not averse to voting on local issues that directly affect them, such as road or zoning decisions. In one area, according to a local resident, a number of them "voted against Clinton" in the 1996 presidential election. In the swing states of Ohio and Pennsylvania, Republicans actively sought the Amish vote in the 2004 presidential elections.

22. Since the beginning of the twenty-first century, I have heard scattered stories of Amish people, under what they perceived to be dire circumstances, seeking social security benefits or receiving other state or governmental assistance.

23. Kraybill (1994b).

24. The Amish specifically refer to Matthew 5:33–48.

25. Ministers frequently quote 1 Corinthians 11:3; 1 Peter 3:1–6; and Titus 2:3–5 in support of male headship.

26. Baby girls are excluded from this requirement, and in some settlements girls do not regularly wear coverings until they are about twelve or thirteen years old.

27. Perhaps for the historical reason of having to travel long distances to church by horse and carriage, the Amish in North America have always held their worship services every other week. Off-Sundays are typically spent at home or visiting other churches, relatives, or friends.

28. "Dutch" is a corruption of the German word *Deutsch*, meaning "German." Their spoken dialect should actually be called Pennsylvania German or Pennsylvania *Deitsch*.

29. "Amish Population by State (2013)."

30. A major exception to this local autonomy is in Lancaster County, Pennsylvania, where bishops meet twice annually to maintain uniformity on most issues.

31. In reality, at least seven affiliations exist, because of ongoing internal divisions. For example, even though Pennsylvania's Nebraska Amish look alike, they have subdivided into at least five distinct groups, each with its own Ordnung. This Pennsylvania settlement acquired its nickname from its ties to an Amish bishop in Nebraska who provided the Pennsylvania group with counsel and oversight at a critical time for them. See Kraybill et al. (2013), 141.

32. See Nolt and Meyers's (2007) excellent book with its insightful and careful analysis of the Indiana Amish.

33. See Hurst and McConnell (2010) for a nuanced treatment of the diversity of Amish affiliations in the Wooster and Canton, Ohio, areas.

34. E. Kline and Beachy (1998).

35. Another split occurred in Holmes County in 1986, resulting in a group known as the *New* New Order Amish. They have many of the same values and tendencies as the original New Order group, including the propensity of their youth to defect

to the Beachy Amish and conservative Mennonite churches. "It's not a large group because many of the youth have left," a New Order member observed.

36. Two of the three largest settlements (in Elkhart/LaGrange Counties in Indiana and Lancaster County, Pennsylvania) are much more homogeneous than the one in Holmes/Wayne/Stark Counties in Ohio. One reason for this is that in the northern Indiana and Lancaster County settlements, the bishops periodically meet to form policies and work out differences. This has resulted in more uniformity there than in the highly diverse settlements in Holmes/Wayne/Stark Counties in Ohio.

37. An Amish affiliation is a "cluster of church districts linked by social and spiritual bonds" (Kraybill et al. 2013, 12). Also see Kraybill (2001), 336; Kraybill and Bowman (2001), 105; and Kraybill and Hostetter (2001), 177–208.

38. Conversation with the author (Jul. 2000). The interviewee was a highly regarded Lancaster County Amish man, recognized as a community historian.

39. For example, Kraybill (2001), 17, 335, estimated Lancaster County's total Amish population in 1960 at 5,570; in 2000 it was 22,300. He stated: "Lancaster's settlement expanded from merely six church districts in 1878 to sixty-five by 1980. In the twenty-year period between 1980 and 2000, the number of districts more than doubled." Note that the reported population of 5,570 in the Lancaster settlement for 1960 is not much larger than the 2013 estimated population for rumspringa-aged youth.

40. S. Stoltzfus (1994) described how the area of one of the original church districts in Lancaster County was divided and subdivided over the years to accommodate a growing population. These divisions dramatically reduced the size of each district.

41. See the section on population and density in Hostetler (1993), 355–60.

42. A possible reason for the increase in Amish young men driving cars after World War II may stem from those youth who had served in the government's alternative Civilian Public Service (CPS) in locations far from home and with Mennonite and other pacifist youth who accepted driving automobiles.

43. Social psychologists call this phenomenon "group polarization." It helps to explain why one's initial tendencies toward certain behaviors or beliefs intensify in the presence of like-minded peers. Myers (2011), 303–11, one of the early researchers in group polarization, wrote an excellent summary of the theory and findings of this phenomenon.

44. Benedict (1934), a sociologist, first described the continuous-discontinuous distinction. Also see Steinberg (2005), 113–18, for a helpful discussion of this topic.

45. One of my Amish readers reminded me that we should expect more fast youth in the large settlements simply because of the comparatively larger numbers of youth. He rightly pointed out that percentage studies are more accurate indicators of whether there is a relative difference.

Chapter 2. Religion

1. For whatever reason, this lack of attention to adolescent religious experiences also occurs in developmental textbooks on adolescence. Typically, authors devote fewer than five pages to this subject.

2. One of my Amish readers wrote that "females do have a large spiritual and religious influence." He related that his wife also prays with their children, a practice that varies markedly from community to community and family to family.

3. Kraybill and Bowman (2001), 114.

4. Kraybill (2001), 186.

5. Some Amish believe that the ability of the young to understand German has actually increased since the rise of the Amish private-school movement and the subsequent instruction time in that language.

6. Although Sunday schools are usually associated with the New Order Amish, a few Old Order churches in Indiana, Iowa, and elsewhere have Sunday school in the summer.

7. Quoted in Bachman (1961), 143.

8. Kraybill et al. (2007, 2010) dealt with this concept extensively. The seminal work on *Gelassenheit* was written by Cronk (1977). Many thoughtful Amish have told me and other researchers that the word *Gelassenheit* is used far more by academics than by the Amish themselves. The concept, however, is very salient among them.

9. Occasionally Amish men and English outsiders teach in Amish schools, but the bulk of the teachers are unmarried Amish women. Regardless of their background, teachers need to be sympathetic with Amish beliefs and practices.

10. *A Devoted Christian's Prayer Book* (1984) is an English-language translation of this book.

11. An Amish bishop estimated that fewer than 15 percent of Amish members have struggles with whether to remain Amish. A nearby married couple in their thirties, however, estimated that almost twice that many experience this conflict. Nobody, of course, knows for sure, but most observers within and outside of the communities believe that it is a small minority.

12. Both periodicals are produced by Pathway Publishers in Aylmer, Ontario. A few of the most conservative affiliations, such as the Swartzentruber Amish and the Lawrence County (Pennsylvania) Amish, do not approve of these publications.

13. Most church districts offer membership instruction annually, following the spring communion. If a young person decides not to enroll in instruction, it could mean a delay of at least a year, and possibly two, unless he or she receives permission to take instruction in a neighboring church district that is on a different yearly schedule.

14. The *Dordrecht Confession of Faith* (1994) is the English-language translation of this document. M. Miller (2008), 114–47, also has a parallel translation of the articles.

15. The latter point was one of the divisive issues that caused Jakob Ammann to split from the main Mennonite body in 1693.

16. In Lancaster County churches and some others, candidates initially may continue to behave outside the Ordnung, but by the third session, they are expected to be in full compliance with its standards.

17. An occasional bishop will receive a previously resistant membership candidate into the church, whatever the time of year, as soon as he or she comes into compliance. This action can reduce the likelihood that the delay might result in such individuals changing their minds before membership classes come around again.

18. All Amish clergy are selected through a screening nomination process in which each church member privately informs the deacon whom his or her choice is. Each candidate for ordination then selects a songbook from the presiding bishop. Only one of the books has a verse of scripture concealed in its pages. The man who has picked the book with the verse inside is then immediately chosen and consecrated as minister for life. The Amish believe that this scriptural method, based on Acts 1:23–26, leaves the final choice to God.

19. Any kind of delay is not without its risks, however—to the candidate, the family, and the church. In Somerset County, Pennsylvania, the ministers turned down a young man's request for membership three times, because they felt that he was too questioning and rebellious. Nobody was surprised when he subsequently left the Amish.

20. A Lancaster County bishop pointed out that in their community, when candidates are asked if they will "support the teachings and regulations," the words "subject to the word of God" follow (*nach dem Wort Gottes*, in High German). In actual practice, this may lead to disagreements as to the validity of particular Ordnung requirements that may or may not be seen as scriptural.

21. The exact wording may differ slightly among the affiliations, but the basic questions remain the same. *Handbuch fur Bischof* (1978), 26; *In Meiner Jugend* (2000), 190–91; and *Gemein Ordnungen von Lancaster Co., PA* (n.d.), 6, demonstrate the variations. The English-language translation used here is from *In Meiner Jugend*.

22. *Handbuch fur Bischof* (1978) details these ministerial procedures.

23. Transcript from *The Amish* (2012).

24. Ibid.

25. Lecture given at Elizabethtown College (May 1993).

26. Quoted in Bachman (1961), 144.

27. In the first edition of this book (R. Stevick 2007), I wrote that each member was asked whether he or she was "in agreement and compliance" with the Ordnung. I was subsequently told by a bishop that "compliance" is not part of the question in their community, only "in agreement with." In actual practice, this probably allows members who are dissatisfied with certain Ordnung stipulations to ignore them without feeling undue guilt for their infractions.

28. As Anabaptists who are deeply committed to adult baptism, some adults are conflicted between their desire to see their children "safely in the fold" and their

concern about whether a fourteen-year-old is really ready to make an informed and responsible lifetime commitment to the Amish way.

29. A number of anonymously written booklets identified as "An Amish Brotherhood Publication" can be found in certain bookstores and tourist venues in Holmes County, Ohio, such as *What Makes for a Strong Nation?*, *A Sure Path for Mankind*, *What Shall I Wear?*, and *Teaching Emphases That Hinder Discipleship*. A longer book, *The Truth in Word and Work*, explains some New Order beliefs and practices in more detail.

30. See A. Lapp (2003) for details on the group's origin and distinctiveness.

31. R. Stevick (2001), 171. The Amish always emphasize the quiet witness of their deeds over theology or creeds.

32. Some New Order churches will switch to English if they have visitors who do not speak Pennsylvania German. At least two Old Order churches provide simultaneous English translation for guests who do not understand their language; Old Order groups, however, regard this as a questionable practice (at best), since, sooner or later, all English-only churches left the Old Order fold.

33. One observer conjectured that the Swartzentrubers and other plain groups may regard direct eye contact during sermons as a lack of humility on the part of the minister.

34. An Old Order man related that when the young men returned late to the church service after an extended break, interrupting the sermon of a visiting minister, the minister stopped preaching and exclaimed, "You boys really get on my nerves coming in late like this." A public rebuke of this type, however, would be very rare from either Old or New Order ministers.

35. Many Old Order churches also reject these practices.

36. One must use caution in extrapolating these findings to all New Order groups. Also, these questions may have been edited or screened by the elders before they were distributed. Finally, some of the supervised gangs in Lancaster County will also offer a question-and-answer period at their semiannual rules meeting.

37. The conservative Swartzentruber Amish also reported disruptions of their singings by other Amish. Therefore the harassment by Old Order young people may have been indiscriminately targeted at any "outside" Amish youth, rather than just at the "goodie-goodies."

38. *Family Life* (Oct. 1968), quoted in Igou (1999), 188.

39. *Family Life* (Dec. 1974), 7.

40. Responding to this statement, one church member said: "It makes me feel sad to hear comments like this, but it is true. Our ministers warn us all the time that this is not the true way to salvation, and deep in their hearts most Amish know this. We are told living the Amish lifestyle is very important, but without salvation it is nothing."

41. Even though New Order youth have fewer cars while at home, many of their parents concede that Old Order youth are likely to give up their cars, while New Order youth with cars are more prone to leave the Amish for a Mennonite group.

42. Only one of this couple's three children joined or "stayed with the church."

43. Data compiled by Kraybill et al. (2013), based on information in the *Ohio Amish Directory* (2009).

Chapter 3. Adolescence

1. The "Fisher Book," edited by Beiler (2009), is a genealogy book for the Lancaster County Amish and its daughter settlements. It is published about every ten years.

2. James Marcia (1994), 70–71, the leading contemporary researcher in adolescent identity issues, defined identity as follows: "Identity refers to a coherent sense of one's meaning to oneself and to others within that social context. This sense of identity suggests an individual's continuity with the past, a personally meaningful present, and a direction for the future."

3. Erikson (1968, 1980).

4. Marcia (1980).

5. P. Stevick (2006).

6. Triandis (1990, 1995).

7. Developmental psychologists Marcia (1980, 1994) and Erikson (1968, 1980) described this period of exploration as a moratorium, a byproduct of a complex society that temporarily relaxes expectations for mature performance and behavior.

8. After reading this paragraph, in a letter to the author (10 Aug. 2004), a mother from a large settlement wrote, "For the most part, yes, but fifty dresses for a teenage girl is 'frugal'?" She reported that by the time her daughters and their friends counted their outfits for Saturday night, Sunday church, and Sunday night, they each had that many dresses. Obviously those teenagers do worry about looking good and keeping up with the latest fashions.

9. An exception to this utilitarian attire is that boys in the conservative horse-and-buggy Amish groups in Lancaster County wear bow ties when they dress up.

10. L. Stoltzfus (1998).

11. An informal survey was taken among Amish attending a county fair and then discussed on an ABC special, *Mystery of Happiness* (aired 15 Apr. 1996).

12. On reading this section, a convert to the Amish wrote: "I agree. The children are *so* loved and accepted."

13. Presentation at Young Center, Elizabethtown College (May 1991).

14. Biswas-Diener et al. (2005) administered several self-reporting surveys on various components of happiness (SWB = Sense of Well-Being) to both Old Order and New Order volunteers in Illinois. The authors concluded that, as a group, the Amish scored significantly higher than "neutral" in their sense of happiness, their memory of positive over negative events, and their perceived happiness, as judged by their friends.

15. Harter (1999).

16. In the faster gangs in the large settlements, a young person's sense of well-being most likely resembles that of the mainstream culture, with its emphasis on

consumerism, pleasure, fashion, and looks. Among these youth, especially, I have observed many more young people wearing orthodontic braces since my research for the first edition of this book (R. Stevick 2007). Identity acquisition for boundary-testing youth is probably tied more closely to the kind of autonomy, achievement, and recognition issues that confront youth in mainstream America.

17. Cassady et al. (2006).

18. My wife felt it was necessary to remind me that this statement was made by an Amish male.

19. See 1 Timothy 2:11–12; and 1 Corinthians 14:34–35.

20. Johnson-Weiner (2001) believed that Old Order Amish women have more autonomy and voice than do women in "higher" Amish circles, such as the Beachy Amish or Fellowship churches. This may relate to the latter groups' interpretation of and greater emphasis on the Apostle Paul's teaching of gender hierarchy and submission.

21. Moustaches are forbidden among all Amish men. They explain this prohibition as a reaction against the moustaches worn by their European military persecutors.

22. Kraybill and Nolt (2004), 208–9, found that 20 percent of Amish businesses are operated by women, but their ownership is traditionally gendered (e.g., women will not own construction businesses or welding shops). Also see Wesner (2010), 12–13.

23. An incident caused a stir in the Holmes County community when Zach Bolinger (2007), a sportswriter for the *Wooster (OH) Daily Record*, ran a series on girls' softball in the area. The front-page lead article of the sports section featured a photo of an Amish girl in her pink uniform dress sliding into base with a trace of her Spandex-covered thigh showing. The caption read, "Girls just want to have fun." The series spawned several letters from upset Amish readers who felt that the editor showed poor taste in printing the article. An Ohio Amish elder expressed concern about the color of the uniforms and the fact that the Amish second baseman/baseperson had traded her traditional head covering for a Mennonite-like doily covering, "because it's hard for them to play wearing our traditional [oatmeal-container type] covering." See the frontispiece for a less scandalous girls' softball photo taken at the same time.

24. When the Amish monthly, the *Diary*, prints its column requesting pen pals, the seekers are virtually all females.

25. This youth never joined the Amish church.

26. Baumrind (1971, 1978).

27. In a conversation with the author (Oct, 2013), Karen Johnson-Weiner told me that in some Swartzentruber settlements, fathers will occasionally use "the strap" on belligerent teenagers, especially sons.

28. An Amish father wrote: "This sets the pattern of a male being dominant, because girls must get rides from boys to go to gangs and singings. Girls are dependent on the boys."

29. This parallels Batson and Ventis's (1982) findings, which indicated that in North America, women typically outnumber men in religious expression and church attendance.

30. Reiling (2002), 155.

31. Wagler (2011).

32. Furlong (2011).

33. If one's family also leaves the Amish, or if several families leave together because of a formal church division or split, the emotional consequences on individuals are probably less severe than if an individual leaves alone. Also, almost all Amish would agree that not joining the church and thereby avoiding shunning is less painful than joining the church and then leaving it.

34. See McNamara (1997).

35. In October 1998, a significant exception to their silence occurred, in an interview with two young men from Amish families that aired on the CBS program *Public Eye*, with Bryant Gumbel. One of them, besides stating his belief that 10–15 percent of Amish youth in his settlement experimented with drugs, then demonstrated in precise detail how he smoked crack cocaine at an Amish party. Another notable exception occurred when several youth from northern Indiana cooperated with Lucy Walker, the director of *Devil's Playground* (2002), and allowed themselves to be interviewed and photographed extensively.

36. Even the young man who demonstrated how to smoke crack cocaine on CBS's *Public Eye* program indicated that he eventually planned to "settle down and join church."

Chapter 4. Schooling

1. Hostetler (1993), 561.

2. Johnson-Weiner (2006) has written the most comprehensive scholarly book on Amish education.

3. Kraybill and Nolt (2004).

4. As far as I can determine, Kraybill (1998) wrote the first article that focused on the intersection of the Amish and the fast-developing options and temptations of electronic communications. Shortly thereafter, *Wired* magazine (Rheingold 1999) featured the first article that dealt exclusively with the Amish and cell phones. Umble (1994, 1996) provides excellent background material regarding telephones and the Amish.

5. Hostetler (1977), 359.

6. See Huntington (1994); and Meyers (2003).

7. See Nolt (2003), 306–7, for excerpts of the *Wisconsin v. Yoder* decision. Also see Kraybill and Bowman (2001), 114.

8. Meyers (2003), chapter 5, "Education and Schooling," extensively covers these past and present conflicts.

9. O. Garrett (1998).

10. Hostetler and Huntington (1992).

11. Ibid., 94.

12. Kraybill et al. (2013), 263–264.

13. Indiana's regulations state that "the teacher will have passed the eighth grade satisfactorily and will make a passing score on a General Education Development [GED] High School Equivalency Test or on a standardized 12th grade achievement test furnished, administered, and graded by the State Department of Public Instruction" (Articles of Agreement, 3). Although some teachers have obtained a GED, according to Johnson-Weiner, in a letter to the author (4 Aug. 2005), nobody in Indiana knows of this regulation being enforced. In some places, such as Pennsylvania, home-school teachers must have either a high school diploma or a GED. At least one New Order church permits their children to attend a local Christian high school if the student needs a diploma for nursing or teaching.

14. An Amish teacher from a plain group in Pennsylvania reported that some of their teachers not infrequently resort to Pennsylvania German for instruction. He recognized that if state education officials learned of this, those particular schools would face serious sanctions.

15. Letter to the author (26 Jul. 2004).

16. From Maryalice Yakutchik, "Among the Amish, Day 5," *Amish Online*, on the *Discovery Channel* website [no longer available on this site].

17. Johnson-Weiner (2006), 261.

18. Hurst and McConnell (2010).

19. Johnson-Weiner (2006), chapter 8, "Publish or Perish," reviewed all of the important curricular materials used by various Amish groups.

20. Occasionally girls as young as fifteen have taught school. Rarely, a teacher from a Mennonite or other Anabaptist group, or even an outsider sympathetic to Amish values, will be hired. These non-Amish teachers are sometimes criticized for "spending too much time on frills rather than the three Rs" and on being too lax in disciplining disobedient students. On the other hand, a convert to the Amish who taught in the Big Valley of Pennsylvania received criticism for pushing his students to learn too much.

21. In certain areas, teacher shortages have reputedly grown in recent years. "What can we expect," complained an Ohio father, "if we don't pay a decent wage to our teachers? Things will only get worse."

22. Letter to the author (26 Jul. 2004). School boards face the perennial challenge of replacing teachers who get married, since most Amish assume that married women belong in the homes and not in the classroom, at least not until their children are grown. The average tenure of Amish teachers is probably less than four or five years.

23. On this issue, see Meyers (2003), 92 and Nolt (2003), 276–78.

24. Librarians in Holmes County, Ohio, indicated that Amish children and youth used their services and borrowed books in disproportionately higher numbers than the library's other youthful patrons, although the former's choices of reading matter tended to be restricted to history, biographies, nature, farming, religion, and family themes.

25. V. Weaver-Zercher (2013) reported that several of these Amish bookstores also offered a collection of Amish romance novels.

26. Until 2013, Byler was writing exclusively for Good Books (a publishing firm in Intercourse, Pennsylvania) and ventured into novels featuring horses and settings in western states. (Good Books filed for bankruptcy in December 2013.)

27. New Order (and some Old Order) parents generally forbid their children to read romance novels, westerns, or any novels portraying violence or fighting.

28. A parent objected to the implied sexual behavior in Wojtasik's (1996) novel and mentioned the word "condom," a term that he thought most Amish readers would find offensive. Both an Old Order and a New Order reader who reviewed a prepublication copy of the present chapter agreed that the word was objectionable, even in that context.

29. V. Weaver-Zercher (2013), chapter 8, "Amish Reading Amish."

30. *One Way Street* (E. Stoll 1972) and many other books published by Pathway typically do not list the author's name. This is a traditional practice, to reduce the likelihood of pride or attention-seeking.

31. The author, Elmo Stoll, shocked the Amish world when he eventually left the Aylmer, Ontario, settlement and started a conservative non-Amish settlement in Cookeville, Tennessee. Wagler (2008–9), in blogs, wrote a detailed and engaging three-part biography of Elmo Stoll, including Wagler's own youthful encounters with and impressions of the bishop.

32. Also see *Family Life* (Aug.–Sept. 1986), 8–10.

33. Several years ago a bishop from Lancaster County required the late Ben Blank, one of his ministers who served on Pathway's board, to terminate his tenure.

34. One youth discovered Thomas Paine and Herman Melville, and read all of Mark Twain's works. As a result, he has gained the nickname "Moby," from Melville's novel *Moby Dick*.

35. Hostetler (1992). For decades, John A. Hostetler (1918–2001) was regarded as the foremost scholar on Amish life and culture. He wrote or coauthored dozens of articles and several books on Amish culture for both professional journals and popular magazines. His most noteworthy was *Amish Society*, published in four editions between 1963 and 1993. D. Weaver-Zercher (2005) analyzed Hostetler's place in Amish studies and compiled some of Hostetler's most important contributions in *Writing the Amish*.

36. Once, when I stopped by to visit, I saw that he had been reading a sizeable tome. I asked him what it was, and he showed me *A History of Russia*. His tastes were broad and catholic.

37. To the dismay of state licensing boards, several Amish "dentists" and dental technicians even extract teeth or make dental plates for Old Order friends and acquaintances.

38. For an example of the kind of critical thinking and precise writing that some Amish achieve, see E. Stoltzfus (1996). Also see Pauline Stevick (2006), chapter 4, "An Amish Intellectual"; and the transcript of "A Reflection on the Nature of the

Ordnung and Why It Changes" (2013), an Amish businessman's presentation about technology and the Ordnung, on the Amish America blog site.

39. Hostetler (1992), 562.

Chapter 5. Parenting

1. See P. Stevick (2006).

2. Kraybill (2001), 16, 333–34. Although these data are from Lancaster County, most Amish cite retention rates that compare with or exceed these figures. Hurst and McConnell (2010) report similar numbers in their Ohio data.

3. Exact numbers for deviants are difficult to obtain. Most estimates are based on observations by the parents of teenagers. Some Amish adults in larger settlements estimate that as many as 50 percent of the youth over the age of sixteen have tried alcohol, and that 25 percent use it weekly. In some of the Lancaster County gangs, all of the males and some of the females drink regularly. Several groups, however, including two whose young men drive motorized vehicles, have little, if any, drinking. The use of alcohol is also rare in most small settlements and in the New Order Amish affiliations.

4. Wittmer (1973).

5. All Amish adults and children know that they are to honor their parents, and that children are to be obedient: "Children, obey your parents in the Lord for this is right. Honor thy father and mother" (Ephesians 6:1–2a). This verse quotes from the Fifth Commandment: "Honor thy father and thy mother that thy days may be long upon the land which the Lord thy God giveth thee" (Exodus 20:12).

6. A notable exception existed in Lancaster County. A non-Amish man, described by the Amish as a "motivational expert," not only conducted Dale Carnegie–type seminars, but also regularly led ten-week sessions on family issues and dynamics. In winter 2003, a hundred plain people enrolled in his family seminar. Another exception occurred in 2005–6, when the *Lancaster New Era* (Burke 2005) reported that dozens of Amish paid $4,975 each to attend a five-day "business/motivational workshop" conducted by an outsider. The bishops eventually agreed to forbid all attendance.

7. A conversation with an Amish woman, related by Donald B. Kraybill to the author.

8. *Blackboard Bulletin* (Apr. 1999), 5.

9. Steinberg (1990, 2001).

10. When asked about this relatively quiet period, a mother from a Lancaster County daughter settlement said: "It is generally true among our people, but it is not nearly so simple for those of us who are more liberal parents. We have more to deal with during those years. Our younger children want the same kind of independence that they see their older brothers and sisters experiencing."

11. *Young Companion* (Jan. 1991), 10.

12. *Family Life* (Jan. 1975), 8.

13. According to Reiling (2002), 151, "the Amish believe that listing the names of those who defect will function to limit defection."

14. A minister who moved to another settlement asked that he not be included as a candidate for bishop there, because his children were "out in the world." His request was honored.

15. This could help explain, in part, the behavior of the Amish parents of the slain children at Nickel Mines, who went to the killer's parents and offered them forgiveness. Perhaps in the Amish world view, the killer's mother and father were the ones who ultimately failed in parenting.

16. *Young Companion* (Jan. 1979), 16–17.

17. Reiling (2002).

18. *Die Botschaft* (2 Dec. 1987), 5.

19. *Budget* (11 Aug. 1960).

20. *Lancaster Intelligencer Journal* (30 Nov. 1984), 9.

21. Varian (1999) chronicled an Amish couple's worst fear when their daughter left their Iowa community to marry a divorced English man. The daughter, Ruth Irene Garret (2001, 2004) has since written her own books.

22. When an English young man became a member of a Lancaster County Amish church, an Amish grandmother asked rhetorically, "Would you want him to marry your granddaughter?" He eventually married an Amish girl and had three children by her, but he subsequently left the church, divorced his wife, and took their oldest child with him. The Amish believe that marrying an outsider increases the likelihood of future problems and of leaving the church. Considerable evidence exists to support their fear. An informal survey conducted by Amish converts found that more than 300 outsiders joined the church in the last several decades but only 100 of them have remained with the church.

23. Nolt (2003), 288.

24. Exact figures are unavailable, but in one western Old Order settlement, all of the young men in CPS reputedly left the Amish.

25. Beechy and Beechy (199–), 140.

26. Nolt (2003), 299–300.

27. One former Old Order man recounted how his volunteer work project among Native Americans put him in contact with more-progressive Anabaptist youth, who influenced his eventual defection to the Mennonites. Ironically, his Amish home-church district had supported the voluntary service involvement that resulted in his leaving. The problem of defection became so worrisome that it led to the formation of the National Steering Committee in the 1960s. Committee members tried to work out alternatives to urban assignments in hospitals.

28. The irony is that the author, Elmo Stoll, eventually left the Amish church and started his own group in Cookeville, Tennessee, in an attempt to have a more biblically based church. After his untimely death, the settlement soon disbanded.

29. The Amish teacher, a woman in her forties and an experienced vocational-school teacher, assigned me the task of also translating a verse. My studies in Penn-

sylvania German gave me a bit of help in that effort, but I hereby confess that I had to get some assistance from my fourteen-year-old desk mate, Marcus King. When it was my turn to stand before the teacher with the attempt in my sweaty hand, I felt like I was back in eighth grade. When she pronounced my work to be good, I felt a rush of non-Amish pride and English relief. It was an unforgettable experience for me.

30. Letter to the author (5 Mar. 2001).

31. *Family Life* (Feb. 1986), 12.

32. Tomlin (2003).

33. An Amish reader, after perusing this section in a prepublication manuscript, took exception to the argument that the Pennsylvania German language is dying or that it is a valid indicator of the health of an Amish settlement or affiliation. He cited a large settlement that he and others regard as using the language far more than in his settlement, but having a lower retention rate. He also reported that his children are much better versed in High German than he was at their age. This illustrates the diversity of opinion surrounding the language issue and its complexity.

34. Kraybill and Nolt (2004), 19–35.

35. For an excellent discussion of the concerns that many Amish have with the decreased percentage of children growing up on farms, see Kraybill and Nolt (2003).

36. Beechy and Beechy (199–), 141.

37. "Singing and Hymns" (1990).

38. Research by Charles Jantzi and the author for presentations at Elizabethtown College in June 2013 on "Amish America: Plain Technology in a Cyber World."

39. See Trollinger (2012) for the most current and extensive treatment of Amish-based tourism.

40. *Die Botschaft* (3 Jun. 1987), 10. Although this statement was made before the advent of supervised groups, it still applies to many youth who are not in those groups or who live in other settlements.

41. *Lancaster New Era* (8 Nov. 1984), 6.

42. *Elkhart (IN) Truth* (8 Sept. 1973)

43. Conversation with the author at the Young Center, Elizabethtown College (Jul. 2013).

44. Since the advent of supervised youth groups and singings around the early years of the twenty-first century, most adults believe that adversarial relationships have decreased significantly between adults and youth.

45. *Budget* (1 Apr. 1909).

46. Associated Press (1999). Thirty years earlier, in an article headlined "Nine Amish Held in Vandalism" (1968), the *Des Moines Register* reported a similar incident from the same community, when these Youngie were picked up for overturning a wagon and a grain elevator, breaking windows, decapitating chickens, and dumping sand and gravel into machinery.

47. *Budget* (29 Sept. 1949).

48. Hurst and McConnell (2010), 41–43.

49. *Die Botschaft* (5 Dec. 1984).

50. One reason such situations are rare is that Amish youth have traditionally been more likely to leave home than to act out. For example, young men might join the armed forces or go west to work on a ranch.

51. *Family Life* (Apr. 1999).

52. An Amish minister claims that a realtor who worked with the Parke County settlement refused to bring certain interested families there to check out the community, "because he knew they didn't fit in."

53. Being small and isolated is no guarantee for concerned parents that life will be like it is in the Parke County, Indiana, settlement. On the other side of the state, another small daughter settlement has the reputation of resembling Lancaster County more than it does Parke County. The youth in this other Indiana settlement dress less conservatively, spend more time with each other, and reputedly violate more community standards than in Parke County. One observer wondered if the former settlement began in an attempt to have more relaxed behavioral expectations than in Parke County. For whatever reasons, these two daughter settlements in the same state provide some contrast in their youth standards.

54. Cited in *Gemeinde Brief* (5 Mar. 1986), a local Indiana Amish publication.

55. Unpublished letter on file in the Heritage Historical Library, Aylmer, Ontario.

56. Copy of a letter in the author's personal files.

57. Reporter's conversation with the author (Jul. 1998).

58. Hurst and McConnell (2010), 75–76.

59. The 2012 guidelines for one of the supervised groups in Lancaster County are remarkably similar to those of the original "rules groups" and quite explicit, as is evident from the following excerpt:

1. The appearance of the members, their way of travel, and their activities should conform to the standards of the church.

2. The goal is to have gatherings that are free from unrighteousness, thus being attractive only to those who desire decent and orderly conduct. At Sunday-night gatherings, supper will normally be served around 5:00 [p.m.]. Youth are asked to be respectful with food and take care of their own trash. Singing will start around 7:00 and last for 1–1/2 hours, using the *Ausbund* and German Lieder books.

3. Saturday nights are "Family Time." For youth to go away with their friends or gather at a friend's home on a Saturday night is discouraged.

4. Youth are asked to avoid all organized sports, including baseball, football, hockey, etc. Volleyball and ice hockey are acceptable, but not to be played in public places.

5. Cell phones, recorded music, videos, etc., should never be part of any of our gatherings. Remember Jesus' statement: "Ye are the light of the world."

6. Smoking is not allowed at our gatherings, and youth are asked to keep themselves free from all uses of tobacco.

7. Vacations for all youth should be planned wisely, and well supervised by the parents. More allowance can be made for older youth who are church members.

8. Week-night activities should be approved by an appointed planner. Encourage singings for the sick or elderly, or other worthwhile activities, rather than birthday parties, etc. Youth should leave week-night activities by 10:00 [p.m.].

Following are some definements [*sic*] of guidelines 1 and 4:

1. No leather, zippered, or hooded coats, sweaters, or jackets. Shoes worn for supper and singings should be black, and girls should wear shoes and nylons at singings.

2. Boys should not have shingled [barber] haircuts and girls' hair [should] be modestly rolled. Let's avoid the worldly styles that would like to slip into our circles. Parents who encourage their children to attend our gatherings are expected to accept and support these guidelines, and help with supervision when they attend. Youth from other groups who accept an invitation to supper and singings must understand that they are accepting the guidelines, along with supervision.

3. Organized sports is defined as: No league or tournament organized games. The "on" week activity nights are encouraged for [our group]-only volleyball games.

4. We expect all youth to uphold high moral standards, with purity in words and action. Dating couples should both be church members. Courtship should be begun with prayer with God's leading.

60. "At an Amish Youth Singing" (2010).
61. Shachtman (2006).

Chapter 6. Teen Culture

1. Hostetler (1977), 358.

2. Hostetler and Huntington (1992), 99.

3. This poem, written by nine-year-old Esther Zook, was one of two poems about work on the cover of the *Diary* (Mar. 1998).

4. For a description of this relief effort, see Unruh (1952), 227–29; and for a fascinating first-hand account, see Newswanger (1996), 110–13.

5. Long hours of work in the heat or cold can become tiresome. An Amish writer from Iowa reminisced about the drudgery of endless hours of picking beans and cucumbers in "Pity Party in the Pickle Patch" (2004).

6. Unpublished letter (dated 2 Apr. 1978), on file in the Heritage Historical Library, Aylmer, Ontario.

7. *Die Botschaft* (23 Jul. 1997), 45.

8. Kissinger (1983), 87–93, devotes an entire chapter to tobacco cultivation and culture.

9. Traditionally, Amish youth turned over the bulk of their earnings to their parents, who either used some or all of it for family expenses or kept it on behalf of their children until they came of age at twenty-one. Many families in large settlements have dropped this practice.

10. The word "frolic" comes from the German word *fröhlich*, which means "joyous." See Hostetler (1993), 243.

11. Kraybill et al. (2013), 366. Also see "Providing Alternate Places of Service" (2012).

12. Shachtman (2006), 196–205, summarizes the struggle between the Amish and OSHA, especially around the beginning of the twenty-first century.

13. Organized sports are an integral part of the youth culture in all three large settlements, and in a few other places as well. A scribe from Mt. Hope, Ohio, wrote in the *Budget* (29 Jul. 1992) that the Holmes County Merchant volleyball team, composed of Amish players, won the state finals and went on to Kansas, where they placed second in the national finals. These tournaments, at the highest levels, continue to attract Amish softball teams.

14. *Young Companion* (Jun. 1993), 7–8.

15. *Young Companion* (May–Jun. 1990), 20.

16. According to informed parents and teens, this non-washing of uniforms by Lancaster County mothers has been largely ignored in recent years.

17. The "Can You Help Me?" (1990) column in one issue of *Young Companion* was devoted to the question of playing ball on Sunday. Predictably, every letter that the editors chose to print stated that Sunday should be kept holy and reserved for worship and visiting.

18. By 2006, a growing number of baptized adults, including parents, had returned to the ballparks to see the Youngie play.

19. As of 2013, many of the supervised youth groups, such as the Eagles and the Hummingbirds, still require their members to abstain from all organized sports teams.

20. E. Stoll (1982).

21. Meyers (1994), 393.

22. Outsiders can watch cornerball at the volunteer fire company auctions and sales held in Lancaster County in late winter and early spring. Sometimes called "mud sales" by outsiders, they attract thousands of buyers and spectators, who inadvertently but inevitably turn the thawing spring ground into a quagmire.

23. Cornerball was also popular among many German-speaking rural Pennsylvanians from the Lutheran, Reformed, and United Church of Christ traditions. J. Kline (1990) wrote an informal history of the game.

24. Some young men have apparently solved this problem by moving to Rexford, Montana, an Amish settlement two miles from the Canadian border. "We get quite a few unattached boys who are here primarily for the hunting," said a longtime resident.

25. Lancaster County has only a handful of serious birders. When I asked a well-known Amish birder and writer from Holmes County, Ohio, about this Pennsylvania dearth, he speculated that "the Lancaster Amish are too busy working to pay off their big farm mortgages." Some Lancaster County residents agreed.

26. The magazine started out as the *Purple Martin News* but broadened its appeal and circulation to cover the entire spectrum of serious birding.

27. Birding, like hunting, apparently is regarded as a male activity, since female birders are fairly uncommon.

28. The oldest of the five brothers has been the editor of *Feathers and Friends*. The brothers took five weeks to bicycle from northern Indiana to the Texas-Mexican border and then returned by train with their bicycles.

29. Shortly after the inline skating craze hit mainstream culture in 1990, roller-blades entered some of the large communities. Major news organizations featured photos of smiling Amish youth skating along rural roads. By the early twenty-first century, not only the youth but many adults were lacing up to go to work or to sales, or simply for fun. For his revision of *The Riddle of Amish Culture*, Kraybill (2001) chose two young women from Lancaster County on rollerblades for his cover photo. In that settlement, rollerblades—and foot-powered scooters—are permitted, even though bicycles are forbidden.

30. "Amish Going Modern, Sort of, About Skating" (1996).

31. An article by Lovelace (2003), reporting that five members of the Blazers hockey team were killed when their Jeep Grand Cherokee collided with a snowplow after competing in a local hockey league, informed many readers for the first time about the involvement of Amish youth in organized ice hockey in Lancaster County, Pennsylvania.

32. See Yassos (2012).

33. All Old Order affiliations prohibit flying, except for health or family emergencies. Three unmarried Old Order members from Lancaster County were temporarily excommunicated for flying to Central America on a Mennonite-sponsored work project. Most New Order groups, however, permit their members to fly.

34. In most Amish communities, some local people (often Mennonites or retirees) supplement their income by "hauling" Amish to nearby and distant destinations when horse-and-buggy transportation is inconvenient or impossible. See Butterfield (1997).

35. As of 2013, Sarasota officials were seeking to have Pinecraft designated as a Cultural Heritage Center.

36. In 2013, there were at least eleven Mennonite churches of various stripes with Sarasota addresses. Despite looking thoroughly English and conversing in English, most of the breakfast crowd, both diners and waitresses, in the family-style back room of Der Dutchman Restaurant in Pinecraft grew up as plain, Pennsylvania German speakers.

37. In 2013, two house churches, in addition to the Amish church house, offered weekly Sunday services during the tourist season for those who were uncomfortable with or admonished to avoid the original church.

38. Belkin (1999); and Jones (1999).

39. Hostetler (1993), 358–60.

40. Writers and headline editors, unaware of the distinction between the Sunday-night singings and Saturday-night parties, have apparently confused the two in their reporting. A headline in the *Elkhart (IN) Truth* proclaimed, "Amish 'Sing' Busted—Two Arrested" (1973). The article then described a Saturday-night party instead of a Sunday singing. The same mistake had been made in that newspaper six years earlier (18 Jul. 1967), when a reporter confused a Saturday-night party with a Sunday-night singing. Anyone observing a band hop or party would recognize that these events are in a different category from a singing.

41. One wag described this activity as the plain communities' form of birth control—having visitors show up unannounced in the bedroom where the courting couple is together.

42. Letter to the author (24 Sept. 1999).

Chapter 7. Singings

1. Conversation with the author (18 Jun. 2004).

2. In some parts of Indiana, this Sunday-evening event is called a "crowd." According to one informant: "Not much singing takes place. It's mostly a bunch of socializing and carrying on." On the other hand, the singing I attended in northern Indiana in December 2012 was very *onstlich* (decent), to use the Amish terms of approval.

3. In some new settlements that are made up mostly of young families, adults may get together at times to sing in the evenings, but children rarely attend youth singings until they turn sixteen. In some cases, singings have been held sporadically, or they have even been suspended when parents refused to host the youth at their homes because of rowdiness. These situations are not typical, however.

4. In the 1990s, older unmarried Amish in Lancaster County formed a gang, calling themselves the Chess Nuts since many of them liked to play chess. By the beginning of the twenty-first century the gang had dissolved, since "most of our gang had gotten married," a bachelor reported. They were soon replaced by the Drifters, a gang of twenty- or thirty-somethings, who boasted a membership of nearly eighty. As of 2013, there were at least three gangs composed of older youth, one of which was named the Dogwoods. Tongue in cheek, a mother referred to them as the Dagwoods. Their oldest members were in their forties and were still clean-shaven, a significant departure from past practices. Drifter member's conversation with the author (10 Oct. 2013).

5. The underlying message may be that it would be disrespectful to parents and other adults to be overly excited about going with the young folk.

6. This practice varies among communities, depending on tradition and income. Sometimes males will receive their carriages in their early teens if the family needs extra transportation for church or visiting. Among the Swartzentruber people in Loyal, Wisconsin, parents reportedly do not give their sons carriages of their own

until they come of age at twenty-one. Within a few communities or families, sons are responsible for obtaining their own carriages. I have yet to hear of a girl receiving a carriage when she turns sixteen.

7. In most of the Amish settlements with a Swiss heritage, adults and rumspringa youth still drive open carriages, such as in Adams and Allen Counties, Indiana.

8. In 2001, a young man in Ohio sported a kind of sunroof in his carriage.

9. Coole (2002). An observer from another large settlement reported seeing a bumper sticker that read, "My parents had sex and all I got was this lousy life," a bumper sticker that only a rumspringa youth would display.

10. See Scott (1981) for a comprehensive treatment of carriage styles in a variety of Amish settlements.

11. Email to the author (21 Apr. 2013). On the other hand, a non-Amish friend married to an English midwife reported in a conversation with the author (1 May 2013) that he saw the inside of a young man's carriage that was totally covered with *Playboy* centerfolds.

12. Goldstein (1997), 40.

13. J. Yoder (1995), 114–17.

14. An older couple recalled that several singings were held "on the lawn under the trees" in Lancaster County in the 1950s, but their son responded: "If we would hold ours outside these days, people would freak out. It would be the joke of the year!"

15. In a few settlements, usually in the Midwest, boys and girls alternate along the benches.

16. E. Lapp (2005).

17. Some of the songs have a decidedly non-pacifist or suggestive bent: "The Battle of New Orleans," "Hello, Viet Nam," "I Died for the Red, White, and Blue," "Geisha Girl," "Rolling in My Sweet Baby's Arms," and "Pistol-Packing Mama," to name a few. In virtually all other settlements, every one of these songs would be "beyond the pale" for singings, underlining their explicitly religious aspect. See Schwartz and Schwartz (1980). Other than for the oldest songs with no copyright restrictions, virtually all of the lyrics appear to have been pirated.

18. Surprisingly, some parents and grandparents from various Old Order districts scattered throughout the larger settlements reported that forty or fifty years ago, all songs were in English.

19. "Bluebird on Your Window Sill," a sentimental piece written by Canadian Elizabeth Clarke in 1948, was the first Canadian song to sell a million copies; see Marsh (2000). It was popularized in the United States by Bing Crosby, Doris Day, and Tex Williams, among others, and obviously caught the attention of many Amish youth.

20. This distinct singing quality may have originated from the nasal singing style common in colonial America and mocked by the British. Or it may simply stem from the continued popularity of country-and-western music among Amish youth. A family in Lancaster County who attended a singing in a midwestern state reported

that the singing was so "loud and shrill" that they wanted to cover their ears. This kind of singing style appears to be diminishing, however.

21. Perhaps the compilers have assumed that because no music notes are included, they need not obtain permission to reprint the words.

22. When asked about the quality of the translations, one informant admitted that occasionally translators "had to sneak in some Pennsylvania Dutch to make things come out right."

23. Letter to the author (Feb. 2013).

24. Unpublished letter on file in the Heritage Historical Library, Aylmer, Ontario.

25. *Die Botschaft* (24 Jan. 1989).

26. *Die Botschaft* (19 Aug. 1987), 14.

27. *Die Botschaft* (30 Jun. 1993), 8.

Chapter 8. Rumspringa

1. "Crank," a street term for (usually lower quality) methamphetamine, was the term used in the documentary.

2. According to an Indiana therapist, in a conversation with the author (8 Jun. 2013), Faron Yoder was in and out of prison after his initial release. Rumors subsequently claimed that he had experienced a Christian conversion and was involved in street witnessing and evangelism.

3. In some settlements, parents maintain that their youth do not participate in Rumspringa, but these adults are defining it as wildness and deviance, the common stereotype promoted by the popular media.

4. L. Miller (1989).

5. *The Amish* (2012).

6. Gibson (2006).

7. According to Langin (1994), in parts of Indiana youth join groups similar to the Lancaster County gangs but do not use the same terminology.

8. *Die Botschaft* (22 Dec. 1993), 36.

9. Some peace-loving parents might have wondered about the types of attitudes and behaviors reflected in gang names such as the Cruisers, Crystals, Diamonds, Drifters, Rangers, Rockies, and Sawed-Off Shotguns (who split from the Shotguns, one of the longest-standing gangs in Lancaster County). Many of the current names are of birds or other nature-related animals.

10. Gideon L. Fisher, in the *Diary* (Aug. 1982), describing the beginning of his Rumspringa.

11. Hostetler (1993). In a conversation with the author (Jul. 2000), the late Abner Beiler, a Lancaster County historian, remembered the Happy Harrys as being the first youth group. He also recalled: "I was in the Chow-Chows. It was called that because we had a real mixture of youth." "Chow chow" is the name of a pickled mixed-vegetable condiment served with meals.

12. Since the drug arrests in 1998, this gang has dissolved.

13. Many Amish elders believe that car ownership or the young men's haircuts are the best indicators of the "decency" of a gang and its members.

14. Some of the counties adjacent to Lancaster County have developed their own, similar gang structure. Nearby Perry County had three gangs in 2001, but they dwindled to only one three years later. At the same time, nearly 400 Amish youth in the ridge-and-valley counties of central Pennsylvania had four gangs to choose from— the Chipmunks, Meadowlarks, Mountaineers, and Rangers. Most of the youth from Brush Valley, Nittany Valley, Sugar Valley, Nippenose, White Deer, Penn's Valley, and Buffalo Valley belonged to one of these groups, although a few youth traveled to Lancaster County on weekends to participate in a gang.

15. Out-of-county teens can also belong to conservative gangs.

16. According to the article "Paying Their Last Respects" (1999), on Memorial Day weekend, five Amish youth from both western Pennsylvania and Lancaster County, traveling from the Sunday-night singing in Lancaster, were killed, along with their driver, in a predawn crash.

17. Most of those who make these long weekend trips have or are interested in finding a special friend.

18. Even if youth are rebellious or running with the fastest youth, a young person almost never appears at church dressed in English clothing. "It's out of respect," an eighteen-year-old explained. A Lancaster County Amish man, however, claimed to have seen an Amish girl dressed in blue jeans at a Sunday church service in one area of a large settlement in Indiana.

19. A father in Holmes County, Ohio, stated that even though they have not had the gang structure that exists in Lancaster County, their church districts have youth on all parts of the adult-centered to youth-centered spectrum, and that it is easy to determine which group a young person identifies and socializes with by the visual clues of his or her apparel.

20. Similar age groupings, or cohort groups, occur in most settlements, but without the "buddy bunch" designation.

21. Conversation with a Lancaster County bishop and wife (Jul. 2009).

22. In developmental psychology terms, an Amish gang is equivalent to an adolescent "crowd" in public schools, a loose aggregation of peers who share common interests and find their identity and status through membership in this group. In contrast, the Amish buddy bunch is similar to what developmentalists call an adolescent "clique," a smaller group of friends that provides intimacy and fulfills socialization needs. See Steinberg (2005), 175–91.

23. Three college students visiting an Orioles group singing thought that all the young women from a particular buddy group could be identified through their distinctive perfume. When asked about it, an Amish mother laughed and said that each girl probably tried on their hostess's perfume before coming down to the singing.

24. Young people in a few smaller settlements also spend part of Saturday and all of Sunday with their peers.

25. The most conservative settlements are often the repositories of games and dances popular in the eighteenth and nineteenth centuries.

26. Unpublished letter on file in the Heritage Historical Library, Aylmer, Ontario.

27. For this reason, some parents refuse to go away overnight during a weekend. "Of course our children say that the group came to our place without an invitation, but either way, it's a mess," reported a father. One couple revealed that the only time they left their farm over a weekend was when their children were out of town. A more recent practice is that some families will notify the police before they go away for a weekend or leave on vacation, in order to avoid having their place used for a party.

28. Crowding can cause its own problems. A news story with the headline "Seven Amish Injured when Barn Collapses" (1977) reported that so many young people had crowded into the barn where the Sunday-night party and dance were being held that the main floor collapsed. No fatalities were reported, but one girl sustained serious back injuries. Some Amish in Lancaster County believe that this event led to the continued decentralizing of gangs and to the eventual downsizing and minimizing of the number of parties.

29. The description of this hop was provided by former student who is a friend of the author.

30. Virtually no females cut their hair short, and, in most places, relatively few who live at home appear anywhere in jeans or shorts.

31. This section of the book was researched in the 1990s; the most popular cigarettes for smokers in the fast circles now are Camel Menthol Silvers.

32. A Beachy Amish historian reports that as an Old Order youth in the 1950s, he knew of two rival gangs in Ohio that would occasionally fight each other at singings. A man from another large settlement (who later left the Amish) stated that when he was a teenager in the early 1960s, at 90 percent of those hoedowns there was always a "big brawl" between one or two of the guys. See McNamara (1997), 214.

33. A couple of weeks later, the young man went back uninvited to show two of his female friends what an Amish party was like. In contrast to his first visit, when he arrived with his Amish friend, the young man was not greeted cordially this second time, and he began to fear that his female companions might be harassed by some of Youngie who were drinking heavily. Consequently, the non-Amish visitors left almost immediately.

34. Despite the subculture of alcohol drinking that has persisted in many places over the years, most Amish believe that, with some exceptions, there are relatively few Amish alcoholics. A bishop offered this explanation: "In mainstream society, young people often drink as self-medication to get away from their troubles. Most of our youth who drink do it for fun with their peers instead of trying to escape from bad situations. When they decide to settle down and join the church, most of them have little trouble in giving up their drinking." Nevertheless, law enforcement officials required fifty youth from Geauga County, Ohio, to receive counseling at Turning Point, an alcohol-prevention program; see Graves (2000).

35. "Hard to Forget" (1969).

36. With characteristic humility, an Amish parent wrote back, thanking the writer for his or her concern, promising to do his best to "plant many seeds of love, joy, peace, and respect" in his children, and, with the Lord's help, to do something to alleviate the problems the writer pointed out. The Amish man's entire letter, from which this excerpt came, filled nearly eighteen column inches in the *Lancaster New Era* (23 May 1981).

37. See Umble (1994), an excellent, albeit somewhat dated, history of the relationship between the Amish and the telephone.

38. Erik Wesner, comments on the author's manuscript (27 Mar. 2013). Also, Wesner (2010), 19, recognized that cell phones had already slipped into many Amish communities.

39. "A Fire in the Land" (2010).

40. When asked about how many young people in one of their youth groups in Perry County, Pennsylvania, had cell phones, a bishop answered, "All of them." His estimate, along with those mentioned in the text, do not represent cell-phone use among all of the youth in the three large settlements. Settlement-wide numbers are hard to come by, but they certainly would be much smaller. As of this writing, my best estimate is that at least 25 percent of Amish youth in the large settlements have cell phones or smartphones.

41. A friend who lives southern Lancaster County tells of going to a nearby drugstore in Quarryville, Pennsylvania, to print some photos and finding that five of the six photo printers were occupied by teenage Amish girls printing pictures of their beach vacation.

42. Charles Jantzi, professor of psychology, Messiah College, Mechanicsburg, Pennsylvania, in a conversation with the author (31 May 2013).

43. The program was eventually repudiated by one of the young actors, Angus T. Jones, who reported that he had experienced a Christian conversion. He labeled the show he starred in "filth" and urged viewers to turn it off.

44. In 2013, brightly colored dress shirts with a ties and dark slacks characterized the fashionably dressed Amish male, a reflection of the then-current mainstream style for males.

45. Jantzi (2013).

46. One girl whose Facebook cover photo featured a professional portrait said that many of these photo shoots would result in costs of $100 or more, depending on how many wallet-sized and large-frame portraits were ordered.

47. I have seen only one Amish male on Facebook displaying the otherwise widely used middle finger.

48. See Wikipedia (2013b).

49. In a conversation with the author (spring 2013), Charles Jantzi reported that the same young woman featured photos of eleven expensive dresses that she was "tired of" and wanted to get rid of.

50. Email to the author (21 Apr. 2013). Also see Cates and Weber (2012).

51. An Indiana youth came back to his vehicle after "bailing," as he put it, when

one of his friends called him on his cell phone to notify him that his vehicle would be towed if he failed to return immediately.

52. Conversation with the author (Oct. 2012).

53. Despite the potential danger of injury or death in this incident, a more likely cause of serious injury or death involves youth driving under the influence. I was told that in one area of a large settlement, the young women will often drive the young men home, because the latter are "too drunk to drive."

54. Email to the author (21 Apr. 2013).

55. Tullis (2006).

56. Conversation with the author (7 Nov. 2012).

Chapter 9. Courtship

1. Hurd (1997), who has done extensive research among the Nebraska Amish in Pennsylvania, pointed out the difficulties that young people in some of the small splinter groups had in finding a spouse from such a limited pool of eligible mates.

2. J. Yoder, (1995), 109–10, 128–29.

3. One oral account claims that on their son's wedding day, as the soon-to-be married couple received the best wishes of the guests, the mother of the groom approached the bride-to-be and expressed her pleasure in finally meeting her new daughter-in-law. Many Amish in some of the traditional communities would view this as a distinct possibility, at least in the past.

4. Research studies by Miller et al. (1986), Thornton (1990), Dorius et al. (1993), and Small and Luster (1994) all show a significant positive correlation between early dating and early sexual intercourse.

5. Functionally, this may result from a developmental difference between males and females.

6. The father added: "A boy gets a desk during his running-around years. He has things, just like the girl does, that his mother made; just not as much."

7. Although the social setting may be non-threatening, the physical setting of walking along a dark road at night in dark-colored clothing is a different matter. A group of horse-and-buggy Mennonites playing Walk-a-Mile after a singing were struck by a car in rural Franklin County, Pennsylvania, and five youth were injured. Also, one Amish mother noted a different concern: "The rule gangs [supervised singings] do not do Walk-a-Mile. They go home an hour after singing time is over. We do not consider Walk-a-Mile a godly practice. It arouses too many lovey [sic] feelings, especially on the boys' behalf."

8. Occasionally, teenage boys have been so humiliated when they were "told off" [refused] that they quit attending the singings.

9. Related in Goldstein (1997), 140–41.

10. Ibid., 141.

11. Hurst and McConnell (2010), 73. A book by Harris (1997) found its way into Amish youth circles, especially the supervised Lancaster County groups. Harris rejected dating around and advocated a hands-off courtship.

12. "Special Section: Journey to Freedom," February 28, 2000.

13. Hurst and McConnell (2010), 71.

14. [Schlabach] ([1980]). The portion of the pamphlet in which this allegation appears, written in High German in the Fraktur script, was translated by Jonathan Lauer, the head librarian at Messiah College.

15. Donnermeyer and Cooksey (2004), 21.

16. Technically, the wedding season runs up to spring communion, but, until recently, first marriages rarely occurred after Christmas. Couples in their thirties or older who are marrying for the first time, however, have more latitude in marrying outside the traditional wedding season.

17. In the same settlement, married couples will occasionally confess in a members' meeting that their courtship was "impure" and ask to be placed in the *Bann*. They are not asked to specifically describe their wrong behavior, however. After being excommunicated for six weeks, they are again accepted into full membership. Some members report that as many as 20 percent of the married couples in their district have made such confessions.

18. Beachy (2011) has posited that Scotch-Irish immigrants first introduced the practice in North America, especially among the frontier people of the Northeast and Midwest. His recounting of the controversy surrounding this practice among the Amish is the most complete that I have found (2: 334–38).

19. Donald Kraybill, in a letter to the author (30 May 2003), related that when he traveled to Switzerland in 1993, an older man recalled bundling as a youth in a rural area in the southern part of that country.

20. See Folsom (1994), in the chapter on "Bed Courtship," 117–18. Folsom reported that among the Nebraska Amish, the pink patches in their normally subdued quilts come from remnants of *Nacht Ruch*. In 2013, a Nebraska father expressed his disgust at seeing bright orange, bright red, and bright green nightdresses hanging on clotheslines. He believed that such a conspicuous display did not bode well for those couples.

21. Furlong (2011), 101–2.

22. See Gingerich (1939), 244.

23. See P. Yoder (1998), 7, 61–62.

24. These include most Swartzentruber affiliations, Pennsylvania's Nebraska and Lawrence County Amish, Ohio's Andy Weaver (or "Dan") group, and a few others. At least two Swartzentruber settlements in Kentucky and one in Tennessee do not practice bed courtship.

25. Folsom (1994); and L. Miller (1989).

26. Several Old Order Amish who knew Levi Miller criticized him for betraying family secrets. Some bookstore managers in Holmes County, Ohio, claim that this is the primary reason that they do not stock or sell this book.

27. A deacon reported that a church member had found condoms while cleaning up after a youth activity.

28. His observation illustrates that an action viewed from two different cultures

(or subcultures) may mean one thing to the person in the culture and something quite different to the person outside the culture.

29. In a letter to the author (spring 2001), an Amish father from a large settlement that once condoned bundling wrote: "[The boy] held his girl on his lap on a rocking chair or the girl laid on the couch and the boy laid on top of her. This latter practice was *very* awkward because the couple could feel each other's body parts through their clothing. Couples in the 1960s hated this and realized it was not a Christian way to court."

30. Letter to the author (6 Nov. 2002).

31. Letter to the author (11 Apr. 1998).

32. Hurst and McConnell (2010), 73.

33. Older informants in the largest settlements say that bundling was widespread, at least through the first half of the twentieth century.

34. Conversation with the author (19 Sept. 2013).

35. Mackall (2007), 78.

36. Folsom (1994), 121, wrote that a minister who spoke out against bed courtship fifty years ago was silenced by his bishop for five years.

37. [Schlabach] ([1980]), 30, 34.

38. Editors and writers in *Family Life* and *Young Companion* wrote against bed courtship almost from the inception of these magazines. In October 1971, *Die Schaedliche Uebung* (The Shameful Practice) strongly criticized bundling. The editor used Martin Luther's Bible German and wrote in the Fraktur script.

39. *Young Companion* (Jan. 1999), 1–8.

40. Burkholder (2006).

41. Two brief sources of information on Amish homosexuality are articles by Cates (2005 and 2007), and a gay ex-Amish website. Hurst and McConnell (2010), 316, 44, related their conversation with an Old Order Ohio man who said he knew of at least six young homosexual men in his settlement, one of whom brought his partner to a family reunion. Not surprisingly, none of them joined the church. An Amish man who grew up in a rural Michigan and lived for a while with several gay rumspringa youth in the Elkhart/LaGrange Counties (Indiana) area started a Facebook page and website to serve the lesbian-gay-bisexual-transgendered Amish. As of 2013, neither site showed activity by responders with Amish-sounding names. As far as reported homosexual activity within Amish communities is concerned, there is one other anecdotal incident. In large settlements, prepubescent boys occasionally engaged in a "game" known as Cows and Bulls, where boys would simulate animal sex by mounting each other. In a conversation with the author (4 Oct. 2012), a therapist reported that occasionally actual penetration occurred. Reports of bestiality also surface from time to time.

42. Her one exception was a girl she knew who had been brought up Amish and was involved in a television reality series on the Amish. In a conversation with the author (Oct. 2012), a counselor in a large settlement stated that in his/her professional practice over the years, more young Amish women have reported that in or-

der to continue being popular with their male peers, they have to be sexually active.

43. Conversation with the author (Jul. 1998).

44. Besides forbidding early dating, the Amish resistance to their youth listening to popular music may also relate to parental concerns about music's relationship to sexual activity. Martino et al. (2006) reported a positive correlation between hours spent listening to popular music and sexual activity, especially when listening to degrading sexual lyrics, such as those found in rap music. In summer 2013, a respected parent overseer from one of the Eagles' supervised youth groups was asked to talk to the young people, at a special meeting, about "worldly" (secular) music, along with concerns about the misuse of the Internet. From the notes on his presentation (in the author's personal files), I found his talk to be informative, measured, and reasonable as he confronted this perennial issue.

Chapter 10. Weddings

1. Scott (1988), an Old Order River Brethren writer, provided a description of wedding customs in Lancaster County, Pennsylvania, and elsewhere. He noted correctly that practices vary considerably among communities after the wedding. Many of the customs described in his book, as well as some in the present volume, reflect traditional practices in Lancaster County, Pennsylvania.

2. In recent years, writers and producers have increasingly focused on the rumspringa experience, but weddings provide a rare opportunity for first-hand observations of an important Amish ritual. Since the Amish rarely write for outsiders about their weddings—or anything else, for that matter—English wedding guests often assume that what they observe in a particular community is true for all Amish. Also, because most guests do not understand either High German or Pennsylvania German, they often miss or misinterpret the meanings and nuances of the ceremony and some of the subsequent activities.

3. A singular exception occurred in the 2013 wedding season, when Karen Johnson-Weiner, professor of anthropology at Potsdam State University in St. Lawrence County, New York and an expert on Swartzentruber Amish life, received invitations to three Swartzentruber weddings, an almost unheard-of occurrence among that affiliation. This also illustrates that over time, it is possible for an "outsider" to earn the trust and affection of these "plainest of the plain."

4. Since the wedding season in Lancaster County had traditionally started in late October, after the fall communion, and offered a maximum of eight Tuesdays and eight Thursdays on which to be married, courting youth faced the formidable task of finding a day that "suited" their families and friends. A tradition-breaking event occurred in 2005, when the Lancaster County community realized that the daughter of a prominent bishop would be married in a June wedding. Except for weddings involving scandal or widow-widower unions, this may have been the first non-emergency wedding held outside the sacred fall wedding season. Weary Amish who hoped that this would be the beginning of a more flexible, less stressful wedding-season option were not disappointed. The Lancaster County wedding season now

runs at least to March, giving overtaxed couples and families a legitimate reprieve from the previously compressed—and often frantic—time frame for weddings.

5. In those settlements in which parents are heavily involved in cooking and serving, a few allow the parents to leave their work for a few minutes in order to witness the taking of vows.

6. A bishop commented that proposing when the strawberries are in flower is not mandatory. "Although this timing may be traditional, there is constant variation," he explained. This is increasingly true, as the now-expanded wedding season and the exponential population growth of the Amish requires more long-term planning for weddings.

7. Deacons in a horse-and-buggy Amish settlement in the province of Ontario read the wedding announcement, or banns, during three successive services before the couple may marry.

8. In other affiliations, such as some New Order groups in Ohio, the young man simply receives verbal approval from the bishop and reports this to his future bride's home bishop. In parts of central Pennsylvania, the *Zeugnis* is mailed to the bishop of the bride.

9. A young Amish man reported that before one of his peers' wedding, his community learned that the young man had had sexual relations with an English girl. As a result, the ministers decided that the couple could not have the traditional attendants during the church service and ceremony, but they would be permitted to have them for the rest of the day's and evening's activities.

10. According to Scott (1988), 9–10, the bride's father may stipulate the age of those who are invited, depending on how much room the family has for guests. If the house or premises are small and the family has many relatives and friends, they may limit invitations to guests who are eighteen and older instead of offering the more typical invitations for sixteen- and seventeen-year-olds.

11. In Kalona, Iowa, not only does the bride-to-be attend church, but her future in-laws and family will also come to her district to hear the announcement.

12. One young man claimed that many youth are relieved when they are not invited, since there are so many weddings and date conflicts in the short Lancaster County wedding season. A grandfather commented that guests are attentive for the first and last weddings of the season, but suffer from "wedding shock" for most of the rest.

13. In the more progressive or affluent sectors of the large settlements, growing numbers of couples are taking delayed honeymoons to Florida or booking Caribbean cruises. According to a bishop's wife, couples rarely disclose their plans to anyone but their immediate family members and close friends.

14. See P. Stevick (2006), chapter 5, "A Wedding and a Wedding Tale."

15. In a conversation with the author (12 Sept. 2013), a couple from Lancaster County, preparing for their youngest daughter's fall wedding, reported that the $5,000 price tag could easily double when parents include the cost of their traditional housekeeping gifts to the newlyweds.

16. The descriptions of the Maryland wedding in this chapter, recounted by an English woman who was an observer at the wedding, appeared in a contribution by George and Marty Kreps in an earlier version of the Amish Heartland website (www.amish-heartland.com) and are used by permission of Amish Heartland. The document is no longer available.

17. In Lancaster County, I was surprised and amused to learn that an unmarried Amish man sells a wedding-preparation manual that he advertises from time to time in his monthly *Diary* column.

18. With the decrease in farming and increase in businesses among many Amish, more families are opting to buy cases of chicken and celery from commercial sources.

19. Printed invitations are common in some of the other large settlements. "In Lancaster County," a mother reported, "invitations are discouraged. Some do send them about a month before. A verbal invitation is encouraged. With the rubber-stamp craze, some make pretty [homemade] invitations with them. Only the 'fastest' people use engraved invitations, a very small percentage." One bride-to-be sent out a "pretty fancy card" that included a photo of the couple, and the bishop required her to ask each person who received the photo to destroy it. See Rutter (2003).

20. Donnermeyer et al. (1999), 153–55, reported that many Amish in their tricounty area of Ohio scheduled their weddings based on the availability of the wagons. One reason this service may not occur in Lancaster County is that even in 2013, the wedding season has still been generally compressed into six weeks and would require an inordinate number of vehicles to meet the intense demand. A Lancaster County father explained that some Amish individuals rent out wedding chests with dishes and silverware, and the owners charge "a meager fee."

21. Ibid., for a description of this service in Holmes County, Ohio.

22. In St. Mary's County, Maryland, the parents hosting the large wedding described by the English visitor invited 100 relatives and friends to help.

23. The day after the wedding, the entire addition is dismantled, and many of the materials may go to a relative or friend whose daughter is getting married in the next few days or weeks. Occasionally, the addition will be incorporated permanently into the house or shop. See Rutter (2003).

24. Scott (1988), 35.

25. In some locales, relatives and neighbors take chickens home with them, cook them, and return in the morning with the deboned chicken, cut up and ready to be added to the *Roascht* mixture.

26. A couple who has been part of the *Grumbierleit* (potato crew) described the difficulty of cooking potatoes for 400 or 500 people: "It's hard to make mashed potatoes for hundreds of people. It's not something you can practice. One time we underestimated how many to do, but fortunately the wedding was at a farm with a bulk food store, and we got powdered potatoes and added them with cream cheese and butter to try and make them taste right." The husband explained that mashing such a huge quantity is physically demanding, so somebody came up with the idea

of breaking down the potatoes with beaters attached to the Makita battery-operated power drills used by carpenters. "Women in the local church district with nothing else to do help to peel and slice the potatoes for cooking," the couple reported.

27. More recently, one or more young married men oversee the hostlers, to avoid some of the past problems of these young teenagers "getting involved in pranks or other mischief."

28. In most places, the couple chooses unmarried siblings who are close to their own age to be side-sitters, the most honored participants in the day's events. If the bride or groom has no available siblings, cousins, nieces, or nephews will be asked. In parts of Lancaster County, however, many couples choose their friends rather than relatives. Tradition there dictates that none of the attendants are to be dating each other. In some Swartzentruber settlements, couples have eight side-sitters (Mackall 2007).

29. A minister's wife reported that a woman who was married in 2006 was "disciplined by the church"—that is, she had to make a public confession at the close of a Sunday service—because she wore a green wedding dress instead of the traditional blue or purple one. The minister's wife said, "The color is not actually written into the Ordnung, but everyone knows what is expected."

30. In some youth gangs and in certain settlements, young men begin wearing the broader-brimmed hat as soon as they join the church.

31. In those settlements where a married woman is expected to be buried in her wedding cape and apron, customs have sometimes been altered, either to provide a new, larger cape and apron, if necessary, or simply to cut the two garments up the back and, after dressing the body, tuck the sides under the corpse.

32. P. Stevick (2006) captured this self-effacing attitude in her observations of several Old Order Amish weddings and a New Order wedding.

33. When the couple initially seeks the church's approval for their marriage, both are approached by their respective deacons and asked if they are free of fornication. A deacon explained, "At this point, nobody admits to an improper courtship. If they would confess to having done wrong, they would have to postpone their wedding, be excommunicated, and placed in the *Bann* for six weeks. Some couples or individuals have voluntarily confessed to an impure courtship and remove themselves from 'full fellowship' for six weeks during the summer." Likewise, some couples may confess to an improper courtship after they are married. Generally these confessions are not detailed.

34. In at least one settlement, the excommunication lasts for only two weeks. Saloma Furlong, conversation with the author (7 Jun. 2013).

35. Letter to the author (8 Aug. 2002).

36. At an Indiana wedding, a bishop counseled the couple to "choose a decent name for your children, not like Casper" (which was his name).

37. A middle-aged couple from one of the most conservative settlements reported that when they were married, their ministers routinely instructed couples that when

they had children they were "not to tell their boys" about menstruation. The couple did not know the reason for such admonitions.

38. Book of Tobit, chapter 8. A father wrote that all ministers urge the couple to follow Tobias and Sara's example of abstaining from sexual relations immediately. A great-grandmother from Ohio stated, "Starting your life together with prayer and fasting is a good way to begin." A newly ordained minister expressed surprise that some of the bishops no longer instruct the new bride and groom to observe the three-night fast. Another bishop remarked, "I think very few follow it." When an elderly father was asked how faithful he thought newlyweds were in abstaining, he answered: "Who knows? Nobody is there to check on them." With regard to the admonishment to abstain, another father replied, "If I was a betting man, I'd bet a million to one that it don't happen."

39. In a settlement in southern Indiana, the deacon is charged with providing counsel to the couple when they seek the church's approval to marry.

40. What is recounted here shows the order of the large-settlement wedding services. Weddings in the other affiliations are similar, although, with some exceptions, such as the selection of hymns and the standing/sitting protocol. M. Miller (2008), 243–88, provided a thorough description of the scriptures, hymns, and prayers used in Lancaster County weddings.

41. In some settlements, if the bride's father is a bishop, he may preach the main sermon and perform the wedding rites.

42. A New Order couple reported that in their affiliation they do not even use the Tobit narration or blessing because "Tobit is apocryphal and has strange passages we shy away from." Similarly, in a letter to the author (8 Aug. 2002), an Old Order minister reported, "This practice is being dropped by the New Order groups and slowly seems to be losing out in the more progressive [Old Order] areas." An elderly couple who was married in Daviess County, Indiana, stated that the book of Tobit was not used in any weddings performed in the early 1940s.

43. Because of the length of the service and the language barrier, non-Amish guests are usually invited to arrive a little before 11:00 a.m., in time for the taking of the vows.

44. In some locales, this question takes place earlier in the service.

45. Pathway Publishers' devotional guide, *In Meiner Jugend*, translates the wedding questions from five different Amish and two Mennonite settlements. Although they are similar in most areas, the Milverton, Ontario, questions are the only ones in which the woman is asked if she will obey her husband. Also see Hostetler (1993), 192–200, for a description of a wedding in central Pennsylvania.

46. Translations from *Die Ernsthafte Christenpflicht* (1996) are from M. Miller (2000).

47. A man who was married in the 1940s recalled that in his settlement, "the ceremony was to take place before 12:00 noon because if the hand on the clock was going up, it was thought that the marriage would be strong." On hearing this,

someone wondered aloud if the functional purpose of this belief was to keep the preachers from preaching on into the afternoon.

48. Hostetler (1993), 198. In a wedding he attended in the Big Valley of Pennsylvania, Hostetler noted that the bride and groom were served baked oysters and ice cream. Oysters were a traditional treat at many weddings in the past. An Amish father from the Big Valley area reported that "oysters were usually served for the evening meal, but lately that has changed, perhaps due to the cost of good oysters! Now it's usually meatloaf, ham, or some other specialty. The bride's parents choose what to serve the guests."

49. In Lancaster County, members of the immediate family, relatives, and close friends sit at the "second table." Everyone else is served in the final sitting.

50. In 2012, according to one young informant, a few Lancaster County bishops attempted to abolish the relatively new practice having the bride's girlfriends sing the songs of her choice while she opened gifts. Possible reasons given for the ruling were that it was something new or, more importantly, that the bride chose an occasional secular love song for her song sheets. The informant, not a church member, thought that this had been issued as an *Abschtelling* (a binding requirement throughout the Lancaster affiliation), but a mother who attended three fall weddings said that it wasn't even mentioned in their church, and that at each of the wedding receptions, the love songs were sung. "We'll see what happens this fall," she said. Abolishing the singing turned out to be a limited effort, not a general requirement.

51. See Lasansky (1990) for a history of the dowry among the Pennsylvania German groups.

52. Wikipedia (2013c) states that the West African custom of stepping or jumping over a broomstick became a common practice among slaves in the American South as a form of marriage ceremony, since legal marriages were not allowed for slaves.

53. Until the early 1990s, a boy had to ask a girl if he could "take her to the table in the evening." This created a further stress for him, since there was the possibility of being rejected by the girl.

54. According to Hostetler (1993), 198, in the past, reluctant sixteen-year-olds were caught by older siblings or friends and forcibly thrust together to enter with their assigned partners.

55. R. Garrett (2004), 162.

56. The change from cigars to beef sticks began in the mid-1980s, probably as a nod to health concerns, the upward slide of tobacco prices, or to propriety. Nobody knows for sure why beef sticks became the replacement. "It gives them something to nibble on instead of smoking," an Amish man conjectured. Couples may order several cases, distributing the beef sticks to well-wishers before the guests leave the wedding.

57. In Lancaster County, the bride's family traditionally has a table set up with leftovers for anybody who still wants to eat something in the evening or before going home. It is called the *Fressdish* (*fresse* being the Pennsylvania German verb used to

describe the ways animals eat and gorge themselves). At Swartzentruber weddings, unmarried youth pair up and eat leftovers just prior to midnight.

58. A fifteen-year-old girl from Lawrence County wrote all of these for me from memory.

59. See Mackall (2007), chapter 5, "The Midnight Table," 69–89, for a detailed discussion of Swartzentruber Amish weddings.

60. Scott (1988), 35–36.

61. According to a parent, the first few couples within a buddy bunch to be married are the ones most likely to be the objects of pranksters. "If you're older, like we were, when you get married, nobody bothers playing tricks on you."

62. *Lancaster Intelligencer Journal* (15 Oct. 1985), 36.

63. *Die Botschaft* (12 Dec. and 19 Dec. 1990).

64. *Die Botschaft* (1 Nov. 1986), 23.

65. Letter to the author (8 Aug. 2002).

66. Increasingly, especially in the large settlements, couples move into their own places shortly after their wedding day.

67. The term "infair" or "infare" is a Middle English word that has virtually disappeared from modern parlance, except among the Amish. According to *Webster's* (1986), *Infair* originally meant "a feast and reception for a newly married couple, usually at the home of the groom's family a day or two after the wedding."

68. Hostetler (1993), 198.

Chapter 11. The Future

1. Luthy (1986).

2. A young father thought that young couples in their twenties or thirties were more vulnerable to leaving and joining liberal or progressive churches, because, when they joined the Amish as teenagers, most had not really thought through or understood their decision.

3. Kraybill et al. (2013), 282, summarized the percentage of families in ten states that derive their primary income from farming. The data came from settlement directories published between 2006 and 2010.

4. Donald B. Kraybill, quoted in Klimuska (1998).

5. Greska and Korbin (2002).

6. Meyers (1994); and Eriksen et al. (1980).

7. See Igou (1999), 113–38, for concerns that many Amish have about father-absence because of the men working away.

8. D. Johnson (1996) has assembled a comprehensive list of studies on the impact of fathers.

9. Most Amish would consider it to be a major loss for their Amish identity if comprehension of Pennsylvania German was not an expectation and prerequisite for membership. Acquiring skill in High German and Pennsylvania German has been one of the chief barriers to assimilating outsiders into the Amish.

10. Meyers (1994).

11. Since these are correlational data, it is difficult to determine whether the proximity of the town influences youthful attitudes and behaviors, or whether being part of a family that chooses to live near town may be the critical ingredient. Perhaps marginalized Amish prefer to live near town, or perhaps proximity to town life allows worldly influences to penetrate the family.

12. Keim (1993) reported that an influential Amish spokesman, who was opposing a governmental program to place conscientious objectors in city environments for their alternative service, wrote, "It would seem that it is not God's plan that people should build and live in large cities."

13. Reiling (2002).

14. Hostetler and Huntington (1992), 30. After reading this quotation, one of my Amish readers concluded that it is overstated, a point I would agree with.

15. Friedrich and Donnermeyer (2003).

16. Iannaccone (1994) provided a comprehensive discussion as to why conservative sects have a stronger holding power. He also cited clear examples of groups on both ends of the strictness–lenience spectrum.

17. Friedrich and Donnermeyer (2003).

18. Data compiled by Kraybill et al. (2013), 163, showed that the two most conservative Amish groups listed in the directory showed only a 6.1 and 2.6 percent defection rate.

19. One New Order spokesman said that his group's attrition rate is inflated, because this affiliation is the last step out for some Old Order members who planned to leave the Amish without being shunned. See Kraybill (1994a).

20. Meyers (1994), 383.

21. Greska and Korbin (2002).

22. Each community periodically prints a directory listing information on each Amish family unit. The number of listed unmarried women is higher than that of single men in almost all settlements. The exception to this may be in Rexford, Montana, a remote settlement two miles south of the Canadian border that attracts a disproportionate number of single males interested in hunting, fishing, and other outdoor pursuits.

23. Batson and Ventis (1982), 36, noted, "There is considerable evidence that women are more likely to be interested and involved in religion than men."

24. Meyers (1994), 385.

25. Nolt and Meyers (2007), 211.

26. The occasional exposé on Amish sexual abuse featured on national-network news programs may lead to exaggerated estimates of the frequency of this problem. Nobody really knows whether incest or other sexual deviances are higher among the Amish than among the non-Amish, or even if it is higher among the plainest groups compared with the progressive ones.

27. Quoted in Reiling (2002), 156. One cannot generalize from one person's experience, however, because individuals vary as to how salient or significant a par-

ticular belief is for them. Many Amish youth who deviate from adult norms apparently feel much less guilt and fear during their Rumspringa.

28. Ibid., 159.

29. Renno (1993), 69.

30. These statistics were collected from a private compilation of data by an Old Order Amish man in Lancaster County (1 Jun. 2013).

31. Reiling (2002), 148.

32. Kraybill (2001), 186–87, has argued that even though this act of joining appears to be freely taken, it is somewhat constrained, since everything in the community has funneled youth into making a decision to join the church. Shachtman (2006) has posited that freedom to explore during Rumspringa is the key to the high retention rate for the Amish.

33. Kraybill (2001), chapters 10 and 11, "The Transformation of Amish Work" and "Managing Public Relations."

34. See www.aboutamish.blogspot.com.

35. See www.mapministry.org.

36. "A Fire in the Land" (2010).

37. Jonathan Stoll (2012). Several follow-up letters appeared in *Family Life* (Jan. 2013), 2–3, one of which contained this verse from a reader in Ontario, Canada:

> *Surfing the web, receiving messages by text,*
> *Audio-recording and viewing videos come next.*
> *Camera all ready and photos to send,*
> *Entertainment, excitement, without any end.*
> *All this and much more in a hand-held device;*
> *Its use is addicting, and it fits so nice*
> *As an extension, or a part of the arm—*
> *The lure of technology, and loaded with charm.*

38. The most requested speaker for Lancaster County gangs was a counselor with Life Ministries, a conservative Anabaptist-related group from Quarryville, Pennsylvania. As of 2013, he had made over two dozen presentations to various Amish youth groups and their parents.

39. A concerned businessman from Ohio suggested to the author that "outside people like you" should come and do a show-and-tell type presentation with current electronic devices, demonstrating their capabilities and their dangers. He subsequently contacted the Lancaster County presenter, a highly respected, conservative Mennonite man who had spoken to many Lancaster youth and parent groups on the dangers of the Internet, to hear his ideas and suggestions on how to reach the Ohio community's parents and youth.

40. P. Stevick (2006).

41. M. Johnson (1999).

42. Ibid.

43. The defense attorney was impressed by the participation and cooperation of the Amish leaders and parents with the legal and judicial systems. He described this case as "the zenith of my legal career."

Epilogue

1. Rob Schlabach, conversion with the author (Jun. 2011).

2. An approach to critics who confronted one of the founders of the Hummingbird youth group was for him to avoid arguing and simply say to them, "Would you please pray for us?"

3. Beachy (2011).

4. Reasons given for the project's demise varied from criticisms that the leader of the movement did not go through enough proper channels and prior vetting, to criticisms for being open on Sundays, accepting tackle football as a new sport, or attracting too many English teens to mix with Amish youth at the facilities.

5. As various bishops and members pointed out to me, non-complying members could much more easily keep their transgressions hidden by using smartphones than, for example, by driving motor vehicles or buying flat-screen televisions.

6. Besides Luthy's *The Amish in America: Settlements that Failed* (1986), Beachy's *Unser Leit* (2011) is replete with descriptions of many more strife-filled settlements and schisms.

7. Karen Johnson-Weiner, telephone conversation with the author (Mar. 2013).

8. Donald B. Kraybill, comments on the author's manuscript (17 Jul. 2013).

Bibliography

Amish, The. 2012. PBS documentary, from the *American Experience* series. http://video.pbs.org/video/2200745636/.

————. 2012. Transcript. www.pbs.org/wgbh/americanexperience/features/transcript/amish-transcript/.

"Amish Going Modern, Sort of, about Skating." 1996. *New York Times*, 11 Aug., 20.

"Amish Population by State (2013)." 2013. Young Center for Anabaptist and Pietist Studies, Elizabethtown College. www2.etown.edu/amishstudies/Population_by_State_2013.asp.

"Amish 'Sing' Busted—Two Arrested." 1973. *Elkhart (IN) Truth*, 22 Sept.

Associated Press. 1999. "Amish Teen Drinking, Vandalism Worries Parents." *Lubbock Avalanche Journal*, 12 Jun.

"At an Amish Youth Singing." 2010. Amish America. http://amishamerica.com/at-an-amish-youth-singing/.

Ausbund, das ist: Etliche schöne Christliche Lieder. 1996. Lancaster, PA: Amish Book Committee.

Bachman, Calvin George. [1941] 1961. *The Old Order Amish of Lancaster County.* Pennsylvania German Society Publications, vol. 60. Lancaster, PA: Franklin and Marshall College.

Bachmann-Geiser, Bridgette. 2009. *Amish: The Way of Life of the Amish in Berne, Indiana.* Rockland, ME: Picton Press.

Batson, C. Daniel, and W. Larry Ventis. 1982. *The Religious Experience: A Social-Psychological Perspective.* New York: Oxford University Press.

Baumrind, Diana. 1971. "Authoritative vs. Authoritarian Parental Control." *Adolescence* 3: 255–72.

————. 1978. "Parental Disciplinary Patterns and Social Competence in Children." *Youth and Society* 9: 239–76.

Beachy, Leroy. 2011. *Unser Leit: The Story of the Amish.* 2 vols. Millersburg, OH: Goodly Heritage Books.

Beechy, William, and Malinda Beechy, comps. 199–. *Experiences of C.O.'s in C.P.S. Camps, in I-W Service in Hospitals, and during World War I.* LaGrange, IN: W. and M. Beechy.

Beiler, Katie K. 2009. *Descendants and History of Christian Fisher, 1756–1838* ["Fisher Book"], 4th ed. [Gordonville, PA]: Pequea Bruderschaft Library.

Belkin, B. Douglas. 1999. "Pennsylvania Dutch Living Easy in Fla." *Boston Globe*, 22 Mar., A3.

Benedict, Ruth. 1934. *Patterns of Culture.* Boston: Houghton Mifflin.

Blackboard Bulletin. 1957–. Aylmer, ON: Pathway Publishers. Published monthly for Old Order teachers.

Biswas-Diener, Robert, Joan Vittersø, and Ed Diener. 2005. "Most People Are Pretty Happy, but There Is Cultural Variation: The Inughuit, the Amish, and the Maasai." *Journal of Happiness Studies* 6: 205–26.

Bolinger, Zach. 2007. "Amish and English Share Diamond." *Wooster (OH) Daily Record*, 30 Jul.

Botschaft, Die. 1975–. Lancaster, PA: Brookshire Publications and Printing. The masthead describes its mission as "a weekly newspaper serving Old Order Amish communities everywhere."

Braght, Thieleman J. van, comp. 2002. *The Bloody Theater; or Martyrs Mirror of the Defenseless Christians, Who Baptized Only upon Confession of Faith, and Who Suffered and Died for the Testimony of Jesus, Their Savior, from the Time of Christ to the Year A.D., 1660.* 2nd English ed., 24th printing. Scottdale, PA: Herald Press. Originally published as *Der blutige Schauplatz oder Märtyrerspiegel der Taufgesinnten oder wehrlosen Christen, die um des Zeugnisses Jesu, ihres Seligmachers, willen gelitten haben und getötet worden sind, von Christi Zeit bis auf das Jahr 1600.* Dordrecht, 1660.

Budget, The. 1890–. Sugarcreek, OH: Sugarcreek Budget Publishers. A weekly newspaper serving Amish and Mennonite communities.

Burke, Daniel. 2005. "Self-Help or Scam?" *Lancaster New Era*, 13 Oct.

Burkholder, Chris. 2006. *Amish Confidential: The Bishop's Son Shatters the Silence.* Argyle, IA: Argyle Publishing.

Butterfield, Jim. 1997. *Driving the Amish.* Scottdale, PA: Herald Press.

"Can You Help Me?" 1990. *Young Companion* (May–Jun.): 20–21.

"Can You Help Me?" 2011. *Young Companion* (Sept.–Oct.): 14–17.

Carr, Nicholas. 2010. *The Shallows: What the Internet Is Doing to Our Brain.* New York: W. W. Norton.

Cassady, Joslyn D., David L. Kirshke, Timothy F. Jones, Allen S. Craig, Ovidio B. Bermudez, and William Schaffner. 2006. "Case Series: Outbreak of Conversion Disorder among Amish Adolescent Girls." *Journal of American Academy of Child and Adolescent Psychiatry* 44 (3): 291–97.

Cates, James A. 2005. "Facing Away: Mental Health Treatment of the Old Order Amish." *American Journal of Psychotherapy* 59 (4): 371–83.

———. 2007. "Identity in Crisis: Spirituality and Homosexuality in Adolescence. *Children and Adolescent Social Work Journal* 24: 369–383.

———. (forthcoming, 2014). *Serving the Amish: A Cultural Guide for Professional Providers*. Baltimore: Johns Hopkins University Press.

Cates, James A., and Chris Weber. 2012. "A Substance Use Survey with Old Order Amish Early Adolescents: Perceptions of Peer Alcohol and Drug Use." *Journal of Child and Adolescent Substance Abuse* 21 (3): 193–203.

———. 2013. "An Alcohol and Drug Intervention with Old Order Amish Youth: Preliminary Results of Culturally Segregated Class Participation." *Journal of Groups in Addiction and Recovery* 8 (2): 112–28.

Clasen, Claus-Peter. 1972. *Anabaptism: A Social History, 1525–1618; Switzerland, Austria, Moravia, South and Central Germany*. Ithaca, NY: Cornell University Press.

Cooksey, Elizabeth C., and Joseph F. Donnermeyer. 2004. "Go Forth and Multiply: Changes in the Timing of Marriage and Childbearing among Young Amish Women." Paper presented at the 69th Annual Meeting of the Population Association of America, Boston, 1–3 Apr.

Coole, Maria. 2002. "It's Plain to See." *Lancaster Sunday News*, 27 Oct.

Cronk, Sandra L. 1977. "*Gelassenheit*: The Rites of the Redemptive Process in Old Order Amish and Old Order Mennonite Communities." PhD diss., University of Chicago.

Devil's Playground. 2002. DVD. Directed by Lucy Walker. Stick Figure Productions. [New York]: Wellspring Media.

Devoted Christian's Prayer Book, A. 1984. Aylmer, ON: Pathway Publishers. English translation of *Die Ernsthafte Christenpflicht*.

Diary, The. 1969–. Gordonville, PA: Pequea Publishers. A monthly periodical devoted to Amish history and genealogy.

Die Ernsthafte Christenpflicht. 1996. Lancaster County, PA: Amischen Gemeinden.

Dillard, Annie. 2000. *For the Time Being*. New York: Vintage Books.

Donnermeyer, Joseph F., and Elizabeth C. Cooksey. 2004. "The Demographic Foundations of Amish Society." Paper presented at the annual meeting of the Rural Sociological Society, Sacramento, 11–15 Aug.

Donnermeyer, Joseph F., George M. Kreps, and Marty W. Kreps. 1999. *Lessons for Living*. Sugarcreek, OH: Carlisle Press.

Dordrecht Confession of Faith. [1964] 1994. Aylmer, ON: Pathway Publishers.

Dorius, Guy L., Tim B. Heaton, and Patrick Steffen. 1993. "Adolescent Life Events and Their Association with the Onset of Sexual Intercourse." *Youth and Society* 25 (1): 3–23.

Dyck, Cornelius J. 1993. *An Introduction to Mennonite History*. 3rd ed. Scottdale, PA: Herald Press.

Eitzen, Dirk. 2008. "Hollywood Rumspringa: *Amish in the City*." In *The Amish and the Media*, ed. Diane Zimmerman Umble and David L. Weaver-Zercher, 133–53. Baltimore: Johns Hopkins University Press.

———. 2008. "Reel Amish: The Amish in Documentaries." In *The Amish and the Media*, ed. Diane Zimmerman Umble and David L. Weaver-Zercher, 43–64. Baltimore: Johns Hopkins University Press.

Ericksen, Julia A., Eugene P. Ericksen, and John A. Hostetler. 1980. "The Cultivation of the Soil as a Moral Directive: Population Growth, Family Ties, and the Maintenance of Community among the Old Order Amish." *Rural Sociology* 45: 49–68.

Erikson, Erik Homburger. 1968. *Identity, Youth, and Crisis.* New York: W. W. Norton.

———. 1980. *Identity and the Life Cycle.* New York: W. W. Norton.

Family Life. 1968–. Aylmer, ON: Pathway Publishers. A monthly Amish periodical.

"Fire in the Land, A." 2010. *Family Life* (Apr.): 8–13.

Fisher, Gideon L. 1978. *Farm Life and Its Changes.* Gordonville, PA: Pequea Publishers.

Folsom, Jan. 1994. *The Amish: Images of a Tradition.* Harrisburg, PA: Stackpole Books.

Friedrich, Lora, and Joseph F. Donnermeyer. 2003. "To Be or Not to Be: An Analysis of the Baptism Decisions of Young Amish Men and Women." Paper presented at the Ritual in Anabaptist Communities Conference, Hillsdale College, Hillsdale, Michigan, 27 Jun.

Furlong, Saloma. 2011. *Why I Left the Amish: A Memoir.* East Lansing: Michigan State University Press.

Garrett, Ottie A., comp. 1998. *True Stories of the X-Amish.* Horse Cave, KY: Neu Leben.

Garrett, Ruth Irene, with Rick Farrant. 2003. *Crossing Over: One Woman's Exodus from Amish Life.* New York: HarperCollins.

Garrett, Ruth Irene, with Deborah Morse-Kahn. 2004. *Born Amish.* Paducah, KY: Turner Publishing.

Gemein Ordnungen von Lancaster Co., PA. [n.d.]. Gordonville, PA: Gordonville Print Shop.

Gibson, Seth A. 2006. "Gang Prevalence and Involvement among Old Order Amish Youth in the Elkhart-LaGrange Settlement: An Interview Project of the Amish Youth Vision Project." Unpublished paper, Shipshewana, IN.

Gingerich, Melvin. 1939. *The Mennonites in Iowa.* Iowa City: State Historical Society of Iowa.

Goldstein, Michael A. 1997. "Party On, Amos." *Philadelphia Magazine* 40 (Aug.): 137–44.

Graney, Tom. 2003. "Devil's Playground (2002)." Hollywood Outsider. www.hollywoodoutsider.com/reviews/devils_playground.htm.

Graves, Amy Beth. 2000. "Amish Seek Help for Underage Drinking." *Cincinnati Enquirer,* 21 May. www.enquirer.com/editions/2000/05/21/loc_ohios_amish_seek.html.

Greksa, Lawrence P., and Jill E. Korbin. 2002. "Key Decisions in the Lives of Old Order Amish: Joining the Church and Migrating to Another Settlement." *Mennonite Quarterly Review* 76 (Oct.): 373–98.

Gross, Leonard, trans. and ed. 1997. *Prayer Book for Earnest Christians.* Scottdale, PA Herald Press. Translation of *Die Ernsthafte Christenpflicht.*

Guidelines in Regards to the Old Order Amish or Mennonite Parochial Schools. [1978] 1981. 4th printing. Gordonville, PA: Gordonville Print Shop.

Handbuch für Bischof [Handbook for Bishops]. [1935] 1978. Trans. Noah G. Good. Gordonville, PA: Gordonville Print Shop.

"Hard to Forget." 1969. *Family Life* (Jul.): 24–25.

Harris, Joshua. 1997. *I Kissed Dating Good-Bye: A New Attitude towards Relationships and Romance*. Sisters, OR: Multnomah Books.

Harter, Susan. 1999. *The Construction of the Self: A Developmental Perspective*. New York: Guilford.

Horst, Irvin B., ed. and trans. 1988. *Mennonite Confession of Faith*: Adopted April 21st, 1632, at Dordrecht, the Netherlands . . . Lancaster, PA: Lancaster Mennonite Historical Society.

Hostetler, John A. 1977. "Old Order Amish Survival." *Mennonite Quarterly Review* 51 (Oct.): 352–61.

———. 1992. "An Amish Beginning." *American Scholar* 61 (Fall): 552–62.

———. 1993. *Amish Society*. 4th ed. Baltimore: Johns Hopkins University Press.

Hostetler, John A., and Gertrude Enders Huntington. 1992. *Amish Children: Education in the Family, School, and Community*. 2nd ed. Fort Worth, TX: Harcourt Brace Jovanovich.

Huntington, Gertrude Enders. 1994. "Persistence and Change in Amish Education." In *The Amish Struggle with Modernity*, ed. Donald B. Kraybill and Marc A. Olshan, 77–95. Hanover, NH: University Press of New England.

Hurd, James P. 1997. "Marriage Practices among the 'Nebraska' Amish of Mifflin County, Pennsylvania." *Pennsylvania Mennonite Heritage* 20 (2): 20–24.

Hurst, Charles E., and David L. McConnell. 2010. *An Amish Paradox: Diversity and Change in the World's Largest Amish Community*. Baltimore: Johns Hopkins University Press.

Iannaccone, Laurence R. 1994. "Why Strict Churches Are Strong." *American Journal of Sociology* 99: 1180–211.

Igou, Brad. 1999. *The Amish in Their Own Words: Amish Writings from 25 Years of "Family Life" Magazine*. Scottdale, PA: Herald Press.

In Meiner Jugend: A Devotional Reader in German and English. 2000. Trans. Joseph Stoll. Aylmer, ON: Pathway Publishers.

Jantzi, Charles. 2013. "You're on Facebook: Amish Youth's Use of Social Media." Paper presented at the Plain People and Cyber Technology Conference, Elizabethtown College, Elizabethtown, Pennsylvania, 7 Jun.

Johnson, C[hristine] C., B[enjamin] A Rybicki, G[regory G.] Brown, E. D'Hondt, B. Herpolscheimer, D. Roth, and C. E. Jackson. 1997. "Cognitive Impairment in the Amish: A Four County Survey." *International Journal of Epidemiology* 2: 381–94. [higher Mini Mental State Examination (MMSE) scores].

Johnson, Deborah J. 1996. "Father Presence Matters: A Review of the Literature." National Center on Fathers and Families. www.ncoff.gse.upenn.edu/publications/literature-reviews/.

Johnson, Mark E. 1999. "Pair Warn Amish of Drugs' Dangers: Led Educational Meetings Here." *Lancaster Intelligencer Journal*, 1 Jul.

Johnson-Weiner, Karen M. 2000. *New York Amish: Life in the Plain Communities of the Empire State.* Ithaca, NY: Cornell University Press.

———. 2001. "The Role of Women in Older Order Amish, Beachy Amish, and Fellowship Churches." *Mennonite Quarterly Review* 75 (Apr.): 231–56.

———. 2006. *Train Up a Child: Old Order Amish and Mennonite Schools.* Baltimore: Johns Hopkins University Press.

Jones, Richard. 1999. "For Anabaptists, a Resort, Plain and Simple Amish and Mennonites for Decades Have Fled the Wintry Cold for Fun in the Fla. Sun." *Philadelphia Inquirer,* 15 Feb., A1.

Keim, Albert N. 2003. "Military Service and Conscription." In *The Amish and the State,* 2nd ed., ed. Donald B. Kraybill, 43–66. Baltimore: Johns Hopkins University Press.

Kelly, Kevin. 2010. *What Technology Wants.* New York: Viking.

Kissinger, Warren S. 1983. *The Buggies Still Run.* Elgin, IL: Brethren Press.

Klimuska, Ed. 1998. "Worldwide Media Gripped by 'Feeding Frenzy.'" *Lancaster New Era,* 13 Jul.

Kline, Edward A., and Monroe Beachy. 1998. "History and Dynamics of the New Order Amish of Holmes County, Ohio." *Old Order Notes* 18 (Fall–Winter): 7–19.

Kline, John B, ed. 1990. *Rural Recreation: The Traditional Adult Game of Cornerball plus Country Schools and Their Recess Games.* Denver, PA: Hill Barn.

Kraybill, Donald B. 1994. "The Amish Encounter with Modernity." In *The Amish Struggle with Modernity,* ed. Donald B. Kraybill and Mark A. Olshan, 21–34. Hanover, NH: University Press of New England.

———. 1994. "Plotting Social Change across Four Affiliations." In *The Amish Struggle with Modernity,* ed. Donald B. Kraybill and Mark A. Olshan, 53–76. Hanover, NH: University Press of New England.

———. 1994. "War Against Progress: Coping with Social Change." In *The Amish Struggle with Modernity,* ed. Donald B. Kraybill and Mark A. Olshan, 35–52. Hanover, NH: University Press of New England.

———. 1998. "Plain Reservations: Amish and Mennonite Views of Media and Computers." *Journal of Mass Medica Ethics* 13 (2): 99–110.

———. 2001. *The Riddle of Amish Culture.* Rev. ed. Baltimore: Johns Hopkins University Press.

———. 2003. *The Amish and the State.* 2nd ed. Baltimore: Johns Hopkins University Press.

Kraybill, Donald B., and Carl F. Bowman. 2001. *On the Backroad to Heaven: Old Order Hutterites, Mennonites, Amish, and Brethren.* Baltimore: Johns Hopkins University Press.

Kraybill, Donald B., and C. Nelson Hostetter. 2001. *Anabaptist World USA.* Scottdale, PA: Herald Press.

Kraybill, Donald B., Karen Johnson-Weiner, and Steven M. Nolt. 2013. *The Amish.* Baltimore: Johns Hopkins University Press.

Kraybill, Donald B., and Steven M. Nolt. 2004. *Amish Enterprise: From Plows to Profits.* Rev. ed. Baltimore: Johns Hopkins University Press.

Kraybill, Donald B., Steven M. Nolt, and David L. Weaver-Zercher. 2007. *Amish Grace: How Forgiveness Transcended Tragedy*. San Francisco: Jossey-Bass.

———. 2010. *The Amish Way: Patient Faith in a Perilous World*. San Francisco: Jossey-Bass.

Kraybill, Donald B., and Mark A. Olshan, eds. 1994. *The Amish Struggle with Modernity*. Hanover, NH: University Press of New England.

Langin, Bernd G. 1994. *Plain and Amish: An Alternative to Modern Pessimism*. Scottdale, PA: Herald Press.

Lapp, Aaron, Jr. 2003. *Weavertown Church History*. Sugarcreek, OH: Carlisle Printing.

Lapp, Esther, comp. *Heartland Hymns*. 2005. Rosenort, MB: PrairieView Press.

Lasansky, Jeannette. 1990. *A Good Start: The Aussteier or Dowry*. Lewisburg, PA: Oral Traditions Project of the Union County Historical Society.

Lovelace, Brett. 2003. "Injured Men Can't Recall Crash that Killed Five." *Lancaster Intelligencer Journal*, 16 Dec.

Luthy, David. 1986. *The Amish in America: Settlements that Failed, 1840–1960*. Aylmer, ON: Pathway Publishers.

———. 2003. "Amish Settlements across America: 2003." *Family Life* (Oct.): 17–23.

———. 2013. *A History of the Printings of the "Martyrs' Mirror," Dutch, German, English, 1660–2012: From the Collection of Heritage Historical Library*. Alymer, ON: Pathway Publishers.

Mackall, Joe. 2007. *Plain Secrets: An Outsider among the Amish*. Boston: Beacon Press.

Marcia, James C. 1980. "Identity in Adolescence." In *Handbook of Adolescent Psychology*, ed. Joseph Adelson, 159–87. New York: Wiley.

———. 1994. "The Empirical Study of Ego Identity." In *Identity and Development: An Interdisciplinary Approach*, ed. Harke A. Bosma, David J. de Levita, Tobi Graafsma, and Harold D. Grotevant, 67–80. Thousand Oaks, CA: Sage.

Marsh, James H. 2000. *The Canadian Encyclopedia*. Toronto: Historica Foundation of Canada.

Martino, Steven C., Rebecca L. Collins, Marc N. Elliott, Amy Strachman, David E. Kanouse, and Sandra H. Berry. 2006. "Exposure to Degrading versus Nondegrading Music Lyrics and Sexual Behavior among Youth." *Pediatrics* 118 (Aug.): 430–41.

McNamara, Timothy. 1997. "Uses of Popular Music by Old Order Amish Youth in Lancaster County, Pennsylvania." PhD diss., Temple University.

Meyers, Thomas J. 1991. "Population Growth and Its Consequences in the Elkhart-LaGrange Old Order Amish Settlement." *Mennonite Quarterly Review* 65 (Jul.): 308–21.

———. 2003. "Education and Schooling." In *The Amish and the State*, 2nd ed., ed. Donald B. Kraybill, 87–108. Baltimore: Johns Hopkins University Press.

———. 2013. "The Old Order Amish: To Remain in the Faith or to Leave?" *Mennonite Quarterly Review* 68 (Jul.): 378–95.

Meyers, Thomas J., and Steven M. Nolt. 2005. *An Amish Patchwork: Indiana's Old Orders in a Modern World*. Bloomington: Indiana University Press.

Miller, Brent C., J. Kelly McCoy, and Terrance D. Olson. 1986. "Dating Age and Stage as Correlates of Adolescent Sexual Attitudes and Behavior." *Journal of Adolescent Research* 3: 361–71.

Miller, Levi. 1989. *Ben's Wayne.* Intercourse, PA: Good Books.

Miller, Mary M., comp. 2008. *Our Heritage, Hope, and Faith.* Rev. ed. Topeka, IN: Mary M. Miller, Our Heritage Books.

"Mose J. Gingerich." 2013. www.amishinthecitymose.com/about/ [accessed 20 May].

Myers, David G. 2011. *Social Psychology.* 10th ed. New York: McGraw-Hill.

Mystery of Happiness: Who Has It, How to Get It. 1996. Video cassette. With John Stossel. Directed by Roger Goodman. ABC News.

Newswanger, Xtian. 1996. *Amishland.* Intercourse, PA: Gordonville Print Shop.

"Nine Amish Held in Vandalism." 1968. *Des Moines Register,* 27 Sept., 19.

Nolt, Steven M. 2003. *A History of the Amish.* Rev. ed. Intercourse, PA: Good Books.

Nolt, Steven M., and Thomas J. Meyers. 2007. *Plain Diversity: Amish Cultures and Identities.* Baltimore: Johns Hopkins University Press.

Ohio Amish Directory: Holmes County and Vicinity, 2010. 2009. Sugarcreek, OH: Carlisle Press.

Oyer, John S., and Robert S. Kreider. 1990. *Mirror of the Martyrs.* Intercourse, PA: Good Books.

"Paying Their Last Respects." 1999. *Lancaster Intelligencer Journal,* 4 Jun.

"Pity Party in the Pickle Patch." 2004. *Plain Interests* (Apr.): 1.

Plain Interests. 2001–. Millersburg, PA. A monthly periodical dedicated to the interests of Plain readers.

Platte, Petra, Joan F. Zelten, and Albert J. Stunkard. 2000. "Body Image in the Old Order Amish: A People Separate from 'the World.'" *International Journal of Eating Disorders* 28 (Dec.): 408–14.

"Problem Corner." 2006. *Family Life* (May): 29–34.

"Providing Alternate Places of Service." 2012. Conservative Anabaptist Service Program (CASP). March 1. https://www.christianaidministries.org/news/providing-alternate-places-of-service.

"Reflection on the Nature of the Ordnung and Why It Changes." 2013. Paper presented at the Plain People and Cyber Technology Conference, Elizabethtown College, Elizabethtown, Pennsylvania, 8 Jun. http://amishamerica.com/2013-amish-conference-an-amishman-on-the-ordnung/.

Reiling, Denise M. 2000. "The Exploration of the Relationship between Amish Identity and Depression among the Old Order Amish." PhD diss., Michigan State University.

———. 2002. "The 'Simmie' Side of Life: Old Order Amish Youths' Affective Response to Culturally Prescribed Deviance." *Youth and Society* 34 (Dec.): 146–71.

Remnick, David. 1998. "Bad Seeds: Letter from Lancaster County." *New Yorker,* 20 Jul., 28–33.

Renno, John R. 1993. *Growing Up Amish*. Petersburg, OH: Pilgrim Brethren Press.

Rheingold, Howard. 1999. "Look Who's Talking." *Wired* 7 (Jan.): 128–31, 161–63. www.wired.com/wired/archive/7.01/.

Rice, Charles Scott, and Rollin C. Steinmetz. 1956. *The Amish Year*. New Brunswick, NJ: Rutgers University Press.

Rutter, John. 2003. "The Marryin' Kind Are in the Marryin' Season: Amish Make Room for Weddings." *Lancaster Sunday News*, 16 Nov.

[Schlabach, Rob R.] [1980]. *Ein Risz in der Mauer: Treatise on Courtship*. Sugarcreek, OH: Schlabach Printers.

Schwartz, Christian, and Elizabeth N. Schwartz. 1980. *Schwartzs' Song-Book*. Gordonville, PA: Gordonville Print Shop.

Scott, Stephen E. 1981. *Plain Buggies: Amish, Mennonite, and Brethren Horse-Drawn Transportation*. Intercourse, PA: Good Books.

———. 1988. *The Amish Wedding and Other Special Occasions of the Old Order Communities*. Intercourse, PA: Good Books.

"Seven Amish Injured When Barn Collapses." 1977. *Lancaster New Era*, 10 Oct.

Shachtman, Tom. 2006. *Rumspringa: To Be or Not to Be Amish*. New York: North Point Press.

"Singing and Hymns." 1990. *Young Companion* (Mar.): 9.

Small, Stephen A., and Tom Luster. 1994. "Adolescent Sexual Activity: An Ecological, Risk-Factor Approach." *Journal of Marriage and the Family* 56: 181–92.

Smart, Gil. 2011. "Hitchin' Up Buggy and . . . Facebook." *Lancaster Sunday News*, 19 Jun., A1.

"Special Section: Journey to Freedom." 2000. *Family Life* (Feb.): 28.

Standards of the Old Order Amish and Old Order Mennonite Parochial and Vocational Schools of Pennsylvania. 2003. Gordonville, PA: Gordonville Print Shop.

Steinberg, Laurence. 1990. "Autonomy, Conflict, and Harmony in the Family Relationship." In *At the Threshold: The Developing Adolescent*, ed. S. Shirley Feldman and Glen R Elliot, 255–76. Cambridge, MA: Harvard University Press.

———. 2001. "We Know Some Things: Adolescent-Parent Relationships in Retrospect and Prospect." *Journal of Research on Adolescence* 11: 1–19.

———. 2005. *Adolescence*, 7th ed. Boston: McGraw-Hill.

Stevick, Pauline. 2006. *Beyond the Plain and Simple: A Patchwork of Amish Lives*. Kent, OH: Kent State University Press.

Stevick, Richard. 2001. "The Amish: Case Study of a Religious Community." In *Contemporary Spiritualities: Social and Religious Contexts*, ed. Clive Erricker and Jane Erricker, 159–72. London: Continuum.

———. 2006. "Pinecraft, Florida, Notes." Unpublished notes, 10 Oct.

———. 2007. *Growing Up Amish: The Teenage Years*. Baltimore: Johns Hopkins University Press.

Stevick, Richard, and Charles Jantzi. 2013. "Amish Youth on the Internet: A Passing Phase or a Fatal Error?" Paper presented at the Plain People and Cyber Technology Conference, Elizabethtown College, Elizabethtown, Pennsylvania, 7 Jun.

Stoll, Elmo. 1972. *One Way Street*. Aylmer, ON: Pathway Publishers.

———. 1982. "Why I See Danger in Games and Sports." *Family Life* (Mar.): 9–12.

Stoll, Jonathan. 2012. "Celling Our Heritage: Cell Phones, Plain People, and the Electronic Age." *Family Life* (Nov.): 8–16.

Stoll, Joseph. 1966. "The Police Came." *Blackboard Bulletin* (Sept.): 27–29.

Stoltzfus, Elmer. 1996. "Plain and Amish: An Alternative to Modern Pessimism," by Bernd Langin" [book review]. *Pennsylvania Mennonite Heritage* (Apr.): 19, 37.

Stoltzfus, Louise. 1998. *Traces of Wisdom: Amish Women and the Pursuit of Life's Simple Pleasures*. New York: Hyperion.

Stoltzfus, Samuel S. 1994. "Our Changing Church District." *Pennsylvania Folklife* (Spring): 124–31.

Subrahmanyam, Karen, and David Smahel. 2011. *Digital Youth: The Role of Media in Development*. New York: Springer.

Swartzentruber, Mara S. 2011. "Retention Rates in Amish Communities, with Special Reference to Nappanee, Indiana." Unpublished paper, Goshen College, Goshen, IN.

"Thin Shadow, A." 1999. *Young Companion* (Jul.): 14–15.

Thornton, Arland. 1990. "The Courtship Process and Adolescent Sexuality." *Journal of Family Issues* 3 (Apr.): 239–73.

Tomlin, Jimmy. 2003. "Be Not Conformed . . ." *Our State* 71 (4): 152–56.

Triandis, Harry C. 1990. "Theoretical Concepts that Are Applicable to the Analysis of Ethnocentrism." In *Applied Cross-Cultural Psychology*, ed. Richard W. Brislin, 34–55. Cross-Cultural Research and Methodology Series, Vol. 14. Newbury Park, CA: Sage.

———. 1995. *Individualism and Collectivism*. Boulder, CO: Westview Press.

Trollinger, Susan L. 2012. *Selling the Amish: The Tourism of Nostalgia*. Baltimore: Johns Hopkins University Press.

Troyer, David A. [1920] 1998. *Hinterlassene Schriften*. In *The Writings of David A. Troyer*, comp. and trans. Paton Yoder. Aylmer, ON: Pathway Publishers.

Tullis, Matt. 2006. "Amish Man Sentenced for Selling Marijuana." *Wooster (OH) Daily Record*, 24 Feb., A1.

Umble, Diane Zimmerman. 1994. "Amish on the Line: Telephone Debates." In *The Amish Struggle with Modernity*, ed. Donald B Kraybill and Mark A. Olshan, 97–112. Hanover, NH: University Press of New England.

———. 1996. *Holding the Line: The Telephone in Old Order Amish and Mennonite Life*. Baltimore: Johns Hopkins University Press.

Umble, Diane Zimmerman, and David L. Weaver-Zercher. 2008. *The Amish and the Media*. Baltimore: Johns Hopkins University Press.

Unparteiische Lieder-Sammlung zum Gebrauch beim oeffentlichen Gottesdienst und der häuslichen Erbauung, Eine ["Baer book"]. 1860 and reprints. Lancaster, PA: Johann Bar's Söhne.

Unruh, John D. 1952. *In the Name of Christ: A History of the Mennonite Central Committee and Its Services, 1920–1951*. Scottdale, PA: Herald Press.

Varian, Nanette. 1999. "Escaping Amish Repression: One Woman's Story." *Glamour* (Aug.): 114–20.

Wagler, Ira. 2008–9. "The Shepherd at Dawn" (6 Jun.), "The Shepherd at Noon" (22 Aug.), and "The Shepherd at Dusk" (30 Jan.). www.irawagler.com/?page _id=23/.

———. 2011. *Growing Up Amish: A Memoir*. Carol Stream, IL: Tyndale House Publishers.

Weaver-Zercher, David. 2001. *The Amish in the American Imagination*. Baltimore: Johns Hopkins University Press.

———. 2005. *Writing the Amish: The Worlds of John A. Hostetler*. University Park: Pennsylvania State University Press.

Weaver-Zercher, Valerie. 2013. *Thrill of the Chaste: The Allure of Amish Romance Novels*. Baltimore: Johns Hopkins University Press.

Weber, Chris, James A. Cates, and Shirley Carey. 2010. "A Drug and Alcohol Intervention with Old Order Amish Youth: Dancing on the Devil's Playground." *Journal of Groups in Addiction and Recovery* 5 (2): 97–112.

Webster's Third New International Dictionary. 1986. Springfield, MA: Merriam-Webster.

Wesner, Erik. 2010. *Success Made Simple: An Inside Look at Why Amish Businesses Thrive*. New York: Jossey-Bass.

Wikipedia. 2013. *"Amish in the City."* http://en.wikipedia.org/wiki/Amish_in_the _City/ [accessed 18 Mar.].

———. 2013. "Hand Signs," under "Gang Signal." http://en.wikipedia.org/wik i/Gang_Signal#Hand_signs/ [accessed 27 Oct.].

———. 2013. "Jumping the Broom." http://en.wikipedia.org/wiki/Jumping_the _broom/ [accessed 27 Oct.].

Wittmer, Joe. 1973. "Amish Homogeneity of Parental Behavior Characteristics." *Human Relations* 26 (2): 143–54.

Wojtasik, Ted. 1996. *No Strange Fire*. Scottdale, PA: Herald Press.

Yassos, Bart. 2012. "Running with the Amish." *Runners World* 47 (4): 92–102.

Yoder, Joseph Warren. [1940] 1995. *Rosanna of the Amish: The Restored Text*. Scottdale, PA: Herald Press. First published by Yoder Publishing, Huntingdon, NY.

Yoder, Paton, comp. and ed. 1998. *The Writings of David A. Troyer*. Aylmer, ON: Pathway Publishers.

———. 2003. "The Amish View of the State." In *The Amish and the State*, 2nd ed., ed. Donald B. Kraybill, 23–42. Baltimore: Johns Hopkins University Press.

Young Companion. 1971–. Aylmer, ON: Pathway Publishers. A monthly periodical directed to Amish youth.

Index

ABOUT THE AUTHOR

Richard Stevick is professor emeritus of psychology at Messiah College in Pennsylvania. His research interests include Amish adolescence and the challenges of parenting Amish teenagers, especially through their late adolescent years. He also continues to teach a course on Amish culture in which he and his students live with Amish host families.

Over the years, Stevick and his wife, Pauline, have been guests at numerous Amish weddings, youth singing socials, and dozens of church services. Because of his close personal connections, Stevick was one of the few outsiders who knew about the crack cocaine problem among Amish youth in Lancaster County, Pennsylvania, before the FBI arrested three youth from Amish homes who were selling drugs to their peers.

Stevick has worked with both Amish youth and adults in arranging mental health evaluations and treatment. He has also served as a consultant to a research team at the National Institute of Mental Health in Bethesda, Maryland. This team is studying bipolar spectrum disorders among Amish children and youth. In addition, Stevick is currently studying the use and impact of Facebook and other social media on youthful Amish users.

Young Center Books in Anabaptist & Pietist Studies

Charles E. Hurst and David L. McConnell, *An Amish Paradox:*
Diversity and Change in the World's Largest Amish Community
Rod Janzen and Max Stanton, *The Hutterites in North America*
Karen M. Johnson-Weiner,
Train Up a Child: Old Order Amish and Mennonite Schools
Peter J. Klassen, *Mennonites in Early Modern Poland and Prussia*
James O. Lehman and Steven M. Nolt,
Mennonites, Amish, and the American Civil War
Steven M. Nolt and Thomas J. Meyers,
Plain Diversity: Amish Cultures and Identities
Douglas H. Shantz, *A New Introduction to German Pietism:*
Protestant Renewal at the Dawn of Modern Europe
Tobin Miller Shearer, *Daily Demonstrators: The Civil Rights Movement in*
Mennonite Homes and Sanctuaries
Janneken Smucker, *Amish Quilts: Crafting an American Icon*
Richard A. Stevick,
Growing Up Amish: The Rumspringa Years, 2nd edition
Duane C. S. Stoltzfus,
Pacifists in Chains: The Persecution of Hutterites during the Great War
Susan L. Trollinger, *Selling the Amish: The Tourism of Nostalgia*
Diane Zimmerman Umble and David L. Weaver-Zercher, eds.,
The Amish and the Media
Valerie Weaver-Zercher,
Thrill of the Chaste: The Allure of Amish Romance Novels

Center Books in Anabaptist Studies

Carl F. Bowman,
Brethren Society: The Cultural Transformation of a "Peculiar People"
Perry Bush,
Two Kingdoms, Two Loyalties: Mennonite Pacifism in Modern America
John A. Hostetler, ed., *Amish Roots: A Treasury of History, Wisdom, and Lore*
Julia Kasdorf, *The Body and the Book: Writing from a Mennonite Life*
Donald B. Kraybill, *The Riddle of Amish Culture*, revised edition

Donald B. Kraybill, ed., *The Amish and the State*, 2nd edition
Donald B. Kraybill and Carl Desportes Bowman, *On the Backroad to Heaven: Old Order Hutterites, Mennonites, Amish, and Brethren*
Donald B. Kraybill and Steven M. Nolt,
Amish Enterprise: From Plows to Profits, 2nd edition
Werner O. Packull,
Hutterite Beginnings: Communitarian Experiments during the Reformation
Benjamin W. Redekop and Calvin W. Redekop, eds.,
Power, Authority, and the Anabaptist Tradition
Calvin Redekop, Stephen C. Ainlay, and Robert Siemens,
Mennonite Entrepreneurs
Calvin Redekop, ed., *Creation and the Environment: An Anabaptist Perspective on a Sustainable World*
Steven D. Reschly, *The Amish on the Iowa Prairie, 1840 to 1910*
Kimberly D. Schmidt, Diane Zimmerman Umble, and Steven D. Reschly,
Strangers at Home: Amish and Mennonite Women in History
Diane Zimmerman Umble,
Holding the Line: The Telephone in Old Order Mennonite and Amish Life
David Weaver-Zercher, *The Amish in the American Imagination*